THE ARDEN SHAKESPEARE
GENERAL EDITORS:
RICHARD PROUDFOOT, ANN THOMPSON
and DAVID SCOTT KASTAN

ROMEO AND JULIET

THE ARDEN SHAKESPEARE

ALL'S WELL THAT ENDS WELL	edited by G. K. Hunter*
ANTONY AND CLEOPATRA	edited by John Wilders
AS YOU LIKE IT	edited by Juliet Dusinberre
THE COMEDY OF ERRORS	edited by R. A. Foakes*
CORIOLANUS	edited by Philip Brockbank*
CYMBELINE	edited by J. M. Nosworthy*
HAMLET	edited by Ann Thompson and Neil Taylor
JULIUS CAESAR	edited by David Daniell
KING HENRY IV Part 1	edited by David Scott Kastan
KING HENRY IV Part 2	edited by A. R. Humphreys*
KING HENRY V	edited by T. W. Craik
KING HENRY VI Part 1	edited by Edward Burns
KING HENRY VI Part 2	edited by Ronald Knowles
KING HENRY VI Part 3	edited by John D. Cox and Eric Rasmussen
KING HENRY VIII	edited by Gordon McMullan
KING JOHN	edited by E. A. J. Honigmann*
KING LEAR	edited by R. A. Foakes
KING RICHARD II	edited by Charles Forker
KING RICHARD III	edited by Antony Hammond*
LOVE'S LABOUR'S LOST	edited by H. R. Woudhuysen
MACBETH	edited by Kenneth Muir*
MEASURE FOR MEASURE	edited by J. W. Lever*
THE MERCHANT OF VENICE	edited by John Russell Brown*
THE MERRY WIVES OF WINDSOR	edited by Giorgio Melchiori
A MIDSUMMER NIGHT'S DREAM	edited by Harold F. Brooks*
MUCH ADO ABOUT NOTHING	edited by Claire McEachern
OTHELLO	edited by E. A. J. Honigmann
PERICLES	edited by Suzanne Gossett
THE POEMS	edited by F. T. Prince*
ROMEO AND JULIET	edited by Brian Gibbons*
SHAKESPEARE'S SONNETS	edited by Katherine Duncan-Jones
THE TAMING OF THE SHREW	edited by Brian Morris*
THE TEMPEST	edited by Virginia Mason Vaughan and Alden T. Vaughan
TIMON OF ATHENS	edited by H. J. Oliver*
TITUS ANDRONICUS	edited by Jonathan Bate
TROILUS AND CRESSIDA	edited by David Bevington
TWELFTH NIGHT	edited by J. M. Lothian and T. W. Craik*
THE TWO GENTLEMEN OF VERONA	edited by William C. Carroll
THE TWO NOBLE KINSMEN	edited by Lois Potter
THE WINTER'S TALE	edited by J. H. P. Pafford*

* Second series

THE ARDEN EDITION OF THE WORKS OF WILLIAM SHAKESPEARE

ROMEO AND JULIET

Edited by
BRIAN GIBBONS

The Arden website is at
http://www.ardenshakespeare.com

The general editors of the Arden Shakespeare have been
W. J. Craig and R. H. Case (first series 1899-1944)
Una Ellis-Fermor, Harold F. Brooks, Harold Jenkins and
Brian Morris (second series 1946-82)

Present general editors (third series)
Richard Proudfoot, Ann Thompson and David Scott Kastan

This edition of *Romeo and Juliet* by Brian Gibbons
first published 1980 by Methuen & Co. Ltd
Reprinted seven times
Reprinted 1997 by Thomas Nelson & Sons Ltd

Editorial matter © 1980 Methuen & Co. Ltd

Published by The Arden Shakespeare
Reprinted 2006 by Thomson Learning

Arden Shakespeare is an imprint of Thomson Learning

Thomson Learning
High Holborn House
50-51 Bedford Row
London WC1R 4LR

Printed in Singapore

All rights reserved. No part of this book may be reprinted or reproduced or utilized in any form or by any electronic, mechanical or other means, now known or hereafter invented, including photocopying and recording, or in any information storage or retrieval system, without permission in writing from the publishers.

British Library Cataloguing in Publication Data
A catalogue record for this book is available from the British Library
Library of Congress Cataloguing in Publication Data
A catalogue record has been requested

ISBN 13: 978-0-17-443584-6 (hbk)
ISBN 10: 0-17-443584-3 (hbk)
ISBN 13: 978-1-903436-41-7 (pbk)
ISBN 10: 1-903436-41-9 (pbk)
NPN 9 8 7 6 5

CONTENTS

PREFACE

This edition of *Romeo and Juliet* was begun from scratch in 1973, and is based on the first 'good' Quarto of 1599; the 'bad' Quarto of 1597 has been taken fully into account, a number of its readings have been adopted, and its readings have been recorded wherever possible. Only a few notes towards his projected edition were made by John Crow before his much regretted death, and collected by Professor M. M. Mahood. However, Crow's views on a number of editorial problems in the play were expressed in an article, 'Editing and Emending', and I have taken them into account both in letter and in spirit.

Among editions of the play I have learned much from those by Furness, Wilson-Duthie, Kittredge, Alexander, Hosley, Williams and Spencer. I have had the privilege of the friendship of three Shakespeare scholars, Philip Brockbank, Bernard Harris and Robin Hood, during the time I have been at work on this edition, and I am grateful to T. W. Craik for helpful discussion of certain problems of staging the play. Brian Morris was kind enough to read a draft of the Introduction and to comment upon it, and I am very deeply indebted to Harold Brooks and Harold Jenkins for the extraordinary generosity and scholarly excellence of their help and advice. Whatever errors and shortcomings remain are my own responsibility.

University of York
March 1979

Brian Gibbons

ACKNOWLEDGEMENTS

Selections from *The Poems of Sir Philip Sidney*, ed. William A. Ringler, Oxford English Texts (1962), are printed by permission of Oxford University Press; those from Brooke's *Romeus and Juliet* are taken from *Narrative and Dramatic Sources of Shakespeare*, Vol. 1, ed. G. Bullough (1958), Routledge & Kegan Paul, Ltd.

ABBREVIATIONS AND REFERENCES

The abbreviated titles of Shakespeare's works are as in C. T. Onions, *A Shakespeare Glossary*, 2nd edn, 1919. Passages quoted or cited are from the complete *Tudor Shakespeare*, ed. Peter Alexander, 1951.

I. EDITIONS

Q1	*Romeo and Juliet* ... Printed by John Danter, 1597.
Q2	*Romeo and Juliet* ... Printed by Thomas Creede, 1599.
Q3	*Romeo and Juliet* ... Printed for John Smethwick, 1609.
Q4	*Romeo and Juliet* ... Written by *W. Shakespeare* ... Printed for John Smethwicke [1622].
Q5	*Romeo and Juliet* Written by *W. Shakespeare* ... Printed by *R. Young* for John Smethwicke, 1637.
F	*Mr. William Shakespeares Comedies, Histories, & Tragedies*, 1623.
F2	*Mr. William Shakespeares Comedies, Histories, & Tragedies*, 1632.
F3	*Mr. William Shakespear Comedies, Histories, and Tragedies ... The third Impression*, 1664.
F4	*Mr. William Shakespear's Comedies, Histories, and Tragedies ... The fourth Edition*, 1685.
Rowe	*The Works of Mr William Shakespear ... Revis'd and Corrected by N. Rowe Esq.*, 1709. [A second edition of the above,] 1709. [A third edition of the above,] 1714.
Pope	*The Works of Shakespear ... Collected and Corrected ... by Mr. Pope*, 1723.
Theobald	*The Works of Shakespeare ... Collated with the Oldest Copies, and Corrected; with Notes ... By Mr. Theobald*, 1733.
Hanmer	*The Works of Shakespear ... Carefully Revised and Corrected by the former Editions*, ed. Thomas Hanmer, 1744.
Warburton	*The Works of Shakespear. The Genuine Text ... settled ... By Mr. Pope and Mr. Warburton*, 1747.
Johnson	*The Plays of William Shakespeare ... To which are added Notes by Sam. Johnson*, 1765.
Capell	*Mr. William Shakespeare his Comedies, Histories, and Tragedies*, ed. Edward Capell, 1768.
Steevens	*The Plays of William Shakespeare ... To which are added notes by Samuel Johnson and George Steevens*, 1773. [A second edition of the above, revised and augmented,] 1778. [A third edition of the above,] 1793.
Malone	*The Plays and Poems of William Shakespeare ... with ... notes by Edmond Malone*, 1790.

Singer	*The Dramatic Works of William Shakespeare with Notes . . . by Samuel Weller Singer*, 1826.
Knight	*The Pictorial Edition of the Works of Shakespeare*, ed. Charles Knight, 1838.
Collier	*The Works of William Shakespeare . . . with the various readings, and notes . . . by J. Payne Collier*, 1842–4. [A second edition of the above,] 1853. [A third edition of the above,] 1858.
Dyce	*The Works of William Shakespeare. The Text revised by the Rev. Alexander Dyce*, 1857. [A second edition of the above,] 1864–7. [A third edition of the above,] 1875–6.
Grant White	*The Works of William Shakespeare*, ed. Richard Grant White, 1857.
Delius	*Shaksperes Werke. Herausgegeben und erklärt von N. Delius*, 1854–60.
Staunton	*The Plays of Shakespeare*, ed. Howard Staunton, 1858.
Camb.	*The Works of William Shakespeare*, ed. William George Clark and John Glover, 1863–6. [Vol. 28, ed. W. A. Wright.]
Globe	*The Works of William Shakespeare*, ed. W. G. Clark and W. A. Wright, 1864.
Keightley	*The Plays of William Shakespeare. Carefully edited by Thomas Keightley*, 1864.
Hudson	*The Complete Works of William Shakespeare* . . . ed. H. N. Hudson, 1881.
Furness	*Romeo and Juliet*, ed. H. H. Furness (New Variorum Shakespeare), 1871.
Daniel	*Romeo and Juliet*, ed. P. A. Daniel, 1875.
Craig	*The Complete Works of Shakespeare*, ed. W. J. Craig, 1891.
Dowden	*Romeo and Juliet*, ed. E. Dowden (Arden Shakespeare), 1900.
Chambers	*Romeo and Juliet*, ed. E. K. Chambers, 1904.
Durham	*Romeo and Juliet* (The Yale Shakespeare), ed. W. H. Durham, 1917.
Kittredge	*The Works of Shakespeare*, ed. G. L. Kittredge, 1936.
Hoppe	*Romeo and Juliet*, ed. H. R. Hoppe, 1947.
Houghton	*Romeo and Juliet*, ed. R. E. C. Houghton, 1947.
Alexander	*William Shakespeare, The Complete Works*, ed. Peter Alexander, 1951.
Hosley	*Romeo and Juliet*, ed. R. Hosley (Yale Shakespeare, revised), 1954.
Sisson	*William Shakespeare, The Complete Works*, ed. C. J. Sisson, 1954.
NCS	*Romeo and Juliet*, ed. John Dover Wilson and George Ian Duthie (New Shakespeare), 1955.
Munro	*The London Shakespeare*, ed. John Munro, 1958.
Hankins	*Romeo and Juliet*, ed. J. E. Hankins, 1960.
Williams	*Romeo and Juliet*, ed. G. W. Williams, 1964.
Spencer	*Romeo and Juliet*, ed. T. J. B. Spencer, 1967.
Riverside	*The Riverside Shakespeare*, textual ed. G. Blakemore Evans, 1974.

2. TEXTUAL COMMENTARIES

Tyrwhitt	Thomas Tyrwhitt, *Observations and Conjectures upon some Passages of Shakespeare*, 1766.
Walker	W. S. Walker, *A Critical Examination of the Text of Shakespeare* [ed. W. N. Lettsom], 1860.
Daniel	*Notes and Conjectural Emendations of certain Doubtful Passages in Shakespeare's Plays*, 1870.
Crow	John Crow, 'Editing and Emending', *Essays & Studies*, 1955.
Sisson	C. J. Sisson, *New Readings in Shakespeare*, 1956.

3. OTHER WORKS

Abbott	E. A. Abbott, *A Shakespearean Grammer*, 1869.
Brooke	Arthur Brooke, *The Tragicall Historye of Romeus and Iuliet, written first in Italian by Bandell, and nowe in Englishe by Ar. Br.*, 1562, reprinted in G. Bullough (ed.), *Narrative and Dramatic Sources of Shakespeare*, Vol. 1, 1957.
Chaucer	Geoffrey Chaucer, *Works*, ed. F. N. Robinson, 2nd edn, 1957.
Cotgrave	*A Dictionary of the French and English Tongues*, 1611.
Daniel, *Poems*	Samuel Daniel, *Poems and A Defense of Ryme*, ed. Arthur Colby Sprague, 1930.
E.E.T.S.	Early English Text Society.
Golding	*Ovid's Metamorphoses, The Arthur Golding Translation* (1567), ed. John Frederick Nims, 1965.
Lyly	John Lyly, *Works*, ed. R. Warwick Bond, 1902.
Madden	D. H. Madden, *The Diary of Master William Silence*, 1907.
Marlowe	Christopher Marlowe, *Works*, ed. C. F. Tucker Brooke, 1910.
MSR	Malone Society Reprints.
Nares	Robert Nares, *A Glossary . . . of Words* . . . ed. J. O. Halliwell and Thomas Wright, 1882.
Nashe	Thomas Nashe, *Works*, ed. R. B. McKerrow, revised F. P. Wilson, 1966.
OED	*Oxford English Dictionary*.
Onions	C. T. Onions, *A Shakespeare Glossary*, 2nd edn, revised, 1919.
Partridge	Eric Partridge, *Shakespeare's Bawdy*, revised edn, 1955.
Puttenham	George Puttenham, *The Arte of English Poesie*, in G. G. Smith (ed.), *Elizabethan Critical Essays*, 1910.
Schmidt	Alexander Schmidt, *Shakespeare Lexicon*, 1923.
Shakespeare's England	ed. Sidney Lee and C. T. Onions, 1916.
Sidney	*The Poems of Sir Philip Sidney*, ed. W. A. Ringler, 1962.
Tilley	M. P. Tilley, *A Dictionary of Proverbs in England in the Sixteenth and Seventeenth Centuries*, 1950.

4. PERIODICALS

JEGP	*Journal of English and Germanic Philology*.
MLN	*Modern Language Notes*.
MLQ	*Modern Language Quarterly*.

MLR	*Modern Language Review.*
N&Q	*Notes and Queries.*
PBSA	*Publications of the Bibliographical Society of America.*
RES	*Review of English Studies.*
SB	*Studies in Bibliography.*
SJH	*Shakespeare Jahrbuch.*
SQ	*Shakespeare Quarterly.*
Sh.S.	*Shakespeare Survey.*
Shaks.S.	*Shakespeare Studies.*
TLS	*Times Literary Supplement.*

INTRODUCTION

1. THE TEXT

Q1. The First Quarto of *Romeo and Juliet* appeared with the following title-page:

> *AN* / EXCELLENT / conceited Tragedie / *OF* / Romeo and Iuliet, / As it hath been often (with great applause) plaid publiquely, by the right Ho-/nourable the L. of *Hunsdon* / his Seruants. / LONDON, / Printed by Iohn Danter. / 1597. /

Q2. A Second Quarto appeared two years later, evidently intended to supplant this Bad Quarto. Its title-page reads:

> THE / MOST EX- / cellent and lamentable / Tragedie, of Romeo and *Iuliet.* / *Newly corrected, augmented, and / amended:* / As it hath bene sundry times publiquely acted, by the / right Honourable the Lord Chamberlaine / his Seruants. / LONDON / Printed by Thomas Creede, for Cuthbert Burby, and are to / be sold at his shop neare the Exchange. / *1599.* /

The statement that Q2 is 'newly corrected, augmented, and amended' means that it is a replacement of the first edition, not a revision of an earlier version of the play. *Romeo and Juliet* Q1 is a Bad Quarto, piratical and dependent on an especially unreliable means of transmission for the text, like the Bad Quartos of the second and third parts of *King Henry VI*, *King Henry V*, *The Merry Wives of Windsor*, *Hamlet* Q1 and *Pericles*.[1] The Bad Quarto of *Romeo and Juliet* provoked the publication of a Good Quarto a couple of years later. This is what happened also in the case of *Hamlet*, and probably *Love's Labour's Lost*: for the claim on the title-page that *Love's Labour's Lost* is 'Newly corrected and augmented' indicates that there was a preceding Bad Quarto, although no copy of it survives; it is probable that the publication of this Good Quarto of *Love's Labour's Lost* (1599) was intended as a twin for that of *Romeo and Juliet*, published in the same year; and

1. The history of the modern bibliographical analysis of Bad Quartos is succinctly given in F. P. Wilson, *Shakespeare and the New Bibliography*, rev. Helen Gardner (1970), pp. 80–95; see also Norman Sanders's account in *Shakespeare, A Select Bibliographical Guide*, ed. Stanley Wells (1973), pp. 11–24. On *Romeo and Juliet* see also W. W. Greg, *The Shakespeare First Folio* (1955), pp. 225–35.

Love's Labour's Lost, like the Good Quartos of *Romeo and Juliet* and *Hamlet*, was printed from 'foul papers', that is, Shakespeare's autograph draft, not a transcription prepared as a prompt-book.

After *Romeo and Juliet* Q1 (1597) and Q2 (1599) there are no further substantive editions, that is, editions having independent authority or suggesting access to new evidence of what Shakespeare wrote. Subsequent derivative editions are Q3 (1609) reprinted from Q2; Q4 (1622) reprinted from Q3, with occasional consultation of Q1; and Q5 (1637) reprinted from Q4. The Folio text is based on Q3 with the exception of a number of passages which follow Q4. These derivative editions exhibit two kinds of change from the substantive editions: errors accumulating through the processes of the printing-house, and attempted corrections, some cogent, some mistaken, but all apparently without authority, none beyond the capacity of a compositor or editor. In these circumstances the fact that the compositor of Q4 made use of a copy of Q1 for occasional consultation when using Q3 as his copy-text indicates a degree of conscientiousness.

Since the hypothesis of memorial reconstruction was first advanced by Greg to explain certain features of the Bad Quarto of *The Merry Wives*,[1] it has come to be accepted that a number of Bad Quartos of Shakespeare's plays were reconstructed from memory by reporters who knew the play on the stage; *Romeo and Juliet* Q1 is such a text. It contains anticipations, recollections, transpositions, paraphrases, summaries, repetitions and omissions of words, phrases or lines correctly presented in Q2. Most of these features are evidence of the faulty memory of the reporters, though certain omissions, and a cut in the required number of players, may indicate that Q1, however abbreviated, derived from a version adapted for acting.[2]

1. This was in 1910, in an edition of the 1602 quarto of *Merry Wives*.

2. H. R. Hoppe, *The Bad Quarto of Romeo and Juliet* (1948), notes that by contrast with Q2, which seems to have no numerical limitations of players in mind and could 'by judicious doubling' have been enacted 'by perhaps 20 players', Q1 could have been handled 'by about 12'; judging by Q1 stage directions Hoppe thinks the abridged version was for a company with no musicians and few supernumeraries: he instances IV. ii where the '*serving men, two or three*' of Q2 are reduced to one in Q1, or IV. iv. 14, where '*three or foure with spits and logs, and Baskets*' in Q2 are reduced to a '*Seruingman with Logs & Coales*'. Elsewhere maskers, torchbearers and servants are cut, perhaps to free actors for more important parts. Cuts in the text may have been intended to reduce the duration of the play in performance, which is evidently what happened in the Bad Quartos of *Henry VI* Parts II and III and in the Bad Quarto of *Orlando Furioso* which Greg analysed, *Two Elizabethan Stage Abridgements, the 'Battle of Alcazar' and 'Orlando Furioso'* (1923).

The title-page of Q1 declares that it was printed by John Danter. In fact only the first four sheets (A–D) came from his press, and the rest from that of Allde. It has been argued by H. R. Hoppe[1] that the rest of the text had to be printed elsewhere because Danter was raided by the Stationers' Company some time between 9 February and 27 March 1597; his presses were seized and subsequently destroyed, and he was charged with printing *The Jesus Psalter* 'and other things without aucthoritie'. Hoppe believes that *Romeo and Juliet* was going through Danter's press at the time of the raid. In discussing the title-page reference to Hunsdon's Men, Hoppe deduces that the Quarto must have been in the press between the beginning of Lent (9 February) and 17 March 1597, when Shakespeare's company ceased to be known by that name.

Recently, J. A. Lavin has argued that it is not evident why sheets E–K must be supposed to have been printed after A–D rather than simultaneously in a shared printing job, as happened in the printing of two books by Greene, shared by Danter and Wolfe. Lavin points out that the title-page date of 1597 is no guarantee that it was not printed in late 1596,[2] and that its bibliographical features do not necessarily indicate interruption of printing in Danter's shop. The conclusion seems acceptable: the printing was probably done some time between the last months of 1596 and March 1597, in a job shared between Danter and Allde.

Q2 is nearly half as long again as Q1; it offers correct versions of corrupt or garbled passages in Q1 and its characteristics indicate that the copy was the author's foul papers from which the prompt-book was derived. In one extended passage and certain other places the Q2 compositor used Q1 as copy, presumably because of obscurity or deficiency in the manuscript.

An analysis by Paul Cantrell and George Walton Williams[3] of the printing of Q2 has determined the shares of the two compositors who set the text, and a study of their work in other books

1. Ibid.; Hoppe's suggestion, that the second printer was Edward Allde, has been confirmed by Standish Henning, 'The Printer of *Romeo and Juliet*, Q1', *PBSA*, LX.

2. 'John Danter's Ornament Stock', *SB*, XXIII. Harold Brooks points out that postdating to make a book seem fresh for as long as possible certainly was practised: the first impression of Oldham's *Satyrs upon the Jesuits* (1681) was certainly on the market in late 1680, probably November. (If *Romeo and Juliet* (1597) was actually published in late 1596 this would strengthen the argument for the play's having preceded *A Midsummer Night's Dream*.)

3. 'The Printing of the Second Quarto of *Romeo and Juliet* (1599)', *SB*, IX.

printed in Creede's shop indicates that both of them were conscientious artisans. Although the New Shakespeare editors of *Romeo and Juliet* describe 'the compositor' as 'slovenly',[1] they also admit that he faithfully reproduces Shakespeare's first and second shots together, as well as words which he found in his copy that do not make sense (due, as they suppose, to a copyist who spelt out *literatim* what he found difficult to read in the foul papers). Indeed it is difficult not to think that this reproduction of anomalies, inconsistencies and duplications in Q2 indicates a conscientious compositor faithfully following his copy with few serious lapses.

Q1 AS MEMORIAL RECONSTRUCTION

A feature of Q1 which indicates that a reporter's[2] memory is playing a part in the transmission of the text is that speeches which properly appear two acts later are anticipated, an error impossible for a scribe or compositor working his way through the text but quite plausible for someone who has acted in or prompted a performance of the play a number of times, and who confuses two different passages because they are in some way parallel.

For instance in I. v, at the end of the feast, Capulet is bidding goodnight to his guests, full of regret that his celebration has come to an end. Q2 reads:

> I thanke you honest gentlemen, goodnight:
> More torches here, come on, then lets to bed.
> Ah sirrah, by my faie it waxes late,

but Q1 at the end of the feast has this:

> Well then *I* thanke you honest Gentlemen,
> I promise you but for your company,
> I would haue bin a bed an houre agoe:
> Light to my chamber hoe.

The reporter has remembered lines from Capulet's speeches in III. iv and misplaces them in the earlier scene: in III. iv Paris visits Capulet who frankly wants him to go home and tells him so:

1. *Romeo and Juliet*, ed. J. Dover Wilson and G. I. Duthie (1955), p. 115.
2. It is convenient to speak of 'a reporter' when discussing a particular passage, though different parts of the play may have been reported by different individuals in the group, while some of the reconstruction may have been collaborative. Presumably the Bad Quarto version was assembled by a group who had been involved in the first authentic production and intended to perform the play, with a reduced cast, on a provincial tour.

> I promise you, but for your companie,
> I would haue bene a bed an houre ago.

Seventeen lines later, almost at the end of III. iv, Capulet says

> Farewell my Lord, light to my chamber ho.

Another instance of anticipation is evident with the arrival of the Nurse with news for Juliet. In Q2 she arrives, flustered, in II. v, with the news of Romeo, and makes the complaint

> Fie how my bones ake, what a iaunce haue I?

Much later (in III. ii) she brings news of Tybalt's death in shocked distress and exclaims

> Ah wheres my man? giue me some Aqua-vitae:

Q1 combines elements from these two speeches in the scene where the Nurse brings news of Romeo; Q1 reads:

> Lord how my bones ake. Oh wheres my man? Give me some aqua vitae.

An instance of anticipation of a passage several scenes away is Romeo's greeting to the Friar at II. iii, where the Q1 reporter remembers the later scene in which Juliet visits the Friar (II. vi). In Q2 Romeo and the Friar share a couplet in II. iii:

> *Ro.* Goodmorrow father.
> *Fri.* Benedicitie.
> What early tongue so sweete saluteth me?

and in Q2 Juliet greets the Friar in II. vi with the line

> Good euen to my ghostly confessor.

Q1 makes Romeo say this line in the earlier scene, spoiling the couplet:

> *Rom:* Good morrow to my Ghostly Confessor.
> *Fri:* *Benedicite*, what earlie tongue so soone saluteth me?

In each of these cases the Q1 version crudely damages the tone and mood of the earlier scene by confusing it with the later: so Capulet becomes impolite, the Nurse a tippler, the light poise of Romeo prosaic.

The reporter's faulty memory also causes him to reproduce phrases or lines later than their proper place. In Mercutio's dying speech at III. i Q1 has the line:

> *Mercutio* was slaine for the first and second cause

which recollects a line already given in its proper place at II. iv (ll. 25–6 in Q2, l. 27 in Q1); and in the passage later in III. i where Benvolio is narrating the events of the brawl between Mercutio, Tybalt and Romeo, Q1 recollects a Q2 line from Benvolio's earlier narrative of the brawl at the beginning of the play (in Q2 it is I. i. 120):

> *Q1:* While they were enterchanging thrusts and blows.

These instances of recollection involve single phrases or fragments. As it happens, however, both places in III. i also provide more generally illustrative material showing that Q1 is a reported text. Mercutio's dying speech is imperfectly remembered, its fragments are pieced together in a mosaic supplemented by pedestrian paraphrasings. Here is the speech in Q2:

> No tis not so deepe as a well, nor so wide as a Church doore, but tis inough, twill serue: aske for me tomorrow, and you shall finde me a graue man. I am peppered I warrant, for this world, a plague a both your houses, sounds a dog, a rat, a mouse, a cat, to scratch a man to death: a braggart, a rogue, a villaine, that fights by the booke of arithmatick, why the deule came you betweene vs? I was hurt vnder your arme.

The Q1 version is:

> I am pepperd for this world, I am sped yfaith, he hath made wormes meate of me, & ye aske for me to morrow you shall finde me a graue-man. A poxe of your houses, I shall be fairely mounted upon foure mens shoulders: For your house of the *Mountegues* and the *Capolets*: and then some peasantly rogue, some Sexton, some base slaue shall write my Epitapth, that *Tybalt* came and broke the Princes Lawes, and *Mercutio* was slaine for the first and second cause. Wher's the Surgeon?

Q1 has misplaced two of the phrases in the Q2 version in an earlier speech (they are the opening and closing lines 'No tis . . . twill serue' and 'why the deule . . . arme') but also anticipates a line which occurs later in Q2, III. i. 112 ('They haue made wormes meate of me'). The middle of the speech in Q1 is not Shakespeare; for his still impatient and headstrong Mercutio, suddenly caught by spasms of physical agony and anguished thoughts, Q1 substitutes pedestrian hack-writing in regular dull rhythm, concluded with a dismally banal sententious couplet. The Q1 version recalls the rough shape and length of the speech, recognizes its dramatic function, but does not reproduce the words.[1]

1. The non-Shakespearean element in this speech may be a deliberate substitution (or 'gag') by the actor concerned, obviously without Shakespeare's endorsement.

In the next instance Benvolio is reporting the brawl between Romeo, Tybalt and Mercutio. Q2 reads as follows:

> *Romeo* he cries aloud,
> Hold friends, friends part, and swifter then his tongue,
> His aged arme beates downe their fatall poynts,
> And twixt them rushes, vnderneath whose arme,
> An enuious thrust from *Tybalt*, hit the life
> Of stout *Mercutio*. (III. i. 169–74)

The version in Q1 is:

> Which *Romeo* seeing cal'd stay Gentlemen,
> And on me cry'd, who drew to part their strife,
> And with his agill arme yong Romeo,
> As fast as tung cryde peace, sought peace to make.
> While they were enterchanging thrusts and blows,
> Vnder yong *Romeos* laboring arme to part,
> The furious *Tybalt* cast an enuious thrust,
> That rid the life of stout *Mercutio*.

Here is a non-Shakespearean paraphrase studded with genuine phrases and words; it is hard to make sense of the sixth line in the extract, and 'rid the life' is obviously a memorial error for the Q2 phrase 'hit the life'. More importantly, the inclusion of a line (the fifth) from the first narrative of brawling in Act I seriously blunts the point of this speech, which is to defend Romeo from any charge of aggressive provocation. Q2 has Romeo's arm beating 'downe their fatall poynts' before he rushes between the combatants; but Q1 misses this out, and adds a line which strongly suggests that Romeo fully joined in the fight, so making it two against one. The bad phrasing of the sixth line makes it appear that Romeo's arm was labouring to strike Tybalt. Here again the faulty memory of the reporter, by confusing two very different passages, damages the dramatic effect and characterization as well as vulgarizing the text.

Sometimes in Q1 roughly equivalent dramatic purposes are served by scenes containing only scattered fragments of Shakespeare. For instance, the meeting at the Friar's cell (II. vi) appears in Q1 in a version with no verbal similarity to Q2; evidently the reporter remembered the narrative content of the scene, wished to retain it for its dramatic function, but had to compose it afresh. Deficient memory also produces a substitute version of the lament over the supposedly dead Juliet at IV. v, where again the Q2 version is wholly different. In the last two acts Q1 increasingly displays these features; some speeches are correctly rendered by

Q1, others contain varying proportions of Shakespeare in varying degrees of accuracy. The Friar's final narration contains occasional fragments of Shakespeare in pedestrian verse of the reporter's own composition; and since Shakespeare's Friar has a tendency to prolixity and tediousness, the Q1 version at least retains something of the original—though we may find it ironic that it omits the Friar's lines

> I will be briefe, for my short date of breath
> Is not so long as is a tedious tale.

In general Q1 abbreviates many speeches and episodes given fully in Q2, evidently as the result of the bad memory of the reporters, especially in the last two acts—such a deterioration towards the end is in fact a characteristic common to the Bad Quartos.

Yet a number of the omissions may indicate deliberate cuts in a recent abridged version in which the reporters had participated.[1] For example, Benvolio's narration of the first brawl in I. i is ten lines long in Q2 but only two lines in Q1. This might very well indicate a cut. It is certain that the compiler of the Q1 text knew the full version of Q2 here, since later on (III. i), as we have seen, one of the lines omitted from Benvolio's narration is inserted in his second narration of the second brawl. The servants who open I. v in Q2 are omitted in Q1; this could also be a cut. In a number of instances a dozen or more lines in Q2 are reduced to one or two in Q1. For example, in II. v, the Q2 lines in which Juliet expresses her frustration (29–37) are cut, and IV. i, where the Friar's plan is explained to Juliet, twenty-one lines in Q2 are reduced to five lines in Q1.

These possible Q1 cuts may be considered alongside other omissions and summaries in Q1 which could equally well be caused by failure of memory, such as the omission of all but the first four lines of Juliet's speech which in Q2 begins III. ii: 'Gallop apace, you fierie footed steedes'. Q1 prints only the first four lines of this, but it does provide a stage direction longer than the equivalent in Q2. It may be that Juliet's speech had been cut partly to reduce the duration of performance, partly in anticipation of a provincial audience eager enough for violent or comic action but impatient with lyric utterance. On the other hand the extremely vivid phrasing of the Q1 direction '*Enter the Nurse wringing her hands, with the ladder of cords in her lap*' is evidently the result of patching together an anticipation of Juliet's 'why dost

1. Cf. Hoppe's views, cited p. 2, n. 2.

thou wring thy hāds?' a few lines later in Q2 (which Q1 omits) and the Nurse's reference to fetching a ladder, recollected from II. v: 'I must prouide a ladder made of cordes' (Q1).

In the opening scene a substantial amount of dialogue in Q2 is omitted in Q1, being simply covered by a long stage direction which only summarizes the Q2 dialogue and accompanying stage directions. As a consequence, according to the Q1 stage direction, Benvolio does not emphatically try to stop the brawl; he loses the memorable and thematically important line

> Part fools, put up your swords, you know not what you do.

and the Q1 stage direction merely reads (after *Enter Benvolio* a line earlier):

> *They draw, to them enters* Tybalt, *they fight, to them the Prince, old* Mountague, *and his wife, old* Capulet *and his wife, and other Citizens and part them.*

The Q2 version preserves an order of events ritually and thematically significant to the whole play:

> *Enter* Benvolio (64) . . . *They fight* (70) . . . *Enter* Tibalt (72) . . . *Enter three or foure Citizens with Clubs or partysons* (79) . . . *Enter old* Capulet *in his gowne, and his wife* (82) . . . *Enter old* Mountague *and his wife* (86) . . . *Enter Prince* Eskales, *with his traine* (88).

Certainly Q2 is wholly superior here, presenting an unmistakably Shakespearean structure of action which will be memorably completed by the final scene of the play. Q1 is by contrast dramatically, not simply verbally, shoddy. The stage direction in Q1 here is summarizing action poorly recollected by the reporter.[1] Even so nobody is omitted in the Q1 directions who should be present.

The influence of stage performance on the reported text of Q1 is apparent in another feature of Q1 not yet discussed here: Q1 contains a number of vulgarizations, interpolations, and additions very characteristic of actors who alter details to suit their interpretation. So in I. iii Benvolio gives Mercutio a cue for the Queen Mab speech in Q1: 'Queen Mab whats she?' In v. iii the Page adds to his whistle the words 'My Lord', and in III. i the business with Mercutio's Page is expanded by making the Page reply to

1. There has been an unconvincing suggestion that the wording of Q1's directions, '*to them*', indicates that it is taken from a theatrical plot, in which the locution is common: see Alfred Hart, *Stolne and Surreptitious Copies* (1942), p. 421; Hoppe, op. cit., p. 80. Some extant theatrical plots are presented in Greg, *Dramatic Documents from the Elizabethan Playhouses* (1931).

the command to fetch a surgeon, and adding a later exchange—'Wher's the Surgeon? / *Boy.* Hee's come sir.' The Nurse is given new lines in prose at IV. iii in Q1 though in Q2 she says nothing; one of the new lines adds a homely touch: 'Well theres a cleane smocke under your pillow, and so goodnight.' Such minor additions as these are probably deliberate, by actors; but there are also many minor vulgarizations, minor paraphrases or variants probably introduced by defective memory.[1] For instance, at I. iii. 98, where Q2 has

> But no more deepe will I endart mine eye

Q1 substitutes 'engage' for 'endart'. I. iv. 47 is a more obvious case: Q2 has

> Fiue times in that, ere once in our fine wits

but Q1 vulgarizes to

> Three times a day ere once in her right wits.

In II. iv. 132 Q1 loses a joke by wrongly correcting the malapropism: Q2 has

> *Nur.* If you be he sir, I desire some confidence with you.
> *Ben.* She will endite him to some supper. (ll. 132–3)

where Q1 reads

> *Nur:* If you be he sir, I desire some conference with ye.
> *Ben:* O, belike she meanes to inuite him to supper.

Some of the vulgarizations can be explained as recollections of similar phrases in other plays; *Arden of Feversham* may explain Q1's variant of I. i. 127:

> A troubled minde driue me to walke abroad (Q2)
> A troubled thought drew me from companie (Q1)
> Disturbed thoughts dryues me from company
> (*Arden of Feversham*, III. v. 1);

and the phrase 'ciuill broyles' in the Q1 Prologue may come from *The True Tragedy of Richard Duke of York*, which has the line: 'take thine oath, to cease these ciuill Broiles', varying from *3 Henry VI*,

1. Hoppe (op. cit., p. 128) makes the point that a compositor whose exercise of memory consists in keeping a line or two in his mind while setting might make this kind of error, might erroneously transpose or substitute a word or phrase; yet no printer of *Romeo and Juliet* after Q2 did make this kind of error of transposition or substitution.

I. i. 196–7: 'take an Oath, / To cease this Ciuill Warre.' These and other instances of recollections in Q1 could indicate the reporters' familiarity with the Bad Quartos of *2 Henry VI*, *3 Henry VI*, *Richard III* and with *Arden of Feversham.*[1]

The stage directions in Q1 are of exceptional interest, since although they are descriptive they are remarkably apt and vivid. Here are some instances (with references keyed to the present edition):

I. v. 121	*They whisper in his eare.*
II. iv. 131	*He walkes by them, and sings.*
151	*She turnes to Peter her man.*
II. vi. 15	*Enter Juliet somewhat fast, and embraceth Romeo.*
III. i. 89	*Tibalt under Romeos arme thrusts Mercutio in and flyes.*
III. iii. 107	*He offers to stab himselfe, and Nurse snatches the dagger away.*
161	*Nurse offers to goe in and turnes againe.*
III. v. 1	*Enter Romeo and Iuliet at the window.*
67	*She goeth downe from the window.*
158	*She kneeles downe.*
234	*She lookes after Nurse.*
IV. iii. 58	*She fals upon her bed within the Curtaines.*
IV. v. [50]	*All at once cry out and wring their hands.*
IV. v. 95	*They all but the Nurse goe foorth, casting Rosemary on her and shutting the Curtens.*
V. i. 11	*Enter Balthasar his man booted.*
V. iii. 11	Paris *strewes the Tomb with flowers.*
147	Iuliet *rises.*
169	*She stabs herselfe and falles.*

Some of these seem to record the impressions of a spectator ('*somewhat fast*'); or they could be the work of someone concerned with production, noting important stage business and portable properties used in performance.[2] In Q1 the stage direction '*She kneeles downe*' accompanies Juliet's line

Good father heare me speake?

1. A. S. Cairncross, 'Pembroke's Men and Some Shakespearean Piracies', *SQ*, XI (1960), pp. 335–49.

2. Compare the Bad Quarto of *The Merry Wives*, which has the descriptive stage direction in III. iii: '*Sir Iohn goes into the basket, they put cloathes ouer him, the two men carries it away: Foord meetes it, and all the rest, Page, Doctor, Priest, Slender, Shallow.*'

In Q2, however, Juliet says

> Good Father, I beseech you on my knees,
> Heare me with patience, but to speake a word
> (ll. 159–60)

and there is no stage direction as such; the action is implied by the dialogue. Similarly, Q1's stage direction for the killing of Mercutio derives from the text, where Mercutio says 'I was hurt vnder your arme'. That it is the Nurse not the Friar who in III. iii prevents Romeo stabbing himself is not apparent from the Q2 text; it is hard to believe it represents Shakespeare's intention, but Q1 probably records what happened in a performed version of the play. In III. v the Q1 directions about action at the window are helpful in suggesting how to stage the scene, though Q1's modified *text* is not to be preferred on grounds of quality or stageworthiness. In Q1 the Nurse is given an entrance, as Romeo exits, to warn Juliet of her mother's approach; Juliet's speech (60–4) is cut and lines of dialogue taken from I. iii. 1–4 are inserted. Juliet's entrance at the lower level is not indicated:

> *Enter Iuliet's Mother, Nurse.*
> *Moth:* Where are you Daughter?
> *Nur:* What Ladie, Lambe, what *Iuliet?*
> *Iul:* How now, who calls?
> *Nur:* It is your Mother.
> *Moth:* Why how now *Juliet?*
> *Iul:* Madam, I am not well.

Q1's directions for IV. iii. 58 and IV. v. 95 (which are quoted above) are vivid but tantalizing; they do not identify the exact location of the bed nor do they make it clear whether it is brought on stage or revealed by opening a curtain or doors; but there does seem to be a visual recollection of authentic stage business. The descriptive direction in IV. v. ('*All at once cry out and wring their hands*') seems intended as substitute for forgotten dialogue, and serves as a substitute for the Q2 text. At III. iii, Q1's directions for the separate entry of the Friar and Romeo probably reflect an actual performance; certainly Q2's direction for joint entry is contradicted by the dialogue which requires a delayed entry for Romeo.

One more feature of Q1 links it to stage performance and memorial reconstruction: this is the fact that the speeches of the Nurse in I. iii are printed in italic. An explanation for this is that the compositor found in his manuscript contrasting types of handwriting; whoever wrote out the speeches of the Nurse did so not in an English but in an italic hand. The compositor followed his copy, supposing that the italic was significant in some way. It does not follow that, because the compositor of Q1 printed all the Nurse's speeches in the scene in italic, they must necessarily have so appeared in the manuscript; a compositor might continue italics to the end of the scene on his own responsibility even though the hand changed back to English after several speeches. The point needs to be made since the text of the Nurse's speeches is remarkably good for the first 34 lines of the scene, but after that its quality and metrical regularity deteriorate. Yet a question remains: why should a manuscript suddenly present a compositor with the speeches of only one character written in italic, though intervening speeches by others continue in an English hand? It has been proposed[1] that the reporters had obtained a fragment of the actor's part of the Nurse, containing the opening speeches written in italic. The one surviving example of an actor's part from an Elizabethan play[2] suggests that this is possible: the part is written out on a long paper roll consisting of strips pasted end to end, written on one side only, including short cues and stage directions. The reporters could have cut this up and pasted it into their copy, writing in intervening speeches in their non-italic hand. When the fragment ended (perhaps at l. 35) they could have resorted once more to memorial reconstruction. At the end of the scene in Q1 the 'Clown's' speech is also printed in italic. Here we may well suppose that the compositor, who had for quite a time been setting alternate speeches in italic and roman, considered that after four lines of verse in roman it was right to print the three lines of comic prose in italic. There is no other reasonable explanation, and the fact adds probability to the theory that the compositor continued setting the Nurse's speeches in italic after his copy reverted to non-italic handwriting.[3]

THE COPY FOR Q2

Major evidence that the copy for Q2 was Shakespeare's own manuscript, not corrected and not prepared for prompter's use, is the very large number of anomalies and inconsistencies and accidents preserved in the text of Q2. Speech prefixes are highly

1. By Greg, *The Editorial Problem in Shakespeare* (1942), p. 62.

2. See Greg, op. cit., pp. 45–6. The part is Alleyn's, the title-role for *Orlando Furioso*; it is at Dulwich: a facsimile is reproduced in Greg, *Dramatic Documents*.

3. This is substantially the view of G. I. Duthie, 'The Text of Shakespeare's *Romeo and Juliet*', *SB*, IV, pp. 9–10.

inconsistent and variable, so that it is virtually impossible to believe that a scribe or editor would not have reduced them to order if he had transcribed the manuscript; nor would he have introduced them. Lady Capulet is *Capu.Wi* (1), *Ca. Wi*(1), *Wife.* (5), *Wi.* (1), *Old La.* (6), *La.* (14), *Mo.* (12), *M.* (4). Although on some occasions it seems that Shakespeare varies her speech prefix according to the way he thinks of her function in a particular scene, on others the variation seems purely arbitrary. Capulet appears as *Capu.* (11), *Cap.* (5), *Ca.* (16), *Fat.* (1), *Fa.* (11). In some scenes he is 'father' when addressing the Nurse, which cannot be explained as the way Shakespeare thought of his function in the scene.[1] Attendants are referred to inconsistently as *Ser.*, *Man.*, *Boy.*, *Page.*, *Clowne.*, *Peter.*, without a system of variation—although Friar Laurence is distinguished from Friar John in v. ii, where he becomes *Law.* instead of the usual *Frier.*

In the stage directions a similar arbitrary variation is to be observed; so in IV. v. 102 the direction '*Enter Will Kemp*' refers to no character but to the clown for whom the part was evidently written. Shakespeare presumably intended the parts of Peter and Balthasar to be doubled or else temporarily confused them, since the direction at v. iii. 21 has '*Enter* Romeo *and* Peter', where Balthasar must be meant; elsewhere in Act v he is referred to as '*Romeo's man*'. Stage directions with variant forms include IV. iv. 1 '*Enter Lady of the house*' for Lady Capulet and IV. v. 32 '*Enter Frier and the Countie*' for Friar and Paris. There are so-called permissive stage directions (for indeterminate numbers of persons) such as that at I. i. 79 '*Enter three or foure Citizens*' or l. 87 '*Enter Prince* Eskales, *with his traine*', or I. v. 16 '*Enter all the guests and gentlewomen to the Maskers*'. There is in addition the strong possibility that the stage direction at III. i. 36 '*Enter* Tybalt, Petruchio, *and others*' reveals a 'ghost' character whom Shakespeare intended to develop, gave the name Petruchio, and then found no lines for when he composed the scene. All these features may be paralleled from other Shakespeare texts which editors agree are printed from foul papers, such as *Much Ado*, which has a 'ghost' character in the stage direction '*Enter Leonato gouernour of Messina, Innogen his wife*, . . .' and in which the speech prefixes for Dogberry in one scene

1. Cantrell and Williams, 'The Printing of Q2', conclude that Compositor A was faithful to his copy, and that the variation in speech prefixes he prints indicates that he is following a manuscript of independent authority 'and following it faithfully'. NCS (p. 115) believes the scribe who transcribed the manuscript was 'unintelligently meticulous' in reproducing Shakespeare's irregularities, while the compositor was 'either very slovenly or a much overdriven mechanic'.

are variously '*Andrew*' (i.e. clown, merry-andrew) and '*Kemp*', and for Verges the actor's name, '*Cowley*'. In *Love's Labour's Lost* proper and generic names for characters are indiscriminately varied, even within a scene, where '*Holofernes*' and '*Pedant*' alternate irregularly;[1] while *Titus Andronicus* offers a characteristic permissive stage direction in '*Enter . . . Aaron the Moor, and others as many as can be. . . .*'

Another important sign of foul papers is the incidence of duplication and confusion in the text itself. So in III. v, lines 177–9 in Q2 read:

> Gods bread, it makes me mad,
> Day, night, houre, tide, time, worke, play,
> Alone in companie, still my care hath bene

Here it seems probable that Shakespeare first wrote 'Day, night,' then considered in turn 'houre', 'tide' and 'time', discarded them, and then wrote 'worke, play'; but he did not score out the discarded words, or if he did, it was too lightly for the Q2 compositor. The latter in any case seems to have followed the manuscript layout, and so both lines 177 and 178 have faulty scansion in Q2. Again, at III. ii. 76 Q2 has:

> Rauenous douefeatherd rauē, woluishrauening lamb,

where presumably Shakespeare's first version is 'Rauenous doue', recast in the second version to provide a double and punning oxymoron. Again the discarded word has been erroneously printed owing to a misunderstanding of the manuscript.

There are other instances of minor duplications of this kind, such as that in V. iii. 102–3, which reads in Q2:

> Why art thou yet so faire? I will beleeue,
> Shall I beleeue that vnsubstantiall death is amorous,

where 'I will beleeue' is evidently Shakespeare's first attempt, not adequately marked for deletion; or IV. i. 111–12 in Q2:

> Be borne to buriall in thy kindreds graue:
> Thou shall be borne to that same auncient vault,

where the first line appears to be a discarded first version

1. Dover Wilson in his edition thinks that generic titles in speech prefixes may be taken 'as clues suggesting revision', and that the Quarto compositor at this point (IV. ii) was dealing with part of the original manuscript which Shakespeare had partially revised. His view is refuted by Greg, *The Shakespeare First Folio*, p. 114, n. 1; Greg notes that McKerrow originally emphasized that varying speech prefixes could be evidence of authorial manuscript.

erroneously printed. In some cases, however, the issue is more complex because the passage is longer and the nature of the revision less obvious, as at II. ii. 189 ff., where four lines assigned to Romeo are repeated, with minor alterations, as the opening lines of the next scene, where they are assigned to the Friar; or at III. iii. 39, where probably alternative versions are printed:

(a) This may flyes do, when I from this must flie,
(b) And sayest thou yet, that exile is not death?
(c) But *Romeo* may not, he is banished.
(d) Flies may do this, but I from this must flie:
(e) They are freemen, but I am banished.

The first three lines, according to Capell, are Shakespeare's first version and to be discarded, since line (a) becomes (d) and line (c) becomes (e) while (b) is developed into the following:

Hadst thou no poyson mixt, no sharpe ground knife,
No sudden meane of death, though nere so meane,
But banished to kill me: Banished?

The hysteria of Romeo expresses itself partly in repetition, but how much repetition? Most editors think that some part of this passage was discarded by Shakespeare during revision, but opinions vary about the nature and extent of the process, and it is possible that no emendation is needed.[1] There is little doubt, however, that in the other passages here cited with their obvious revisional duplications, emendation is required.

From the evidence surveyed here it seems we may visualize Shakespeare's manuscript as sometimes including first and second versions as part of the continuous dialogue and sometimes as marginal additions and corrections, perhaps with, perhaps without, signs to show where they are to be inserted. Such directions to a copyist would not be necessary, of course, if one were able to suppose that Shakespeare knew that he himself would be producing a fair copy; indeed in that case he might very well leave some lines unfinalized and write on, preferring not to risk losing his poetic impetus.[2]

1. Spencer does not emend the Q2 passage.

2. E. A. J. Honigmann, *The Stability of Shakespeare's Text* (1965), pp. 16, 33. Honigmann has suggested that Shakespeare may have tidied up these tangles if or when he wrote a fair copy for the playhouse, where he probably also deposited his foul papers for safe keeping. 'When, two or more years later, the foul papers were passed on to the printers, their occasional deviation from the acted version could easily escape notice.' Honigmann, op. cit., p. 21, suggests that authors closely connected with one company, such as Shakespeare or

It remains to add that we need not suppose the manuscript used by the Q2 compositor as copy, Shakespeare's foul papers, to be homogeneous, especially if Shakespeare wrote his plays on loose sheets of paper: some sheets might be first drafts, some transcripts or first-draft fair copies.[1]

In 1879 Robert Gericke noticed[2] that the Q2 compositor set the Nurse's part at the beginning of I. iii in italic, as in Q1, though he obviously had access to different copy after line 34. On the basis of this bibliographical link he argued that a long passage, from I. ii. 46 to I. iii. 34, was reprinted from Q1 by the Q2 compositor. Other bibliographical links between Q1 and Q2 have since been identified, and various theories proposed to explain them, separately or together.[3] Although there is a complex history of

---

Fletcher, may have handed their foul papers over to the playhouse not because they were compelled to but because, 'in an age when lodgings could be searched and papers removed (e.g. Kyd's), and when "pirates" tried to steal plays, the theatre was the best place for safe deposit'.

1. Fredson Bowers, *Textual and Literary Criticism* (1959), citing the work of Cantrell and Williams, notes that Williams proposes the hypothesis that the manuscript was not homogeneous: the pattern of speech prefixes for Capulet and Lady Capulet could indicate that a regular usage becomes varied and irregular after III. v, while at the same point a marked increase in the use of capitals in the text appears; so the manuscript up to III. v might be a revision, a draft fair copy; after III. v the manuscript might be an earlier, more provisional draft. See also Bowers, *On Editing Shakespeare* (1955), pp. 110–11.

2. '*Romeo and Juliet* nach Shakespeare's Manuscript', *SJH*, XVI, pp. 270–2.

3. A. W. Pollard and J. Dover Wilson in 1919 argued (in the *TLS*) that links at II. iv. 40–6 and III. v. 27–32 and elsewhere indicated a common manuscript source. Greta Hjort, 'The Good and Bad Quartos of *Romeo and Juliet* and *Love's Labour's Lost*', *MLR*, XXI (1926), supposed that the copy for Q2 was an exemplar of Q1 which had been collated with an authentic manuscript; additions and corrections were written into the Q1 margins and between the lines or on inserted slips of paper. R. B. McKerrow in 'A Note on the "Bad Quartos" of *2* and *3 Henry VI* and the Folio Text', *RES*, XIII (1937), independently arrived at Gericke's theory. Sidney Thomas, in 'The Bibliographical Links between the First Two Quartos of *Romeo and Juliet*', *RES*, XXV (1949), disputed whether there would have been space in an exemplar of Q1 for all the corrections and additions to be written in; he also pointed out that where Q1 served as copy for Q2 in I. ii–iii it was not corrected or annotated; he rejected the evidence for other bibliographical links. In 1952 G. I. Duthie in 'The Text of Shakespeare's *Romeo and Juliet*', *SB*, IV, argued that the copy for Q2 was a scribal transcript from manuscript together with certain leaves torn out of an exemplar of Q1 and corrected in ink by reference to the manuscript. Duthie supposed the scribe tore out and corrected the Q1 leaves on which the passage identified by Gericke is printed; also probably leaves D1, E1 and G3 were removed from Q1 and added to the bundle of papers comprising the transcription from manuscript. Duthie conjectured that the similarity in the setting up of the Prologue in Q1 and Q2 might indicate that another leaf, A3, was added to the copy for Q2,

editorial interpretation of details, it is possible to distinguish two basic general theories to account for the Q2 text. Theory A is that, except for the passage identified by Gericke, where Q1 was followed, Q2 was set from Shakespeare's or a transcription of Shakespeare's manuscript—but with occasional consultation of Q1. Theory B is that an exemplar of Q1 was corrected and amplified by reference to a manuscript and used as sole copy. W. W. Greg, in *The Shakespeare First Folio* (1955), expressed the conviction that the copy for Q2 was Shakespeare's foul papers, except for one extended passage from I. ii to I. iii detected by Gericke, and certain other places where bibliographical links indicated that Q1 had been consulted. In the same year J. Dover Wilson defended the alternative theory in an article,[1] and with G. I. Duthie published an edition of the play based on the assumption that the copy for Q2 was an exemplar of Q1 corrected and annotated by a scribe who had collated it with a manuscript. Dover Wilson cited a large number of places in which he saw bibliographical links with Q2 in the pages of Q1 'which cannot be explained on any theory of mere consultation of Q1 by those responsible for Q2'.[2] This assertion has been challenged by Richard Hosley, who notes[3] that in the article Dover Wilson 'does not demonstrate the hypothesis of annotated-quarto copy' but 'merely demonstrates that Q1 occasionally influenced the text of Q2 during the printing of that edition'. This evidence clearly commands attention and may now be investigated along with a second proposition of Dover Wilson's, which is that a copyist is just as likely as a compositor to reproduce faithfully the confusions and duplications in Q2 which have been thought to point to the use of foul papers.[4]

To begin with the reprinted passage in I. ii to I. iii, the most substantial bibliographical link between Q1 and Q2; the very close similarities in spelling, misprint and type—especially in the Nurse's speeches and the setting up of the 'letter' (I. ii. 67–72)—and the very scarce substantive variants, constitute a biblio-

---

even though the Q2 Prologue is so different that it would have had to be 'almost completely rewritten'. Duthie changed his mind, when collaborating with J. Dover Wilson on their edition of *Romeo and Juliet*, adopting the theory of annotated Quarto copy.

1. 'The New Way with Shakespeare's Texts, II: Recent Work on the Text of *Romeo and Juliet*', *Sh.S.*, *8* (1955).

2. Ibid., p. 84.

3. Richard Hosley, 'Quarto Copy for Q2 *Romeo and Juliet*', *SB*, IX, p. 132n.

4. 'The New Way', p. 89.

graphical link. Although Gericke thought it began at l. 46 ('*Ben.* Tut man . . .') there are four substantive and other incidental variants in the next few lines, whereas if l. 53 ('*Romeo.* For your broken shin') is taken as a starting point, there is no variation for 18 lines, where the Q2 omission of '*and*' is very probably a compositor's error. The only other substantive variants are 'you' for Q1 'thee' at l. 81, '*an*' for '*a*' (I. iii. 11), Q2's misprint '*stal*' for Q1 '*shall*' (I. iii. 17) and Q2's correction '*the Dugge*' for Q1 '*Dugge*' (I. iii. 31). After l. 34 the variant '*yeares*' for Q1 '*yeare*' may indicate return to manuscript copy at l. 35, and certainly l. 36 has a substantive variant '*run and wadled all about*' for Q1's '*wadled up and downe*'. Thereafter the quality of Q1 deteriorates sharply. The evidence points to the conclusion that the Q2 compositor used as copy for this passage the Q1 text unrevised and uncorrected by scribal intervention.

In 1919 Pollard and Dover Wilson identified bibliographical links between Q1 and Q2 in two other places: II. iv. 37–47 and III. v. 26–35. In the first instance the alternatives from Q1 and Q2 are as follows:

Q1] *Ben:* Heere comes *Romeo.*
Mer: Without his Roe, like a dryed Hering. O flesh flesh how art thou fishified. Sirra now is he for the numbers that Petrarch flowdin: *Laura* to his Lady was but a kitchin drudg, yet she had a better loue to berime her: Dido a dowdy Cleopatra a Gypsie, *Hero* and *Hellen* hildings and harletries: *Thisbie* a gray eye or so, but not to the purpose. Signior *Romeo* bon iour there is a French curtesie to your French flop: yee gaue vs the counterfeit fairely yesternight.

Q2] *Ben.* Here Comes *Romeo*, here comes *Romeo.*
Mer. Without his Roe, like a dried Hering, O flesh, flesh, how art thou fishified? now is he for the numbers that Petrach flowed in: *Laura* to his Lady, was a kitchin wench, marrie she had a better loue to berime her: Dido a dowdie, Cleopatra a Gipsie, *Hellen* and *Hero*, hildings and harlots: *Thisbie* a grey eye or so, but not to the purpose. Signior *Romeo*, *Bonieur*, theres a French salutation to your French slop: you gaue vs the counterfeit fairly last night.

There is a coincidence in the use of capitals and colons, and in eight proper names, five in italic, three in roman; the inconsistent pattern is exactly reproduced in Q2, evidently because the compositor consulted Q1. At the same time Q2 contains a number of substantive variants ('wench' for 'drudg', 'marrie' for 'yet', 'harlots' for 'harletries', '*Bonieur*' for 'bon iour', 'salutation' for 'curtesie', 'last night' for 'yesternight'). Q2's '*Bonieur*' is italic, has a capital, is undivided, and misreads/misprints *e* for *o*; this seems such a complex deviation from Q1 that a manuscript form is a preferable alternative explanation. While the other variants are consistent with the hypothesis that the Q2 compositor used as copy an exemplar of Q1 corrected by a transcriber from the manuscript, neither scribal correction of Q1 nor Q2 compositorial error is persuasive as an explanation of '*Bonieur*'. This probably is, as Hosley says,[1] a manuscript link between Q2 and foul papers.

The passage from III. v discussed by Pollard and Dover Wilson is as follows:

Q1] *Jul:* It is, it is, be gone, flye hence away.
It is the Larke that sings so out of tune,
Straining harsh Discords and vnpleasing Sharpes.
Some say, the Larke makes sweete Diuision:
This doth not so: for this diuideth vs.
Some say the Larke and loathed Toad change eyes,
I would that now they had changd voyces too:
Since arme from arme her voyce doth vs affray,
Hunting thee hence with Huntsvp to the day.
So now be gone, more light and light it growes.

Q2] *Iu.* It is, it is, hie hence be gone away:
It is the Larke that sings so out of tune,
Straining harsh Discords, and vnpleasing Sharpes.
Some say, the Larke makes sweete Diuision:
This doth not so: for she diuideth vs.
Some say the Larke and loathed Toad change eyes,
O now I would they had changd voyces too:
Since arme from arme that voyce doth vs affray,
Hunting thee hence, with Huntsup to the day.
O now be gone, more light and light it growes.
(III. v. 26–35)

Here the correspondences are in the capitals for 'Larke', 'Toad' and 'Huntsvp'. But on the next line there is a variant speech prefix in Q2:

Q1] *Rom:* More light and light, more darke and darke our woes.

1. 'Quarto Copy', p. 136. The Q2 compositor supposed *Bonieur* to be a proper name, in italic. Reference to Q1 would have corrected his misunderstanding.

Q2] *Romeo.* More light and light, more darke and darke our woes.

This is not likely to be a scribal correction or alteration since a scribe who saw '*Romeo*' in the manuscript would see no need to correct '*Rom*:' which is correct already. The compositor who set this page has been studied by Paul L. Cantrell and George Walton Williams;[1] his preferred form for the speech prefix for Romeo is '*Ro.*', but he faithfully follows the Q1 form '*Rom*:' when reprinting Q1 sig. B3 (I. ii. 55, 60, 64 and 66) and he very rarely uses the form '*Romeo.*' which stands at III. v. 36 above. It seems probable that here too the manuscript was directly used as copy for Q2, and that the compositor faithfully printed '*Romeo.*' because that is what stood in the foul papers.[2]

A similar example occurs at II. i. 10–13. Here the passage reads:

Q1] Pronounce but Loue and Doue, speake to my gossip *Venus* one faire word, one nickname for her purblinde sonne and heire young *Abraham: Cupid* hee

Q2] Crie but ay me, prouaunt, but loue and day,
Speake to my goship *Venus* one faire word,
One nickname for her purblind sonne and her,
Young *Abraham: Cupid* he . . .

Without doubt the coincidence of the erroneous colon between the names *Abraham* and *Cupid* is a bibliographical link between Q1 and Q2; but the reading 'Pronounce' in l. 10 of Q1 is clearly right and no scribe would have altered it to 'prouaunt'. This must be a misreading of the handwritten form 'pronounc' or 'pronounce'. Here, then, a bibliographical link between Q1 and Q2 is accompanied by an adjacent manuscript link between Q2 and foul papers.

These examples indicate that the copy for Q2 was Shakespeare's foul papers with an exemplar of Q1 used for consultation—that is, Theory A. The rival Theory B cannot account for '*Bonieur*', '*Romeo.*', or '*prouaunt*'.

It remains true that a significant number of minor bibliographical links between Q1 and Q2 may be traced, and to examine them gives a clearer sense of the way the Q2 compositor used his Q1 exemplar. An instance is II. iv. 106–7 in Q2, where a stage direction is misplaced in the middle of Romeo's speech,

1. Op. cit.

2. 'Quarto Copy', p. 136; Dover Wilson does not mention the *Rom:/Romeo.* variant when discussing the passages in 'The New Way', p. 85.

resulting in incorrect lineation. Apparently the compositor was influenced by the arrangement in Q1:

Q1] *Rom:* Heers goodly geare.
Enter Nurse and her man.
Mer: A saile, a saile, a saile.
Ben: Two, two,

Yet Q1's assigning of the last two speeches is not reproduced in Q2, which indicates that the Q2 compositor was using his manuscript copy, but being guided in location and typography by Q1:

Q2] *Ro.* Heeres goodly geare. *Enter Nurse and her man.*
A sayle, a sayle.
Mer. Two two,

Earlier in I. iii there are two examples where the Q2 compositor imitated the lineation of Q1's turned-over lines (2–4 and 12–14) quite needlessly. It is obvious in the following instance, II. ii. 159–64, that a bibliographical link exists:

Q1] *Iul:* *Romeo*, *Romeo*, O for a falkners voice,
To lure this Tassell gentle backe againe:
Bondage is hoarse and may not crie aloud,
Els would I teare the Caue where Eccho lies
And make her airie voice as hoarse as mine,
With repetition of my *Romeos* name.

Q2] *Iuli.* Hist *Romeo* hist, ô for a falkners voyce,
To lure this Tassel gentle back againe,
Bondage is hoarse, and may not speake aloude,
Else would I teare the Caue where Eccho lies,
And make her ayrie tongue more hoarse, then
With repetition of my *Romeo*.

Here the coincidence in typography in ll. 160 and 162, where the words 'Tassel(l)' 'Caue' and 'Eccho' are all printed with capitals, constitutes a minor bibliographical link, especially as there are variants which indicate that the Q2 compositor had manuscript copy. There are one or two conjectured links which seem unconvincing. At III. i. 1–4 Hosley believes[1] the Q2 compositor followed the Q1 arrangement of ll. 1–2 as verse, then reverted to manuscript for ll. 3–4 (not in Q1) which he found, and so printed, as prose. Hosley's view that ll. 3–4 are 'unmetrical' and rightly printed as prose is hard to accept. In two instances of omitted

1. 'The Bad Quarto', p. 23.

speech prefixes it has been suggested that the Q2 compositor was influenced by Q1. II. ii. 184 in Q2 reads:

> Good night, good night.
> Parting is such sweete sorrow.

Supposedly the speech prefix '*Romeo.*' before 'Parting' has been omitted by Q2's compositor, under the influence of Q1; the layout derives from manuscript, in which, as a new speech by Romeo, 'Parting . . . sorrow' stood directly under 'Good . . . night.' The second instance is for III. iii. 84–6 in Q2:

> *Nur.* O he is euen in my mistresse case,
> Iust in her case. O wofull simpathy:
> Pitious prediccament, euen so lies she,

where it is conjectured that Q1 has omitted the speech prefix '*Friar*' before 'O wofull' and '*Nurse*' before 'euen so', and been followed by Q2. The conjecture, by Farmer and Walker, has been frequently adopted by editors.

In this connection it is worth noting Hosley's assumptions,[1] based on interesting evidence: 'from time to time Compositor A seems to have consulted Q1 as he began setting a new page of type, for the influence of Q1 is occasionally apparent at the head of a Q2 page but notably lacking at the foot of the preceding page.' Hosley cites, for example, Q1–2 '*Abraham: Cupid*' which occurs in the first line of Q2 sig. D1v, whereas Q2 'prouaunt' and 'day' (Q1 'Pronounce' and 'Doue') occur in the third line from the bottom of D1. Q1–2 'Passado', 'Punto', 'Hay' and 'Poxe' (Q2 'Pox') occur in the first four lines of Q2 sig. E2v, whereas Q2 'Prince of Cats', 'Complements' and 'dualist a dualist' (Q1 'prince of cattes', 'complements' and 'Duallist a Duellist') occur in the last five lines of E2. In these instances the Q2 compositor consulted his exemplar of Q1 presumably for guidance in layout and setting up, when beginning the new page; on other occasions he may have consulted Q1 because of some obscurity or doubtful reading in the manuscript, and set up directly from Q1 the line or two he could carry in his head. When, after doing so, he again needed to consult copy, he returned to his chief copy, Shakespeare's foul papers.

THIS EDITION

1. Since Q1 is a reconstruction from memory by reporters (one of the 'stolne, and surreptitious copies, maimed, and deformed by

1. 'Quarto Copy', p. 137, n. 19.

the frauds and stealthes of iniurious impostors' referred to by Heminge and Condell) it must be suspected in every case—though since it does derive independently (not through any extant text) from Shakespeare's manuscript, it is still substantive, however untrustworthy, and there is always the chance that a reporter remembers correctly what the Q2 compositor accidentally omits, misreads, or otherwise gets wrong. It follows that a corrupt passage or error in Q2 must be considered in its own immediate textual, bibliographical and literary context before Q1 is consulted, and even then the fact that the Q1 reading may be a memorial error or substitution must always induce editorial caution.

The present edition is therefore based on Q2 with the exception of the extended passage in I. ii and I. iii reprinted from Q1; but due consideration has been given to Q1 throughout and a number of Q1 readings have been adopted. The Q4 compositors consulted Q1 while basing their text on Q3. There is no firm evidence that the Q4 compositors actually had access to independent evidence of what Shakespeare wrote, but one or two Q4 readings are so shrewd it is tempting to think them more than mere guesswork (cf. IV. i. 85, 100).

2. Copies of all five Quartos and four Folios were in fact collated in the preparation of the present edition, together with a number of important later editions (Cambridge, Variorum, N.C.S., Alexander, Williams, Spencer, Riverside); but, in accordance with Arden practice, the collation actually records only:

(a) Substantive editions providing evidence by an independent route of what Shakespeare wrote: that is, in the case of *Romeo and Juliet*, Q2, and wherever practicable (in view of the Bad Quarto's frequently wide divergence) Q1.

(b) Editions forming part of the chain of transmission to F: that is, Q3 (reprinting Q2) and Q4. F1 is also recorded in full, even though it is not, in the case of *Romeo and Juliet*, substantive.

(c) Readings from other editions having a serious claim to consideration or being otherwise of interest.

This edition, in accordance with Arden practice, aims to establish the text in the light of the evidence and of editorial opinion, but not to record its complete history; it does not therefore record *in full* Q5, F2, F3, F4 or any subsequent edition.

Unless the sense or the transmission is affected, the collation ignores:

(a) Accidentals, minor literals, details of punctuation, spelling, italicization, and variant forms of proper names.
(b) Variant forms of stage directions later than F, and of locations.
(c) Alternative Elizabethan spellings where they are unambiguous: these are silently modernized. Lemmas are given in the modernized form, the citations following in the original. Agreement between the Quartos and F1 is recorded in the form Q2–4, F, Q1; Q1, as a Bad Quarto, is cited last except when its reading is preferred; '*subst.*' (=substantially) means that any variation is immaterial to the point under consideration; '*var. Q1*' means that the Q1 text diverges too far to be recorded, though having a rough equivalent. Routine normalization is marked by '*ed.*' This does not indicate that the reading appears for the first time in this edition.

3. In modernizing, a number of archaic verbal and grammatical forms have been retained (*washing*, *open-arse*, *nyas*, *phantasimes*, *injuried*, *mishaved*, *lign'd*, *wanny*) for reasons discussed in the commentary. On the other hand *to/too*, *then/than*, etc., are made to conform to modern usage; *and* meaning *if* is spelt *and* not *an*.

In the verse in this edition *-ed* indicates the syllabic past verb ending, *'d* the non-syllabic. In the prose this distinction is not observed and uncontracted modern forms are adopted throughout. There are a number of cases in which Q2 is inconsistent in the printing of elisions in second person singular verbal forms (e.g. II. ii. 62, *camest*; II. v. 23, *shamest*; III. i. 128, *gavest*). F correctly elides in a number of these cases, and also correctly expands a Q2 contraction (III. v. 226, *Speakest*). In the present text such elisions have been silently made consistent with the requirements of the metre. In one or two cases other simple minor emendations have been made to correct the metre (e.g. III. iii. 142, III. v. 106, V. i. 15).

Punctuation has been modernized and regularized, in accordance with Arden practice.

4. Act and scene divisions follow the traditional arrangement of the Cambridge edition; there are no divisions in the Quartos and F has only the initial 'Actus Primus. Scaena Prima.' The scene divisions at I. v, II. ii, IV. iv and IV. v are made for convenience of reference where, on the Elizabethan stage, action would have been continuous.

Stage directions in Q2, which was printed mainly from foul papers, are often inadequate or inaccurate, while those in Q1 probably record details of the first staging of the play. Many Q1 directions have therefore been included. Additions and alterations to the directions in the Quartos and F are indicated by square brackets; the collation and commentary record the significant details.

Locations are not given in the stage directions, since they are the invention of editors and often obscure or contradict the principles and practices of the Elizabethan stage, but a limited selection of editors' imaginary settings of the scene is included in the collation.

2. THE DATE

The latest possible date for *Romeo and Juliet* is 1596. By March 1597 Shakespeare's play had been performed, and the reporters of the Q1 version had had time to make their reconstruction, and sell it to the printer. This sequence of events must have required several months at least, indicating that Shakespeare completed his play no later than the spring of 1596. In fact it has been usual to assign the play to 1595.[1] There are no allusions to it before 1598.[2]

The earliest date that has been seriously proposed for first performance is 1591, at about the time of *King Henry VI* Parts 2 and 3. This would make *Romeo and Juliet* one of the very earliest of Shakespeare's works, which most scholars have considered, on stylistic grounds, it cannot be. There have been two arguments in favour of 1591, neither conclusive.

(i) It was proposed by Tyrwhitt[3] that the earthquake alluded to by the Nurse in I. iii is the English earthquake of 1580: 'And since that time it is eleven years', says the Nurse, thus pinpointing the date at 1591. Unfortunately there were a number of earthquakes in England in the period, and scholars were also able to add earthquakes recorded in Verona, which lies near a region of northern Italy subject to periodic serious earthquakes. So Hunter in 1845[4] proposed the earthquake near Verona of 1570 because it was large and more suited to the story; Sidney Thomas[5] suggested the English earthquake of 1584, giving a date for the play of 1595, which he considered preferable. Sarah Dodson[6] favoured this 1584 event since tremors were, according to her,

1. E. K. Chambers, *William Shakespeare* (1930), Vol. 1, p. 345; J. G. McManaway, 'Recent Studies in Shakespeare's Chronology', *Sh.S.*, 3 (1950), pp. 22–33.

2. Chambers, op. cit., p. 346; the first allusion is by Marston to a performance at The Curtain.

3. Furness, *Variorum*, p. 43.

4. Ibid., p. 44.

5. *MLN*, LXIV (1949), pp. 417–19.

6. *MLN*, LXV (1950), p. 144.

apparently widely felt in the Alps and must have excited gossip in Verona. She also proposed as alternatives a landslip in Dorset in 1583 and a sinking of the earth in Kent in 1585, on 4 August, only four days too late to fit the Nurse's exact 31 July. The fact that Shakespeare could rely on some memory of earthquakes in England would have made the Nurse's claim sound plausible to those spectators (the great majority) who would not recognize this as a touch of local Veronese colour. It is also apparent that the Nurse's appetite for circumstantial evidence is like Mistress Quickly's in *Henry IV* or Pompey's in *Measure for Measure*, so that a judge does well to adopt the scepticism of an Escalus. The allusion to an earthquake can support a date of 1591, 1595 or 1596 (if we dismiss Hunter's proposal which gives 1581), so that even if we could suppose a particular earthquake to be in mind, the issue would be unresolved.

(ii) A. S. Cairncross has argued that there are reciprocal recollections in four Bad Quartos (of *King Henry VI* Parts 2 and 3, *Richard III* and *Romeo and Juliet*) which he dates at 1590–1. His evidence in fact only suggests that the reporters of *Romeo and Juliet* knew the other plays, not vice versa, and though a single recollection of *Romeo and Juliet* in *The True Tragedy* (the Bad Quarto of *3H6*) might be valid, that text was published in 1595, conjecturally as a result of the breaking of Pembroke's Men in 1593.[1] In any case, *Romeo and Juliet* cannot have been as early as 1591 because of its own borrowings (of which Cairncross is evidently unaware) from Daniel's *Complaint of Rosamund* (1592 and 1594)[2] and poems by Du Bartas published in Eliot's *Ortho-Epia* of 1593;[3] These borrowings indicate 1593 as the earliest possible date for *Romeo and Juliet*.

It is necessary to take account of the relationship with *Two Gentlemen of Verona*, in which Shakespeare makes use of Arthur Brooke's poem *The Tragicall Historye of Romeus and Iuliet* (1562), and to discuss certain connections with *The Comedy of Errors* and *Titus Andronicus*; it will then be appropriate to deal with the group of plays sharing lyrical feeling—*Romeo and Juliet*, *Love's Labour's Lost*, *A Midsummer Night's Dream* and *Richard II*—which probably provide the strongest indication of the play's date.

1. 'Pembroke's Men and Some Shakespearian Piracies', *SQ*, XI. Cairncross notes that *The True Tragedy* has the lines 'that I / Shall be valiant and stand to it, for if / I would, I cannot runne awaie' (p. 618). There is no equivalent in *3H6*, IV. i, and the lines appear to recall *Rom.*, I. i. 8–9.

2. Cf. notes in the present edition to I. i. 212, I. iv. 107–11, III. ii. 5, V. i. 61, V. iii. 92–6, 112–15.

3. Cf. notes in the present edition to III. v. 1–7, 22.

The dates of *The Comedy of Errors, Two Gentlemen* and *Titus* are not certain, but it is generally agreed that all were written before 1594. The Arden editor of *The Comedy of Errors*, R. A. Foakes, notes that *Two Gentlemen* has closer links with *Errors* than with any other play of Shakespeare's, sharing many phrases, jests, relatively unusual words, and certain comic routines, and Foakes believes that *The Comedy of Errors* was written 'not long before or immediately after the long spell of plague which caused all acting to be prohibited in London throughout most of the year 1593, and which probably turned Shakespeare to writing his narrative poems'.[1] Clifford Leech dates *Two Gentlemen* in 1593–4,[2] and we may suppose that Shakespeare completed it soon after *The Comedy of Errors*. *Two Gentlemen* is relevant to the dating of *Romeo and Juliet* since Brooke's poem appears to be the source for certain episodes in *Two Gentlemen*, and several parallels have also been noted between it and Brooke's poem.[3] Brooke is recalled in the episode in which Valentine plans to ascend to his love's window by means of a rope-ladder at night; Silvia's father plans to marry her against her will to a colourless suitor, Thurio; Valentine, on being banished from Verona to Mantua, bewails his fate and is counselled to be patient, as is Romeo by Friar Laurence; and when he meets the outlaws, Valentine tells them he was banished for killing a man in Verona. Later Eglamour meets Julia by Friar Patrick's cell, where she should go to confession, and as they proceed towards Mantua (we learn from the Duke), 'Friar Laurence met them both / As he in penance wandered through the forest'. As Geoffrey Bullough remarks, 'Obviously Shakespeare had been reading Brooke's poem before writing *The Two Gentlemen of Verona*'.[4]

There are artistic uncertainties in *Two Gentlemen* which are probably due to Shakespeare's difficulties in this, his first attempt to shape romance narrative into dramatic comedy; it is notable that in *The Comedy of Errors* a strong frame is taken from classical comedy to contain the romance narrative material, and this may indicate that Shakespeare was indeed deeply exercised with the problem of evolving dramatic forms in which to deal with this particular kind of story. It seems consistent with Shakespeare's evident interest in this subject-matter, and with his ambitious—

1. Op. cit., Introduction, p. xxviii. 2. Arden edition (1962), Introduction.

3. Cf. *Brooke's 'Romeus and Juliet'*, ed. J. J. Munro (1908), Appendices I and II. Shakespeare borrows from Brooke's poem in *3H6*, v. iv, showing that he knew it at least as early as 1591.

4. G. Bullough, *Narrative and Dramatic Sources of Shakespeare*, Vol. 1 (1961), p. 209.

indeed daring—versatility in the first part of his career, that he should decide soon after completing *Two Gentlemen* to write a tragedy based on Brooke's poem. He had already written a tragedy, *Titus Andronicus*, performed at the latest in 1594 and usually dated 1591–2 (though 1589 has been proposed), and in constructing a dramatic version of Brooke's tragic poem Shakespeare drew on his experience in *Titus.*[1] These relations with *Two Gentlemen* and *Titus* point to a date of 1594–5 for *Romeo and Juliet*. The fact that there are certain significant reminiscences of *The Comedy of Errors* in *Romeo and Juliet*[2] may partly be accounted for by the important performance of *The Comedy of Errors* at the Gray's Inn Revels on 28 December 1594, when Shakespeare was writing *Romeo and Juliet*: *Errors* was fresh in his mind.

From the point of view of style, *Romeo and Juliet* is recognizably one of a group of lyrical plays usually dated at 1594–5. Evidently, the span of years from 1590 to 1596 is one in which Shakespeare explored an astonishingly wide diversity of poetic and dramatic styles; he must have written with great rapidity, and at this period of rapid and intense development, his art might be expected to show some features reminiscent of his earliest work, while in general the style he had just developed prevails. Certainly the finished state of artistic and structural unity in *Romeo and Juliet* gives little encouragement to speculation that the play might have been begun in about 1591,[3] then laid aside, and only completed a year or two later. In any case our concern here is with the play completed for performance, and there is convincing stylistic evidence closely relating it to *Love's Labour's Lost*, from which it may be seen to develop certain themes.

Love's Labour's Lost was in Shakespeare's mind when he began *Romeo and Juliet*. It is usually dated at 1594–5,[4] and it shares with *Romeo and Juliet* a concern with literary and social fashions in love and love-melancholy, and both plays have youthful central

1. Cf. G. K. Hunter, 'Shakespeare's Earliest Tragedies', *Sh.S.*, 27 (1974), pp. 1–10; Hunter is non-committal about the date of *Titus*. Chambers, op. cit., p. 317, thinks *Titus* no later than *R3* or *Errors*, proposing 1593; J. G. McManaway (in *Sh.S.*, 3) cites Peter Alexander's support of 1591–2, but problems of authorship, revision, and possible confusion with a non-Shakespearean *Titus* remain. R. F. Hill (*Sh.S.*, 10) concludes that *Titus*, if wholly Shakespeare's, is his earliest play, prior to *H6*, that is to say, 1589 or earlier.

2. Cf. the servants' disgruntlement in II. ii, mock conjuring in II. i, and notes to the present edition: II. iv. 143, V. i. 59, V. ii. 21.

3. The basis for such speculation remains the allusion to Brooke's *Romeus* in *3H6*, V. iv. 1–32. Yet because Shakespeare knew Brooke's poem in 1591 it does not follow that he was writing *Romeo and Juliet* then.

4. Chambers, op. cit., p. 335.

characters. Both plays give prominence to sonnets and sonneteering and contain echoes of Shakespeare's own early sonnets and his poem *Venus and Adonis* (1593). There are parallels in the formal counterpoint of lyrical poetry and comic prose, and between Mercutio and Berowne. The possibility of a date for *Love's Labour's Lost* in 1594–5 fits well with the probability that Shakespeare went on to write *Romeo and Juliet* very soon after completing it.

A Midsummer Night's Dream is first mentioned in 1598 in Meres' *Palladis Tamia*,[1] but is usually dated at 1595–6. It is reminiscent of *Romeo and Juliet* in its opening situation, where the Duke is called upon to arbitrate in a family quarrel between a choleric father and his wayward daughter who prefers her own lover to the one her father chooses, and there are many similarities of imagery, especially at the beginning. The burlesque love tragedy of Pyramus and Thisbe performed at the end of *A Midsummer Night's Dream* is taken from Book IV of Ovid's *Metamorphoses*, but there are additional details recalling the story of Romeo and Juliet, such as the assurance that 'the wall is down that parted their fathers', and the inclusion of the parents in Quince's original casting.[2] George Pettie regarded the story of Pyramus and Thisbe as parallel to that of *Romeo and Juliet* in his *Petite Pallace of Pettie his Pleasure* (1576) where he says 'such presiness of parents brought Pyramus and Thisbe to a woful end, Romeo and Julietta to untimely death'.[3] It is significant that Shakespeare sympathizes with the children in both plays, although Brooke censures Romeo and Juliet for neglecting parental advice.

These features point to a closeness in composition between the two plays. Since Shakespeare knew Brooke's poem at least as early as 1591 (it is echoed in *3H6*, v. iv) his additions to 'Pyramus and Thisbe' might derive from the poem; only if we suppose that the artisans' difficulties with staging—'You can never bring in a wall'—allude to the scene in *Romeo and Juliet* where Romeo says he has leapt Capulet's orchard wall, can we argue that *Romeo and Juliet* was performed earlier than *A Midsummer Night's Dream*.[4]

1. Ibid., p. 247.

2. C. L. Barber, *Shakespeare's Festive Comedy* (1959), p. 152, n. 25. The threat of death to Hermia in the first scene of *MND* suggests a recollection of Brooke, ll. 1945 ff.

3. G. Bullough, op. cit., Vol. 1, p. 374.

4. Cf. *A Midsummer Night's Dream*, ed. Harold F. Brooks in the Arden edn (1979), Introduction, pp. xliii–xliv—though Brooks believes in an actual wall on stage in *Rom.* as I certainly do not (see II. i. 5). Brooks has an account of the

Indeed, it may not be altogether appropriate to consider the two plays in terms of Shakespeare's linear development as an artist; one might see them, rather, as a kind of diptych, portraying the attraction and repulsion of opposites—love and hate, light and darkness, wit and folly, action and dream—in opposed modes, of tragedy and comedy, written close together about 1595.

This date gains further support by consideration of *Richard II*, provisionally dated at 1595 by Peter Ure.[1] *Richard II* shares the lyrical feeling, prolific use of formal rhetorical patterns and devices, rhyme, motifs of imagery and occasional extreme elaboration of conceits, common to the group.

In conclusion, the allusions to Daniel and Eliot indicate 1593 as the earliest possible date for *Romeo and Juliet*, the Bad Quarto makes 1596 the latest. Whether it is supposed that the play precedes or follows *A Midsummer Night's Dream* makes little difference to the date, since the style and themes show the two plays must have been written very close together, between 1594 and 1596.[2]

---

stylistic devices common to *LLL*, *Rom.*, *MND* and *R2*, on pp. xlv–li of his Introduction, which is convincing.

1. In his Arden edition (1956), Introduction, p. xliv.

2. The Montagues and Capulets had been of special interest to the family of the Earl of Southampton, Shakespeare's patron, since George Gascoigne wrote a masque (1575) for a double marriage in the Montague family, that of Southampton's mother, the Dowager Countess, from whom he derived such claims to ancient blood as he had. Gascoigne was asked to devise a masque to explain the Venetian dress already chosen by eight gentlemen who 'had determined' to appear in a masque. Gascoigne, 'calling to minde that there is a noble house of the Mountacutes in Italie', decided to bring in a boy-actor who would declare himself a descendant of the Italian Mountacutes, and that 'his father being slaine at the laste warres against the Turke, and he there taken, he was recovered by the Venetians'. The boy wore a token of the 'Mountacutes of Italie' in his cap, which he explained in these words:

> This token which the *Mountacutes* dyd beare alwaies, for that
> They covet to be knowne from *Capels* where they passe,
> For ancient grudge which long ago 'twene these two houses was.

M. C. Bradbrook has recently suggested (*Shakespeare the Poet in his World*, 1978, pp. 100–1) that events in the real life of the Earl of Southampton in 1594 may be connected with Shakespeare's writing of *Romeo and Juliet*: 'At celebrations for his coming of age on 6 October, Southampton was at Titchfield in Hampshire, feasting his tenants but also concealing a friend who had just killed his foe in a feud. Two brothers, Sir Charles and Sir Henry Danvers, were involved in a quarrel with the family of Sir Walter Long; in a fight at an inn, Henry Long had wounded Sir Charles with his sword, whereupon Sir Henry Danvers shot Long dead. Both fled to the Earl of Southampton who concealed them.' Taken

3. SOURCES

Originating in folklore, the story of Romeo and Juliet was developed by a series of European writers of *novelle* in the fifteenth and sixteenth centuries, and it gained considerable currency in England after its first translation into English in 1562 by Arthur Brooke: there are twelve allusions to Romeo by English writers between 1562 and 1583.[1] The popularity of Italian *novelle* generally in England at this time is attested by Gosson's attack[2] on Painter's *Palace of Pleasure* in 1582 as one of the books 'ransackt to furnish the Play houses in London', and Painter includes a version of Romeo and Juliet in his second volume, published in 1567.[3] In the preface to his 1562 translation Brooke says 'I sawe the same argument lately set forth on stage with more commendation than I can look for', but if there was indeed an early play of Romeo and Juliet no trace of it survives, and Brooke gives no indication of whether it was in English, French or Latin. His poem continued to be popular; Tottell obtained a licence to reprint it in 1582 and it was reissued in 1587 by Robert Robinson, with a title-page declaring it 'a rare example of true constancie, with the subtill counsells and practises of an old fryer and their ill event'. It is against this background of current popularity that Gascoigne's use of the story in his masque is to be seen. The story was well established in the 1580s and Shakespeare may have known it for a number of years before 1591, in more than one version, before he decided to dramatize it. It was compared to Pyramus and Thisbe as a famous love tragedy,[4] and Shakespeare shows a boldness in choosing so famous a story so early in his career somewhat comparable to that shown in his choice of the *Menaechmi*, probably the best known of all classical plays in the

---

with the echo from Gascoigne in the Prologue to *Romeo and Juliet*, where the phrase 'ancient grudge' recurs, the suggestion of some allusion to the Earl of Southampton seems possible, though scarcely indicating that the play owed its genesis to the Southampton–Danvers incident. Certainly this incident emphasizes that a feud between important families was a contemporary English phenomenon as well as something traditionally and typically Italian.

1. Collected by René Pruvost, *Matteo Bandello and Elizabethan Fiction* (1937); see Leo Salingar, *Shakespeare and the Traditions of Comedy* (1974), p. 314.

2. Stephen Gosson, *Plays Confuted* (1582), in *The Elizabethan Stage*, ed. Chambers, Vol. IV, pp. 215–16.

3. So popular were *novelle* in England that there were three editions of Vol. I of Painter's *Palace of Pleasure* (1566, 1569, 1575) and two of Vol. II (1567, 1580?).

4. Salingar, op. cit., p. 314.

sixteenth century, as the main source of *The Comedy of Errors*, written not long before.

At another level, Shakespeare's interest in the Romeo story may be seen in relation to his deep-seated preoccupation with certain motifs which are treated in five of his plays, *Romeo and Juliet*, *The Merchant of Venice*, *Much Ado*, *All's Well* and *Measure for Measure*, all based on a group of *novelle* concerned with broken nuptials and their social and rational reconciliation. It seems probable that Shakespeare knew all the *novelle* in this group at the outset, before writing any of the plays,[1] and certainly such motifs had a strong appeal for him throughout his career. Shakespeare is selective in his choice among the many *novelle* current at the time in England, and in this he is distinctive, though he is not the first dramatist to see the value of following Boccaccio and his successors, who give a feeling of modernity, through detailed setting and characterization, to tales which have their origins deep in folklore.

J. J. Munro[2] has considered the early analogues to the Romeo and Juliet story in a number of 'separation' and 'potion' romances, among which the *Ephesiaca* of Xenophon of Ephesus (third century AD) combines both motifs. The wife Anthia is separated from her husband and rescued from robbers by Perilaus; to avoid marrying him she obtains from a physician a draught which she believes to be mortal poison but which is only a sleeping potion. She awakes in the tomb and is carried off by tomb-robbers to further adventures.

In the fifteenth century the story reappears in more detailed form in the thirty-third of the *Cinquante Novelle* of Masuccio Salernitano (Naples, 1476). In Siena, Mariotto secretly marries Giannozza with the help of a bribed Friar. In the course of a quarrel Mariotto kills a prominent citizen, and he is banished. After asking his brother to keep him informed of events in Siena he goes in exile to Alexandria. Giannozza now comes under pressure from her angry father to marry a suitor he thinks satisfactory. She bribes the Friar to make her up a sleeping potion, which she drinks after sending a message to her husband. She is buried, is delivered from the tomb by the Friar, and sails for

1. Ibid., p. 305.

2. In his edition of *Brooke's 'Romeus and Juliet'* (1908), Introduction, pp. ix–lx. Carol Gesner, *Shakespeare and the Greek Romance* (1970), pp. 63–4, adds the *Babylonica* of Iamblichus as an early analogue. There was only one thirteenth-century manuscript, in Florence; it was first printed in 1601. Donald McGrady convincingly establishes, in *Shakespeare Studies* (ed. Barroll, 1969), that *Romeo and Juliet* has no Spanish source.

Alexandria. Her messenger having been captured by pirates, Mariotto, on hearing of her supposed death, returns to Siena disguised as a pilgrim. He tries to open her tomb but is seized and subsequently beheaded. Giannozza comes back to Siena and dies of grief in a convent.

Masuccio stresses that the events of the story took place in his own lifetime. Luigi da Porto, who published a version of the legend in 1530,[1] sets the scene in Verona and says that the lovers lived in the days of Bartolommeo della Scala. Da Porto seems to be the origin of the belief that the legend is historically true; it is repeated by Corte in his history of Verona of 1594.[2] In fact there were two real families named Montecchi and Capelletti who belonged to political factions in the thirteenth century, but only the Montecchi lived in Verona: the Capelletti were of Cremona, and the sole connection between the two is in a line of Dante's *Purgatorio* VI (106) which mentions them together as examples of civil dissension. The legend has long since ceased to be treated as historical truth, but its imaginative attraction still draws visitors to the supposed tomb and balcony of Giulietta in present-day Verona.

In da Porto the lovers are named Romeo and Giulietta and the two families of Montecchi and Capelletti are at feud. There is a Friar Lorenzo, and da Porto invents Marcuccio, Thebaldo and the Conte di Lodrone (Shakespeare's Paris). Romeo goes disguised as a nymph to a carnival ball at his enemy's house in the hope of seeing a lady who scorns his love. Giulietta falls in love with him at first sight and, in a dance, a change of partners brings him next to her. On the other side of her is Marcuccio, who we are told has very cold hands. Giulietta takes Romeo's hands and tells him that he makes one of her hands warm even if Marcuccio freezes the other. The lovers meet often in due course at Giulietta's balcony until one night when it is snowing Romeo begs admittance to her room; Giulietta rejects him with modest scorn, declaring that when she is his bride she will give herself to him and follow him anywhere. Friar Lorenzo, a friend of Romeo, marries the pair, hoping to bring peace to the feuding families. Then in a brawl Romeo at first avoids harming any Capelletti, but when his own side are in peril he kills Thebaldo. He flees to Mantua, leaving a message that the Friar is to keep him in touch with events in Giulietta's house. Since she is eighteen, her parents interpret her grief as a sign that she wishes for marriage

1. *Historia novellamente ritrovata di due nobili amanti* (Venice, 1530).
2. Munro, op. cit., p. xxxvi.

and arrange a match with Lodrone. She refuses, and so angers her father. She asks the Friar for poison but he substitutes a sleeping potion intended to last for forty-eight hours. Giulietta professes obedience to her father, but takes the potion: next morning she is discovered apparently dead and is buried in the family vault. A message from Friar Lorenzo fails to reach Romeo, but the servant, believing Giulietta to be dead, gives him the fatal news. Romeo returns disguised as a peasant and carrying poison; he goes to the tomb, laments over Giulietta, takes the poison and embraces her. She awakes and speaks to him before he dies. The Friar arrives and tries to persuade her to enter a convent but she commits suicide by holding her breath until at last with a great cry she falls on Romeo's body. The two families become reconciled and the lovers are buried with great ceremony.

Da Porto's invention of many telling details and incidents develops the psychological interest of the story; his ending, which differs from that of Masuccio, may be influenced by the story of Pyramus and Thisbe in Ovid, *Metamorphoses* IV.

The basis of Shakespeare's play is apparent in da Porto; the line of transmission runs from da Porto to Bandello and then Brooke, although adaptations of da Porto were made in French, by Adrian Sevin in *Halquadrich and Burglipha* (1542), and in Italian by Clizia in 1553. Luigi Groto wrote a play in 1578 called *Hadriana* based on da Porto; it has a nightingale which sings when the lovers part, but it seems very unlikely that Shakespeare knew of it.

Bandello published his version of the story in his *Novelle*, the second volume of which was published in 1554. Bandello gives more emphasis to Romeo's initial love-melancholy, and the feud between the families is active. Romeo attends the ball, not disguised as a nymph, but in a masque with several other young gentlemen; he removes his vizard and is recognized, but is so young and handsome that nobody insults him. Mercutio is said to be 'audacious among maidens as a lion among lambs', though his hands remain icy, as in da Porto; Bandello introduces the character of the Nurse and a character corresponding to Shakespeare's Benvolio; the Conte Lodrone is called Paris. Romeo only learns Julietta's identity from a friend as he leaves the ball, and Julietta finds out who he is from the Nurse. When he waits under Julietta's window she speaks of the danger; they decide at the first nocturnal meeting to marry. The Nurse is persuaded to help, and Romeo's servant Pietro gives her a rope-ladder by which Romeo visits Julietta before the marriage. This is consummated in the Capulet garden. After the brawl in which Romeo slays Tibaldo only after trying to make peace, he shelters in the Friar's cell; he refuses Julietta's request to accompany him to Mantua disguised as a page, so she appeals to the Friar who suggests the sleeping potion scheme. Just before drinking the potion Julietta expresses terror. Friar Lorenzo's messenger, Friar Anselmo, fails to reach Romeo because of plague quarantine, and when Romeo hears the fatal news from Pietro he attempts suicide with a sword. He returns disguised as a German to Verona. In the tomb, when Julietta awakes she is at first alarmed at Romeo's disguised figure and fears the Friar has betrayed her; but then she recognizes him, the lovers mutually lament their misfortune, and Romeo regrets killing Tibaldo and urges Julietta to live on after his own death. The remainder of the story follows da Porto.

Bandello's plain narrative was translated into French by Boaistuau in 1559;[1] in this version there are many additions of moralizing and sentiment, and the characters indulge in rhetorical outbursts. The visit to the apothecary is described, and in the tomb Romeo dies before Juliet awakes. Pietro and the Friar arrive, but hurriedly leave when they hear a noise, whereupon Juliet stabs herself with Romeo's dagger. The two men are arrested by the Watch, and the bodies of the lovers are set out on a public stage as the Prince holds an inquiry. The Friar and Pietro are pardoned, the Nurse banished, the apothecary hanged, the families reconciled and the lovers solemnly buried.

Brooke's translation, 3020 lines in length, is a faithful version of Boaistuau, though Brooke also makes additions to the story in his turn, under the influence of the greatest romance narrative in his own language, Chaucer's *Troilus and Criseyde*.[2] Brooke's chief contribution is his emphasis on the power of the 'blyndfold goddesse' 'fierce Fortune' throughout the story, providing a perspective which distinctly recalls Chaucer, and without which the verbal borrowings or echoes would have little significance. Brooke's Preface speaks of unhonest desire, of the neglect of authority and parental advice, the shame of stolen contracts, the moral to be drawn by the pious reader;[3] but his poem itself shows

1. *Histoires Tragiques extraictes des oeuvres italiennes de Bandel, et mises en nostre langue Françoise, par Pierre Boaistuau*, Vol. 1 (Paris, 1559).

2. Cf. Munro, op. cit., Introduction and Appendix II; J. W. Hales, 'Chaucer and Shakespeare', *Quarterly Review*, 1873; Nevill Coghill, 'Shakespeare's Reading in Chaucer', *Elizabethan and Jacobean Studies presented to F. P. Wilson*, ed. H. Davis and H. Gardner (1959), pp. 86–99; John Lawlor, '*Romeo and Juliet*' in *Early Shakespeare*, ed. J. R. Brown and Bernard Harris (1961).

3. Shakespeare transfers these sentiments, in part, to Friar Laurence.

a warmer understanding of youth, which keeps the reader half-conscious of the spirit of Chaucer for much of the time. No doubt Troilus and Criseyde were commonly linked with Romeo and Juliet as patterns of tragic love,[1] but it is Brooke who could have provided Shakespeare with immediate stimulus to recall Chaucer's poem, as he did, when writing *Romeo and Juliet*. Brooke recognizes the limitations of his *novella* narrative as a source for a tragic poem, and he makes use of Chaucer when presenting moments of heightened emotion.[2] Chaucer's importance for Shakespeare's play is in giving a powerful precedent for the idea of the shared private world of intensity created by the lovers and contrasted to the background of unstable forces, indifferent to individual desires and always felt as threatening them. Chaucer's English poem, so much more powerful, as art, than the versions of the *novella* story of Romeo and Juliet available to Shakespeare, influences the deep structure of emotional experience which is the play's basis, and Thomas Kyd, in *The Spanish Tragedy*, provided a practicable dramatic model for the presentation of such a tragedy of fate, giving the audience a superior knowledge of the story from the outset, reducing the hero's role to bring into prominence the complex patterns of action, and finally presenting a graphic stage-image for the audience to interpret. Chaucer's strategy in matching the tender intensity of his lovers against the ironic maturity of Pandarus evidently influences the general mode of *Romeo and Juliet*, while the verbal echoes of Marlowe's *Hero and Leander* and *Tragedy of Dido* suggest that a contemporary stimulus interested Shakespeare in the special quality imparted by sheer speed of action and recklessness of passion to stories of tragic love.

4. THE PLAY

Although Shakespeare imposes his own emphatic pattern on the story,[3] he follows Brooke's poem with very close attention in other respects. Many close verbal parallels testify to Shakespeare's willing dependence on Brooke's detailed descriptions of Verona, and suggest his pleasure in the account of places, of detailed reactions

1. Furness, *Variorum*, cites an instance in 1583 (p. 407).

2. Brooke's imitation of sunrises, threats of suicide, and extreme displays of grief and despair, in *Troilus*, are cited in Munro, op. cit., Appendix II.

3. See R. A. Law, 'On Shakespeare's changes of his source material in *Romeo and Juliet*', *Studies in English*, 9 (University of Texas, 1929).

of characters to one another, of customs and manners. Brooke is enthusiastic about the Italian quality of the place and people, and something of this is transmitted by Shakespeare, although the domestic life of the Capulet and Montague families resembles that of English merchants rather than Renaissance Italian nobility.[1] However, the impression of Italian summer weather, hot days, warm nights, sudden thunderstorms, is absorbed by Shakespeare from Brooke, and much enlivened in the process. The closeness with which Shakespeare read Brooke is attested by occasional allusions in the play to incidents in Brooke which Shakespeare did not dramatize, and by the frequency with which Shakespeare preserved material from Brooke while altering its context or transferring it to another character; so the Nurse's account of Juliet's childhood, for example, is recounted to Juliet and her mother in the play (I. iii), but is told to Romeo by the Nurse in Brooke, and there are a number of similar episodes to support the impression that Shakespeare had a copy of Brooke by him as he wrote the play.[2]

Shakespeare absorbs from Brooke the vivid atmosphere and lively detail, but adapts his rambling and episodic narrative with a clear awareness of the need to give it greater emotional power, to enact a completed trajectory. Shakespeare strengthens the symmetrical pattern of the action, increasing the importance of a number of minor characters to provide parallels and interweave motives; he also greatly develops one or two in order to alter the balance of Brooke's poem, giving a variety of comic moods as a foil to the tender and intense lyricism, and to the bloody violence. He cuts the imaginary time taken by the story from several months

1. Gunnar Sjögren, *SQ*, XIII (1961), pp. 161–3, gives some entertaining illustrations of Italian Renaissance noblemen taking a fussy interest, like Capulet, in household affairs.

2. (a) In Brooke the story begins at Christmas, which probably accounts for Shakespeare's apparent assumption that it is winter in episodes when feasts are prepared, though it is summertime in the rest of the play. See I. ii. 20 n., I. v. 26 n.

(b) In IV. v Capulet proclaims he is speechless but then laments clamorously; the same inconsistency occurs in the same place in Brooke, l. 2454.

(c) Shakespeare's Romeo (III. iii. 118) is rebuked for railing on his birth, which he has not done, except in Brooke, l. 1325.

(d) Capulet, as in Brooke, makes great preparations for the feast (IV. ii, Brooke, ll. 2281–7) yet in III. iv. 27 Shakespeare makes him say the celebrations will be very muted; Brooke has been followed in one place but not in another.

(e) In Brooke, ll. 897–8, the Nurse offers the lovers a field-bed for the night; in the play Mercutio jests about a field-bed when looking for Romeo who is in the Capulet garden (cf. II. i. 40).

in Brooke to four or five days, and he provides a very firm basic structure: the opening and closing of the play, and the central scene, involve the whole community, and are marked by the appearance of the Prince, to use his authority on his turbulent city. The strong design is reinforced by the use of an identical structure for all three of these episodes.

The pattern of repetition in scenes involving the Prince is bold and simple, but it provides the basis for the more intricate patterning Shakespeare imposes on Brooke's story. In the opening few scenes of the play Shakespeare introduces the main characters (in contrast with Brooke who often allows the reader to wait until a character is immediately needed by a turn in the plot before mentioning him) and their strongly contrasting personalities and actions give immediate momentum to the plot, while the alternation from public to private life generates an interest in the interplay of the two main themes, the family feud and the course of true love. Shakespeare develops the character of Benvolio from a few lines in Brooke: and indeed Benvolio, the man of good will, is set against Tybalt, the embodiment of violent aggression, in the opening moments of the play. Tybalt is only present in Brooke's poem in the affray when Romeo kills him; Shakespeare introduces him at once, and deepens his menacing potential by making him recognize Romeo at the Capulet feast and attempt an affray there and then. The rival heads of houses enter hard on the heels of Benvolio and Tybalt in the first brawl. Shakespeare develops them and contrasts them from the first moment, as Lady Capulet ridicules her ageing husband's martial pretension and Lady Montague shows dark anger and commitment to family honour; both sets of parents will soon be seen in private domestic life to substantiate these first impressions. Shakespeare is concerned in these scenes to create the impression of a web of relationships, a detailed depiction of the various elements in the community. The Nurse, whose garrulity is an invention of Brooke's, is much developed by Shakespeare, especially as a comic character; she is emphatically coarse in her vitality, providing a foil for Juliet's lightness and natural delicacy. Juliet's age is reduced by Shakespeare from Brooke's sixteen to fourteen:[1] strong emphasis is given the point to add to the

1. The audience is evidently meant to think of her as young for marriage. In later plays Marina is fourteen and Miranda fifteen, but stress is placed there too on the fact that they are very young. Heroines such as Viola or Beatrice approach more closely to what historians consider as the Elizabethan norm, of marriage in late adolescence: cf. Peter Laslett, *The World We Have Lost* (1965),

impression of youth, freshness, and vulnerable innocence in the heroine. The Nurse's reminiscences give density to the background of Juliet's life; a comparable function in Romeo's case is served by Mercutio, who is greatly developed from a hint in Brooke to become a buoyant companion, a detached critical observer, a debunker of the fashionable and a lively example of a young gallant.

Mercutio is a foil to Romeo the lover, and to Tybalt the swordsman; Shakespeare invents the scene in which the young gallants prepare to enter the Capulet feast and Mercutio delivers his fantastic speech about Queen Mab. The episode in which Mercutio and Benvolio seek the concealed Romeo is also Shakespeare's invention, and so too is the meeting of Mercutio and the Nurse which results in an exuberant display of comic bawdy (so bringing out their matched roles in relation to the lovers). Shakespeare again alters his sources in having Mercutio take up Tybalt's challenge to Romeo, and in having Tybalt kill Mercutio under Romeo's arm as he tries to part the two men. This is Shakespeare's invention, and it results in Romeo's accepting the obligation to revenge; though Romeo does kill Tybalt in the source story too, in Shakespeare his motivation is different. The act is woven into the complex pattern: Tybalt's death binds the public drama of the opening moments of the play to the private drama of Romeo and Juliet. Romeo, who had been in solitary love-melancholy while Tybalt fought the opening brawl of I. i, is at last forced to accept the honour code.

The movement which concludes in Tybalt's death is matched by a subsidiary movement in which Romeo is contrasted to Paris. In Shakespeare, not in Brooke, Paris is first introduced (in I. ii) in close juxtaposition to Romeo; as Romeo leaves the stage lamenting his unhappy love for Rosaline, Paris enters, talking to Capulet about his suit to Juliet. It is also Shakespeare's invention that Paris is invited to the ball to woo Juliet, but he says nothing there, while fortune smiles on Romeo as he meets Juliet. Paris is next seen much later, after the death of Tybalt, again discussing the proposed marriage to Juliet (III. iv.; cf I. ii). Here Shakespeare

---

ch. 4. Laslett (p. 88) says that in Tuscany at about the time the action of *Romeo and Juliet* is supposed to take place, girls could have been as young as fourteen at marriage, though men would be nearer thirty. The second Earl of Exeter married Elizabeth Manners in 1589 when she was thirteen, and she bore a child when she was fourteen and five months; but this seems to have been exceptional, even for the privileged, in Shakespeare's time.

follows Brooke, so that the structural parallel between the scenes emphasizes the persistence of Paris as a threat to the hopes of the lovers, and when the Capulet parents, on the spur of the moment, name a day for the wedding, an ominous note is sounded. Shakespeare invents another scene in which Paris meets Juliet at the Friar's cell; this keeps up the pressure and strengthens the role of Paris as rival to Romeo in the second half of the play, once Tybalt and Mercutio are dead and Benvolio fades from the action. As in Brooke, Paris arrives on his wedding morning, entering with the Friar to hear that Juliet is dead; he joins in a chorus of lament, but Shakespeare only gives him conventional phrases, in contrast to the powerful, terse and memorable words in which Romeo reacts to the news brought by Balthasar: 'Is it e'en so? Then I defy you, stars'. The alterations made to Brooke's ending by Shakespeare also give added importance to Paris; his visit to the tomb is Shakespeare's invention, as is the challenge, fight, and his death at Romeo's hands. Thus Shakespeare develops Paris into a noble rival to Romeo; he has public acceptability and observes the rules of conventional courtship, so contrasting with Romeo's secret and unconventional love. The final encounter in the tomb matches the desperate, passionate and isolated hero against this orthodox antagonist who understands so little and whose death ironically recalls the futile deaths of Tybalt and Mercutio. The rival suitor is granted a place in death beside Juliet in recognition of his integral part in the pattern.

Shakespeare makes the plot depend crucially on messages. He invents the episode in which Romeo, Benvolio and Mercutio learn by accident from Capulet's illiterate servant of the proposed ball. This scheme is repeated when the Nurse haphazardly encounters the young gallants, and Romeo lightheartedly identifies himself amidst the bawdy mockery of his friends. Later, the Nurse brings Juliet a happy reply (II. v). In the second, tragic movement of the play, the Nurse brings Juliet the news of Tybalt's death and Romeo's banishment in a scene structurally similar to the earlier one (III. ii; cf. II. v). Shakespeare stresses in both scenes the ease with which messages can go wrong; so Juliet at first thinks it is Romeo, not Tybalt, whom the Nurse saw bedaubed in gore-blood. This second scene is Shakespeare's invention, intended to point up the pattern of repetition. In the closing movement of the play Balthasar brings Romeo the false report of Juliet's death (V. i); immediately afterwards, as Romeo leaves the stage by one door, bearing a phail of poison, Friar John enters by another to begin the next scene by telling Friar Laurence how he failed to get through with the message that Juliet is drugged, not dead. Here again Shakespeare's stagecraft supports his selective emphasis on the source story, giving prominence to the mechanism of fate. A further minor addition to the story, in which Shakespeare makes Capulet impulsively bring forward the wedding day of Juliet and Paris from Thursday to Wednesday, increases the feeling of impending doom created by the complex pattern of repeated episodes and situations in the two halves of the play. It is this which constitutes Shakespeare's structural equivalent to those passages in Chaucer and Brooke which dwell on the lamentable power of Fortune over the lovers; at the same time Shakespeare follows Chaucer in using leitmotivs in the dramatic poetry, creating a sense of deep inner coherence in the action to which the characters testify, as if by subconscious prompting—as when Romeo and Juliet speak of stars, lightning, torches and rich jewels in darkness, or when Capulet compares Verona's youth to buds and flowers and their fathers to limping winter, or when Romeo compares himself to a mariner risking shipwreck, or when the Friar observes 'The earth that's nature's mother is her tomb'. The intensive and recurrent use of a group of leitmotivs gives a distinctively sharp lyric quality to the tragedy. In Shakespeare's later love tragedies the importance of leitmotivs increases as their number diminishes, indicating that for him they are especially important in creating the structure of feeling which characterizes this mode of tragedy.[1]

For Shakespeare the period immediately preceding the composition of *Romeo and Juliet* was one of intense exploration of different kinds of love poetry; the play begins with a sonnet, spoken as Prologue, and there are indeed general analogies between the play and a sonnet sequence, in which leitmotivs have dramatic and thematic functions, and where the private emotional experience of lovers is intently explored in isolation and in relation to their social context and to ideas of love, destiny and death. Arthur Brooke himself prefaced his poem with two sonnets to the reader and another presenting The Argument of the poem, so recognizing the affinities between the sonnet form and his subject. Shakespeare's Prologue has the same purpose, attun-

1. Cf. the studies of the language of *Othello* and *Antony and Cleopatra* in G. Wilson Knight, *The Wheel of Fire* (1930) and *The Imperial Theme* (1931).

ing the audience to the play's verbal music and, subliminally, to its sonnet-like symmetries and intensities of feeling and design. The opening phase of the play is marked by recurrent transitions from blank verse into rhyme; talk of love induces couplet-rhyming by Benvolio and Romeo, and when Capulet talks of Juliet's tender youth he does so in rhyme; furthermore, this is directly followed by Benvolio's proposing through a sonnet-like sestet that Romeo seek a new mistress and prompting Romeo to answer him, in corresponding sestet form, with the soon-to-be-broken vow of fidelity to Rosaline. These small-scale, compressed sonnets, composed of a quatrain and a couplet, finely tune the audience's expectations in preparation for the moment when Romeo, after his ecstatic reaction to the first sight of Juliet, takes her hand and begins what is to become a full-length sonnet, whereupon she joins him in a duet, so completing the poem: its argument and outcome is their first kiss. Shakespeare creates a perfect symbol of the absorption of the sonnet mode into the art of the play, enacting experience which the sonnet poet must *re*collect and *re*create. Moreover, this moment of artistic triumph is itself only a part of Shakespeare's full originality here, which is in the invention of a means to realize, on the stage, what had hitherto only been depicted in non-dramatic poetry: each lover's intimate and delicate states of consciousness, subtle and potent movements of feeling, intuitions of heart's mysteries. The spectator at the theatrical performance, a public occasion so potentially inimical to intimate response, is here involved in an experience equivalent to that created in the imagination of the solitary reader.

Among sonnet-sequences of the period the first in quality and the closest in feeling to *Romeo and Juliet* is Sidney's *Astrophil and Stella*.[1] Nashe, in his preface to the unauthorized edition of 1591, characterized it in the evocative phrase 'the tragicommody of love . . . performed by starlight',[2] and he recognized its firm overall structure in the succinct description: 'The argument cruell chastitie, the Prologue hope, the Epilogue dispaire'. To establish clearly Shakespeare's achievement in creating, in *Romeo and Juliet*, a dramatic equivalent to the sonnet-sequence as we find it in *Astrophil and Stella*, it is well worth while turning to

1. Malone was the first to note the parallels between *Romeo and Juliet* and Daniel; K. Muir, *Shakespeare's Sources* (1957), notes the link between Sonnet 85 of *Astrophil and Stella* and Romeo's final speech. Among recent studies may be cited that of Watson, Daniel and Sidney in Inge Leimberg, *Shakespeares Romeo und Julia, von Sonettdichtung zur Liebestragödie* (Munich, 1968).

2. Cited in *The Poems of Sir Philip Sidney*, ed. W. A. Ringler (1962), p. xlix. Quotations from Sidney are taken from this edition.

Sidney and examining his sequence in detail for a few moments. This should then help to illuminate the particular lyric quality of *Romeo and Juliet* and to illustrate the course of Shakespeare's inspired response to Sidney's great work.

Sidney presents a sequence of scenes in *Astrophil and Stella*, as is implied in Nashe's description of the work as a 'Theater of pleasure', and no scene is more moving or dramatically important (and none closer in feeling and conception to *Romeo and Juliet*) than that presented in the fourth song, where Astrophil meets Stella in a garden by moonlight and seeks with his 'whispering voyce' to persuade her; each stanza concludes in his plea and her response, varying in tenderness, urgency and acknowledged feeling but always increasing his pain:

Take me to thee, and thee to me.
'No, no, no, no, my Deare, let be.'

The atmosphere of seclusion, darkness and tender intimacy is created in intently simple language, candidly pure diction; tiny details of sensation, sound and image suggest nature approving a union secret and ecstatic:

Night hath closd all in her cloke,
Twinckling starres Love-thoughts provoke:
Danger hence good care doth keepe,
Jealousie it selfe doth sleepe:
Take me to thee, and thee to me.
'No, no, no, no, my Deare, let be.'

Better place no wit can find,
Cupid's yoke to loose or bind:
These sweet flowers on fine bed too,
Us in their best language woo:
Take me to thee, and thee to me.
'No, no, no, no, my Deare, let be.'

This small light the Moone bestowes,
Serves thy beames but to disclose,
So to raise my hap more hie;
Feare not else, none can us spie:
Take me to thee, and thee to me.
'No, no, no, no, my Deare, let be.'

The complete stillness and harmony evoked in the description of the moonlit garden suggests the ideal happiness of love; Stella seems to assent to the ideal but deny the act, and Astrophil gives a piquant intensity to the sense of shared seclusion by reminding Stella how very close is the household held in 'Dumbe sleepe', how remote the chance of another such meeting between them, how urgent the pressure of 'Niggard Time'; but the final stanza has a darker note:

> Wo to me, and do you sweare
> Me to hate? But I forbeare,
> Cursed be my destines all,
> That brought me so high to fall:
> Soone with my death I will please thee.
> 'No, no, no, no, my Deare, let be.'

Stella's responses are tender in their admission of love, the pain of denial. Her gravity expresses a fuller understanding than Astrophil's. It is Stella's tone which gives the poetry its complexity, it is Stella who consistently draws Astrophil to a more profound and finally tragic view of love, so intensifying their shared experience of each other's nature. This intimate voice, this fine communion of consciousness, is the heart of Sidney's achievement in the poem. The episode presented in the fourth song is placed between sonnets exploring Astrophil's state of mind in anticipation and reflection; so in Sonnet 85 the excited emotion mounts freely through each line to a simply expressed gesture:

> I see the house, my heart thy selfe containe,
> Beware full sailes drowne not thy tottring barge:
> Least joy, by Nature apt sprites to enlarge,
> Thee to thy wracke beyond thy limits straine.
> Nor do like Lords, whose weake confused braine,
> Not pointing to fit folkes each undercharge,
> While everie office themselves will discharge,
> With doing all, leave nothing done but paine.
> But give apt servants their due place, let eyes
> See Beautie's totall summe summ'd in her face:
> Let eares heare speech, which wit to wonder ties,
> Let breath sucke up those sweetes, let armes embrace
> The globe of weale, lips *Love's* indentures make:
> Thou but of all the kingly Tribute take.

Sonnet 89 by contrast expresses Astrophil's subsequent restless, impatient and obsessive condition through a sequence of rapid antitheses which generate, yet persistently frustrate, syntactic and emotional energies:

> Now that of absence the most irksome night,
> With darkest shade doth overcome my day;
> Since *Stella's* eyes, wont to give me my day,
> Leaving my Hemisphere, leave me in night,
> Each day seemes long, and longs for long-staid night,

The night as tedious, wooes th'approch of day;
Tired with the dusty toiles of busie day,
Languisht with horrors of the silent night,
Suffering the evils both of the day and night,
While no night is more darke then is my day,
Nor no day hath lesse quiet then my night:
With such bad mixture of my night and day,
That living thus in blackest winter night,
I feele the flames of hottest sommer day.

This transition from Sonnet 85's expression of hope, vulnerable only in its whole-heartedness, to the frustrated bitterness of Sonnet 89, may seem at first sight only negative and destructive, but in the sequence as a whole it can be seen as part of Astrophil's development towards his final tragic maturity. He comprehends his fate and faces despair steadily, without betraying or denying his ideals or his love. To look back to Sonnet 1 from the eleventh song, where Astrophil seeks consolation beneath Stella's window in the dark night, only for their colloquy to be interrupted by members of her household, or from the final sonnet, where Astrophil cries out:

Ah what doth Phoebus' gold that wretch availe,
Whom iron doores do keepe from use of day?

is to recognize how much tragic irony lay unsuspected in the apparently encouraging advice of the Muse, 'looke in thy heart and write'.

The sonnet-sequence as a form is particularly suited to the presentation of a young man in love; individual sonnets in *Astrophil and Stella* present many separate moments and moods, including doubt, self-pity, delight, impatience, dejection, self-deception; and Sidney is prepared to allow considerable emphasis to fall on the erratic, unstable and intermittent progress of Astrophil in self-knowledge and in love of Stella. As Sonnet 1 announces:

I sought fit words to paint the blackest face of woe,
Studying inventions fine, her wits to entertaine:

the work is concerned from the outset with style and tone, and Astrophil's self-consciousness about his poetry, which is the specific subject of several sonnets, quickly develops beyond any mere conventional sonneteer's interest in technique to become a quest for self-realization. The full expression of his emotion for Stella would be one kind of fulfilment, and indeed finally Stella leads him to a kind of spiritual and emotional self-realization.

The subtlety and insight of Sidney in creating the character of Astrophil is nowhere more impressive than in those moments when he feels speech itself an enemy, since it confirms his separateness, and the sonnet form a prison. A contrast between the first and last sonnets shows the sequence to be a dramatic record of spiritual and artistic self-discovery; Astrophil at first is imposed on by the mechanics of sonnet form, and as he adventures into undiscovered emotional country he often does so by inventively deploying old formulae, and he may still have to guard against rhyme's temptations to sententiousness and attitudinizing. Self-consciousness, self-criticism, reflected by Stella, are the means to true growth:

> My Muse may well grudge at my heav'nly joy,
> If still I force her in sad rhymes to creepe:

Such, then, is the lyric narrative which was in Shakespeare's mind when he composed *Romeo and Juliet.*

When we first hear of Romeo in Shakespeare's play he is described in the attitude of a typical Elizabethan melancholy lover; he is young and untried, but there is at first an element of parody in Shakespeare's presentation of him; his conventionality and bookishness are obvious in the first words he speaks, all absurdly stereotyped paradox and similitude, like a young lord in *Love's Labour's Lost*; it is only the unusually rapid and intense alternations of mood, and a certain musical sensitivity in diction, that enliven his speech:

> O heavy lightness, serious vanity,
> Misshapen chaos of well-seeming forms!
> Feather of lead, bright smoke, cold fire, sick health,
> Still-waking sleep that is not what it is!
> This love feel I that feel no love in this. (I. i. 176–80)

Again:

> Love is a smoke made with the fume of sighs;
> Being purg'd, a fire sparkling in lovers' eyes;
> Being vex'd, a sea nourish'd with lovers' tears;
> What is it else? A madness most discreet,
> A choking gall, and a preserving sweet. (I. i. 188–92)

Paris, Romeo's rival, lacks this sweetness of tone and volatile temperament, and is actually likened to a book (without intentional irony) by Lady Capulet. Shakespeare's emphasis on this predictable, literary mode of perception and feeling may also be recognized in Capulet's description of the young ladies invited to the feast as 'Earth-treading stars that make dark heaven light';

he also compares them to 'fresh female buds', delighted with the approach of 'well-apparelled April'. When Romeo and Juliet meet for the first time, Juliet gently mocks Romeo when she says 'you kiss by th'book', though her debate with him in their shared sonnet shows them equal in wit. Act II begins, like Act I, with a sonnet prologue, but it contributes little beyond a re-statement of the sonnet form; indeed, from this point forward, the emergence of deeper and finer feeling is expressed not in rhyme but in blank verse. The play progressively distinguishes between characters who contentedly express themselves through received verbal and rhetorical conventions, and the hero and heroine who learn that greater maturity and fulfilment require language true to their own particular selves.

When Romeo enters Capulet's garden Shakespeare effects a transition, through the use of blank verse, somewhat comparable in its effect to Sidney's transition from the tight patterning of feeling in Sonnet 85 to the sustained, even rhythm of the fourth song, allowing the gradual creation of a delicate atmosphere in which tender and intimate feeling can find expression. Juliet's first soliloquy in this scene (II. ii) enacts her yearning, its supple syntax constantly reaching forward through the pentameters, her youth and candour palpable in the clear, absolute quality of language and thought:

> What's Montague? It is nor hand nor foot
> Nor arm nor face nor any other part
> Belonging to a man. O be some other name.
> What's in a name? That which we call a rose
> By any other word would smell as sweet;
> So Romeo would, were he not Romeo call'd,
> Retain that dear perfection which he owes
> Without that title. (II. ii. 40–7)

In this atmosphere Romeo too finds a new language:

> I am no pilot, yet wert thou as far
> As that vast shore wash'd with the farthest sea,
> I should adventure for such merchandise.
> (II. ii. 82–4)

As the episode unfolds, their voices alternate in an increasingly complex rhythm; the Nurse's interruption causes an excited acceleration of pace, after which, when Juliet returns to the window, she acts out in reality a sonnet scenario, herself the falconer, Romeo her tassel gentle. Shakespeare presents the scene as a visual symbol in the spectators' eyes, *and* as it is to the lovers, *and* as it might be re-created by a sonnet poet in his art. Juliet acknowledges the fusion of art and living experience in this moment; her consciousness of it gives such joy that her conceits become inspired with airy fantasy and humour:

I would have thee gone,
And yet no farther than a wanton's bird,
That lets it hop a little from his hand
Like a poor prisoner in his twisted gyves,
And with a silken thread plucks it back again,
So loving-jealous of his liberty. (II. ii. 176–81)

and Romeo can share the fantasy:

I would I were thy bird.

From this point in the play onwards, rhyme becomes associated with formality, as in the Friar's first scene (II. iii) or Benvolio's account of the fray in III. i, or Juliet's first exchanges with Paris at the Friar's cell in IV. i, or the sestets spoken by Paris and by the Prince in V. iii.

Romeo's development, however, is not achieved without uncertainties, hesitations, and false notes: when Romeo and Juliet meet at the Friar's cell to be married (II. vi) the contrast reveals Juliet's greater emotional maturity and comprehension:

Romeo. Ah, Juliet, if the measure of thy joy
Be heap'd like mine, and that thy skill be more
To blazon it, then sweeten with thy breath
This neighbour air, and let rich music's tongue
Unfold the imagin'd happiness that both
Receive in either by this dear encounter.
Juliet. Conceit more rich in matter than in words
Brags of his substance, not of ornament.
They are but beggars that can count their worth,
But my true love is grown to such excess
I cannot sum up sum of half my wealth.
(II. vi. 24–34)

Here again we may think of the analogy between Romeo and Astrophil, Juliet and Stella. Such emotional power and authentic voice, already secure in Juliet, emerge in Romeo's language at the dawn parting:

Let me be ta'en, let me be put to death,
I am content, so thou wilt have it so.
I'll say yon grey is not the morning's eye,
'Tis but the pale reflex of Cynthia's brow.
Nor that is not the lark whose notes do beat

The vaulty heaven so high above our heads.
I have more care to stay than will to go.
(III. v. 17–23)

In this sequence Romeo and Juliet share a complex mood, their intimacy touched by the chill of imminent parting, tense with the unspoken knowledge of how 'Fate does Iron wedges drive / And alwaies crouds itself betwixt'.[1] The mutual tenderness in the debate between nightingale and lark, the recognized, self-conscious handling of the formal motifs, once again serves to measure the increasing distance between their earlier poetic artifice and their present experience.

Marriage, the act of union, and the closeness of violent death, have brought Shakespeare's characters, by contrast with Astrophil and Stella, to a fiercer sense of the imperatives of the moment: their commitment is to precipitate action, which heightens their sensitivity to the detailed texture of experience with its constant possibilities of violence, cruelty and pain.

By the beginning of the last scene, Romeo's transformation of personality is expressed in a new note of resolution and command, compressed, resonant and personal. This is made explicit in the formal contrast Shakespeare presents between Paris and Romeo at the beginning of the scene. Paris enters to perform obsequies at the tomb:

Sweet flower, with flowers thy bridal bed I strew.
O woe, thy canopy is dust and stones
Which with sweet water nightly I will dew,
Or wanting that, with tears distill'd by moans.
The obsequies that I for thee will keep
Nightly shall be to strew thy grave and weep.
(v. iii. 12–17)

but Romeo's entrance interrupts him. Romeo is desperate and resolute:

The time and my intents are savage-wild,
More fierce and more inexorable far
Than empty tigers or the roaring sea.
(v. iii. 37–9)

The contrast measures the distance between Romeo now and the distant youth who once wept for Rosaline: as he was then, he himself might have versified no better than Paris; now, language is his to command. In his final speech, over the body of Juliet, Romeo deliberately attempts a summation of his experience. The recapitulation of tragic leitmotivs, which could have been a

1. Andrew Marvell, 'The Definition of Love'.

distracting artifice, is expressed with direct and fresh emotion; the images are felt as both spontaneous and inevitable products of the moment. 'Lightning before death', hitherto for Romeo no more than a proverb, suddenly reveals itself to be an unsuspected tragic symbol. The sight of Juliet at the point of his own death shocks Romeo like a flash of lightning, yet her beauty turns the tomb into a feasting presence full of light, and makes Romeo's heart light with joy. Paris had likened Juliet to a sweet flower; now for Romeo death becomes a bee sucking the honey of her breath, the flower's crimson petals then become a flag of battle, a valiant forlorn hope on beauty's field, defying Death's pale legion. The image of death the warrior dissolves into that of death the rival lover, at once insubstantial and abhorrently actual, the tomb his dim palace, worms his chambermaids. These gothic and macabre images seem to be telepathically communicated from Juliet: Romeo intuitively shares the nightmarish fears that assailed her at the moment of draining the cup:

> Death that hath suck'd the honey of thy breath
> Hath had no power yet upon thy beauty.
> Thou art not conquer'd. Beauty's ensign yet
> Is crimson in thy lips and in thy cheeks,
> And Death's pale flag is not advanced there.
>
> Shall I believe
> That unsubstantial Death is amorous,
> And that the lean abhorred monster keeps
> Thee here in dark to be his paramour?
> (v. iii. 92–6, 102–5)

To turn away from Romeo's intense eloquence at this momen requires an act of will, yet if we do so in order to compare the lines in Daniel's *Rosamund* which are here recalled, we are struck by the extraordinary transformation they undergo in Romeo's passionate imagination. Here is Daniel:

> When naught respecting death, the last of paines,
> Plac'd his pale collours, th'ensigne of his might,
> Upon his new-got spoyle before his right;
>
> Ah how me thinks I see death dallying seekes,
> To entertaine it selfe in loues sweet place:
> Decayed Roses of discoloured cheekes,
> Doe yet retaine deere notes of former grace:
> And ougly death sits faire within her face;
> Sweet remnants resting of vermilion red,
> That death it selfe, doubts whether she be dead.
> (ll. 605–7, 673–9)

Daniel's even, melancholy cadence, his mood of resignation, turn into defiant, sensuously alive personification in Romeo's speech.

Even more remarkable, however, is the relation between Romeo's final lines and Sonnet 85 of *Astrophil and Stella.* It is as if Astrophil in his final mood of tragic despair were to rewrite his earlier sonnet of happy anticipation, for with sharp irony Romeo recalls, only bitterly to redirect, its opening lines; Astrophil's

> Beware full sailes drowne not thy tottring barge:
> Least joy, by Nature apt sprites to enlarge,
> Thee to thy wracke beyond thy limits straine.

becomes Romeo's

> Thou desperate pilot now at once run on
> The dashing rocks thy seasick weary bark.
> (v. iii. 117–18)

Romeo's sails are full of despair, not joy, his verse moves to imminent wreck, where Astrophil only invokes the idea as an implausible hyperbole and his syntax remains buoyant. The pattern of close ironic correspondence between Romeo's speech and this sonnet reveals the acuteness of Romeo's feeling. Where Astrophil bids his eyes

> See Beautie's totall summe summ'd in her face

Romeo cries 'Eyes, look your last!' Instead of his arms embracing 'The globe of weale', Romeo's are bid take their 'last embrace'. Romeo, unlike Astrophil, can make no appeals to his ears: Juliet's voice is stilled. Romeo's lips, which once indeed did '*Love's* indentures make', must now

> seal with a righteous kiss
> A dateless bargain to engrossing Death.
> (v. iii. 114–15)

It is a close and intricate tragic reworking.

So, at last, the rote-learned sonneteering paradoxes are lived out actually; in the intensity of the tragic climax fire and ice are simultaneously felt, drugs at once quick and deadly. To kiss is to die in earnest: the living moment and the poem coincide.

Time, which has exerted cumulative pressure on the lovers, achieves a triumph here. Romeo, nervea up for the act of suicide, fearing the imminent intrusion of the Watch, his breath and pulse still recovering from the fierce violence of killing Paris, carries the body into the tomb, where he receives new shocks at the sight of the body of Juliet, and then Tybalt: 'liest thou there in thy bloody sheet?' With time hurrying near, Romeo the love poet misreads the signs of Juliet's revival. Less than a minute's hesitation here would have saved his life and Juliet's, but Romeo acts in passionate haste.

At the play's opening Romeo lives only to dream; it is not he but his family who burst on to the stage, weapons drawn in the sunlit city street, to fight the Capulets. Immediately afterwards Romeo's father, despite the fact that he is himself still heated from this dangerous brawl, laments Romeo's love of introspective solitude: to him that appears to be an alarming tendency. In these opening moments much stress is laid on questions of time. Benvolio's report of the fray is emphatic about the exact sequence of events, the Prince gives precise orders that Capulet must go with him 'now' and Montague report 'this afternoon'. On the other hand stress is also laid on extended and indefinite periods of time: the brawl juxtaposes vigorous youth and decrepit age; Montague describes the quarrel as 'ancient', the Prince recalls that this is the third of a series of outbreaks; Romeo's melancholy has continued for an indefinite period. Still, the encounter between Benvolio and Romeo, the one having just fought Tybalt, the other associated with solitude, dawn, dew, silence and Nature, seems to promise an abrupt intrusion of the daylight world and clock-time into Romeo's dreams:

Romeo. Is the day so young?
Ben. But new struck nine.

As the play develops Shakespeare sustains the emphasis on the continuous counterpoint between extended periods and an exactly stipulated day, hour, moment. Motifs of imagery drawn from the stars, the seasons and flowers invoke powerfully normative measures of extended time: the period of the bud's development gives special beauty and meaning to the moment when it first opens to the sun. Yet if Capulet's annual feast marks the fulfilment of one cyclical rhythm, of love and kinship, the brawl fulfils another cycle, of hate. Both are 'old-established'. Time brings new hope of reconciliation through the ardour of the young lovers; but it also brings new menace through the equally hot irascibility of the young Tybalt and Mercutio. Nature may foster the new-born infants of the spring, but it is in the morn and liquid dew of youth that contagious blastments are most imminent.

The opening statement of the counterpoint between extended

time and the specific moment is complex; it is, furthermore, reflected in the play's larger rhythms of dramatic narrative. Shakespeare stresses the temporal as well as the physical location of the scenes of the play.[1] This is consistent with his concern to impose a firm overall dramatic structure on the loosely episodic *novella* of Brooke's version (the action of which he has compressed from a period of nine months to a few days), but there are further important artistic repercussions to be noticed. The play's scenes are composed in a temporal rhythm of which the movements conclude in dawn. At the beginning of the play, before he enters, Romeo is described walking in a grove of sycamore at dawn; the second dawn rises as he leaves Capulet's orchard; the third as he descends from Juliet's window after the wedding night; the fourth when Juliet's drugged body is found by the Nurse; a final dawn rises[2] as the Prince surveys the dead bodies in the tomb. The scenes of Act I mark the passing of a day from nine in the morning, through the afternoon, when both Capulet and his wife stress the feast to come 'this night', to the coming of darkness when Benvolio, Mercutio and Romeo enter bearing torches to light them to the feast. The brilliantly lit, crowded feast is succeeded by the contrasting night scene, lit only from Juliet's window, dark and

1. Granville Barker, *Prefaces to Shakespeare*, Vol. II (1930), p. 12, observes that Shakespeare's chief technical resource in the play is the vivid contrast of pace and mood between scene and scene, in swift succession. A valuable discussion of the handling of time in the play is by G. Thomas Tanselle, *SQ* (1964), pp. 349–61. Although the action, as McGinn observes, 'is dated throughout with a most exact attention to hours', there are a number of minor anomalies (discounting the internal contradictions of the Nurse's reminiscences), such as Lady Capulet's statement that Romeo 'lives' in Mantua, when he has hardly had time to get there after being banished, or Juliet's remark that the Nurse has praised Romeo 'So many thousand times', when scarcely two days have elapsed in the play (though of course months pass in Brooke).

2. An anomaly which has aroused commentators concerns the time which is supposed to elapse between Juliet's taking the potion and the end of the play. The Friar (IV. i. 90–1) says: 'Wednesday is tomorrow; / Tomorrow night look that thou lie alone.' Since the wedding-day is advanced, she presumably takes it on *Tuesday* night. She is to drink the potion which will last 'two and forty hours'. Evidently if the Friar had said either 'four and twenty' or 'eight and forty' this would make the time-scheme exact; so that Juliet would be buried on Wednesday afternoon, to awaken near dawn on Thursday or Friday. Nevertheless in the theatre Shakespeare's specific references to time will give an audience a continuous sense of firm location and urgent haste, and they will not notice a problem only shown up by close attention in the study. Shakespeare stresses that Juliet's taking of the potion is followed by a dawn scene, and her awakening and suicide is followed by another dawn; this is the timing that is dramatically important, and it is very clear. In Brooke the Friar's message is that Juliet will awake 'the next night' (l. 2479).

private. It ends with dawn. The whole play's action is plotted according to a chronological plan in which time is accounted for as deliberately as it is in this act.

The Nurse's account of Juliet's life in I. iii is a kind of *reductio ad absurdum* of the process which relates extended time and stipulated moments; her narrative is packed with particular references. She can tell Juliet's age unto an hour, Juliet will be fourteen come Lammas Eve at night, she twice says it is eleven years since the earthquake, she swears by her maidenhead at twelve year old, and she will remember the story of Juliet saying 'Ay' if she lives a thousand years. Now the Nurse is completely confident that this is what constitutes knowledge of Juliet; Juliet's identity and development, as she supposes, are the product of communal family life, are the sum of the impressions shared in the family memory; but the Nurse does not notice the discrepancy between her idea of the girl and the unmistakable note of gravity, expressing a private identity, in Juliet's answer that, as to marriage, 'It is an honour that I dream not of'.

At the Capulet feast (I. v), in an atmosphere of pastime, the sight of Juliet produces in Romeo a state of ecstatic waking dream:

> It seems she hangs upon the cheek of night
> As a rich jewel in an Ethiop's ear.

This is abruptly juxtaposed to Tybalt's instant, violent impulse to action:

> This by his voice should be a Montague.
> Fetch me my rapier, boy.

In their first kiss Romeo and Juliet withdraw into a private world of intimacy, suspending the world's ordinary time and replacing it with the rival time of the imagination. Yet no sooner do they draw apart than they find themselves bound to take heed of the alien public world and its imperatives, of time calculated in days and hours, of love reduced to appetite, happiness to jesting and farce, vitality to violence. The first meeting of the lovers is separated from the second by an exuberantly comic and bawdy interlude involving Benvolio and Mercutio; meanwhile Romeo has leaped the orchard wall, into another world of unknown joy. A distinct and separate atmosphere and rhythm is established by sudden contrast, as the laughter of the two young men fades away and Romeo stands silently in darkness gazing at the house. Juliet's appearance at a window is the dawn in a rival world from which the moon is banished:

It is the east and Juliet is the sun!
Arise fair sun and kill the envious moon.

Time and mutability do not exist in the world of ideal love; it has no local habitations and no names, it is free from Verona and the feud. Juliet prays that Romeo will discard his name and he vows he 'never will be Romeo'. The first part of the scene is composed of soliloquies, the expression of separate inner lives, yet here spontaneously in harmony, filled with images of aspiration and release from the world's weight of physical and social laws; but as soon as Juliet realizes that Romeo is actually there, these laws press in around her: 'Art thou not Romeo, and a Montague?' There is a struggle between the self that takes Romeo at his word and says 'Ay' and the self that automatically adopts worldly caution, 'form' and 'compliment'. In this second dialogue, Juliet wishes that she might take back her vow in order to give it again, prolonging the moment by wave-like repetition to infinity, yet there is no escape from time: both lovers must bow to it: Juliet must ask 'What o'clock tomorrow / Shall I send to thee', and Romeo answer 'By the hour of nine'.

Juliet's reaction, ''Tis twenty year till then', sustains the lovers' preoccupation with the relativity of time; at her next appearance in II. v she is intensely impatient:

The clock struck nine when I did send the Nurse,
In half an hour she promis'd to return.
Perchance she cannot meet him. That's not so.
O, she is lame. Love's heralds should be thoughts
Which ten times faster glides than the sun's beams
Driving back shadows over lowering hills.
Therefore do nimble-pinion'd doves draw Love,
And therefore hath the wind-swift Cupid wings.
Now is the sun upon the highmost hill
Of this day's journey, and from nine till twelve
Is three long hours, yet she is not come.
Had she affections and warm youthful blood
She would be as swift in motion as a ball:
My words would bandy her to my sweet love,
And his to me. (II. v. 1–15)

In the world she shares with Romeo, messages travel by thought, at ten times the speed of light. In her imagination she seizes the slow, round sun, the rotund plodding Nurse and the infuriating regular clock, squeezes them all into one ball and makes it fly at the pace of a hotly contended point in a tennis match. 'Wisely and slow: they stumble that run fast', the watchword of Friar

Laurence, reminds us that the rival views of time are embodied in different generations: Romeo responds to the Friar with the telling rebuke 'Thou canst not speak of that thou canst not feel'.

As the hour of wedding approaches, Romeo restates Juliet's faith in the imagination's capacity to triumph over time: eager for Juliet's arrival he tells the Friar

> come what sorrow can,
> It cannot countervail the exchange of joy
> That one short minute gives me in her sight.
> (II. vi. 3–5)

Shakespeare deploys intent artistry in designing this sequence of episodes: he imposes a marked rhythm which will bring out the interplay of conflicting time scales. The meeting of the lovers at the Friar's cell, and their departure for marriage in church, awakens the keenest anticipation in the audience; yet the expectations thus aroused are at once dissipated by the bored and desultory conversation of Mercutio and Benvolio, out in the street on a hot afternoon with nothing to do. Only when this slack atmosphere is established does Tybalt burst in to fracture it: a rapid build-up to a climax of excitement ensues with the fight and killings; then the entrance of the Prince produces a solemn period for the grave implications to be absorbed. It is now that Shakespeare switches directly back to Juliet, still unaware of the killings, only just married and still full of innocent excitement, which for her has been unbroken since II. vi when she was last on stage. Shakespeare imposes on the audience here another abruptly unexpected change of tempo as he faces them with Juliet's irresistible passion: they are made to feel directly the collision between opposed time scales, between Verona in July and the inner universe created by the lovers. Juliet's soliloquy is the climactic expression of the lovers' desire: if they do not make their sun stand still, they will make him run, inventing anew, and in private, a ceremony to rival the world's old-accustomed epithalamium:

> Gallop apace, you fiery-footed steeds,
> Towards Phoebus' lodging. Such a waggoner
> As Phaeton would whip you to the west
> And bring in cloudy night immediately.
> Spread thy close curtain, love-performing night,
> That runaway's eyes may wink, and Romeo
> Leap to these arms untalk'd-of and unseen.
> Lovers can see to do their amorous rites
> By their own beauties; or, if love be blind,

It best agrees with night. Come, civil night,
Thou sober-suited matron, all in black,
And learn me how to lose a winning match
Play'd for a pair of stainless maidenhoods.
Hood my unmann'd blood, bating in my cheeks,
With thy black mantle, till strange love grow bold,
Think true love acted simple modesty.
Come night, come Romeo, come thou day in night,
For thou wilt lie upon the wings of night
Whiter than new snow upon a raven's back.
Come gentle night, come loving black-brow'd night,
Give me my Romeo; and when I shall die
Take him and cut him out in little stars,
And he will make the face of heaven so fine
That all the world will be in love with night,
And pay no worship to the garish sun. (III. ii. 1–25)

The allusion to Phaeton, however, especially when accompanied by a Marlovian tone and a verbal link with Golding's version of that tragic story,[1] sets up an ominous cross-current in the speech. In Golding the boldness of Phaeton is so certainly, so inevitably disastrous from the first moment, that moral reproof of his youthful rashness is subdued by pity for his fate, as Jove hurls 'at the Wagoner a flash of lightning' and Phaeton 'fire yet blasing stil among his yellow haire' shoots 'headlong downe . . . like to a starre in Winter nights'.[2] Juliet's invocation of night is ostensibly sanctioned by epithalamium convention, as in Spenser:[3]

Ah when will this long weary day have end,
And lende me leaue to come unto my love?
. . . Hast thee O fayrest Planet to thy home.

Yet in Juliet's version there is an intensity of pressure, an urgency, which is not orthodox. The speech is full of imperatives: 'Gallop', 'Spread', 'Come', 'Hood', 'Come', 'Come', 'Come', 'come', 'Give', 'Take', 'cut'; and Juliet presses into service a variety of concepts of night each of which she discards impatiently as it fails to satisfy. At such a hectic pace the magic or religious rituals cannot begin to work properly, since they derive their power from anciently established incantatory rhythms and ceremonies. Juliet speaks directly from her young heart, revealing her poignant prematurity when she gives mythological figures of such mystery and authority as Cupid and Night these practical, domestic, humble

1. Cf. the note to the present edition at III. ii. 1.
2. Ovid, *Metamorphoses*, trans. Arthur Golding (1567), II, ll. 404–6.
3. 'Epithalamium', ll. 278–9, 282.

jobs: drawing curtains, teaching a child to play a game, hooding a falcon, cutting stars out of silver paper. Juliet's epithalamium is improvised from her own youthful experience; its strength is in its impetus, but this too is qualified: the bride who is eager to 'put on perfection and a woman's name' is still in part an 'impatient child that hath new robes and may not wear them'. The repeated emphasis on night, subliminally linked with the associations of Phaeton, innocently awakens those forbidding companions of Blind Cupid, Fortune and Death.[1] In *Venus and Adonis* Shakespeare had lamented Amor's aspect as a god of death: here, intuitively, Juliet in her soliloquy moves from the first line towards the idea of her own death and Romeo's. By using the image of the stars to symbolize the eternal quality of their love, Juliet unconsciously admits awareness of impending malign fate; but, simultaneously, she transforms that star-crossed love into a symbol of ultimate triumph:

> Give me my Romeo; and when I shall die
> Take him and cut him out in little stars,
> And he will make the face of heaven so fine
> That all the world will be in love with night,
> And pay no worship to the garish sun.

1. On this important Renaissance poetic theme see Erwin Panofsky, *Studies in Iconology* (1939), pp. 112–14, and Edgar Wind, *Pagan Mysteries in the Renaissance* (1967), ch. x. Shakespeare had already treated the theme in his narrative poems; Venus furiously abuses Death in *Ven.*, ll. 930–54, and the fable that Death and Love exchanged arrows is alluded to in ll. 947–8:

> Love's golden arrow at him should have fled,
> And not death's ebon dart to strike him dead.

Kyd's *Soliman and Perseda* opens with a dispute between Love, Fortune and Death as to which of them should preside over the action:

> *Loue.* What, *Death* and *Fortune* crosse the way of *Loue*?
> *Fortune.* Why, what is *Loue* but *Fortunes* tenis-ball?
> *Death.* Nay, what are you both, but subiects vnto *Death*?

Tancred and Gismund, first published in 1591–2, opens with the entrance of Cupid, drawing in his left hand 'Vaine hope, Brittle joy', and in his right 'Faire resemblance, Late Repentance'. He asserts his power over the world and his determination to wreak much woe to restore awe at his name, recently the object of scorn and scoffing as 'A brat, a bastard, and an idle boy'. Cupid leaves Vaine Hope and Faire Resemblance at the threshold of Tancred's palace, and as he enters gives the warning 'after me, comes death, and deadly paine'. N. J. Halprin, 'The Bridal Runaway' (*Sh. Soc. Papers*, II (1845), p. 14), has some valuable commentary on Juliet's speech. A more recent interesting commentary is by Gary M. McCown, 'Runnawayes Eyes and Juliet's Epithalamium', *SQ*, XXVIII (1976), pp. 150–70.

This prayer is answered, with exact and tragic irony, in the final moments of the play when the Prince begins the concluding sestet with the words

> A glooming peace this morning with it brings:
> The sun for sorrow will not show his head.
> (v. iii. 304–5)

That the sun will not shine for sorrow on the final morning of the play is not only a tribute to Ovidian precedent,[1] for this unnaturally arrested dawn, prolonged and glooming, neither night nor day, memorably concludes a complex double pattern beginning with the play's setting in high Italian summer, where a cool fresh dawn of dispersing cloud and dewy grass may harden under a burning sun into an oppressive noon, menacing with thunder, and where a balmy moonlit night is dependent on the heat of the preceding day, its dark, velvet delicacy intensified by contrast with the sun's unmitigated glare. In the charmed darkness of a silent summer night it is easy to lose touch with the noisy world of day, so distinct, objective, unveiled. The play incorporates these seasonal features of July into the dramatic rhythm; they underscore and at certain points prominently influence character and action.

July is a season of extremes, and so a particularly appropriate choice by the stars for the imposition of their malevolent design. The opposition of the stars to the lovers, though plainly announced in the Prologue, works with mischievous equivocal art, in the play itself, through the natural order and the casual appearance of daily life; so Capulet cheerfully invites Paris to meet 'Earth-treading stars, that make dark heaven light', and it is easy enough to be persuaded by his tone to underestimate or even entirely overlook the fact that 'dark heaven' also means malevolent fate. Capulet only seeks to be polite, but the air of impersonality in his contrived, artificial language undermines the hyperbolic idea that the beauty and will of the human spirit can triumph over fate figured in the drift of stars.

At first sight Juliet appears to Romeo as an auspicious star, a rich jewel adorning night's cheek; she is the guide to his wandering bark,[2] a dazzlingly bright and supremely joyful 'consequence'

1. To mark the fall of Phaeton in Ovid's *Metamorphoses* 'A day did pass without the sun'.

2. The conceit is developed e.g. in Spenser, *Amoretti* 34, and Shakespeare, Sonnet 116.

after his dark forebodings. Later, gazing up from the dark garden, Romeo replaces the stars with Juliet's eyes; it is an ardently vivid imagining; but the stars shine still. They are silent witnesses to the fatal contract made by their light and the light of the moon, 'the inconstant moon'. At the Capulet feast Romeo finds Juliet 'Beauty too rich for use, for earth too dear' but he does not detect, at that moment, the keenly ironic ambiguities alive in his words,[1] while Juliet's impulsive premonition after the contract, that it is 'too rash, too unadvis'd, too sudden, / Too like the lightning' involuntarily expresses a mysterious intuition of the inseparability of such ecstasy from death. Juliet's momentary fear, however sharply felt, must yield to more dominant emotions, the brilliant and violent delights of love at first sight:

> It lies not in our power to love, or hate,
> For will in us is over-rul'd by fate.[2]

So, in the play's larger rhythms, the ordinary events of daily life, with their insignificantly arbitrary quality, can become suddenly endowed with extreme, reckless energies. The brawl in the opening scene builds up out of a clear sky as suddenly and unpredictably as a July thunderstorm. To the Prince the feud itself appears a kind of sudden plague, a 'cankered hate', related to 'cankered peace'. So a populous city, confined by the protection of its walls, breeds a stifling atmosphere with its own kinds of fearful menace. Elizabethan Londoners needed no reminder that the infectious heat of summer can have fatal consequences in cities, and indeed there would be for an Elizabethan audience a cruelly familiar plausibility, as well as apt symbolic significance, in the outbreak of plague which prevents Friar John from getting through to Romeo with the fateful message in Act V. Again, because of the Nurse's obvious garrulity and whimsical randomness when recalling the past in I. iii, an audience may not take altogether seriously her memories of how, on the very day Juliet was weaned, there was an earthquake; yet this is a sign traditionally not without portent and one which probably makes a subliminal contribution to our sense of instability and violence as

1. M. M. Mahood, *Shakespeare's Wordplay* (1957), pp. 62–3, notes quibbles on *use* as 'employment, interest, wear and tear', *earth* as 'mortal life' and 'the grave', *dear* as 'cherished' and 'costly', possibly *beauty* and 'booty' (as in *1H4*, I. ii. 28), and observes: 'Juliet's beauty is too rich for use in the sense that it will be laid in the tomb after a brief enjoyment; but for this very reason it will never be faded and worn. And if she is *not* too dear for earth since Romeo's love is powerless to keep her out of the tomb, it is true that she is too rare a creature for mortal life.'
2. Marlowe, *Hero and Leander*, I. 167–8.

constituent elements of the atmosphere. The high sensitivity of the lovers makes them intuitively aware, at the very moment of decision, of some ulterior force's presence, and though they acknowledge it only obliquely in verbal conceits, a pressure of wit expresses anxiety which is clear even though it cannot be rationalized. When the lovers part at dawn after their wedding night in III. v, Juliet makes a movingly courageous attempt to recapture the tone of happy loving banter as she disputes:

> Yond light is not daylight, I know it, I.
> It is some meteor that the sun exhales
> To be to thee this night a torchbearer
> And light thee on thy way to Mantua.
>
> (III. v. 12–15)

Juliet feels that to preserve the completeness of her intimacy with Romeo at this moment she must release the unspoken foreboding which threatens to imprison each of them in spiritual isolation, so she daringly admits her fear, but with a fantastic conceit borrowed from Romeo's imagination she simultaneously turns the ominous meteor into a mere torchbearer and Romeo's flight into a continuation of nocturnal revelry; yet his flight remains surreally lit, through a Petrarchan hyperbole in which Nature herself bows before the greater power of human beauty. Juliet's conceit is precisely expressive of her feeling, for if neither lover now needs reminding by merely outward signs of the stars' malignity, equally they know the pricelessness of their fortune in the possession of each other. So although the audience, forewarned by the Prologue, may suppose the moment darkly ill-omened, Juliet senses it to be hopeful as well as fearful. Torchbearers frame the scene at the Capulet feast but also at the Capulet tomb; the lovers may begin to fulfil an ironic design in the first brilliant moment of rapture, yet their faith and fearlessness discover in the very darkness of that design a mysterious and exalting path to light.

It is a consequence of the imaginative energy with which Shakespeare invests the forces of comedy in the play that the power of hope should continue to resist with such vitality at this stage of the action, where each new scene seems to add weight by ironic parallel and cumulative misfortune to the impending probability of tragedy. The two modes of tragedy and comedy are opposed, so generating the central dynamic of the action, but there are subterranean connections between them which make an antithetical structure complex like a living organism. The play's comedy is notable for the latent presence, even in scenes of the greatest ease, of a pressure of energy ready to turn into violence, while the insistent patterning of the action is matched by the readiness with which emotional, instinctual and physical energies threaten to overrun all bounds. Two key comic scenes are focused on very long solo performances by the matched comedians, the Nurse and Mercutio (I. iii. 12–57; I. iv. 53–103); in both cases the disproportionate prolixity of the speakers generates a comic anarchy expressly emphasizing unbridled appetites; in both speeches, also, the connections and oppositions between tenderness and brutality, imaginative fantasy and physical mindlessness seem, once released, to proliferate with self-generating speed, inducing an irresistible comic response at once, demanding the actor's whole repertory of vocal and gestural skills for the large-scale low farce of the Nurse and the contrasting air and fire of Mercutio, balletic and rapid in acceleration, dancing a breathtakingly various sequence of instant caricatures. And yet, in their sheer length, both performances reveal the limitations which are the obverse of their strengths, for they embody an essentially reductive view of life in this appropriate art of farce, which uses the mechanisms of jokes and comic routines to exploit stock responses, building up comic pressure and triggering its release, stretching the actor's own physical art to its limits to carry the audience away as subjects to a tyrannous comic spirit.

Yet energy in the theatre remains a delight, and the comic forces released in such abundance in the first three acts provide enormous dynamic power for the action. The variety of impressions and the speed with which they are presented through all the resources of drama are remarkable, with the colourful excitement of action and costume and spectacle, masking, dancing and music, the remembered images of childhood and the past, crowding into a present already densely peopled by strong diverse attitudes and colliding intentions. The absurdity of youth's postures is matched with the folly of declining age, the language of parody and ridicule invests its butts with surprising attractive vitality even as it mocks them, and love-idealizing poetry releases a stream of submerged exuberant bawdy. In the early scenes especially, the characters have an air of freedom to shape time into whatever kind of enjoyable or energetic experience they choose; they are full of zest for novelty and excitement, for making things happen, confident in the promise of pleasure. Here and indeed throughout the play their language is sensuously responsive to the world, which they feel and see with distinct precision: the rosebud unfolding, wormwood laid to a woman's nipple, an empty hazelnut, grasshoppers' wings, a piece of marzipan, a toe plagued with corns, a rich jewel in an Ethiop's ear, a falconer's call, poison in the infant rind of a weak flower; and, later, a poultice for aching bones, a silk button, a cat's scratch, a light footstep on everlasting flint, a bloody discarded sword at the entrance to a tomb.

This vivid responsiveness to the physical texture of life is centred in the human body itself, the very instrument of the art of theatre, from the first moment of the play, as the coarse talk of the servants generates through many active verbs a quick awareness of the body as an instrument of physical brutality and sexual aggression: severing, beating, violating, dismembering. It is seen in action at once as a riotous brawl is fought on stage. The entrance of the ageing heads of houses makes us consider the body's vulnerability to time, if not to violence, and their wives, the first women to appear, are no longer young or desirable, so making the subsequent first impression of Juliet more vividly youthful. The whole span of the body's life is displayed in a cameo when the young girl and her mother listen to the old Nurse, for whom even a slow walking pace is now an effort which leaves her breathless and aching, as she recalls Juliet as an infant, taking her first uncertain steps as she learned to walk.[1]

The play celebrates the active beauty of the body and its endurance of suffering and decline, giving intense expression to its imperatives of food, exercise, sexual desire and rest, and to the human ceremonies in which they are satisfied. The sheer energies of the appetites generated produce a kind of pleasure even in the negative experiences of destruction, hatred, lust, exhaustion. The body's strengths and frailties are graphically demonstrated in its separate parts and in their coordinated action, whether it is

1. Cf. I. iii. Shakespeare's Nurse serves a dramatic purpose at this point somewhat like the Nurse in Marlowe's *Tragedy of Dido*, IV. v, who unwittingly supposes Cupid to be the child Ascanius, and becomes powerfully affected by the god's presence: as the old woman feels young again, and looks forward in imagination to the child's manhood, the audience witness the child-god's power: the Nurse cries 'That I might liue to see this boy a man! / How pretilie he laughs, goe ye wagge, / Youle be a twigger when you come to age. / Say *Dido* what she will I am not old, / Ile be no more a widowe, I am young. / Ile haue a husband, or els a louer.' And Cupid mocks her: 'A husband and no teeth!' (1389–94). In *Hamlet*, v. i, a darker context surrounds the Prince's memory of his childhood, when Yorick bore him on his back a thousand times, recalled as he gazes at Yorick's skull, at the grave-side.

brutal or feeble, skilfully disciplined or spontaneously graceful: stumbling, limping, fencing, dancing, kissing. Finally, in darkness, comes concentration on its mysterious inner life, of emotion, of thought, of imagination. The life-giving and death-dealing drive of instinctual life is the beginning of the play, though the ending presents an image of the body in its most mysterious state, stillness.

The pattern of action is marked by simple physical signs: the hands of Montague and Capulet are first seen brandishing weapons; Romeo takes Juliet's hand as a sacrament as he first speaks to her; Capulet takes Montague's hand in reconciliation as the play ends. In a similar pattern, Romeo and Juliet kiss on four occasions: at the feast, at the Friar's cell, at dawn after the wedding night, and at death. Romeo kills Tybalt and Paris by the sword, but himself dies by poison; Juliet evades marriage to Paris by taking a potion, but she dies on Romeo's blade. Each feels the agonizing stroke of death as love ecstasy, for at the centre of their experience is the paradox that only through the body can the limits of the body and the self be transcended:

> 'Tis but thy name that is my enemy:
> Thou art thyself, though not a Montague.
> What's Montague? It is nor hand nor foot
> Nor arm nor face nor any other part
> Belonging to a man. O be some other name.
> What's in a name? That which we call a rose
> By any other word would smell as sweet;
> So Romeo would, were he not Romeo call'd,
> Retain that dear perfection which he owes
> Without that title. Romeo, doff thy name,
> And for thy name, which is no part of thee,
> Take all myself. (II. ii. 38–49)

Later, when Romeo is racked with frenzied grief, this speech is ironically recalled:

> In what vile part of this anatomy
> Doth my name lodge? Tell me that I may sack
> The hateful mansion. (III. iii. 105–7)

The Friar fears that Romeo is becoming lost in madness, but warns him with homiletic orthodoxy that only his body, 'a form of wax', is still recognizable as Romeo, and, again, that he is like a soldier blown to pieces by his own gunpowder as he prepares a charge in his musket. Yet Juliet, with transcendent passion, had imagined the dying Romeo cut into stars and strewn all across the heavens, in an image which fuses sexual ecstasy and extinction.

The Friar's mode of expression is formulaic and sententious, uncreatively dependent on the stereotypes of proverb lore, and it is this which persistently allows him to express even the darkest paradoxes in quasi-rational terms and so to proceed, step by step, with an air of caution, along a path leading in the event recklessly to destruction. Here there are important connections between the roles of the Friar, Mercutio and the Nurse, for like him they too underestimate the depth, mystery and danger of the lovers' experience. Mercutio and the Nurse share an ultimately mechanistic view of life: of emotion as instinctual, of personality in terms of type and role, of identity as socially derived; both in their individual styles express unquestioning acceptance of the conventions of society, mundane, material, public. Each is ready to offend certain particular conventions, but only those recognized as proper to fulfilment of their own type and role, and they do so in an emphatically conservative spirit. Relying on custom and convention, simplistically conceiving the spirit of comedy as merely play, they fail to recognize the dark aspect of the Dionysiac[1] even as it visibly expresses itself through them.

The role of the Nurse seems at first designed to temper Juliet's cool, tentative air with earthy vigour and indulgently humorous acceptance of sexual desire and enjoyment, while the Nurse's lower social position enables her to give practical help in advancing the cause of love. She acts as messenger, deceives the Capulet household, assists at the dangerous and clandestine wedding night; yet later, in the crisis of Romeo's banishment, when the Nurse's love and understanding of Juliet are really tested, it is apparent that the girl she nursed has grown into a womanly maturity far beyond her comprehension. All she can suggest is a deceit of the most callous kind, her tone of coy and cosy assurance failing to disguise a brutal opportunism and moral blindness. The spirit of comic anarchy looks suddenly ugly and destructive:

> I think it best you married with the County.
> O, he's a lovely gentleman.
> Romeo's a dishclout to him. (III. v. 217–19)

Although the personality of Mercutio, with so much air and fire, is in strong contrast to the Nurse's, his relationship with Romeo follows a parallel pattern, for all Mercutio's affectionate concern and deliberately infectious exuberance in countering

1. C. L. Barber, *Shakespeare's Festive Comedy* (1959), has an illuminating discussion of the saturnalian ritual element in Shakespeare's comedies.

Romeo's melancholy is based on a radical misconception of Romeo's true nature. The comic ritual of exorcism must fail, and in failing it exposes the magician as only a charlatan. In his first scene Mercutio derides the idea of an unsounded self to be sought in dreams, and he at once prescribes Romeo a course of vigorous exercise to clear the melancholy humour from his blood, and love-making to satisfy his frustrated appetite: 'Prick love for pricking and you beat love down.' Dreams, to Mercutio, are simply the product of physical appetites and anxieties, all other explanations of them being nonsensical superstition—a modern intelligence like his can expose them as rapidly as his breath can form the words to do so; he will not submit himself to an unknown fear.

The Queen Mab speech is a burlesque show, debunking a motley assembly of folk-tale figures, contemporary urban caricatures and jest-book types, proverbial rural superstitions, old wives' tales and ancient myth. It proceeds at an ever-increasing pace which makes dream-like changes and inconsistencies of scale seem absurdly abrupt, and fearful distortions only ridiculous.[1] It consciously exhibits its own process of free association of ideas and words as further evidence of the crudely mechanical causes of fantasy, its spiritual nullity. Mercutio offers to caricature the working of the imagination, yet his speech displays his own real imaginative creativity, assembling under the pressure of excitement a fascinating rival to the objective everyday world. There is wit and vitality in his improvisation which belies the reductive argument. Furthermore, though ostensibly intended to expose the sham mystery, it also summons up an awareness of the many names and forms by which, since ancient times, the hidden forces of the irrational have been known. The power released in his grotesque vision is able to generate independently a spirit which intoxicates and takes possession of Mercutio; he is lost to it when Romeo interrupts and brings him to himself again.

In performance Mercutio's role here demands a continuous accompaniment of mime and quick physical caricature at an ever-

1. Mab begins in size no bigger than an agate stone but later is as big as a man, wielding a pig's tail and pressing maids on their backs. She is like the nightmare demon or incubus in ll. 92–3, but also like elves who punish slatterns, or Robin Goodfellow, described in *MND*, II. i. 34–59. Among Mercutio's sources one obvious case is Chaucer, *Parliament of Fowles*, ll. 99–105 (first pointed out by J. W. Hales, *Quarterly Review*, 1873, pp. 246–7). There is a strongly English flavour to the Queen Mab speech which links it closely to *MND* and concedes little to the Italian location of the play. There may be a recollection of Petronius, *Satyricon*, but if so it is indirect.

accelerating pace which may approach physical frenzy; it is an extreme of sheer physical excitement through which may be glimpsed something awesome in the life of the body at its most intense, where it touches madness and religious vision as well as erotic ecstasy. Inspiration and self-possession, the terms of the play's deep dialectic, are shown in a teasingly intricate, paradoxical relationship in this dazzlingly original use of comedy.

Mercutio the jester insists in the name of common sense that love is inseparable from appetite and violence, that society's fixed rules and beliefs have a wholly tolerable degree of absurdity in them, that unconventionality is probably foolish if not perverse. Nevertheless the rebellious pressure in his mockery and wit is so continual and general that it unbalances his actual relationship to the world: there is something manic in him:

> The pox of such antic lisping affecting phantasimes, these new tuners of accent. By Jesu, a very good blade, a very tall man, a very good whore! Why, is not this a lamentable thing, grandsire, that we should be thus afflicted with these strange flies, these fashion-mongers, these 'pardon-me's', who stand so much on the new form that they cannot sit at ease on the old bench? O their bones, their bones! (II. iv. 28–36)

His intensity of excitement communicates itself infectiously, either as comic wit or, as Benvolio observes, in anger; but what decisively separates Mercutio from Benvolio and, more importantly, from Romeo, is the sheer violence and lewdness of his mind. The anticipation of Romeo's 'It is my lady, O it is my love! / O that she knew she were!' in Mercutio's aggressively coarse mock 'O Romeo, that she were, O that she were / An open-arse and thou a poperin pear!' is like the compulsive charge of lewdness in his answer to the Nurse, 'the bawdy hand of the dial is now upon the prick of noon'. Mercutio's estimate of her may be shrewd in its way, but remains gratuitously cruel. It is striking that in the wit-duel between Mercutio and Romeo all the assertively lewd jesting comes from Mercutio, only for Romeo to neutralize it without his noticing: this is indeed a sign of the widening gap between him and Romeo, for the increasing differences are precisely focused in attitudes to sex and anger. Romeo seeks joy and harmony where Mercutio delights in exacerbated conflict, so that Romeo begins to find his friend inflexible, superficial, content with fixed ideas, whereas at the same time Mercutio concludes that Romeo's dreams are mere aberrations, and thinks Romeo only restored to his true self when jesting. The actual polarization of their attitudes is marked in Mercutio's over-confident assumption of success in restoring an exclusive masculine order:

> Why, is not this better now than groaning for love? Now art thou sociable, now art thou Romeo; now art thou what thou art, by art as well as by nature. For this drivelling love is like a great natural that runs lolling up and down to hide his bauble in a hole. (II. iv. 88–93)

Yet if Mercutio makes a decisive misjudgement of Romeo here, there is the equally fierce irony that, partly as a consequence, Romeo comes to underrate Mercutio's other, shrewder insights into the way of the world. Just before Romeo's entrance in this same scene Mercutio had given a bravura demonstration of the twinned arts of fencing and dancing, ebulliently cavorting with the old trope of the danger of Venus to Mars:

> Alas poor Romeo, he is already dead, stabbed with a white wench's black eye, run through the ear with a love song, the very pin of his heart cleft with the blind bow-boy's butt-shaft. And is he a man to encounter Tybalt? (II. iv. 13–17)

It is as if some unacknowledged premonition like Romeo's were inducing this train of thought,[1] and indeed under the surface differences of style and humour Mercutio and Romeo have natural affinities, feel brotherly affection, brotherly rivalry. Romeo is a willing victim to love, Mercutio incites the god to anger: there might be the germ of a Benedick in him as well as a Hotspur, but the speed and violent intensity of the play polarize roles. Mercutio is drawn magnetically to Tybalt as is Romeo to Juliet; his diversion of the quarrel to himself is ironically comparable to a rival lover's act of seduction. Indeed, to kill Tybalt seems a pleasure in itself, an honourable duty, is to emulate Romeo, and perhaps, more obscurely, satisfies envy of Romeo's dedication to love. So, for Mercutio, Romeo's disastrous intervention in the duel is precisely expressive of the malevolent power of Venus (though he never learns of Romeo's marriage) and Romeo's impulse for peace strikes him as unbearably ironic, agonizingly absurd. Their mutual incomprehension and mutual affection are given balletic clarity in the fatal action. Mercutio's exultant dance as he fights Tybalt is broken by his friend's dream-guided intervention; the moment's hesitation gives death its chance. In an instant the whole course of the play alters decisively,

1. The exact irony with which fate punishes Mercutio is reminiscent of the mode of Ovid's *Metamorphoses* as well as the malicious wit of the angry Cupid in *Tancred and Gismund*, offended at scoffers and bent on deadly punishment.

and the scene which began with jesting about quarrelling ends with the solemn bearing of a dead body from the stage. The isolation of the hero and heroine in a tragic action must now begin.

In *Romeo and Juliet* the play's decisive events occur with instantaneous suddenness: servants brawl on sight, the lovers fall in love at first sight, the shock of the tragic catastrophe converts the parents suddenly and completely from hate to love. The contrast to the rhythm of dream consciousness is extreme. Shakespeare is indeed much concerned with disproportion in this play; he imposes a clear dramatic structure on the story, but there is a pressure towards opposed extremes felt in all areas of the work, in the internal shaping of the rhythms of emotion, the emphasis on collisions between time-scales, attitudes, even the major dramatic modes, comedy and tragedy, which indicates a central concern with reconciliation only to be achieved through ultimately bloody, intense and spectacular violence.

The *novella* as a form and mode tends to exploit the bizarre, violent, erotic or sensational, but in a context of generally realistic detailed settings; it often defies the artist's power to give it imaginative coherence as narrative. In certain of his comedies and late romances Shakespeare exploits the *novella*'s potentiality for the creation and exploration of extreme states of feeling, and its provision of realistic narratives which test concepts of Fortune and Providence to breaking point. In *Romeo and Juliet*, as in *Othello*, which also has *novella* origins,[1] Shakespeare allows scope to these unbalanced narrative energies in schemes of intrigue, involving the Friar and Nurse in the earlier play, and Iago and Emilia in the later, yet at the same time the lovers are from the outset withdrawn in an experience of sublime purity and intense suffering which renders them spiritually remote from other characters and the concerns of the ordinary world. The single clear line of ideal aspiration in love is set against the diversified complex intrigues which proliferate in the ordinary world, and contact between the two has tragic consequences; whereas in *Much Ado* or *Measure for Measure*, plays in which Shakespeare reworks similar *novella* material[2] with less emphasis on the isolated, extreme devotion of lovers, a comic action results.

1. The story is based on Giraldi Cinthio, *Hecatommithi*, III. vii.

2. See the discussion by Salingar, *Shakespeare and the Traditions of Comedy*, pp. 314–21.

In *Romeo and Juliet* the two kinds of life touch in an explosive flash as Romeo intervenes in the duel and then commits himself to angry revenge:

> Away to heaven respective lenity,
> And fire-ey'd fury be my conduct now!

The sudden crisis awakens primitive instincts which momentarily overwhelm his finer nature. When he recovers self-possession he is appalled at his act, yet half-conscious of the prompting of fate: 'O, I am fortune's fool'. Tybalt may have abused his good will, may have killed Mercutio treacherously and dishonourably, whereas Romeo fought Tybalt fairly by the laws of duelling; yet, however understandably, Romeo allowed himself to be infected by the tragic disease of anger, giving new impetus to the blood-feud, betraying his own higher principles. In the scenes which follow, both Romeo and Juliet are seen absorbing the disaster which threatens their very identities, bringing them to the edge of madness and the disintegration of their ideals. To Juliet in her grief, sanity itself is dependent on Romeo's life:

> I am not I if there be such an 'I',
> Or those eyes shut that makes thee answer 'Ay'.

yet if Romeo killed Tybalt he may be no longer truly Romeo:

> O nature what hadst thou to do in hell
> When thou didst bower the spirit of a fiend
> In mortal paradise of such sweet flesh?
> (III. ii. 48–9, 80–2)

We may think of the fearful experience of Adriana in *The Comedy of Errors*, who is similarly confronted by unrecognizably alien behaviour in her husband; it seems to threaten her deepest selfhood and perception of reality:

> How comes it now, my husband, O, how comes it,
> That thou art then estranged from thyself?
> Thyself I call it, being strange to me,
> That, undividable, incorporate,
> Am better than thy dear self's better part.
> For know, my love, as easy mayst thou fall
> A drop of water in the breaking gulf,
> And take unmingled thence that drop again
> Without addition or diminishing,
> As take from me thyself, and not me too.
> (*Err.*, II. ii. 118–28)

Romeo receives the news of his banishment with hysterical

passion, declaring exile to be death, life and selfhood to be inseparable from Juliet: then, seeing his act through her eyes, he fears he has destroyed her in betraying himself. Romeo's attempted suicide (III. iii) marks the nadir of his struggle with his own immaturity, but it proves at the same time to be an important point of self-discovery, a tempering. His tragic role may be clarified by contrast with that of Hamlet. Shakespeare withholds from Romeo the full experience of evil, the capacity for unbounded and ruthless self-analysis, the conscious acceptance of responsibility for society at large, with which he endows Hamlet. It is the special poignancy of Hamlet's fate that he must confront it alone; for Romeo and Juliet there is the consolation and the exultation of sharing love as they undergo a shared fate. In *Romeo and Juliet* Shakespeare's earliest emphasis is on the communal life of Verona and the two opposed prominent families, each with its own complex of internal bonds, hardened by collective memory and fixed allegiances, committed to honour; but in *Hamlet* the deepest of all kinship bonds imposes direct stress on the hero, as he learns that his own father was murdered by the new king whom his mother has married. The ghost demands blood vengeance of him, and his first attempt to execute it results in the killing of Polonius, father of the woman he loves. By contrast Romeo and Juliet love one another before knowing each other's names, later swearing to abandon their names and be newly baptised, so loosening the bonds of kinship. Though Romeo kills Tybalt, Tybalt was no more than Juliet's kinsman, and provoked the quarrel. These mitigating circumstances allow the lovers to overcome the doubt and threat of madness in a new access of love. Shakespeare controls and directs the audience's sympathy to withhold radical questioning or qualification of the lovers' ideals. As misfortune follows misfortune in the lovers' dealings with the world, an audience will recognize that a sacrificial ritual is taking place to purge Verona of its disease, yet at the same time Shakespeare stresses that the lovers experience in their private selves a fine tempering, they become stronger in dedication to their own rival world of spiritual nobility. Since they remain unwilling victims of dark fortune, always knowing less than the audience about their situation, a deep pathos gathers in the cruel moment when Romeo kills Paris and dies on Juliet's breast seconds before she awakes.

The issue of tragic responsibility is not to be separated from the context in which Shakespeare presents it. From the moment Romeo leaves for Mantua in banishment, increasing sympathy is directed towards the lovers, and Verona is presented as claustrophobic, stultifyingly formal, hard and predictable. The vitality and wit of Mercutio, the good humour of Benvolio, grace it no more; the Nurse reveals a callous nature which earns her Juliet's fierce contempt, and the Capulet parents become impatient and then hostile and threatening. Paris presses his suit with a kind of stubbornness at Friar Laurence's cell, exchanging with Juliet a willed, formal dialogue which gives mutual pain; the audience will contrast it with the happy meeting of Romeo and Juliet earlier in the play on their wedding day. Finally the Friar's potion scheme focuses sympathy on the isolated heroine, demanding of her an act of lonely courage and faith in love:

My dismal scene I needs must act alone.

Having witnessed Juliet's pathetic fears and movingly fierce resolution, an audience must view with partiality the ensuing stage image which explicitly defines the opposed worlds of the play, as the Capulet household bustles in communal excitement and practical business to make ready for the wedding feast, completely oblivious of the fact that in their midst Juliet has already embarked on a fearful and heroic adventure into stillness.

The unfolding of the play's final movement widens the gap between what any character can perceive of the situation and what is apparent to the audience. This has the effect of distancing the audience from the action so that certain distinct stage images may be contemplated in sharp focus, enhancing awareness of their wide symbolic meanings, their silent eloquence. So when the Nurse draws the bed-curtains apart she discovers the still form of Juliet to her family, and the sight instantly reawakens in Juliet's parents suppressed tender love for their only daughter. The episode is a first statement of the major theme of the final movement: what passionate active eloquent youth finds impossible is achieved at once by its still silent lifeless image.

The scenic form of this episode is repeated with cumulatively powerful effect in the action which follows, where intensely vigorous, confused activity is arrested by the discovery of human figures that have no motion and no breath. Romeo is forced by Paris to fight a duel to the death, re-enacting the fight with Tybalt in III. i; the audience will recognize the complexity of the parallel and its fierce ironies, for once more Juliet awaits union with Romeo, unaware of his entanglement in the world's great snare as she lies concealed in the tomb. Romeo opens the tomb and drags Paris into it, then the sight of Juliet dazzles him. The impact of the spectacle on him is part of a larger spectacle apparent only to the audience, who see a tableau symbolizing the world's instinctive antipathy to the exceptional being, the ideal of perfection. Romeo cannot enter the metaphysical feasting presence except at the cost of killing Paris; and beside Juliet, an image of human beauty more than mortally fine, lies Tybalt, the human form in its most graphically corruptible state, wrapped in a bloody sheet. In Shakespeare's playhouse, moreover, the unchanging tiring-house façade remains a visible background to this scene. The window from which Romeo descended on parting from Juliet after the wedding night, now darkened, bears silent witness to the bitter contrast between the lovers' first bedchamber and their last, blighted by the bodies of Tybalt and Paris in token of death's challenge as a rival lover. It is against such desolation that the true force of Romeo's response to the sight of Juliet must be measured. Romeo sees in her such beauty as transcends mutability itself; he is filled with such joy that he experiences death as regeneration, vanquishing his ultimate rival. There is a further meaning here for the audience, however, for they know, as Romeo cannot, that medicine artifically suspends life and death in Juliet's beauty; yet very soon, when Juliet awakes, the audience will learn that they too were deceived: the ultimate sign in which Romeo rejoiced as he gazed on Juliet's sculptured stone-cold beauty, the crimson in her lips and cheeks, was life: the moment in which life, and with it mutability, revives in her perfect still form, is the moment which inspires Romeo to drink the poison. Shakespeare ironically reorders the fable of Pygmalion;[1] we see the beloved statue awakening to life on the feast day of Venus, yet here a new mysterious meaning is present, for Shakespeare's lovers must undergo a metamorphosis out of Nature, into the artifice of eternity. We must think not only of Pygmalion but also of Lucrece in the moment when Tarquin's dark gaze is blinded by her beauty, discovered as he draws the bed-curtains:

> Her hair, like golden threads, play'd with her breath—
> O modest wantons! Wanton modesty!—
> Showing life's triumph in the map of death,
> And death's dim look in life's mortality.
> Each in her sleep themselves so beautify,
> As if between them twain there were no strife,
> But that life liv'd in death, and death in life.
>
> (*Lucr.*, ll. 400–6)

1. See Ovid, *Metamorphoses*, x.

Such perfection must partake as much of death as of life; here is a first, non-dramatic statement of a motif which becomes a profound symbol of reconciliation in Shakespeare's mature art, in *Antony and Cleopatra*, *Cymbeline* and *The Winter's Tale*.

In *Lucrece* acute revulsion from atrocity contributes vitally to the drive to transfiguration. Shakespeare focuses intensively on the two protagonists, he confines the action to the climax of the fable: in this poem it is symbolic stasis, not dramatic process, which embodies the tragic myth, and it is in the activity of Shakespeare's poetry rather than the characters' experience that the riddle of mutability's longing for perfection is adumbrated. Tarquin's Dionysiac violence ironically results in a triumphant affirmation of beauty's Apollonian image, yet the poem does not speak with a play's directness or inclusiveness: in the theatre an audience can share possession of experience, responding communally as much as individually.

In the close of *Romeo and Juliet* the discovery of the lifeless figures of the lovers yields the widest communal reawakening of love, and the audience are brought through a remarkably shaped emotional passage to a last point of rest. As Romeo dies in Juliet's arms silence and stillness fall on the stage, allowing for the contemplation of the tableau of tragic love-death. Yet this is not the end, and the tableau is an illusion, fittingly and abruptly broken by the entrance of the Friar, figuratively accompanied by all the encumbrances of the *novella*-story. The effect of the scene on the Friar is so appalling that he loses his nerve. The sight of Paris steeped in blood awakens gothic shudders, then one of the figures stirs: Juliet's waking to the sight of Romeo dead beside her brings home to the Friar his worst forebodings, asserts his impotence, but at the same moment the sound of the Watch approaching is more than he can bear: under the intense pressure to act quickly he panics; his desertion of Juliet earns her curt dismissal; the sound of the Watch outside the tomb accelerates her brief final speech and prompts the swift decision with which she seizes Romeo's dagger to win her escape. The scene which filled the Friar with terror is for her inspiring and ecstatic. The forms of the lovers, truly at last united in their wedding bed of death, now become the focus of the action as, successively, the Watch, Romeo's man, the Friar, the Prince, Capulet, Lady Capulet and Montague, bereaved of his wife, enter in turn to behold the scene in the tomb. The audience hear the reactions of confusion, grief and repentance in the world of Verona gathering on the stage. Romeo and Juliet lie together, immune at last to rude will, confusion, accident and change. Yet, paradoxically, in this moment when the two kinds of life in the play seem supremely and finally separate, the image of love and beauty works a potent transformation on the city and its values.[1]

As the Prince and the lovers' families stand silent in grief, the Friar gives a virtually uninterrupted account, forty lines in length, of the strange, erratic trajectory of the story: the audience watch as successive revelations have their deep impact on the parents, the Prince and the populace. This narrative awakens pity, compassion and guilt in them, and as he delivers it the Friar begins his expiation in the act of confession. The dangerous folly of his meddling in natural magic now apparent, his good intentions may speak in mitigation of his guilt. Moreover, his narrative has such cumulative effect that the Prince himself, in pronouncing judgement, includes his own name among the guilty, and in that confession prepares the way for full reconciliation:

> Where be these enemies? Capulet, Montague,
> See what a scourge is laid upon your hate,
> That heaven finds means to kill your joys with love;
> And I, for winking at your discords too,
> Have lost a brace of kinsmen. All are punish'd.
> (v. iii. 290–4)

So, converted by the sight of the lovers and the revelation of their heroic fidelity, Capulet offers his hand to Montague, sealing the bond of marriage between the two families in a dowry of love, not gold. Both families are bereft of an heir, and the exchange of promises that each father shall erect a statue of the other's child, in gold, symbolizes the alchemical transmutation of worldly wealth, property, earth, into the spiritual riches of the heart and the imagination. When the play ends the image of the lovers lying side by side remains in the mind's eye, the passionate speed of young love commemorated already in sculpture, an art which is free from the dimension of time. The youth of the lovers is made immutable, the violence and darkness in their story absorbed in the golden, still image.

Romeo and Juliet is a drama in which speed is the medium of fate, though at first it appears that fate is only a function of speed. In the close, the awesome silent tableau prompts the audience to

1. The play must suffer serious mutilation if the final scene is significantly cut, as it was in the production by Franco Zeffirelli (1960), which is otherwise, by general agreement, the most brilliant of recent years. A vivid and illuminating account of it is by John Russell Brown, *Sh.S.*, 15 (1962).

the recognition that the unique quality of this tragic experience is created by the impetuous rashness of youth. The myth is essentially dramatic.

Reconciliation, of the play's opposed modes, of the two families, of the city itself, is the play's conclusion, and in this sense it is a natural successor to Shakespeare's first historical tetralogy and a tragic counterpart of *A Midsummer Night's Dream*, where love and night have also their part to play; but in its concern with the defiance of time, its rejection of the stereotype of cruel Fortune, its celebration of the power of faith to awaken the human spirit to a greater good, it also looks forward to the far end of Shakespeare's works, to the last Romances.

THE MOST EXCELLENT AND LAMENTABLE TRAGEDY OF ROMEO AND JULIET

DRAMATIS PERSONÆ

ESCALUS, *Prince of Verona.*
MERCUTIO, *a young gentleman and kinsman to the Prince, friend of Romeo.*
PARIS, *a noble young kinsman to the Prince.*
Page to Paris.

MONTAGUE, *head of a Veronese family at feud with the Capulets.*
LADY MONTAGUE.
ROMEO, *Montague's son.*
BENVOLIO, *Montague's nephew and friend of Romeo and Mercutio.*
ABRAM, *a servant to Montague.*
BALTHASAR, *Romeo's servant.*

CAPULET, *head of a Veronese family at feud with the Montagues.*
LADY CAPULET.
JULIET, *Capulet's daughter.*
TYBALT, *Lady Capulet's nephew.*
Capulet's Cousin, an old gentleman.
NURSE, *a Capulet servant, Juliet's foster-mother.*
PETER, *a Capulet servant attending on the Nurse.*
SAMPSON, GREGORY, ANTHONY, POTPAN, *Servingmen*, } *of the Capulet household.*

FRIAR LAURENCE, FRIAR JOHN, } *of the Franciscan Order.*
An Apothecary, of Mantua.
Three Musicians (Simon Catling, Hugh Rebeck, James Soundpost).
Members of the Watch, Citizens of Verona, Masquers, Torchbearers, Pages, Servants.
CHORUS.

THE MOST EXCELLENT AND LAMENTABLE TRAGEDY OF ROMEO AND JULIET

THE PROLOGUE

[*Enter* Chorus.]

Chorus. Two households both alike in dignity
(In fair Verona, where we lay our scene)
From ancient grudge break to new mutiny,
Where civil blood makes civil hands unclean.
From forth the fatal loins of these two foes
A pair of star-cross'd lovers take their life,
Whose misadventur'd piteous overthrows
Doth with their death bury their parents' strife.
The fearful passage of their death-mark'd love
And the continuance of their parents' rage,
Which, but their children's end, nought could remove,
Is now the two hours' traffic of our stage;
The which, if you with patient ears attend,
What here shall miss, our toil shall strive to mend.
[*Exit.*]

Prologue

S.D.] *Dyce; not in Q2–4,F,Q1.* 1–14.] *Q2–4; not in F; with variants as below, Q1.* 1. households both] *Q2–4; houshold Frends Q1.* 3. ancient . . . mutiny] *Q2–4; ciuill broyles broke into enmitie Q1.* 4. Where . . . blood] *Q2–4; Whose . . . warre Q1.* 6. take] *Q2–4; tooke Q1.* 7. misadventur'd] *Q2–4; misadventures, Q1.* 8–10.] *Q2–4; Through the continuing of their Fathers strife, / And death-markt passage of the Parents rage Q1.* 11.] *Q2–4; not in Q1.* 14. shall . . . strive] *Q2–4; we want wee'l studie Q1.* mend] *Q2–4; amend Q1.* S.D.] *Capell; not in Q2–4,F,Q1.*

[ACT I]

[SCENE I]

Enter Sampson *and* Gregory, *with swords and bucklers, of the house of Capulet.*

Samp. Gregory, on my word we'll not carry coals.
Greg. No, for then we should be colliers.
Samp. I mean, and we be in choler, we'll draw.
Greg. Ay, while you live, draw your neck out of collar.
Samp. I strike quickly being moved.
Greg. But thou art not quickly moved to strike.
Samp. A dog of the house of Montague moves me.
Greg. To move is to stir, and to be valiant is to stand: therefore if thou art moved thou runn'st away.
Samp. A dog of that house shall move me to stand. I will take the wall of any man or maid of Montague's.

ACT I

Scene I

Act I Scene I] *F* (*Actus Primus. Scoena Prima.*); *not in Q2–4,Q1.* *Location.*] *The Street in Verona. Rowe; A public Place. Capell.* 1. on] *Q2–4;* A *F;* of *Q1.* 3. and] *Q2–4;* if *F,Q1.* 4. of] *Q2,3;* of the *Q4,Q1;* o'th *F.*

1. *carry coals*] A current expression which meant 'to submit to insult or humiliation'; cf. Nashe, *Have With You, Works,* III, p. 53.

2. *colliers*] Proverbial not only for grime but for dishonesty.

3. *choler*] anger.

4. *draw . . . collar*] A proverbial expression meaning 'to avoid the hangman's noose' (Tilley C 513, N 169).

5. *moved*] aroused—Sampson seems deliberately to invite quibbles with this choice of word.

7. *dog*] A contemptuous reference to the Montague servants. The talk of dogs, proverbially bad-tempered in hot weather (the dog days), recurs in the analogous situation in III. i. 24–6.

11. *take the wall*] keep to the preferred side of the path nearest the wall and least foul. Hence an assertion of superiority. Cf. Lyly, *Endimion,* v. ii. 1–4: '*Top. Epi,* love hath iustled my libertie from the wall, and taken the vpper hand of my reason. *Epi.* Let mee then trippe vp the heeles of your affection, and thrust your goodwill into the gutter.'

Greg. That shows thee a weak slave, for the weakest goes to the wall.

Samp. 'Tis true, and therefore women, being the weaker vessels, are ever thrust to the wall; therefore I will push Montague's men from the wall, and thrust his maids to the wall.

Greg. The quarrel is between our masters and us their men.

Samp. 'Tis all one. I will show myself a tyrant: when I have fought with the men I will be civil with the maids, I will cut off their heads.

Greg. The heads of the maids?

Samp. Ay, the heads of the maids, or their maidenheads; take it in what sense thou wilt.

Greg. They must take it in sense that feel it.

Samp. Me they shall feel while I am able to stand, and 'tis known I am a pretty piece of flesh.

Greg. 'Tis well thou art not fish; if thou hadst, thou hadst been Poor John. Draw thy tool—here comes of the house of Montagues.

Enter two other Servingmen [ABRAM *and* BALTHASAR].

14. 'Tis true] *Q2–4;* True *F;* Thats true *Q1.* weaker] *Q2–4,F;* weakest *Q1.* 21. civil] *Q2,3,F;* cruel *Q4; not in Q1.* 22. I will cut] *Q2–4;* and cut *F; not in Q1.* 26. in sense] *Q1,Q4;* sense *Q2,3,F.* 30–1. comes of] *Q2–4,F;* comes two of *Q1.* 31. house of] *Q2–4;* House of the *F; not in Q1.* S.D.] *ed.; Enter two other seruing men. Q2–4,F; Enter two Seruing men of the* Mountagues. *Q1.*

12–13. *weakest . . . wall*] the weakest succumb in a struggle; proverbial, cf. Tilley W 185.

14–15. *weaker vessels*] See 1 Peter iii. 7, which was the source of the proverbial expression (Tilley W 655).

16–17. *thrust to the wall*] i.e. in amorous assault. The emphasis on confined urban streets and animal reactions is strongly marked.

21. *civil*] An easy minim misreading is possible; but Q2 may be simply defended: there is the antithesis *fought* with the men, *be civil* with the *maids*, and the paradox that cutting off their heads is being *civil*; but since taking *maidenheads* is assumed to be giving pleasure, the jest is that the act is indeed literally *civil.*

26. *in sense*] Punning on 'meaning' and 'feeling'.

27. *stand*] With a quibble on the bawdy sense 'have an erection'.

28. *pretty piece of flesh*] Cf. *Ado*, IV. ii. 79, and *Tw.N.*, I. v. 27. Quibbling on the senses (i) pretty fellow, (ii) one sexually well endowed.

30. *Poor John*] dried salted hake, poor Lenten food, certainly not flesh that would stand; often ancient; cf. *Temp.*, II. ii. 22.

30–1. *comes of*] Q1's reading has some support from the S.D. in Q2; Williams compares other instances of the partitive genitive in *Ham.*, III. ii. 44–5, and the *King James Bible*, Numbers xiii. 20, 23, and elsewhere.

31. S.D. *Abram and Balthasar*]

Samp. My naked weapon is out. Quarrel, I will back thee.

Greg. How, turn thy back and run?

Samp. Fear me not.

Greg. No, marry! I fear thee!

Samp. Let us take the law of our sides: let them begin.

Greg. I will frown as I pass by, and let them take it as they list.

Samp. Nay, as they dare. I will bite my thumb at them, which is disgrace to them if they bear it.

Abram. Do you bite your thumb at us, sir?

Samp. I do bite my thumb, sir.

Abram. Do you bite your thumb at us, sir?

Samp. Is the law of our side if I say ay?

Greg. No.

Samp. No sir, I do not bite my thumb at you, sir, but I bite my thumb, sir.

Greg. Do you quarrel, sir?

Abram. Quarrel, sir? No, sir.

Samp. But if you do, sir, I am for you. I serve as good a man as you.

Abram. No better.

Samp. Well, sir.

Enter BENVOLIO.

Greg. Say 'better', here comes one of my master's kinsmen.

Samp. Yes, better, sir.

41. disgrace] *Q2,Q1;* a disgrace *Q3,4,F.* 45. of] *Q2–4,F;* on *Q1.* 51. But if] *Q2–4;* If *F,Q1.* 57. sir] *Q2–4; not in F,Q1.*

Romeo's servant in v. i and v. iii is called Balthasar; Abram is so called in speech prefixes but not named in the dialogue.

32. *naked weapon*] Peter quibbles in the same sense at II. iv. 155.

34. *turn . . . run*] Gregory takes (or pretends to take) *I will back thee* to mean 'I will turn my back'.

40. *bite my thumb*] 'to threaten or defie by putting the thumbe naile into the mouth, and with a ierke (from the upper teeth) make it to knack' (Cotgrave).

57–78. *Samp. Yes, better . . . seek a foe.*] Q1 substitutes the S.D.: *They draw, to them enters* Tybalt, *they fight, to them the Prince, old* Mountague, *and his wife, old* Capulet *and his wife, and other Citizens and part them.*

Abram. You lie.

Samp. Draw if you be men. Gregory, remember thy washing blow. *They fight.*

Ben. Part, fools, put up your swords, you know not what you do.

Enter TYBALT.

Tyb. What, art thou drawn among these heartless hinds?
Turn thee, Benvolio, look upon thy death.

Ben. I do but keep the peace, put up thy sword,
Or manage it to part these men with me.

Tyb. What, drawn, and talk of peace? I hate the word,
As I hate hell, all Montagues, and thee:
Have at thee, coward. [*They*] *fight.*

Enter three or four Citizens *with clubs or partisans.*

Citizens. Clubs, bills and partisans! Strike! Beat them down! Down with the Capulets! Down with the Montagues!

Enter old CAPULET *in his gown, and* LADY CAPULET.

60. washing] *Q2,3,F;* swashing *Q4; not in Q1.* 63–4.] *As Pope; prose in Q2–4,F; not in Q1.* 67. drawn] *Q2–4;* draw *F; not in Q1.* 69. S.D. [*They*] *fight*] *F* (*Fight*); *not in Q2–4; var. Q1.* 69. S.D. Citizens] *ed.; Offi. Q2–4, F; not in Q1.*

60. *washing*] Cf. Ovid, *Metamorphoses*, trans. Golding (1567, ed. Nims, 1965), v. 252: 'Astyages . . . Did with a long sharpe arming sworde a washing blow him give'. *Swashing* has the same meaning in Stanyhurst's *Aeneis*, I. 19: 'This Queene wyld lighteninges from clowds of Iuppiter hurling Downe swasht theyre nauy' (1582), but there is no need of emendation to the Q2 reading.

63. *heartless hinds*] A quibble: (i) cowardly menials, (ii) female deer without a male hart to protect them. Tybalt accuses Benvolio of ignobility in drawing on servants rather than a worthy opponent of gentle rank.

64. *Benvolio*] i.e. of good will (in Italian). The name is not in the sources, and is expressive of his peace-making role; Tybalt may be glancing ironically at this.

69. S.D. *partisans*] broad-headed spears, about nine feet long.

70. *bills*] a long-handled weapon with a concave blade, or a kind of concave axe with a spike at the back and a spear-tipped shaft (OED).

72. S.D. *gown*] Capulet's entrance presents a vivid and simple image of violated domestic peace and dignity, and suggests the implications of the feud. Disturbed by the riot, he has thrown on a dressing-gown and dashed out with characteristic rashness. The opening scene of *Othello*, also presenting violation of domestic order, similarly has Brabantio '*in his gown*'.

Cap. What noise is this? Give me my long sword, ho!
Lady Cap. A crutch, a crutch! Why call you for a sword?

Enter old MONTAGUE *and* LADY MONTAGUE.

Cap. My sword I say! Old Montague is come,
And flourishes his blade in spite of me.
Mont. Thou villain Capulet! Hold me not! Let me go!
Lady Mont. Thou shalt not stir one foot to seek a foe.

Enter Prince ESCALUS *with his* Train.

Prince. Rebellious subjects, enemies to peace,
Profaners of this neighbour-stained steel—
Will they not hear? What ho! You men, you beasts!
That quench the fire of your pernicious rage
With purple fountains issuing from your veins,
On pain of torture from those bloody hands
Throw your mistemper'd weapons to the ground
And hear the sentence of your moved prince.
Three civil brawls bred of an airy word

74. *Lady Cap.*] *ed.; Wife. Q2–4,F; not in Q1.* S.D.] *As Spencer; after l. 77 in Q2–4,F; var. Q1.* 78. *Lady Mont.*] *ed.; M. Wife 2. Q2–4; 2 Wife. F; not in Q1.* one] *Q2–4;* a *F; not in Q1.* 87. brawls] *Q2–4,Q1;* Broyles *F.*

73. *long sword*] an old-fashioned weapon, useless against the rapier because so much heavier, even were Capulet still strong enough to wield it. His wife mockingly reminds him of his advanced age.

76. *spite*] scorn.

78. S.D. *Escalus*] The only occurrence of the name in the play; elsewhere *Prince*. Brooke calls him *Escalus*, Painter, *Lord Bartholemew of Escala* (della Scala, the ruling family of Verona). In fact Bartolommeo della Scala ruled Verona in the period in which Luigi da Porto and Bandello set the story of Romeo and Juliet.

83. *fountains*] Perhaps there is an ironic play on the fact that Verona (according to Brooke and Painter) is graced with many fountains and clear springs; or cf. *Tit.*, II. iv. 22–4: 'Alas, a crimson river of warm blood, / Like to a bubbling fountain stirr'd with wind, / Doth rise and fall between thy rosed lips'.

85. *mistemper'd*] The steel is *tempered*, made hard and resilient by beating, but put to wrong use as a result of the *intemperate* (violent) conduct of its owners. Sir John Smyth noted in 1590 that rapier blades are 'made of a verie hard temper to fight in priuat fraies' (OED sb I 5). *Tempered* also meant properly proportioned or constituted (of a state or city) and the keeping of correct pitch in music.

86. *moved*] offended and angry.

87. *Three*] Neither Brooke nor Painter specifies the number; Shakespeare's Prince, by reiterated emphasis on *three*, gives the events something of a ritualized formality, as in a fable, while insisting on the recurrent oppressiveness of the feud.

airy] Cf. Brooke, l. 37: 'first hatchd of trifling stryfe'.

By thee, old Capulet, and Montague,
Have thrice disturb'd the quiet of our streets
And made Verona's ancient citizens
Cast by their grave-beseeming ornaments
To wield old partisans, in hands as old,
Canker'd with peace, to part your canker'd hate.
If ever you disturb our streets again
Your lives shall pay the forfeit of the peace.
For this time all the rest depart away;
You, Capulet, shall go along with me,
And Montague, come you this afternoon,
To know our farther pleasure in this case,
To old Freetown, our common judgement-place.
Once more, on pain of death, all men depart.
Exeunt [all but Montague, Lady Montague and Benvolio].

Mont. Who set this ancient quarrel new abroach?
Speak, nephew, were you by when it began?

Ben. Here were the servants of your adversary
And yours, close fighting ere I did approach.
I drew to part them; in the instant came
The fiery Tybalt, with his sword prepar'd,
Which, as he breath'd defiance to my ears
He swung about his head and cut the winds,
Who nothing hurt withal, hiss'd him in scorn.
While we were interchanging thrusts and blows
Came more and more, and fought on part and part,

99. farther] *Q2,4,Q1;* Fathers *Q3,F.*
101. S.D.] *Hudson; Exeunt. Q2–4,F,Q1.*

90. *ancient*] long-established and advanced in age; accustomed to peace for so long that their weapons are rusty with disuse (*Canker'd with peace*).

91. *grave-beseeming*] suitably sober: but probably there is a quibble on *grave*, anticipating that of Mercutio in his final speech (and of Claudius in *Ham.*, IV. vii. 78–81).

100. *Freetown*] The name of Capulet's castle, in Painter, is Villafranca, and in Brooke, Freetown. Shakespeare visualizes Capulet as living in a merchant's house rather than a castle. This dignity he transfers to Escalus.

102. *set . . . abroach*] The phrase was used of a cask (of liquor or gunpowder) pierced and running. The image is taken up by Benvolio's description of the *fiery Tybalt.*

109–10. *He . . . scorn*] Benvolio's mockery is ingenious, and may owe something to Spenser, *Faerie Queene*, I. vii. 12, or Marlowe, *Tragedy of Dido*, II. i. 548–9: 'he disdaining whiskt his sword about, / And with the wind thereof the king fell down'; and cf. *Ham.*, II. ii. 466–8.

112. *on part and part*] on one side and the other.

Till the Prince came, who parted either part.
Lady Mont. O where is Romeo, saw you him today?
Right glad I am he was not at this fray.
Ben. Madam, an hour before the worshipp'd sun
Peer'd forth the golden window of the east
A troubled mind drive me to walk abroad,
Where underneath the grove of sycamore
That westward rooteth from this city side
So early walking did I see your son.
Towards him I made, but he was ware of me,
And stole into the covert of the wood.
I, measuring his affections by my own,
Which then most sought, where most might not be found,
Being one too many by my weary self,
Pursu'd my humour, not pursuing his,
And gladly shunn'd who gladly fled from me.
Mont. Many a morning hath he there been seen,
With tears augmenting the fresh morning's dew,
Adding to clouds more clouds with his deep sighs;
But all so soon as the all-cheering sun

114. *Lady Mont.*] *ed.; Wife. Q2–4, F, Q1.* 115. I am] *Q2, Q1;* am I *Q3 4, F.* 118. drive] *Q2;* draue *Q3,4,F;* drew *Q1.* 120. city] *Q2–4,F;* Citties *Q1, Malone.* 127. humour] *Q2,4;* honour *Q3,F,Q1.*

116–31. *an hour . . . sighs*] The atmosphere of heated brawling in the streets is banished with the introduction of Romeo's name, which is accompanied by associations of dawn, dew, silence and Nature.

118. *drive*] This form, as a past tense, occurs in Fletcher, *Bonduca*, I. i. 114 (MSR) and Spenser, *Faerie Queene*, I. ix. 38, 5; V. xi. 5, 8 (Crow, NCS).

119. *sycamore*] Cf. *LLL*, V. ii. 89–94: Boyet tells how he sought the cool shade of a sycamore, was interrupted by the approach of the lords and stole into a 'neighbour thicket' to escape their company. In *Oth.*, IV. iii, the sycamore is associated with love-sickness; probably there is a pun: *sickamour*.

120. *city side*] Malone follows Q1, but the non-possessive form is not uncommon in Shakespeare (cf. III. i. 88 and III. iii. 17, or *John*, II. i. 234).

123. *covert*] concealment.

125. *then . . . found*] then specially sought out places where I was least likely to be found.

126. *Being . . . self*] The pursuit of a conceit displays the artificiality of the pose to the point of absurdity.

127. *Pursu'd . . . his*] Indulged my own inclination for solitude by avoiding the opportunity of discovering Romeo's mood.

130–1. *With . . . sighs*] Cf. *Tit.*, III. i. 212–30.

Should in the farthest east begin to draw
The shady curtains from Aurora's bed,
Away from light steals home my heavy son
And private in his chamber pens himself,
Shuts up his windows, locks fair daylight out
And makes himself an artificial night.
Black and portentous must this humour prove
Unless good counsel may the cause remove.

Ben. My noble uncle, do you know the cause?

Mont. I neither know it nor can learn of him.

Ben. Have you importun'd him by any means?

Mont. Both by myself and many other friends.
But he, his own affections' counsellor,
Is to himself—I will not say how true—
But to himself so secret and so close,
So far from sounding and discovery,
As is the bud bit with an envious worm
Ere he can spread his sweet leaves to the air
Or dedicate his beauty to the sun.
Could we but learn from whence his sorrows grow,
We would as willingly give cure as know.

Enter ROMEO.

144. other] *Q2–4;* others *F; not in Q1.* 145. his] *Q3,4,F;* is *Q2; not in Q1.* 151. sun] *Pope, conj. Theobald;* same *Q2–4,F; not in Q1.*

134. *Aurora's*] The goddess of the dawn, married to Tithonus, whose bed she supposedly left each morning.

135. *heavy*] Punning, as frequently in the play, on the emotional and physical senses of the word (cf. l. 176 below).

139. *humour*] In ancient and medieval physiology four chief fluids were supposed to determine, according to their relative proportions, bodily and mental qualities and disposition. Black choler, or melancholy, was one of the four fluids, or humours, and Romeo's father fears it may be gaining dominance in Romeo.

140. *counsel*] advice.

145. *affections'*] loving attachment, love-passion, as in *Oth.*, I. iii. 112.

148. *sounding and discovery*] Nautical images, of gauging the depth, and sailing, in uncharted waters; the image of the *unsounded self* is an important and recurrent one in Shakespeare.

149. *bud . . . worm*] Cf. Sonnet 35: 'loathsome canker lives in sweetest bud'.

151. *sun*] Theobald's emendation is welcome for the stronger emphasis it gives to the metaphor; he writes 'there is some power else besides *balmy air* that brings forth and makes the tiny buds spread themselves'. Crow observes 'Theobald's emendation . . . is not strictly necessary . . . But the emender could encourage himself with clear evidence that the mistake could be made, and was made, in Shakespeare's time.'

Ben. See where he comes. So please you step aside;
I'll know his grievance or be much denied.
Mont. I would thou wert so happy by thy stay
To hear true shrift. Come, madam, let's away.
Exeunt [*Montague and Lady Montague*].
Ben. Good morrow, cousin.
Romeo. Is the day so young?
Ben. But new struck nine.
Romeo. Ay me, sad hours seem long.
Was that my father that went hence so fast?
Ben. It was. What sadness lengthens Romeo's hours?
Romeo. Not having that which, having, makes them short.
Ben. In love?
Romeo. Out.
Ben. Of love?
Romeo. Out of her favour where I am in love.
Ben. Alas that love so gentle in his view
Should be so tyrannous and rough in proof.
Romeo. Alas that love whose view is muffled still
Should without eyes see pathways to his will.
Where shall we dine? O me! What fray was here?
Yet tell me not, for I have heard it all.
Here's much to do with hate, but more with love.
Why then, O brawling love, O loving hate,

157. S.D.] *Capell; Exeunt. Q2–4,F; not in Q1.*

155. *grievance*] source of sorrow.

158. *Is . . . young?*] Romeo has been up before dawn, so to him 9 a.m. seems late; and he is so preoccupied with melancholy musings that he has lost track of time. Shakespeare makes the strongest possible contrast between the heated and exciting atmosphere of the street brawl and the abstracted mood of the solitary Romeo. To judge from Romeo's question at l. 171, he does not listen to Benvolio's remark that it is 9 a.m.

168. *in proof*] when experienced.

169. *muffled*] Alluding to Cupid's blindness. Sometimes, as in Botticelli's *Primavera*, Cupid is shown blindfolded; Benvolio burlesques the convention at I. iv. 4. E.K.'s gloss on *Swaine* in Spenser, *The Shepheardes Calender*, March, holds Cupid to be 'described of the Poetes to be a boye . . . blindfolded, because he maketh no difference of personages'; he cites as authorities Propertius and Moschus (in Politian's translation). Cf. Erwin Panofsky, *Studies in Iconology* (1939), ch. IV.

173. *with hate . . . love*] With hate, because of the feud and brawl, with love, because Rosaline is a Capulet. But if we read *to-do*, the meaning is that Romeo's inner turmoil, caused by love, seems to him greater than that apparent in the public brawl.

O anything of nothing first create!
O heavy lightness, serious vanity,
Misshapen chaos of well-seeming forms!
Feather of lead, bright smoke, cold fire, sick health,
Still-waking sleep that is not what it is!
This love feel I that feel no love in this.
Dost thou not laugh?

Ben. No coz, I rather weep.

Romeo. Good heart, at what?

Ben. At thy good heart's oppression.

Romeo. Why such is love's transgression.
Griefs of mine own lie heavy in my breast,
Which thou wilt propagate to have it press'd
With more of thine. This love that thou hast shown
Doth add more grief to too much of mine own.
Love is a smoke made with the fume of sighs;
Being purg'd, a fire sparkling in lovers' eyes;
Being vex'd, a sea nourish'd with lovers' tears;
What is it else? A madness most discreet,
A choking gall, and a preserving sweet.
Farewell, my coz.

Ben. Soft, I will go along;
And if you leave me so, you do me wrong.

175. create] *Q1;* created *Q2–4*,F. 177. well-seeming] *Q4;* welseeing *Q2,3,F;* best seeming *Q1.* 184. mine] *Q2,3,F;* my *Q4,Q1.* 190. lovers'] *Pope;* louing *Q2–4,F;* a louers *Q1.*

175. *of nothing first create*] A conceit upon the proverb 'nothing can come of nothing'.

create] Abbott (§ 342) notes of *create* in *MND*, v. i. 412: 'Such words being directly derived from Latin participles . . . may themselves be regarded as participial adjectives without the addition of "d".'

176. *serious vanity*] weighty emptiness.

177. *well-seeming*] Q2 offers another instance of an omitted letter; cf. *his*, l. 145.

181. *coz*] i.e. cousin.

185. *propagate*] The image is taken from propagation by layering, where a branch of a vine or other trailing plant is bent down to the ground and a stone or other weight placed on it, causing it to put down roots and form a separate plant. Romeo says that Benvolio's concern adds a grief to the love-melancholy he has already.

190. *lovers'*] Possibly Q2's compositor was distracted by the repetition of *-ing* endings to *Being*, *sparkling*, *Being*; but the balance with l. 189, *lovers' eyes*, is essential.

191. *discreet*] showing discernment; also cautious, civil.

Romeo. Tut, I have lost myself, I am not here.
This is not Romeo, he's some other where.
Ben. Tell me in sadness who is that you love?
Romeo. What, shall I groan and tell thee?
Ben. Groan? Why no, but sadly tell me who.
Romeo. Bid a sick man in sadness make his will?
A word ill-urg'd to one that is so ill.
In sadness, cousin, I do love a woman.
Ben. I aim'd so near when I suppos'd you lov'd.
Romeo. A right good markman; and she's fair I love.
Ben. A right fair mark, fair coz, is soonest hit.
Romeo. Well, in that hit you miss; she'll not be hit
With Cupid's arrow, she hath Dian's wit,
And in strong proof of chastity well arm'd
From love's weak childish bow she lives uncharm'd.

195. Tut] *Q2–4,F1–2,Q1;* But *F3–4.* lost] *Q2–4,F,Q1;* left *Daniel, conj. Allen.* 200. Bid a] *Q1,Q4;* A *Q2,3,F.* make] *Q1,Q4;* makes *Q2,3,F.* 201. A] *Q2–4,F;* Ah *Q1.* 209. uncharm'd] *Q2–4,F;* unharmd *Q1.*

195. *Tut*] The speech begins in Q2 on page B2r; the preceding page has the catchword *But*; the first word on B2r in Q2 however is *Rom.* so that reliance on the catchword seems ill-advised. Williams suggests that the correct catchword '*Rom.* Tut' had been accidentally omitted; the compositor looking for it at the top of the wrong page found, on B4r, the first word *But.*

lost myself] Cf. l. 148 and n. above. Daniel's emendation would pick up Benvolio's *leave*; misreading *o* for *e* is easy. Cf. Brooke, ll. 419–20: 'And whilst I talkt with him, hym selfe he hath exylde, / Out of himself'; and I. iv. 104.

197. *in sadness*] seriously.

198. *groan*] Quibbling on the other sense of sad: melancholy.

205. *right . . . hit*] Quibbling bawdily on terms from archery, as in *LLL*, IV. i. 101–31; *mark* = target.

206. *hit*] shot.

207. *Dian's wit*] Although Romeo is complaining that Rosaline is as skilful as Diana in preserving her chastity, her effect on him suggests that she may be another instance of a favourite Renaissance motif, Venus in disguise, which had already been applied by Spenser in *The Shepheardes Calender* (gloss to April) to Queen Elizabeth, who is likened to Venus visiting Aeneas disguised as 'one of Dianaes damosells'. Clouet painted Diane de Poitiers as Venus in disguise, and Isaac Oliver did the same in a portrait of Queen Elizabeth I.

208. *proof*] well-tried armour, impenetrable by shot.

209. *weak childish bow*] Cupid's youth attracts, with paradoxical effect, these adjectives to his dangerous bow.

uncharm'd] The minim difference between Q1 and Q2 makes either reading graphically plausible, and both ideas are indeed implicitly suggested by *Cupid's bow*; but *uncharm'd* better expresses the special power of Cupid while not obscuring his harmful potential.

She will not stay the siege of loving terms
Nor bide th'encounter of assailing eyes
Nor ope her lap to saint-seducing gold;
O she is rich in beauty, only poor
That when she dies, with beauty dies her store.
Ben. Then she hath sworn that she will still live chaste?
Romeo. She hath, and in that sparing makes huge waste.
For beauty starv'd with her severity
Cuts beauty off from all posterity.
She is too fair, too wise, wisely too fair,
To merit bliss by making me despair.
She hath forsworn to love, and in that vow
Do I live dead, that live to tell it now.
Ben. Be rul'd by me, forget to think of her.
Romeo. O teach me how I should forget to think.
Ben. By giving liberty unto thine eyes:
Examine other beauties.
Romeo. 'Tis the way
To call hers, exquisite, in question more.
These happy masks that kiss fair ladies' brows,

211. bide] *Q2–4;* bid *F; not in Q1.* 212. ope] *Q2–4,Q1;* open *F.* 213. rich in beauty,] *Q1,Q3,4,F;* rich, in bewtie *Q2.* 216. makes] *Q4;* make *Q2,3,F; not in Q1.* 225. *Ben.*] *Q2,F; Ro. Q3,4; not in Q1.*

210. *siege*] A conventional military image for courtship; cf. *Wiv.*, II. ii. 225–6.

212. *ope her lap*] Though locked in a tower of bronze, Danaë was taken by Jove in a shower of gold. Romeo's phrasing contrives to suggest a commercial transaction *and* an erotic act. It is unlike Romeo to think of *buying* her favours, and we may suppose his immaturity has allowed the conceit to get out of hand. He had intended to stress her saint-like resolution; cf. Daniel, *The Complaint of Rosamond* (1592), ll. 232–5, 'Doost thou not see how that thy King thy *Ioue*, / Lightens foorth glory on thy darke estate: / And showres downe golde and treasure from aboue, / Whilst thou doost shutte thy lappe against thy fate'.

213–14. *rich . . . store*] The central idea of the first seventeen Sonnets. See also Daniel, *Rosamond*, ll. 239–52.

216. *sparing . . . waste*] her thrift is very wasteful. There is a quibble on *waste* and *waist* (as in *2H4*, I. ii. 139–142) which makes an impossible paradox: that chastity makes her heavily pregnant. By saving her virginity Rosaline *wastes* the chance of increasing her *waist* (by carrying a child). Cf. Sonnet I: 'makes huge waste'.

217. *starv'd*] brought to death.

219. *wisely too fair*] Quibbling on *fair* (i) beautiful, and (ii) just.

227. *call . . . in question*] bring her beauty into my thoughts (but her beauty will be called into question in another sense when set beside Juliet's).

Being black, puts us in mind they hide the fair.
He that is strucken blind cannot forget
The precious treasure of his eyesight lost.
Show me a mistress that is passing fair;
What doth her beauty serve but as a note
Where I may read who pass'd that passing fair?
Farewell, thou canst not teach me to forget.

Ben. I'll pay that doctrine or else die in debt. *Exeunt.*

[SCENE II]

Enter CAPULET, PARIS *and a* Servant.

Cap. But Montague is bound as well as I,
In penalty alike, and 'tis not hard I think
For men so old as we to keep the peace.

Paris. Of honourable reckoning are you both,
And pity 'tis you lived at odds so long.
But now my lord, what say you to my suit?

Cap. But saying o'er what I have said before.
My child is yet a stranger in the world,
She hath not seen the change of fourteen years.
Let two more summers wither in their pride

Scene II

SCENE II] *Capell; not in Q2–4,F,Q1.* *Location.*] *A Street. Capell.* S.D.] *Rowe; Enter* Capulet, *Countie* Paris, *and the Clowne. Q2–4,F; Enter Countie* Paris, *old* Capulet. *Q1.* 1. But] *Q2;* And *Q4; not in Q3,F,Q1.*

236. *I'll pay . . . debt*] I'll keep trying to teach you that lesson: until my death, if necessary.

Scene II

1. *bound*] bound over to keep the peace. Capulet and Montague have now both been to see the Prince and been warned.

4. *reckoning*] There is a quibble, in the next line's *at odds*, on the senses of social esteem and manner of computing. Paris is made to reveal his interest in Capulet's wealth while elaborating a compliment to the long-established dignity of the family. In a parallel situation in *Ado*, Shakespeare invites directly ironic feeling towards the practical attitude to dowries shown by Claudio (cf. *Ado*, I. ii. 256–7).

9. *fourteen*] Shakespeare has reduced her age from Painter, where it is eighteen, and Brooke, where it is sixteen. This emphasis on Juliet's youth is repeated, and the audience is evidently meant to think of her as young for marriage.

Ere we may think her ripe to be a bride.
Paris. Younger than she are happy mothers made.
Cap. And too soon marr'd are those so early made.
Earth hath swallow'd all my hopes but she;
She is the hopeful lady of my earth.
But woo her, gentle Paris, get her heart,
My will to her consent is but a part,
And she agreed, within her scope of choice
Lies my consent and fair according voice.
This night I hold an old accustom'd feast
Whereto I have invited many a guest
Such as I love, and you among the store:
One more, most welcome, makes my number more.
At my poor house look to behold this night
Earth-treading stars that make dark heaven light.
Such comfort as do lusty young men feel
When well-apparell'd April on the heel

14. Earth] *Q2,3,F;* The earth *Q4; not in Q1.* 15. She is] *Q4;* Shees *Q2,3,F; not in Q1.* 18. agreed] *Q2;* agree *Q3,4,F; not in Q1.*

13. *marr'd*] Puttenham in *The Arte of English Poesie* (1589) has 'The maide that soone married is, soone marred is'. Cf. *All's W.*, II. iii. 294.

14–15. *Earth . . . earth*] Some editors have suspected corruption here; Dr Johnson found l. 15 'not very intelligible'; Williams supposes both lines to have been inadequately marked for deletion in the manuscript and printed in error. The absence of rhyme in a passage of otherwise regular couplet rhyme, metrical irregularity, and the repetition in l. 15 of key words from l. 14, are the evidence advanced by editors who omit the two lines; but the two lines do not repeat the one assertion; Capulet takes up Paris's remark which he answers with a proverb, then quibbles on *earth* as associated not only with the grave but with fertility; *earth* = body at III. ii. 59. Juliet is the fruit of his loins and she alone will inherit his property, his *lands*; he has planted her and hopes to make her full of growing: she is to carry on his line. The simplest explanation for the broken rhyme is that the compositor misread a final word; error cannot be demonstrated, though it may be suspected.

20. *old accustom'd*] In Brooke and Painter the story begins near Christmas, which is the occasion for the feast, so that Romeo's misery is echoed in the chill and dreary weather, and the light and warmth of the banquet present a rich contrast; but Shakespeare fills the play with summer, warmth and light. See Intro., p. 38.

27. *well-apparell'd April*] The familiar allusion suggests a figure from a country festival procession or game, as in Sonnet 98's 'When proud-pied April dressed in all his trim / Hath put a spirit of youth in everything' and Spenser, *The Shepheardes Calender*, May, ll. 1–33.

Of limping winter treads, even such delight
Among fresh female buds shall you this night
Inherit at my house. Hear all, all see,
And like her most whose merit most shall be;
Which, on more view of many, mine, being one,
May stand in number, though in reckoning none.
Come go with me. [*To servant.*] Go sirrah, trudge about
Through fair Verona, find those persons out
Whose names are written there, and to them say,
My house and welcome on their pleasure stay.
Exeunt [*Capulet and Paris*].

Ser. Find them out whose names are written here. It is written that the shoemaker should meddle with his yard, and the tailor with his last, the fisher with his pencil, and the painter with his nets, but I am sent to find those persons whose names are here writ, and can never find what names the writing person hath here writ. I must to the learned. In good time.

Enter BENVOLIO *and* ROMEO.

29. female] *Q1,F2;* fennell *Q2–4,F.* 32. on] *Q4;* one *Q2,3,F; not in Q1.* 37. S.D.] *Rowe; Exit. Q2–4,F; Exeunt Q1.* 38. written here. It] *Dyce;* written. Here it *Q2–4,F; var. Q1.*

28. *limping winter*] Cf. Golding's *Ovid*, xv. 233 f.: 'Then ugly winter last / Like age steales on with trembling steppes'.

29. *female*] A minim misreading is possible; support for Q2's *fennell* comes from Lyly, *Sapho and Phao*, II. iv. 61: 'fancie is a worm, that feedeth first vpon fenell' (an emblem of flattery). Durham comments that fennel 'was thrown in the path of brides'; but the association of *young men* with *well-apparell'd* April suggests that the delight they will experience will be, appropriately, in *female* buds—cf. I. i. 149–51, where Romeo is described as a *bud*; cf. also I. iii. 77–8, where Paris is called a *flower*.

30. *Inherit*] Receive.

32–3. *Which . . . none*] And when you have had a more thorough view of many of the girls, my daughter, who will be one of those there, may be one of the number you will consider for first place—except, of course, for the old saying, that one isn't a number (Spencer). Cf. Tilley O 52.

34. *trudge*] Puttenham notes that the word is used properly only of rogues, lackeys, and such manner of people.

39–42. *shoemaker . . . writ*] Parodying Lyly, *Euphues, the Anatomy of Wit* (ed. Bond), p. 180: 'The shomaker must not go aboue his latchet, nor the hedger meddle with anye thing but his bill. It is vnsemely for the Paynter to feather a shaft, or the Fletcher to handle the pensill. All which thinges make most against me, in that a foole hath intruded himselfe to discourse of wit.'

40. *yard*] With a bawdy quibble on *yard* = penis; cf. Partridge, s.v. *yard*, and *LLL*, v. ii. 661.

Ben. Tut man, one fire burns out another's burning,
One pain is lessen'd by another's anguish;
Turn giddy, and be holp by backward turning.
One desperate grief cures with another's languish;
Take thou some new infection to thy eye
And the rank poison of the old will die.
Romeo. Your plantain leaf is excellent for that.
Ben. For what, I pray thee?
Romeo. For your broken shin.
Ben. Why, Romeo, art thou mad?
Romeo. Not mad, but bound more than a madman is:
Shut up in prison, kept without my food,
Whipp'd and tormented and—good e'en, good fellow.
Ser. God gi' good e'en; I pray, sir, can you read?
Romeo. Ay, mine own fortune in my misery.
Ser. Perhaps you have learned it without book. But I pray
can you read anything you see?
Romeo. Ay, if I know the letters and the language.
Ser. Ye say honestly; rest you merry.

46. One] *Q1,Q3,4,F;* On *Q2.* 49. thy] *Q2,Q1;* the *Q3,4,F.* 56. good e'en] *Q2–4,F, Q1* (Godden). 57. God gi' good e'en] *Q2–4,F,Q1* (Godgigoden). 59–60.] *As prose, Pope; as verse Q2–4,F,Q1.*

45. *one fire . . . burning*] Cf. Brooke, ll. 207–8, and *Gent.*, II. iv. 188–9, and Tilley F 277. Benvolio's speech is rhymed, appropriately urging love as a cure for love with a string of proverbial commonplaces.

51. *plantain leaf*] The leaf was used to bind wounds or cure bruises. Romeo mocks Benvolio's suggested remedies for a broken heart by giving the common remedy for a broken shin; he seeks to evade any discussion of his feelings while indicating that they are too deep for Benvolio to comprehend. Costard, in *LLL*, III. i. 69–70, enters with a broken shin, misunderstands Armado's call for *some enigma* and *l'envoy* as highfalutin foreign remedies, and cries instead for *a plantain*, the tried local salve.

52. *Romeo. For . . .*] From about this point until I. iii. 34 Q1 served as the copy from which Q2 was printed.

57–63. *God . . . read*] Shakespeare emphasizes the element of chance in the action. The servant Capulet has chosen happens to be illiterate, a fact which his master has forgotten in the heat of the moment. The meeting with Romeo is sheer accident and after the servant turns away, by chance Romeo regrets his off-hand answer and takes the list: Romeo's allusion to fortune at l. 58 is ironically apt.

59. *without book*] Hence 'by heart' or 'by ear'. 'By heart' applies aptly to Romeo.

62. *Ye say . . . merry*] The servant understands him to mean he knows neither letters nor language and cannot read, so bids him farewell.

Romeo. Stay, fellow, I can read. *He reads the letter.*
Signor Martino and his wife and daughters;
County Anselm and his beauteous sisters;
The lady widow of Utruvio;
Signor Placentio and his lovely nieces;
Mercutio and his brother Valentine;
Mine uncle Capulet, his wife and daughters;
My fair niece Rosaline and Livia;
Signor Valentio and his cousin Tybalt;
Lucio and the lively Helena.
A fair assembly. Whither should they come?
Ser. Up.
Romeo. Whither to supper?
Ser. To our house.
Romeo. Whose house?
Ser. My master's.
Romeo. Indeed I should have asked you that before.
Ser. Now I'll tell you without asking. My master is the great rich Capulet, and if you be not of the house of Montagues I pray come and crush a cup of wine. Rest you merry. *Exit.*
Ben. At this same ancient feast of Capulet's
Sups the fair Rosaline, whom thou so loves,
With all the admired beauties of Verona.

64–72.] *As verse, Dyce*[2], *conj. Capell; as prose Q2–4,F,Q1.* 64. *daughters*] *Q2–4,Q1; daughter F.* 65. *Anselm*] *Q2–4,F,Q1* (Anselme); Anselmo *Dyce*[2], *conj. Capell.* 70. *and*] *Q1; not in Q2–4,F.* 72. *lively*] *Q2–4,F,Q1;* lovely *Rowe*[1]. 75–6. Whither to supper? / *Ser*. To our house] *Q2–4,F,Q1* (*subst.*); Whither? / *Ser*. To supper; to our house *Theobald, conj. Warburton;* Whither? / *Ser*. To our house *Capell.* 79. you] *Q2–4,F;* thee *Q1.* 83. S.D.] *F; not in Q2–4,Q1.*

63. the letter] A stage-property 'letter', i.e. a folded paper; it is strictly speaking a list of names.

74. *Up*] Not to be outdone in witty quibbling the servant plays upon the phrase *come up* (cf. II. v. 63) expressing amused or indignant contempt.

75–6. *Whither . . . house*] Theobald and Warburton transfer *To supper* to the Servant, and receive the following rebuke from Dr Johnson: 'When a man reads a list of guests, he knows that they are invited to something, and, without any extraordinary good fortune, may guess, to a supper.' Capell considers the phrase *To supper* redundant; Williams that it is a reporter's anticipation of Benvolio's *Sups the fair Rosaline* of l. 85.

82. *crush a cup*] drink, quaff (OED *crush* v 7). Steevens notes 'We still say, in cant language, *to crack a bottle*'.

Go thither and with unattainted eye
Compare her face with some that I shall show
And I will make thee think thy swan a crow.

Romeo. When the devout religion of mine eye
Maintains such falsehood, then turn tears to fire,
And these who, often drown'd, could never die,
Transparent heretics, be burnt for liars.
One fairer than my love! The all-seeing sun
Ne'er saw her match since first the world begun.

Ben. Tut, you saw her fair, none else being by:
Herself pois'd with herself in either eye.
But in that crystal scales let there be weigh'd
Your lady's love against some other maid
That I will show you shining at this feast,
And she shall scant show well that now seems best.

Romeo. I'll go along, no such sight to be shown,
But to rejoice in splendour of mine own. [*Exeunt.*]

91. fire] *Q2–4,F,Q1;* fires *Pope.* 101. she shall scant show well] *Q2–4,Q1;* she shew scant shell, well *F* (*some copies*); she shall scant shell, well *F* (*some copies*). seems] *Q2,Q1;* shewes *Q3,4,F.* 103. S.D.] *Pope; not in Q2–4,F,Q1.*

87. *unattainted*] not infected; cf. l. 49 above.

91. *fire*] Pope prefers a plural form for the sake of the rhyme, but Q2 reads *fier:* and the colon is definitely not a half-printed *s*.

92. *often drown'd*] i.e. with weeping for love of Rosaline; cf. III. v. 130–7 and Donne, *A Valediction of Weeping*, l. 20.

93. *Transparent*] Quibbling on the senses 'self-evident' and 'seen through'. Spencer conjectures a reference to the testing of those suspected of being in league with the devil, by seeing if they would start to drown: if they kept afloat they obviously had supernatural help and were evidently heretics, so suffered death by burning.

97–9. *Herself . . . maid*] 'Romeo's eyeballs are the two pans of a scale; both in l. 97 holding an image of Rosaline, while in ll. 98–9 her image is balanced against that of another' (NCS).

[SCENE III]

Enter LADY CAPULET *and* NURSE.

Lady Cap. Nurse, where's my daughter? Call her forth to me.
Nurse. Now by my maidenhead at twelve year old,
I bade her come. What, lamb. What, ladybird.
God forbid. Where's this girl? What, Juliet!

Enter JULIET.

Juliet. How now, who calls?
Nurse. Your mother.
Juliet. Madam, I am here, what is your will?
Lady Cap. This is the matter. Nurse, give leave awhile,
We must talk in secret. Nurse, come back again,
I have remember'd me, thou's hear our counsel.
Thou knowest my daughter's of a pretty age.
Nurse. Faith, I can tell her age unto an hour.
Lady Cap. She's not fourteen.
Nurse. I'll lay fourteen of my teeth—
And yet, to my teen be it spoken, I have but four—

Scene III

SCENE III] *Capell; not in Q2–4,F,Q1.* *Location.*] *A room in Capulet's house. Capell.* 1. *Lady Cap.*] *ed.; Wife. Q2–4,F,Q1.* 2–4.] *As verse, Johnson; as prose Q2–4,F,Q1.* 3. bade] *Q2,3,F,Q1 (bad); had Q4.* 7. *Lady Cap.*] *ed.; Wife. Q2–4,F; W: Q1.* 7–10.] *As verse, Capell; as prose Q2–4,F,Q1.* 11. an] *Q2–4,F; a Q1.* 12. *Lady Cap.*] *ed.; Wife. Q2–4,F,Q1.* 13. teen] *Q2–4,F,Q1;* teeth *F2.* 12–15.] *As Steevens 1793; prose Q2–4,Q1;* Ile . . . teeth, / . . . spoken, / . . . fourteene, / . . . tide? / *F.*

1 ff.] Most editors since Capell print this scene as verse, though Hosley follows Q2, which prints ll. 2–63, and the Nurse's part thereafter to l. 78, as prose.

1–4. *Nurse . . . Juliet*] The parallel with IV. v. is insistent: Lady Capulet there tells the Nurse to fetch Juliet, and the Nurse goes to do so with almost identical words (evidently those she has used to Juliet all her life): *lamb, lady, love, sweetheart,* then a bawdy jest (ll. 5–7) and the apology *God forgive me!* Then she finds Juliet apparently dead.

2. *maidenhead . . . old*] The joke is that she could not swear safely by her maidenhead at thirteen; this is also a very direct return to emphasis on the earliest age when a girl might marry: the conversation stresses (to comic extremes) that Juliet will be fourteen in a few weeks.

3. *ladybird*] Possibly a word for light o' love as well as sweetheart (NCS); which explains the Nurse's apology *God forbid*; but she may also mean 'God forbid anything has happened to her'.

9. *thou's*] thou shalt. A colloquialism: Abbott (§ 461).

13. *teen*] sorrow.

She's not fourteen. How long is it now
To Lammas-tide?
Lady Cap. A fortnight and odd days.
Nurse. Even or odd, of all days in the year,
Come Lammas Eve at night shall she be fourteen.
Susan and she—God rest all Christian souls—
Were of an age. Well, Susan is with God;
She was too good for me. But as I said,
On Lammas Eve at night shall she be fourteen.
That shall she; marry, I remember it well.
'Tis since the earthquake now eleven years,
And she was wean'd—I never shall forget it—
Of all the days of the year upon that day.
For I had then laid wormwood to my dug,
Sitting in the sun under the dovehouse wall.
My lord and you were then at Mantua—
Nay I do bear a brain. But as I said,
When it did taste the wormwood on the nipple
Of my dug and felt it bitter, pretty fool,
To see it tetchy and fall out with the dug.

15. *Lady Cap.*] *ed.; Wife. Q2–4,F,Q1* 16–48.] *As verse, Capell; as prose Q2–4,F,Q1.* 22. That] *Q2,3,F,Q1; then Q4.*

15. *Lammas-tide*] 1 August, in the early English church a harvest festival for the first ripe corn, from which loaves were made and consecrated (OED). These associations with early ripening chime happily with Juliet's birth; the Nurse may also make the popular, fallacious assumption that *Lammas* derives from Lamb and Mass: hence her pet name for Juliet carries an added resonance. Hosley suggests that Shakespeare, inheriting a heroine named Juliet, gave her a birthday in July.

16. *Even or odd*] The Nurse misunderstands Lady Capulet, who means 'a few' by *odd.*

18. *Susan and she*] Evidently the Nurse's closeness to Lady Capulet partly derives from her having had a daughter of the same age, this child's early death, and the compensation of nursing Juliet. Ironically Juliet too will prove to be too good for the Nurse, and the momentary shadow is ominous, like Romeo's images of cankered buds.

23. *the earthquake*] Attempts to identify an actual earthquake alluded to here have been numerous (see Intro., pp. 26–7).

26. *wormwood*] oil from the leaves of the plant *Artemisia absinthium*, proverbially bitter and medicinal.

29. *Nay . . . brain*] Brooke observes of the Nurse's tale of giving Juliet suck: 'when these Beldams sit at ease . . . part they say is true, and part they do devise, / Yet boldly do they chat of both, when no man checkes theyr lyes' (ll. 663, 665–6).

Shake! quoth the dovehouse. 'Twas no need, I trow,
To bid me trudge.
And since that time it is eleven years.
For then she could stand high-lone, nay, by th'rood,
She could have run and waddled all about;
For even the day before she broke her brow,
And then my husband—God be with his soul,
A was a merry man—took up the child,
'Yea', quoth he, 'dost thou fall upon thy face?
Thou wilt fall backward when thou hast more wit,
Wilt thou not, Jule?' And by my holidame,
The pretty wretch left crying and said 'Ay'.
To see now how a jest shall come about.
I warrant, and I should live a thousand years
I never should forget it. 'Wilt thou not, Jule?' quoth he,
And, pretty fool, it stinted, and said 'Ay'.

Lady Cap. Enough of this, I pray thee, hold thy peace.

Nurse. Yes, madam, yet I cannot choose but laugh
To think it should leave crying and say 'Ay';
And yet I warrant it had upon it brow
A bump as big as a young cockerel's stone,
A perilous knock, and it cried bitterly.
'Yea', quoth my husband, 'fall'st upon thy face?
Thou wilt fall backward when thou comest to age,
Wilt thou not, Jule?' It stinted, and said 'Ay'.

35. eleven] *Q2–4,Q1 (a leuen); a* eleuen *F.* 36. high-lone] *Q2 (hylone), Q1; a lone Q3; alone Q4,F.* 43. Jule] *Q2–4,F;* Juliet *Q1.* 46. should] *Q2,Q1; shall Q3,4,F.* 47. Jule] *Q2–4; Julet F;* Juliet *Q1.* 49. *Lady Cap.*] *ed.; Old La. Q2–4,F; not in Q1.* 57. Jule] *Q2–4,F;* Juliet *Q1.*

33. *Shake . . . dovehouse*] A picturesque way of saying the dovehouse shook.

33–4. *'Twas no need . . . trudge*] i.e. I needed no second warning to take myself off. NCS compares Golding's *Ovid*, II. 502: 'It was no neede to bid him chaufe.'

36. *high-lone*] quite alone, without support (OED).

by th'rood] by Christ's cross.

38. *broke her brow*] fell and cut her forehead.

43. *holidame*] A corrupt form of 'halidom', holiness, hence any holy relic; it was a common error to suppose its origin to be 'holy dame' or 'our Lady'.

48. *stinted*] ceased.

52. *it*[2]] Neuter possessive pronoun; Abbott (§ 228) says it is used especially when a child is mentioned; cf. *Wint.*, III. ii. 98.

53. *stone*] testicle.

Juliet. And stint thou too, I pray thee, Nurse, say I.
Nurse. Peace, I have done. God mark thee to his grace,
Thou wast the prettiest babe that e'er I nurs'd.
And I might live to see thee married once,
I have my wish.
Lady Cap. Marry, that marry is the very theme
I came to talk of. Tell me, daughter Juliet,
How stands your dispositions to be married?
Juliet. It is an honour that I dream not of.
Nurse. An honour. Were not I thine only nurse
I would say thou hadst suck'd wisdom from thy teat.
Lady Cap. Well, think of marriage now. Younger than you
Here in Verona, ladies of esteem,
Are made already mothers. By my count
I was your mother much upon these years
That you are now a maid. Thus then in brief:
The valiant Paris seeks you for his love.
Nurse. A man, young lady. Lady, such a man
As all the world—why, he's a man of wax.
Lady Cap. Verona's summer hath not such a flower.
Nurse. Nay, he's a flower, in faith a very flower.

59–62.] *As verse, Pope; as prose Q2–4,F,Q1.* 60. wast] *Q2–4,F; wert Q1.* 63. *Lady Cap.*] *ed.; Old La. Q2–4,F; Wife: Q1.* 65. dispositions] *Q2–4;* disposition *F; not in Q1.* 66. honour] *Q1;* houre *Q2–4,F.* 67–8.] *As verse, Pope; as prose Q2–4,F,Q1.* 67. honour] *Q1; houre Q2–4,F.* thine] *Q2,3,F; thy Q1; not in Q4.* 68. wisdom] *Q2,3,F,Q1; thy wisdom Q4.* 69. *Lady Cap.*] *ed.; Old La. Q2–4,F; Wife: Q1.* 71. mothers. By] *F;* mothers by *Q2–4; not in Q1.* 72. your] *Q2–4,F, Q1;* a *Knight.* 75–6.] *As verse, Pope; as prose Q2–4,F; not in Q1.* 77. *Lady Cap.*] *ed.; Old La. Q2–4,F; Wife: Q1.*

61. *once*] ever, at any time.

66, 67. *honour*] Q2's reading *houre* is a possible minim misreading of manuscript *honor*. L. 66's *houre* makes sense, but not when taken with l. 67's *houre*. Dr Johnson prefers *hour* as 'more seemly from a girl to her mother'.

72. *your mother*] There is every reason for assuming that Lady Capulet is old, like Lady Montague and the heads of the two houses; but the Q1, Q2 *your mother* could make her, by strict computation, twenty-seven or twenty-eight; cf. III. v. 165. In V. iii. 206 Lady Capulet says that the sight of death is as a bell *That warns my old age to a sepulchre*. Lady Montague has just died of grief, and the parallel between the two mothers is emphatic. The speech prefixes designate her *Old Lady* six times in the present scene in Q2.

76. *man of wax*] faultless, as if modelled in wax; cf. Lyly, *Euphues and his England* (ed. Bond), p. 166: 'you make . . . your Louer . . . so exquisite that for shape hee must be framed in wax'.

Lady Cap. What say you, can you love the gentleman?
This night you shall behold him at our feast;
Read o'er the volume of young Paris' face
And find delight writ there with beauty's pen.
Examine every married lineament
And see how one another lends content;
And what obscur'd in this fair volume lies,
Find written in the margent of his eyes.
This precious book of love, this unbound lover,
To beautify him only lacks a cover.
The fish lives in the sea; and 'tis much pride
For fair without the fair within to hide.
That book in many's eyes doth share the glory
That in gold clasps locks in the golden story.
So shall you share all that he doth possess,
By having him, making yourself no less.
Nurse. No less, nay bigger. Women grow by men.
Lady Cap. Speak briefly, can you like of Paris' love?
Juliet. I'll look to like, if looking liking move,
But no more deep will I endart mine eye

79. *Lady Cap.*] *ed.; Old La. Q2–4,F; not in Q1.* 83. married] *Q2;* seuerall *Q3,4,F; not in Q1.* 91. many's] *Q2–4,F;* many *Q5; not in Q1.* 95. bigger. Women] *F* (bigger: women)*;* bigger women *Q2–4; not in Q1.* 96. *Lady Cap.*] *ed.; Old La. Q2–4,F; Wife: Q1.* 98. endart] *Q2–4,F;* engage *Q1.*

81–2. *Read . . . pen*] His face is like an open book in which beauty has written delight.

83. *married lineament*] harmoniously proportioned features; *lineament* could also mean outline (carrying on the idea of *book* and *pen*).

85–6. *what . . . eyes*] what cannot be found in his face will appear in his eyes, the page-margins where subtler details are explained.

88. *cover*] Taking up *unbound* from l. 87; he needs to be *bound* to you in love to be made complete, as is a book with a *cover*. The idea of embracing may also be present; it is, more clearly, in l. 92's *gold clasps.*

89–90. *fish . . . hide*] a fish is in its element in the sea, and a handsome man (*the fair within*) is finely suited with a beautiful wife (*fair without*) and her binding love.

92. *gold clasps*] Quibbling on the clasps by which a book can be locked shut: the joyful embraces of wedded love, symbolized by golden rings.

95. *nay bigger*] The sense is 'women grow bigger'.

Women grow] i.e. in pregnancy.

97. *look to*] expect.

98. *endart*] The conceit derives from conventional sonneteering: the lady's piercing eyes have the effect of Cupid's shafts. Ironically, Juliet does in the event act in opposition to parental wishes.

Than your consent gives strength to make it fly.

Enter a Servingman.

Ser. Madam, the guests are come, supper served up, you called, my young lady asked for, the Nurse cursed in the pantry, and everything in extremity. I must hence to wait, I beseech you follow straight. *Exit.*

Lady Cap. We follow thee; Juliet, the County stays.

Nurse. Go, girl, seek happy nights to happy days.

Exeunt.

[SCENE IV]

Enter ROMEO, MERCUTIO, BENVOLIO, *with five or six other* Masquers [*and*] Torchbearers.

Romeo. What, shall this speech be spoke for our excuse?
Or shall we on without apology?

99. it] *Q1, Q4; not in Q2,3,F.* 103. S.D.] *F; not in Q2–4,Q1.* 104. *Lady Cap.*] *ed.; Mo. Q2–4,F; not in Q1.*

Scene IV

SCENE IV] *Steevens; not in Q2–4,F,Q1.* *Location.*] *A street before Capulet's house. Theobald.* S.D.]*Q2–4,F; Enter Maskers with* Romeo *and a Page Q1.* 1. *Romeo.*] *Q2–4,F,Q1; Ben. / Capell.*

101. *cursed*] Probably because she has the keys; in IV. iv. she is given keys to fetch spices, and has been called for to get dates and quinces.

Scene IV

S.D. *Enter . . . Torchbearers*] The gentlemen are disguised in preparation for a masquerade—traditional disguising and dancing associated with Christmas and other festivals, a custom of Italian origin though influenced by English mummery; essentially social and impromptu in character, like that of the Lords in *LLL*, V. ii. 157 ff. The masquerade by Henry VIII in *H8*, I. iv. 65 ff., closely follows Holinshed's account, and both these examples have the regular form, the masquers being introduced by a Presenter whose speech greets the host or compliments the ladies and apologizes for the intrusion; dancing and flirtation are expected to follow. The host normally regarded such an intrusion as a compliment. On masquerades see Welsford, *The Court Masque*, p. 102, Chambers, *The Medieval Stage*, I, ch. xvii, *The Elizabethan Stage*, I, p. 152. Cf. also *Ado*, II. i. 71 ff., *Tim.*, I, ii. 124 ff.

1. *Romeo.*] Capell supposed this speech to be misattributed, like the next: certainly a persuasive suggestion, especially in view of the tangle at l. 53 in Q1, where the prefix *Mer.* is omitted so that the Queen Mab speech is attributed to Benvolio. Q2 misattributes l. 23 to *Horatio*. Since Q2 is dependent on Q1 at this point error may be suspected though not proved.

this speech] The masquers have prepared a speech according to custom.

Ben. The date is out of such prolixity.
We'll have no Cupid hoodwink'd with a scarf,
Bearing a Tartar's painted bow of lath,
Scaring the ladies like a crowkeeper,
Nor no without-book prologue, faintly spoke
After the prompter, for our entrance.
But let them measure us by what they will,
We'll measure them a measure and be gone.
Romeo. Give me a torch, I am not for this ambling.
Being but heavy I will bear the light.
Mer. Nay, gentle Romeo, we must have you dance.
Romeo. Not I, believe me. You have dancing shoes
With nimble soles, I have a soul of lead
So stakes me to the ground I cannot move.
Mer. You are a lover, borrow Cupid's wings
And soar with them above a common bound.
Romeo. I am too sore enpierced with his shaft
To soar with his light feathers, and so bound

3. *Ben.*] *Q2–4,F,Q1; Mer.* / *Capell.* 7–8.] *Q1, Pope; not in Q2–4,F.*
20. so bound] *Q2–4;* to bound *F; not in Q1.*

3. *the date . . . prolixity*] 'such rigmaroles are out of date' (NCS).

4. *hoodwink'd*] blindfolded (cf. I. i. 169) with subsidiary quibbles on the hood used to cover a hawk's eyes, so mastering it (Cupid is winged too), and on the game, blind-man's buff.

5. *Tartar's . . . lath*] Cupid is conventionally depicted with an oriental or Tartar's bow, which is lip-shaped and very powerful by comparison to the English bow which has the shape of a segment of a circle. The phrase mocks the god of love with his toy weapon of flimsy cheap wood (*painted lath*) traditional for theatrical properties such as the Vice's dagger. The common paradox that Cupid is both a weak infant and an awesomely powerful divinity is invoked and seen as absurd.

6. *crowkeeper*] a scarecrow with a bow tucked under his arm (cf. *Lr*, IV. vi. 88), or a boy employed to scare off birds; both ideas apply in a suitably derogatory way to Cupid. Cf. Intro., pp. 58–9, II. iv. 15–16 and n.

7–8. *Nor no . . . entrance*] The omission of these lines from Q2 must be ascribed to carelessness by the compositor.

7–8. *prologue . . . prompter*] Cf. Moth's performance in *LLL*, V. ii. 157 ff.

10. *measure . . . measure*] Quibbling on the senses 'standard', 'give', 'apportion', 'dance'.

11. *torch*] Torchbearers at masques always looked on, never taking part.

ambling] artificial, acquired way of walking or dancing; cf. *Ham.*, III. i. 145.

18. *common bound*] Quibbling on the senses 'normal limit', 'unimpressive leap' and 'rogue in chains'.

20. *soar*] This quibble is made along with others in *LLL*, IV. ii. 56–60.

I cannot bound a pitch above dull woe.
Under love's heavy burden do I sink.
Mer. And, to sink in it, should you burden love—
Too great oppression for a tender thing.
Romeo. Is love a tender thing? It is too rough,
Too rude, too boisterous, and it pricks like thorn.
Mer. If love be rough with you, be rough with love;
Prick love for pricking and you beat love down.
Give me a case to put my visage in:
A visor for a visor. What care I
What curious eye doth quote deformities?
Here are the beetle brows shall blush for me.
Ben. Come, knock and enter, and no sooner in
But every man betake him to his legs.
Romeo. A torch for me. Let wantons light of heart
Tickle the senseless rushes with their heels,
For I am proverb'd with a grandsire phrase—
I'll be a candle-holder and look on.
The game was ne'er so fair, and I am done.

23. *Mer.*] *Q4; Horatio. Q2,3,F; not in Q1.* 31. quote] *Q3,4,F;* cote *Q2;* coate *Q1.* 34. betake] *Q2,4,F;* betakes *Q3; not in Q1.* 39. done] *Q1,F;* dum *Q2;* dun *Q3,4.*

21. *pitch*] height from which a hawk stoops to kill; cf. *2H6*, II. i. 5–15.

23. *it*] In making love you would be a burden on the woman and her tenderest part; with a bawdy quibble linked to *tender thing*.

28. *Prick*] There is an obvious bawdy quibble (cf. II. iv. 112) but irony in Mercutio's delight in punning on *prick* = stab: the 'king of cats' scratches him to death. The sense of *beat love down* includes 'causing sexual detumescence'.

29. *case*] cover.

30. *visor . . . visor*] Mercutio considers his face as grotesque as a mask; NCS compare the proverb 'A well-favoured visor will hide an ill-favoured face' (Tilley V 92): or, more simply, his face is itself just a mask.

31. *quote*] observe.

32. *beetle brows . . . blush*] Evidently the mask has heavy overhanging eyebrows and red cheeks.

34. *betake . . . legs*] Quibbling on 'dance' and 'run away'; cf. I. i. 8–9.

36. *Tickle . . . rushes*] Rushes were strewn on the floors of rooms and also perhaps on the stage; cf. *Shr.*, IV. i. 41–2. *senseless* = incapable of feeling; in modern slang a pianist may be said to 'tickle the ivories'.

37. *proverb'd . . . phrase*] i.e. 'A good candle-holder proves a good gamester' (Tilley C 51); hence 'a good old-fashioned proverb applies to me: the spectator sees the best of the game'.

grandsire] long lived, and, quibblingly, 'often used by grandfathers'.

39. *The game . . . fair*] The proverb recommended leaving the gambling table when the game was at its best.

done] Romeo is echoed by Mercutio (*dun's the mouse*) so Q2's reading here

Mer. Tut, dun's the mouse, the constable's own word.
If thou art dun, we'll draw thee from the mire
Of—save your reverence—love, wherein thou stickest
Up to the ears. Come, we burn daylight, ho.
Romeo. Nay, that's not so.
Mer. I mean sir, in delay
We waste our lights in vain, light lights by day.
Take our good meaning, for our judgement sits

41–2. mire / Of] *Q1;* mire / Or *Q2,3;* mire. / Or *F.* 42. save your reverence] *F;* saue you reuerence *Q2–4;* this surreuerence *Q1.* 44. Nay] *Q2,3,F,Q1; not in Q4.* in] *Q2–4,Q1;* I *F.* 45. lights in vain, light lights] *Daniel, conj. Nicholson;* lights in vaine, lights lights *Q2–4;* lights in vaine, lights, lights, *F;* lights by night, like Lampes *Q1;* lights in vain, like lights *Dr Johnson;* lights, in vain light lights *Williams.*

dum cannot be right. NCS thinks *dum* a minim misreading of *done*; Hosley and Williams follow Rowe in printing Q3's *dun*, arguing that Romeo's verbal play is on *dun* (brown) and *fair*, and *dun—done*.

40. *dun's the mouse*] Mercutio quibbles on Romeo's *done* and answers proverb with proverb. Perhaps because a brown mouse would be invisible in the dark, and mice are proverbial for quiet movement (cf. 'not a mouse stirring', *Ham.* I. i. 10), the phrase came to mean 'be still', a fitting watchword for the constable on night duty (cf. *Ado,* III. iii. 31–7). Mercutio seeks to encourage Romeo to be sociable, to enter into the spirit of the adventure which could well end up with a nocturnal brush with the Watch.

41. *If thou art dun*] Quibbling on 'dun-in-the-mire', a dull fellow, a stick-in-the mud (*Dun* was a common name for a horse, and horses often stuck in the mud of Elizabethan roads), and the Christmas game, in which a log representing Dun the horse is pulled by all the company's combined efforts out of imaginary mire. (Gifford says he has often played the game and seen 'much honest mirth at it'.) The gist of Mercutio's reply is that Romeo is dull and heavy as if he were a bogged cart-horse, that being in love is like being up to the ears in ordure (see next note), and he must be freed from the misery by dancing.

42. *save your reverence*] Mercutio makes a mock-apology for almost uttering an indecency, since *sirreverence* was a euphemism for human dung, but his apology itself (*save your reverence*) quibbles on this slang term.

45. *waste . . . day*] Mercutio's *we burn daylight* (l. 43) quibbles on the proverbial sense (= waste time by delaying). Romeo chooses to be literal-minded (because it is actually night) so Mercutio has to explain they are wasting (= using up) their torches to no effect, as in broad daylight. The repeated emphasis on the darkness is important as scene-setting. Cf. *LLL,* I. i. 77: 'Light, seeking light, doth light of light beguile'.

46–7. *Take . . . wits*] i.e. be good enough to take our intended (*good*) meaning, for our good sense is to be found in that five times more often than in the words which refer to sense-experience through our five senses (*wits*); *judgement* = understanding, good sense.

Five times in that ere once in our five wits.
Romeo. And we mean well in going to this masque,
But 'tis no wit to go.
Mer. Why, may one ask?
Romeo. I dreamt a dream tonight.
Mer. And so did I.
Romeo. Well what was yours?
Mer. That dreamers often lie.
Romeo. In bed asleep, while they do dream things true.
Mer. O then I see Queen Mab hath been with you.
She is the fairies' midwife, and she comes
In shape no bigger than an agate stone
On the forefinger of an alderman,
Drawn with a team of little atomi
Over men's noses as they lie asleep.
Her chariot is an empty hazelnut

47. five wits] *Malone, conj. Wilbraham;* fine wits *Q2–4,F;* right wits *Q1.* 53. *Mer.* O then . . . you. / She is] *Q2–4,F; Mer:* Ah then . . . you. / *Ben:* Queene Mab what's she? / She is *Q1.* 54–91.] *As verse Q1; as prose Q2–4,F.* 55. an] *Q2–4,Q1; not in F.* 57. atomi] *Q1;* ottamie *Q2;* atomies *Q3,4,F.* 58. Over] *Q2–4,F;* Athwart *Q1, Pope.* 58–70.] *Lineation and order of lines as Daniel, conj. Lettsom. Prose in Q2–4. See n. below.*

47. *Five*] Malone refers to II. iv. 73–4.

50. *I dreamt*] Romeo's dream remains undisclosed, though ll. 106–13 suggest that it may be darkly ominous. The isolation of the hero is achieved by Shakespeare through a series of such moments where his mood, tone and thoughts contrast strikingly with those of his companions. There may be a deliberate anticipatory linking of hero and heroine when in I. iii. 66 Juliet says of marriage: 'It is an honour that I *dream* not of'. In dreams begin responsibilities.

52. *while*] sometimes (cf. OED sv adv. A1).

53. *Queen Mab*] The suggestion by W. J. Thoms that this is the Irish fairy, *Mabh*, might gain support from H. Ellis's report of a Warwickshire phrase *Mab-led*, meaning led astray by a will o' the wisp (see Brand, *Popular Antiquities*, III, p. 218, ed. 1841). *Queen* may be *quean*, a slattern or low woman, though the line in *Jacob and Esau*, v. vi. (1568): 'Come out thou mother Mab, out olde rotten witche' might support *Mab's* connection with magic.

54. *fairies' midwife*] 'This does not mean the midwife *to* the fairies, but that she was the person *among* the fairies whose department it was to deliver the fancies of sleeping men of their dreams, those *children of an idle brain*' (Steevens).

55–6. *agate . . . forefinger*] Agate was commonly used for seal-rings; a figure would be cut in the stone, set in a ring; cf. *Ado*, III. i. 65, *2H4*, I. ii. 10–11.

57. *atomi*] atoms, tiny creatures.

59–61. *Her chariot . . . coachmakers*] Lettsom's rearrangement involves placing these three lines about the

Made by the joiner squirrel or old grub,
Time out o' mind the fairies' coachmakers;
Her waggon-spokes made of long spinners' legs,
The cover of the wings of grasshoppers,
Her traces of the smallest spider web,
Her collars of the moonshine's watery beams,
Her whip of cricket's bone, the lash of film,
Her waggoner a small grey-coated gnat,
Not half so big as a round little worm
Prick'd from the lazy finger of a maid;
And in this state she gallops night by night
Through lovers' brains, and then they dream of love;
O'er courtiers' knees, that dream on curtsies straight;

64. Her] *Q2–4,F;* The *Q1.* spider] *Q2–4;* spiders *F; not in Q1.* 66. film] *F2* (filme); Philome *Q2–4,F;* filmes *Q1.* 69. Prick'd] *Q2–4,F;* Pickt *Q1.* maid] *Q1, Pope;* man *Q2–4,F.* 72. O'er] *Q1;* On *Q2–4,F.* curtsies] *Q2–4,F* (Cursies), *Q1.*

chariot itself before the description of its parts. In Q2 they follow l. 69. NCS believes that Q2 at this point was set up from a copy of Q1 corrected, and with additional material. The Q2 compositor, 'baffled by the problem of lineation', set up the bulk of the speech as prose, wrongly placing the marginal addition of ll. 59–61. There is a likelihood of more general corruption: in Q1 ll. 59–61 are omitted; so also ll. 64 (absorbed into l. 65), 73. See Appendix I for the Q1 version of the Queen Mab speech.

60. *joiner . . . grub*] The squirrel has chisel-like teeth, the grub bores holes; both are necessary to fashion joints and secure them with dowels in this fantastic version of the trade of joinery.

62. *spinners'*] Probably craneflies'; this insect (the Daddy-long-legs) is still called a *spinner* in Scotland according to Andrew S. Cairncross (*N&Q*, ns 22, 1975, pp. 166–7). The long legs of the cranefly would be appropriate for wheelspokes, the thinner web of the spider for the traces. In *MND*, II. ii. 20–1: 'Weaving spiders, come not here: / Hence you long-legg'd spinners, hence', the reference seems to be clearly to spiders, however, so that though in this context in *Rom.* the sense *craneflies* is attractive, it may not be what Shakespeare meant.

65. *watery*] The moon was associated with dew and with the tides; cf. *MND*, II. i. 162. There is an obvious play on *watery*, 'weak, thin', and on *collars*—colours.

66. *film*] gossamer.

69. *lazy . . . maid*] Worms were humorously said to breed in the fingers of lazy maids; cf. *All's W.*, I. i. 36, where Parolles adapts the idea perversely: 'Virginity breeds mites, much like a cheese'. Harry Keil, 'Scabies and the Queen Mab passage in *Romeo and Juliet*' (*JHI*, XVIII, June 1957, pp. 394–410), offers to identify the condition.

maid] Hoppe suggests Q2's reading is evidence for the manuscript reading *maie* (maiden).

72. *curtsies*] gestures of respect.

straight] immediately.

O'er lawyers' fingers who straight dream on fees;
O'er ladies' lips, who straight on kisses dream,
Which oft the angry Mab with blisters plagues
Because their breaths with sweetmeats tainted are.
Sometime she gallops o'er a courtier's nose
And then dreams he of smelling out a suit;
And sometime comes she with a tithe-pig's tail,
Tickling a parson's nose as a lies asleep;
Then dreams he of another benefice.
Sometime she driveth o'er a soldier's neck
And then dreams he of cutting foreign throats,
Of breaches, ambuscados, Spanish blades,
Of healths five fathom deep; and then anon
Drums in his ear, at which he starts and wakes,
And being thus frighted swears a prayer or two
And sleeps again. This is that very Mab
That plaits the manes of horses in the night

73. dream] *Q2–4; dreamt F; not in Q1.* 74. on] *Q1,Q3,4,F;* one *Q2.* 76. breaths] *Q1* (breathes)*;* breath *Q2–4,F.* 78. dreams] *Q2,4,F,Q1;* dreame *Q3.* 79. a] *Q2–4,Q1; not in F.* 80. as a] *Q2–4,F;* that *Q1.* 81. dreams he] *Q1, Pope;* he dreams *Q2–4,F.* 86. ear] *Q2–4,Q1;* eares *F.*

77. *courtier's*] The repetition of *courtier's* (after l. 72) may indicate re-writing—Shakespeare's first version being printed by the confused compositor. NCS argues that *smelling out a suit* suggests a legal officer of some kind, noting that Collier proposes *counsellor* (i.e. barrister), and compare *Meas.*, I. ii. 103, in support.

78. *smelling . . . suit*] For a fat fee the courtier will undertake to gain the royal favour (NCS).

79. *tithe-pig*] The parson was entitled to a tenth of every litter of pigs as part of his full *tithe*, or tenth of income of the parish.

81. *benefice*] ecclesiastical living.

84. *breaches*] i.e. in defensive walls during assaults.

ambuscados] ambushes; OED says this is an affected refashioning of *ambuscade* after the Spanish, and cites this line.

Spanish blades] Spanish steel was famed for its excellence in swords, Toledo being proverbial for the quality of the weapons made there. There may be a quibble on *blade* = a young gallant, possibly repeated at II. iv. 30 (OED sb 11).

85. *healths . . . deep*] Cf. *2H4*, v. iii. 52; Humphreys (Arden) cites 'One that will drink deep, though it be a mile to the bottom' from *The Eighth Liberal Science: or a new-found Art and Order of Drinking.*

89. *plaits . . . night*] Superstition attributed tangled and matted human or horse hair to the action of elves; cf. *Lr*, II. iii. 10. Elves supposedly hated slatterns and punished them (cf. *Wiv.*, v. v. 42–3).

And bakes the elf-locks in foul sluttish hairs,
Which, once untangled, much misfortune bodes.
This is the hag, when maids lie on their backs,
That presses them and learns them first to bear,
Making them women of good carriage.
This is she—

Romeo. Peace, peace, Mercutio, peace.
Thou talk'st of nothing.

Mer. True, I talk of dreams,
Which are the children of an idle brain,
Begot of nothing but vain fantasy,
Which is as thin of substance as the air
And more inconstant than the wind, who woos
Even now the frozen bosom of the north
And, being anger'd, puffs away from thence
Turning his side to the dew-dropping south.

Ben. This wind you talk of blows us from ourselves:
Supper is done and we shall come too late.

Romeo. I fear too early, for my mind misgives
Some consequence yet hanging in the stars
Shall bitterly begin his fearful date
With this night's revels, and expire the term
Of a despised life clos'd in my breast
By some vile forfeit of untimely death.
But he that hath the steerage of my course

90. elf-locks] *Q1,Q4;* Elklocks *Q2,3,F.* 103. side] *Q2–4,F;* face *Q1.* 112. steerage] *Q2–4,F* (stirrage), *Q1.*

92–3. *maids . . . bear*] The nightmare (*hag*) is an incubus. The superstitions surrounding erotic dreams are ancient, but Mercutio pursues a flippant line of thought to a bawdy quibble.

94. *carriage*] Quibbling on 'deportment', 'bearing children', 'taking a lover's weight'.

96. *nothing*] Quibbling on the bawdy sense, vagina (cf. Partridge, sv *O*).

107–11. *Some . . . death*] *date* is linked with *expire* and *term*; cf. Daniel, *Rosamond*, ll. 241–2: 'But that those rayes which all these flames doe nourish, / Canceld with Time, will haue their date expyred'. Romeo has mortgaged his life from a date set as that evening, the mortgage will be forfeit because by the end of the period (*term*) agreed, he will not be able to pay and will lose his life. The repeated emphasis on darkly ominous feelings counterpoints the approaching feast.

Direct my suit. On, lusty gentlemen.
Ben. Strike, drum.

[Scene V] *They march about the stage, and* Servingmen *come forth with napkins.*

First Ser. Where's Potpan that he helps not to take away?
He shift a trencher! He scrape a trencher!
Second Ser. When good manners shall lie all in one or two

113. suit] *Q2–4,F* (sute); saile *Q1*.

Scene V

Scene v] *Steevens; not in Q2–4,F,Q1.* *Location.*] *A hall in Capulet's house. Theobald.* S.D.] *ed.; They . . . napkins. Enter* Romeo. *Q2–4; They . . . their napkins. Enter Seruant, F; not in Q1.* 1. *First Ser.*] *ed.; Ser. Q2–4,F; not in Q1.* 3. *Second Ser.*] *ed.; 1. Q2–4,F; not in Q1.* all] *Q2–4; not in F,Q1.*

113. *suit*] Dr Johnson considers *suit* to refer to 'the sequel of the adventure'. Spenser, *Faerie Queene*, v. viii. 3, has 'Suite of his auowed quest' with the sense of 'pursuit of an object or quest'; the word is also used of hunting and courtship and, legally, of the prosecution of a cause, all appropriate subsidiary associations with the main idea of Romeo's quest, controlled by destiny. Q1's *saile* seems, as Steevens observes, 'more congruous to the metaphor in the preceding line', and, it might be added, to the wider association in the play of destiny with sea-voyaging; cf. II. ii. 82–4, III. v. 130–7, v. iii. 116–18: so also *Oth.*, v. ii. 270–1. Yet it is highly characteristic of Shakespeare's style at this period to intensify the metaphoric richness of the language by joining together, unexpectedly, heterogeneous ideas: the variable senses of *suit* are more effective in this than the simpler *sail*.

114. *Scene* v] Scene IV ends here according to Steevens, who is followed in this division by many editors.

Scene V

S.D. *They march . . . napkins.*] In Q2 there is no formal scene change here; the action of marching about and the entrance of servingmen establishes the new locality. Romeo has not left the stage, so Q2's '*Enter* Romeo' is an error.

1–10. *Where's . . . Potpan.*] Evidently these two are established household servants taking a share of the delicacies for the feast and having their own party later, to which Susan Grindstone and Nell are invited.

2. *trencher*] According to Harrison's *Description of England* (1587) wooden trenchers were giving way to plate in the houses of gentlemen, merchants, and other wealthy citizens in the early part of Elizabeth's reign, and as we learn in l. 7 below Capulet has plate on display; perhaps the trenchers are necessary for the large numbers invited (Lincoln's Inn in 1827 was still using wooden trenchers in hall, according to Singer).

3. *good manners*] There is a quibble on *hands* in l. 4, playing on the root in Latin, *manuarius*, 'belonging to the hand' (OED).

men's hands, and they unwashed too, 'tis a foul thing.

First Ser. Away with the joint-stools, remove the court-cupboard, look to the plate. Good thou, save me a piece of marchpane, and as thou loves me, let the porter let in Susan Grindstone and Nell—Anthony, and Potpan!

Third Ser. Ay boy, ready.

First Ser. You are looked for and called for, asked for and sought for, in the great chamber.

Fourth Ser. We cannot be here and there too. Cheerly, boys! Be brisk awhile, and the longer liver take all.

Exeunt [*Servingmen*].

Enter [CAPULET, LADY CAPULET, JULIET, TYBALT, NURSE *and*] *all the* Guests *and* Gentlewomen *to the Masquers.*

Cap. Welcome, gentlemen, ladies that have their toes

6. *First Ser.*] *ed.; Ser. Q2–4,F; not in Q1.* 8. loves] *Q2–4;* lovest *F; not in Q1.* 11. *Third Ser.*] *ed.; 2. Q2–4,F; not in Q1.* 12. *First Ser.*] *ed.; Ser. Q2–4,F; not in Q1.* 14. *Fourth Ser.*] *ed.; 3. Q2–4,F; not in Q1.* 15. S.D. (i)] *ed.; Exeunt. Q2–4,F; not in Q1; They retire behind. Malone.* S.D. (ii)] *Furness; Enter all . . . Maskers. Q2–4,F; Enter old* Capulet *with the Ladies. Q1.* 16. *Cap.*] *ed.; 1. Capu. Q2–4,F; Capu: Q1.*

6. *joint-stools*] common wooden stools (chairs were scarce even in important houses); in a large hall they were packed with their legs turned inwards under the long tables, resting on the stretchers, when the meal was over (*Shakespeare's England*, II, p. 121).

6–7. *court-cupboard*] Court-cupboards stood at the ends of the hall and contained wine, fruit, cordials, spoons and table linen; silver plate might be displayed on them (ibid., p. 123). The court-cupboard is to be removed to give more room and, possibly, because it is valuable. It would not normally be removed after meals.

8. *marchpane*] marzipan: for special occasions sometimes garnished 'with prettie conceipts, as birdes and beasts, being cast out of standing moldes', sometimes gilded, or moulded in letters, knots and other devices (*Delightes for Ladies*, 1608, quoted by Nares).

11, 12, 14. S.P.] The assignment of these speeches is very vague in Q2; presumably the third and fourth servingmen are Anthony and Potpan.

13. *great chamber*] Presumably the servingmen are already in the hall, the obvious place for dancing; perhaps Capulet's mansion is imagined as having an ante-room adjoining the hall.

15. *longer . . . all*] Proverbial (Tilley L 395); the *longer liver* is Death, so the proverb encourages the enjoyment of life while it lasts.

16. *Welcome*] Addressed to Romeo and his masked companions.

Unplagu'd with corns will walk a bout with you.
Ah my mistresses, which of you all
Will now deny to dance? She that makes dainty,
She I'll swear hath corns. Am I come near ye now?
Welcome, gentlemen. I have seen the day
That I have worn a visor and could tell
A whispering tale in a fair lady's ear,
Such as would please. 'Tis gone, 'tis gone, 'tis gone,
You are welcome, gentlemen: come, musicians, play.
A hall, a hall, give room! And foot it girls!

Music plays and they dance.

More light, you knaves, and turn the tables up.
And quench the fire, the room is grown too hot.
Ah sirrah, this unlook'd-for sport comes well.
Nay sit, nay sit, good cousin Capulet,
For you and I are past our dancing days.
How long is't now since last yourself and I
Were in a masque?

Cousin Cap. By'r Lady, thirty years.

Cap. What, man, 'tis not so much, 'tis not so much.
'Tis since the nuptial of Lucentio,
Come Pentecost as quickly as it will,
Some five and twenty years: and then we masqu'd.

17. walk a bout] *Daniel;* walke about *Q2–4,F;* haue about *Q1.* 20. ye] *Q2, 3,F;* you *Q4,Q1.* 26. A hall, a hall] *Q2–4;* A Hall, Hall *F; not in Q1.* 33. *Cousin Cap.*] *ed.; 2. Capu. Q2–4,F; Cos: Q1.* 34. *Cap.*] *ed.; 1. Capu. Q2–4, F; Cap: Q1.* 35. Lucentio] *Q1,F;* Lucientio *Q2–4.*

17. *walk a bout*] Q1 supports the reading *a bout* (= some kind of round dance). The sense is 'dance a turn' (Sisson).

19. *makes dainty*] primly hesitates.

20. *Am I . . . now?*] Am I near the mark? Cf. *1H4*, I. ii. 12.

26. *A hall, a hall*] Clear the floor!

27. *turn the tables up*] Trestle tables are dismantled by removing fixing-pegs, lifting off the tops, and stacking tops and trestles against the walls.

28. *quench the fire*] In Brooke the feast takes place near Christmas; possibly when writing these lines Shakespeare forgot that he set the action in July (see I. iii. 14–15); cf. I. ii. 20 n., and Intro, p. 38.

29. *Ah sirrah*] Perhaps to his cousin, perhaps to himself, as Onions suggests; cf. l. 125.

unlook'd-for sport] Alluding to the unexpected arrival of the masked party of strangers.

30. *cousin*] Used as an affectionate form of address to any kinsman.

31. *past our dancing days*] Proverbial; cf. Tilley D 118.

36. *Pentecost*] Whit-Sunday.

Cousin Cap. 'Tis more, 'tis more, his son is elder, sir:
His son is thirty.
Cap. Will you tell me that?
His son was but a ward two years ago.
Romeo. What lady's that which doth enrich the hand
Of yonder knight?
Ser. I know not, sir.
Romeo. O, she doth teach the torches to burn bright.
It seems she hangs upon the cheek of night
As a rich jewel in an Ethiop's ear—
Beauty too rich for use, for earth too dear.
So shows a snowy dove trooping with crows
As yonder lady o'er her fellows shows.
The measure done, I'll watch her place of stand,
And touching hers, make blessed my rude hand.
Did my heart love till now? Forswear it, sight.
For I ne'er saw true beauty till this night.
Tyb. This by his voice should be a Montague.
Fetch me my rapier, boy. [*Exit Boy.*] What, dares the slave
Come hither, cover'd with an antic face,
To fleer and scorn at our solemnity?
Now by the stock and honour of my kin,
To strike him dead I hold it not a sin.
Cap. Why how now, kinsman, wherefore storm you so?

38. *Cousin Cap.*] *ed.; 2. Capu. Q2–4; 2. Cap. F; Cos: Q1.* 39. *Cap.*] *ed.; 1. Capu. Q2–4; 3. Cap. F; Cap: Q1.* 41. lady's] *Q2* (Ladies), *Pope;* Ladie is *Q3,4,F,Q1.* 45. As] *Q2–4,F;* Like *Q1.* 47. snowy] *Q2,3,F;* snowe *Q4;* snow-white *Q1.* 52. For I ne'er] *Q2–4;* For I never *F;* I neuer *Q1.* 54. S.D.] *Collier*[2]*; not in Q2–4,F,Q1.* 59. *Cap.*] *ed.; Capu. Q2–4; Cap. F; Ca: Q1.*

40. *a ward*] A minor, under the control of a guardian until he reached the age of twenty-one.

42. *yonder knight*] Cf. Brooke, l. 246: 'With torche in hand a comly knight did fetch her foorth to daunce'.

44. *It seems she*] Absurdly, Knight defended the F2 reading, 'Her beauty' (which he admitted involves the rejection of 'an undoubted ancient reading'), because it 'has passed into common use wherever our language is spoken . . . Here, it appears to us, is a higher law to be observed than that of adherence to the ancient copies.'

45. *rich . . . ear*] Cf. III. ii. 17; Marlowe, *Hero and Leander*, II. 240: 'Rich iewels in the darke are soonest spide'.

47. *shows*] appears.

55. *antic face*] Alluding to Romeo's mask.

56. *fleer*] grin contemptuously.
solemnity] celebration.

Tyb. Uncle, this is a Montague, our foe:
A villain that is hither come in spite
To scorn at our solemnity this night.
Cap. Young Romeo is it?
Tyb. 'Tis he, that villain Romeo.
Cap. Content thee, gentle coz, let him alone,
A bears him like a portly gentleman;
And, to say truth, Verona brags of him
To be a virtuous and well-govern'd youth.
I would not for the wealth of all this town
Here in my house do him disparagement.
Therefore be patient, take no note of him.
It is my will, the which if thou respect,
Show a fair presence and put off these frowns,
An ill-beseeming semblance for a feast.
Tyb. It fits when such a villain is a guest:
I'll not endure him.
Cap. He shall be endur'd.
What, goodman boy! I say he shall! Go to,
Am I the master here or you? Go to.
You'll not endure him! God shall mend my soul,
You'll make a mutiny among my guests,
You will set cock-a-hoop, you'll be the man!
Tyb. Why, uncle, 'tis a shame.
Cap. Go to, go to.

63. *Cap.*] *ed.; Capu. Q2–4; Cap. F; Ca: Q1* (*so also at ll. 75, 81, 120*). 64. *Cap.*] *Q2,F; Capu. Q3,4; Ca: Q1.* 68. this] *Q2–4,Q1;* the *F.* 79. my] *Q2–4,Q1;* the *F.* 80. set] *Q2,3,F,Q1;* sꞇt a *Q4.*

65. *portly*] well-mannered, of good deportment.

66. *brags*] talks with just pride (OED records only the more usual sense, 'boast').

69. *disparagement*] impoliteness.

73. *semblance*] expression.

76. *goodman boy*] Capulet slights Tybalt's youth with *boy* and his ill-bred attitude with *goodman*, prefixed to the names of persons below the rank of gentleman, especially yeomen and farmers (OED 3 b). Cf. *Lr*, II. ii. 41.

Go to] Expressing protest and impatience.

80. *set cock-a-hoop*] abandon all restraint (with a subsidiary sense 'have things your own way'); OED calls it 'of doubtful origin', noting associations with the boastfulness of a fighting (or crowing) cock, and with unrestrained drinking, when the *cock* (spigot) is removed from the barrel and placed on its *hoop* on top.

be the man] play the man, give the orders.

You are a saucy boy. Is't so indeed?
This trick may chance to scathe you. I know what.
You must contrary me. Marry, 'tis time—
Well said, my hearts—You are a princox, go
Be quiet, or—More light! More light!—For shame,
I'll make you quiet. What, cheerly, my hearts!

Tyb. Patience perforce with wilful choler meeting
Makes my flesh tremble in their different greeting.
I will withdraw; but this intrusion shall
Now seeming sweet, convert to bitt'rest gall. *Exit.*

Romeo. If I profane with my unworthiest hand
This holy shrine, the gentle sin is this:
My lips, two blushing pilgrims, ready stand
To smooth that rough touch with a tender kiss.

Juliet. Good pilgrim, you do wrong your hand too much,

91. bitt'rest] *Q2;* bitter *Q3,4,F,Q1.* 93. sin] *Q2–4,F,Q1;* fine *Theobald, conj. Warburton;* pain *NCS.* 94. two] *Q2–4,Q1;* to *F.* ready] *Q1;* did ready *Q2–4,F.*

82. *saucy boy*] Both terms are stronger than in modern English: Capulet, having suddenly become angry, tells Tybalt he is insolent and childish.

83. *scathe*] injure.

I know what] i.e. I know what I am doing, I mean what I say.

84. *Marry, 'tis time*] i.e. it is time I rebuked you for quarrelling (or, possibly, it is time you accepted my rebuke). There is irony as well as comedy in Old Capulet's sudden rage at the same family characteristic in Tybalt.

85. *Well . . . hearts*] Bravo, good friends! (to the dancers).

You . . . go] Addressed once more to Tybalt, who is called an impertinent youth. Cf. Nashe, *Pierce Pennilesse, Works*, I, p. 23: 'A Caualier of the first feather, a princockes that was but a Page the other day in the Court'.

88. *Patience . . . choler*] Tybalt considers *himself* patient, and *Capulet* wilfully choleric.

89. *different greeting*] the meeting of opposed states (of patience and choler).

92–105. *If . . . take*] Romeo's first words to Juliet begin a sonnet which Juliet shares and which ends in a kiss. The motifs of hands and pilgrimage are intertwined by the lovers in a series of conceits that advance courtship while exalting, purifying and intensifying feeling; the lovers are separated from the rest of the company in a special and quite new tone. Romeo may choose the pilgrimage motif in self-conscious play upon the meaning of *romeo* in Italian, which Florio records as *roamer, wanderer* or *palmer*. Even if the rather implausible suggestion that his masking costume is a pilgrim's is dismissed, there is a private meaning for him in the conceit, since he feels himself, unlike his companions, dedicated to love and its service; the pursuit of the ideal is a journey to a 'straunge stronde' and not without hazard.

93. *gentle sin*] Q1's *sinne* supports the Q2 reading; cf. III. iii. 39. Harold Jenkins proposes *gentler sin*: if Romeo profanes her hand (by holding it) he could atone by a *gentler* sin, defined in the next two lines.

Which mannerly devotion shows in this;
For saints have hands that pilgrims' hands do touch,
And palm to palm is holy palmers' kiss.
Romeo. Have not saints lips, and holy palmers too?
Juliet. Ay, pilgrim, lips that they must use in prayer.
Romeo. O then, dear saint, let lips do what hands do:
They pray: grant thou, lest faith turn to despair.
Juliet. Saints do not move, though grant for prayer's sake.
Romeo. Then move not, while my prayer's effect I take.
[*He kisses her.*]
Thus from my lips, by thine, my sin is purg'd.
Juliet. Then have my lips the sin that they have took.
Romeo. Sin from my lips? O trespass sweetly urg'd.
Give me my sin again. [*He kisses her.*]
Juliet. You kiss by th'book.
Nurse. Madam, your mother craves a word with you.
Romeo. What is her mother?
Nurse. Marry bachelor,
Her mother is the lady of the house,
And a good lady, and a wise and virtuous.
I nurs'd her daughter that you talk'd withal.
I tell you, he that can lay hold of her
Shall have the chinks.

98. that] *Q2–4,F;* which *Q1.* 105. S.D.] *Rowe (after l. 106); not in Q2–4,F, Q1.* 109. S.D.] *Capell; not in Q2–4,F,Q1.*

97. *mannerly*] decent, modest; with a quibble on 'belonging to the hand'; cf. I. v. 3 n.

98. *saints*] i.e. stone statues or images of saints.

99. *palm to palm*] Pilgrims who had visited the Holy Sepulchre at Jerusalem originally bore a palm branch or leaf to signify the fact; Juliet quibbles on the sense 'palm of the hand'. Cf. Brooke, l. 267: 'Then she with tender hand his tender palme hath prest'.

104. *Saints . . . move*] Juliet answers that a statue, as Romeo has called her, does not move, though the saint may grant a prayer.

106–9. *Thus . . . book*] A fresh sonnet begins, but is interrupted by the Nurse.

108. *urg'd*] put forward in argument.

109. *by th'book*] 'As if you had learned from a book of etiquette' and also 'by means of sonnet rhymes and conceits'. The playful criticism is not intended to discourage, though elsewhere Shakespeare's characters use the phrase with strong disparagement, as in III. i. 103.

111. *bachelor*] young gentleman: perhaps the word was suggested by Brooke, l. 163.

116. *the chinks*] plenty of money: probably with a bawdy innuendo as in *MND*, v. i. 157, 174.

Romeo. Is she a Capulet?
O dear account. My life is my foe's debt.
Ben. Away, be gone, the sport is at the best.
Romeo. Ay, so I fear; the more is my unrest.
Cap. Nay, gentlemen, prepare not to be gone,
We have a trifling foolish banquet towards.
They whisper in his ear.
Is it e'en so? Why then, I thank you all;
I thank you honest gentlemen, good night.
More torches here. Come on then, let's to bed.
Ah sirrah, by my fay, it waxes late,
I'll to my rest.
[*Exeunt Capulet, Lady Capulet, Guests, Gentlewomen and Masquers.*]
Juliet. Come hither Nurse. What is yond gentleman?
Nurse. The son and heir of old Tiberio.
Juliet. What's he that now is going out of door?
Nurse. Marry, that I think be young Petruchio.
Juliet. What's he that follows here, that would not dance?
Nurse. I know not.
Juliet. Go ask his name. If he be married,
My grave is like to be my wedding bed.
Nurse. His name is Romeo, and a Montague,
The only son of your great enemy.
Juliet. My only love sprung from my only hate.
Too early seen unknown, and known too late.
Prodigious birth of love it is to me
That I must love a loathed enemy.
Nurse. What's this? What's this?

121. S.D.] *Q1; not in Q2–4,F.* 126. S.D.] *ed.; Exeunt. Q1; not in Q2–4,F; Exeunt all but Juliet and Nurse. Malone.* 129. of] *Q2,3,F,Q1;* of the *Q4.* 131. here] *Q2–4,F;* there *Q1.* 134. wedding] *Q2–4,Q1;* wedded *F.* 141. this? ... this?] *F;* tis? ... tis? *Q2–4;* this? ... that? *Q1.* What's] *Q2,3,F,Q1;* What *Q4.*

117. *dear account*] terrible reckoning.

118. *sport ... best*] Proverbial; see I. iv. 39 n.

121. *banquet*] light refreshment of fruit, wine and delicacies.

123. *honest*] honourable.

141. *this ... this*] Q1's reading seems to be a typical memorial error; Williams (*MLR*, Jan. 1960, p. 79) argues that *tis* is not a misprint but a common dialect or subliterary pronounciation of *this*.

Juliet. A rhyme I learn'd even now
Of one I danc'd withal. *One calls within:* 'Juliet'.
Nurse. Anon, anon!
Come let's away, the strangers all are gone. *Exeunt.*

141. learn'd] *Q2–4,Q1* (learnt)*;* learne *F.* 143. all are] *Q2,3,F;* are all *Q4; not in Q1.*

[ACT II]

[PROLOGUE]

[*Enter*] CHORUS.

Chorus. Now old desire doth in his deathbed lie
And young affection gapes to be his heir;
That fair for which love groan'd for and would die,
With tender Juliet match'd, is now not fair.
Now Romeo is belov'd and loves again,
Alike bewitched by the charm of looks,
But to his foe suppos'd he must complain
And she steal love's sweet bait from fearful hooks.
Being held a foe, he may not have access
To breathe such vows as lovers use to swear;
And she as much in love, her means much less
To meet her new beloved anywhere.
But passion lends them power, time means, to meet,
Tempering extremities with extreme sweet. [*Exit*.]

ACT II

Prologue

ACT II PROLOGUE] *Camb.; not in Q2–4,F,Q1.* S.D.] *Camb.; Chorus. Q2–4,F; not in Q1.* 1. *Chorus.*] *Camb.; not in Q2–4,F,Q1.* 1–14.] *Q2–4,F; not in Q1.* 4. match'd] *Q3,4,F;* match *Q2.* 14. S.D.] *Theobald; not in Q2–4,F,Q1.*

Chorus.] The whole 14 lines (in form a sonnet) are omitted in Q1. Dr Johnson observed: 'The use of this chorus is not easily discovered. It conduces nothing to the progress of the play, but relates what is already known, or what the next scenes will shew; and relates it without adding the improvement of any moral sentiment.'

2. *gapes*] Used of those eagerly awaiting a large inheritance; cf. Jonson, *Volpone*, I. ii. 95–7.

3. *fair*] i.e. Rosaline.

groan'd for] Rowe conjectures a misreading of MS. *sore*. The duplication is compared by Hudson to *AYL*, II. vii. 139.

6. *Alike*] As she that loves him.

7. *foe*] Because Juliet is a Capulet.

complain] make love-laments.

14. *Tempering extremities*] Mollifying hardships. Since the verb *temper* can mean the process of bringing steel to a

[SCENE I]

Enter ROMEO *alone.*

Romeo. Can I go forward when my heart is here?
Turn back, dull earth, and find thy centre out.
[*Withdraws.*]

Enter BENVOLIO *with* MERCUTIO.

Ben. Romeo! My cousin Romeo! Romeo!
Mer. He is wise,
And on my life hath stol'n him home to bed.
Ben. He ran this way and leapt this orchard wall.

Scene I

SCENE I] *Ulrici; not in Q2–4,F,Q1.* *Location.*] *The Street. Rowe; Wall of Capulet's Garden. Capell.* 1–29.] *As Q2–4,F; prose in Q1.* 2. S.D.] *ed.; not in Q2–4, F,Q1; Exit. Rowe; Leaps the Wall. Capell; He climbs the wall, and leaps down within it. Camb.* 3. Romeo! Romeo!] *Q2–4,F; Romeo. Q1.*

suitable hardness and resilience by heating, or tuning a musical instrument, the idea of melting or softening is accompanied by the resulting greater hardness, tautness, or high pitch: all appropriate to the situation.

Scene I

2. *dull earth*] Romeo thinks of himself as a dull and muddy-mettled rascal; he must find Juliet, the centre of his microcosm now (Brooke, l. 829); cf. *Troil.*, IV. ii. 102–4.

5. *leapt . . . wall*] Cf. *2H6*, IV. x. 6–7, where Cade says he has climbed a brick wall into Iden's garden. The present scene can be staged with the utmost simplicity, Romeo entering through a door, concealing himself behind a stage post when Mercutio and Benvolio enter seeking him; the words alone create an intense sense of place, and control the mood; no support is actually needed from elaborate staging, and there is a danger, should it be used, of upsetting the pace and rhythm which are calculated with great care in this scene. The joke in *MND*, III. i, when Snout protests 'You can never bring in a wall' is probably connected—but as a *joke*—with the present scene in *Rom.* Although it has been suggested that a practicable wall was erected on stage for this scene, there are several objections to the proposal. The atmosphere of the scene must not be endangered by bathetic accidents or some obtrusive, or cumbrous, or unconvincing property; sight-lines must not be obstructed. A wall big enough to suggest a real orchard wall, and to make Romeo's leap impressive, could be cumbrous, must be dismantled after only one scene, and would obstruct sight lines. A token small wall would be as distractingly ridiculous as that impersonated by Snout in *MND.* J. W. Saunders, in *Sh.S.*, 7 (1954), suggests that Romeo, followed by Benvolio and Mercutio, enters at yard level; Romeo vaults up on to the stage, which then becomes the orchard; his friends remain at yard level. This seems practicable, except that some groundling spectators would not be able to see what was going on, which is probably a decisive objection. Yet such speculations imply that Shake-

Call, good Mercutio.
Mer. Nay, I'll conjure too:
Romeo! Humours! Madman! Passion! Lover!
Appear thou in the likeness of a sigh,
Speak but one rhyme and I am satisfied.
Cry but 'Ay me!' Pronounce but 'love' and 'dove',
Speak to my gossip Venus one fair word,
One nickname for her purblind son and heir,
Young Abraham Cupid, he that shot so trim

6. *Mer.*] *Q1,Q4; not in Q2,3,F.* 7. Romeo!] *Q1,Q4; Mer. Romeo Q2,3,F.* Madman] *Q2,3,F,Q1;* madam *Q4.* Lover] *Q2–4,F;* liver *Q1.* 9. one] *Q1,Q3,4,F;* on *Q2.* 10. Cry] *Q2–4,Q1;* Cry me *F.* Pronounce] *Q1,Q4;* prouaunt *Q2,3,F;* Couply *F2;* couple *Rowe.* dove] *Q1;* day *Q2,3,F;* die *Q4.* 12. heir] *Q1,Q4;* her *Q2,3,F.* 13. Abraham] *Q2–4,F,Q1* (*subst.*); Adam *Steevens 1778, conj. Upton;* auburn *conj. Warburton.* trim] *Q1, Steevens;* true *Q2–4,F.*

speare here sought, quite uncharacteristically, a literal-minded kind of stage realism which is not sought anywhere else in the play's stagecraft, with its swift and simple shifts of imagined location, and I do not find these suggestions at all plausible.

6. *Mer.*] The placing of the speech prefix in Q1 may be a genuine and correct memory; it makes much more sense than in Q2, where Benvolio says *Nay I'll conjure too* only for the actual conjuring to be done by Mercutio; Q4 must be an intelligent guess.

conjure] Mercutio burlesques the ritual summoning of a spirit by calling its different names; when the right one is spoken the spirit, it is supposed, will appear and speak. The names are mocking synonyms for Romeo.

7. *Lover*] Q1 reads *liver* for *lover.* Since the liver is the seat of the disease of love, Greg (*Aspects of Shakespeare*, ed. J. W. MacKail, p. 147) considers this reading plausible.

10. *Pronounce*] Q1's *pronounce* makes very good sense. The compositor of Q2 obviously ignored Q1 and followed the manuscript which must have been difficult to decipher. The word in the manuscript may have appeared in Shakespeare's idiosyncratic spelling, without the final *e.* In hand D (the possibly Shakespearean part of the MS. of *Sir Thomas More*) appear the spellings *obedyenc, insolenc, offyc.* The error of *day* for *doue* must also be ascribed to misreading of manuscript. *Provant* as a verb = to provision (Nashe, 1599, cited in OED).

11. *gossip*] Originally a godmother, hence a woman invited to be present at a birth as a familiar friend, hence a merry or convivial old woman.

13. *Abraham Cupid*] Many emendations have been proposed for this reading. Upton supposed *Abraham* a misreading of *Adam*, an allusion to the proverbially skilful archer Adam Bell (cf. *Ado*, I. i. 244), but this would be more graphically plausible if the text had the shortened form *Abram*, even though the short and long form are equal alternatives. *Abraham-Abram* (auburn) meaning blond is found e.g. in *Cor.*, II. iii. 20, and this is possible here. Knight proposed an allusion to the 'cheat—the "Abraham-man"—of our old statutes' and NCS has the note 'The sly rogue Cupid, with nothing but a scarf about his loins, is like the abraham men, who wandered

When King Cophetua lov'd the beggar maid.
He heareth not, he stirreth not, he moveth not:
The ape is dead and I must conjure him.
I conjure thee by Rosaline's bright eyes,
By her high forehead and her scarlet lip,
By her fine foot, straight leg, and quivering thigh,
And the demesnes that there adjacent lie,
That in thy likeness thou appear to us.

Ben. And if he hear thee, thou wilt anger him.

Mer. This cannot anger him. 'Twould anger him
To raise a spirit in his mistress' circle
Of some strange nature, letting it there stand
Till she had laid it and conjur'd it down:
That were some spite. My invocation
Is fair and honest; in his mistress' name
I conjure only but to raise up him.

15. stirreth] *Q2,4,F;* striueth *Q3; not in Q1.* 16. and] *Q2–4; not in F,Q1.* 17. thee] *Q2,4,F,Q1;* the *Q3.* 25. there stand] *Q2–4;* stand *F;* there to stand *Q1.* 28. in] *Q2;* and in *Q3,4,F,Q1.*

half-naked about the world begging and stealing'; cf. *Lr*, II. iii. 9–20. Hoppe sees an allusion to the proverbial phrase 'old as Abraham' which is the basis for the conceit on Cupid's eternal youth, as in *LLL*, v. ii. 11: 'he hath been five thousand year a boy'. These ideas of extreme old age yoked to extreme youth, of slyness, of blond hair, near nakedness (of beggar and god) all seem appropriate to the present context; the teeming allusiveness seems altogether characteristic of the young Shakespeare. An editor, lacking evidence of corruption, may not emend.

trim] Q1 preserves the wording of the line in the ballad of King Cophetua and the Beggar Maid: 'The blinded boy that shoots so trim', alluded to in *LLL*, I. ii. 106–7, IV. i. 66–8, *R2*, v. iii. 80, and *2H4*, v. iii. 104. Shakespeare evidently knew it well.

14. *King . . . maid*] In *LLL*, IV. i. 66–82, some detail is given; R. David (Arden ed.) believes from scattered allusions, which he cites, that it had scurvy words and tune, not at all like the version in Percy's *Reliques* (1st series, II. 6), which is insufficiently old and too dainty. David thinks there had been a drama on the subject also.

16. *ape is dead*] Evidently alluding to a fairground trick in which an ape lies feigning death until revived by his master with some fustian ceremony (Strunk, *MLN*, XXXII, pp. 215–21).

17. *Rosaline's*] Mercutio remains unaware of the change in Romeo's affections in the previous scene.

24. *raise . . . circle*] Bawdy quibbling after l. 16's *conjure*, on *spirit* (i) demon, (ii) penis, and *circle* (i) conjuror's magic circle, (ii) vagina.

25. *strange*] belonging to a stranger, not to Romeo.

stand] With a bawdy quibble (on sexual erection).

26. *laid . . . down*] i.e. made it powerless and caused it to depart (with a bawdy quibble).

29. *raise up him*] With a bawdy quibble, as on *stand* in l. 25 above.

Ben. Come, he hath hid himself among these trees
To be consorted with the humorous night.
Blind is his love, and best befits the dark.
Mer. If love be blind, love cannot hit the mark.
Now will he sit under a medlar tree
And wish his mistress were that kind of fruit
As maids call medlars when they laugh alone.
O Romeo, that she were, O that she were
An open-arse and thou a poperin pear!
Romeo, good night. I'll to my truckle-bed.
This field-bed is too cold for me to sleep.
Come, shall we go?
Ben. Go then, for 'tis in vain
To seek him here that means not to be found.
Exeunt [Benvolio and Mercutio].

38. open-arse and] *NCS;* open-arse or *Hosley;* open, or *Q2,3,F;* open *Et cetera, Q1;* open *&* *catera,* and *Q4.* 42. S.D.] *ed.; Exit. Q2,3; Exeunt. Q4,F; not in Q1.*

31. *consorted*] associated.

humorous] damp, but also whimsical, full of fantastic notions (Kittredge).

33. *mark*] target (with a bawdy quibble; cf. Partridge, sv *mark*).

36. *medlars*] A fruit, proverbially 'never good till they be rotten' (Tilley M 863), thought to resemble the female genitalia, with an additional quibble on *medlar/meddler* (*meddle* = to have sexual intercourse with: OED v 5).

38. *open-arse*] A dialect name for the medlar. Farmer and Henley, *Slang and its Analogues* (1902), suggested that Q2's *open, or* meant *open-arse* and Hosley was the first editor to adopt the reading. OED records Q2's form as a variant spelling of *open-arse*, or *openers* (as in Chaucer, *Reeve's Prol.*, l. 17). Presumably Q2's compositor misunderstood and Q1's reporter replaced the word by the euphemism *etc.*

poperin] Bawdy quibbles on (i) the *name* of a kind of pear from Poperinghe, near Ypres, and (ii) (*poperin* = pop her in) on its *shape*, resembling the male genitalia.

39. *truckle-bed*] A small bed on wheels which was pushed under a higher bed when not in use; normally a servant or child slept in it.

40. *field-bed*] Punning on the portable or camp bed, as used by soldiers during a campaign, and the literal sense 'bed on the ground'. No doubt Mercutio's jest lies in pretending he sleeps on a truckle-bed; the subsidiary puns and associations develop this; he imagines Romeo to be still listening, so the talk of beds has added point. Brooke, ll. 897–8, has: 'she shewd a fieldbed ready dight / Where you may, if you list, in armes, revenge yourself by fight'. The motif of love as war recurs, immediately before we hear Romeo and Juliet declare the perfect harmony of their feelings for each other.

[Scene II]

[*Romeo comes forward.*]

Romeo. He jests at scars that never felt a wound.

[*Enter* JULIET *above.*]

But soft, what light through yonder window breaks?
It is the east and Juliet is the sun!
Arise fair sun and kill the envious moon
Who is already sick and pale with grief
That thou her maid art far more fair than she.
Be not her maid since she is envious,
Her vestal livery is but sick and green
And none but fools do wear it. Cast it off.
It is my lady, O it is my love!
O that she knew she were!
She speaks, yet she says nothing. What of that?
Her eye discourses, I will answer it.
I am too bold. 'Tis not to me she speaks.
Two of the fairest stars in all the heaven,
Having some business, do entreat her eyes

Scene II

SCENE II] *Hanmer; not in Q2–4,F,Q1.* *Location.*] *Capulet's Garden. Theobald.* S.D.] *Spencer; not in Q2–4,F,Q1.* 1. S.D.] *Capell; not in Q2–4,F,Q1.* 6. art] *Q2,3,F,Q1;* at *Q4.* 8. sick] *Q2–4,F;* pale *Q1, Singer*[2]. 16. do] *Q1,Q3,4,F;* to *Q2.*

Scene II

S.D.] Romeo has not left the stage; he emerges from behind whatever concealment he has found, or takes the centre of the stage. It is traditional, and hence convenient for reference, to mark a new scene here, but the opening line rhymes with Benvolio's last line, revealing the actual continuity.

1. *felt a wound*] An ironic anticipation of later events which almost imperceptibly adds to the cumulative sense of fatefulness in the action.

S.D.] According to Q1 Juliet appears at a window in the tiring-house façade, not at a balcony.

2–3. *But . . . sun*] Cf. Marlowe, *The Jew of Malta*, II, i. 680–1: 'But stay, what starre shines yonder in the East? / The Loadstarre of my life, if Abigall'.

8. *vestal*] virginally chaste and pure (originally, resembling a priestess at the Temple of Vesta in Rome); cf. *Locrine* (1595), V. iv. 54: 'the girle is wise, and well would seeme to make a vestall Nunne'.

sick and green] To prefer Q1's *pale* to Q2's *sick* is to obscure the reference to 'green-sickness', a disease incident to maids; cf. III. v. 156.

9. *none but fools*] White and green had been the royal livery in Henry VIII's reign; but the emphasis here is on motley: the court jester's coat of motley would include green.

To twinkle in their spheres till they return.
What if her eyes were there, they in her head?
The brightness of her cheek would shame those stars
As daylight doth a lamp. Her eyes in heaven
Would through the airy region stream so bright
That birds would sing and think it were not night.
See how she leans her cheek upon her hand.
O that I were a glove upon that hand,
That I might touch that cheek.

Juliet. Ay me.

Romeo. She speaks.
O speak again bright angel, for thou art
As glorious to this night, being o'er my head,
As is a winged messenger of heaven
Unto the white-upturned wondering eyes
Of mortals that fall back to gaze on him
When he bestrides the lazy-puffing clouds
And sails upon the bosom of the air.

Juliet. O Romeo, Romeo, wherefore art thou Romeo?
Deny thy father and refuse thy name.

20. eyes] *Q1, Pope;* eye *Q2–4,F.* 23. how] *Q2–4,F;* now *Q1.* 31. lazy-puffing] *Q2–4,F;* lasie pacing *Q1, Pope;* lazy-passing *Ulrici, conj. Collier.*

17. *spheres*] Alluding to the concentric spheres of the Ptolemaic system, in which the planets were supposed to move, with the earth as centre.

28. *winged messenger*] angel.

29. *white-upturned*] turned up so far that the whites show clearly.

31. *lazy-puffing*] Defending Q2, White observes 'the lazy-puffing clouds are the slow-moving cumuli that puff themselves out into swelling breasts of rose-tinted white' but he notes the attraction of *pacing* in connection with *bestrides* and its anticipation of *Mac.*, I. vii. 21–3: 'pity like a naked new-born babe, / Striding the blast, or heaven's cherubin hors'd / Upon the sightless couriers of the air'. One argument for *passing* is that the *ssi* and *ffi* ligatures are very similar and easily confused, lying in adjacent sections of the compositor's box; a concurrent minim misreading of *a* for *u* must also be supposed. Q1's *pacing* may be a homophonic substitution for *passing*; but *lazy-pacing* or *lazy-passing* are much easier readings than *lazy-puffing*. On literary grounds any one of the three alternatives would be acceptable, since they are all successively produced in the quick forge and working house of thought: the messenger *bestrides* the clouds as he would a horse *passing/pacing lazily*; the puffed-out clouds suggest *bosom*, or the winged heads drawn in old maps puffing out the wind; puffed-out clouds are also like a ship's billowing sails, carrying the messenger on the *bosom*, not of the deep, but *of the air.* Since Q2's more authoritative *puffing* is more conceitful, and on the principle of *praestat difficilior lectio*, I prefer it.

Or if thou wilt not, be but sworn my love
And I'll no longer be a Capulet.
Romeo. Shall I hear more, or shall I speak at this?
Juliet. 'Tis but thy name that is my enemy:
Thou art thyself, though not a Montague.
What's Montague? It is nor hand nor foot
Nor arm nor face nor any other part
Belonging to a man. O be some other name.
What's in a name? That which we call a rose
By any other word would smell as sweet;
So Romeo would, were he not Romeo call'd,
Retain that dear perfection which he owes
Without that title. Romeo, doff thy name,
And for thy name, which is no part of thee,
Take all myself.

40–2. What's Montague . . . other name.] *As Malone;* Whats *Mountague*? it is nor hand nor foote, / nor arme nor face, ô be some other name / Belonging to a man. *Q2–4,F;* Whats *Mountague*? It is nor hand nor foote, / Nor arme, nor face, nor any other part. *Q1;* O be some other name! What's Montague? / It is nor hand, nor foot, nor arm, nor face, / Nor any part belonging to a man. *NCS.* 41. nor any other part] *Q1, Malone; not in Q2–4,F.* 42.] *So Malone;* ô be some other name / Belonging to a man. *Q2–4,F; not in Q1.* 43. What's in a name] *Q2–4,Q1;* What? in a names *F.* 44. word] *Q2–4,F;* name *Q1, Pope.*

39. *though . . . Montague*] even if you take some other name than Montague.

40–2. *What's . . . name*] Malone takes the phrase *nor any other part* from Q1 and inserts it in l. 41, rearranging the subsequent phrases from Q2 so that O *be some other name* follows, rather than precedes, *Belonging to a man.* The presumption is that Shakespeare, revising the lines, accidentally marked the phrase *nor any other part* for deletion, or was so understood by the compositor. Malone's version involves the least violence to the text and includes all the material from Q1 and Q2, and makes good sense; Q2 as it stands does not. NCS prints Alice Walker's arrangement which supposes that a corrected copy of Q1 was used by the copyist/compositor here: 'The collator copied into the margin the three additions from the foul papers ("Thou art thyself, though not a Montague", "O, be some other name", "belonging to a man") . . . but did so in such a manner that the compositor took the shorter ones to be continuous and inserted them at the wrong point, though in the right order, not topsy-turvy as Malone supposed' ('The New Way', p. 91).

43. *rose*] The implicit comparison of Romeo to a rose is developed in the ambiguous syntax of l. 45's *So Romeo would* following l. 44's *smell as sweet.*

44. *word*] The passage is strewn with exchanges between *name* and *word*, down to l. 58, which supports the view that Shakespeare calls a name, as a thing apart from a person, a *word*; cf. *Tw.N.*, III. i. 16–24, where Feste asserts 'her name's a word'. Q2 makes sense and should stand, despite the irrational pressure of proverbial familiarity attaching to *name* as the choice in many earlier editions.

46. *owes*] owns.

Romeo. I take thee at thy word.
Call me but love, and I'll be new baptis'd:
Henceforth I never will be Romeo.
Juliet. What man art thou that thus bescreen'd in night
So stumblest on my counsel?
Romeo. By a name
I know not how to tell thee who I am:
My name, dear saint, is hateful to myself
Because it is an enemy to thee.
Had I it written, I would tear the word.
Juliet. My ears have yet not drunk a hundred words
Of thy tongue's uttering, yet I know the sound.
Art thou not Romeo, and a Montague?
Romeo. Neither, fair maid, if either thee dislike.
Juliet. How cam'st thou hither, tell me, and wherefore?
The orchard walls are high and hard to climb,
And the place death, considering who thou art,
If any of my kinsmen find thee here.
Romeo. With love's light wings did I o'erperch these walls,
For stony limits cannot hold love out,
And what love can do, that dares love attempt:
Therefore thy kinsmen are no stop to me.
Juliet. If they do see thee, they will murder thee.
Romeo. Alack, there lies more peril in thine eye
Than twenty of their swords. Look thou but sweet
And I am proof against their enmity.
Juliet. I would not for the world they saw thee here.
Romeo. I have night's cloak to hide me from their eyes,
And but thou love me, let them find me here.
My life were better ended by their hate
Than death prorogued, wanting of thy love.

59. thy tongue's uttering] *Q2–4,F;* that tongues utterance *Q1*. 61. maid . . . dislike] *Q2–4,F;* Saint . . . displease *Q1*. 62. cam'st] *Q1,F;* camest *Q2–4*. 65. kinsmen] *Q1,Q3,4,F;* kismen *Q2*.

53. *counsel*] private talk.

66. *o'erperch*] fly over; cf. Brooke, ll. 829–30.

67. *stony limits*] Unconsciously anticipating the tomb.

75. *night's cloak*] Cf. III. ii. 15, where Night the sober-suited matron is asked to use her *black mantle*, and Brooke, l. 457; Daniel, *Rosamond*, ll. 432–4.

78. *prorogued*] postponed, deferred.

Juliet. By whose direction found'st thou out this place?
Romeo. By love, that first did prompt me to enquire.
He lent me counsel, and I lent him eyes.
I am no pilot, yet wert thou as far
As that vast shore wash'd with the farthest sea,
I should adventure for such merchandise.
Juliet. Thou knowest the mask of night is on my face,
Else would a maiden blush bepaint my cheek
For that which thou hast heard me speak tonight.
Fain would I dwell on form; fain, fain deny
What I have spoke. But farewell, compliment.
Dost thou love me? I know thou wilt say 'Ay',
And I will take thy word. Yet, if thou swear'st,
Thou mayst prove false. At lovers' perjuries,
They say, Jove laughs. O gentle Romeo,
If thou dost love, pronounce it faithfully.
Or, if thou think'st I am too quickly won,
I'll frown and be perverse and say thee nay,
So thou wilt woo; but else, not for the world.
In truth, fair Montague, I am too fond,
And therefore thou mayst think my haviour light,
But trust me, gentleman, I'll prove more true
Than those that have more cunning to be strange.

83. wash'd] *Q1,Q4;* washeth *Q2;* washet *Q3,F.* 89. compliment] *Q2–4,F;* complements *Q1.* 90. love me? I] *Q2–4;* Love? I *F;* love me? Nay I *Q1.* 93. laughs] *Q2–4;* laught *F;* smiles *Q1.* 99. haviour] *Q1;* behaviour *Q2–4,F.* 101. more cunning] *Q1;* coying *Q2,3,F;* more coying *Q4;* more coyning *F2;* the coyning *Williams.*

82–4. *pilot . . . merchandise*] The image of Romeo as a merchant venturer relates to the tragic motif of voyaging in the play (cf. I. iv. 112, V. iii. 117–18); cf. Brooke, ll. 1361–78 or 799–808.

89. *compliment*] conventional rules of polite speech; modest formality.

92–3. *At . . . laughs*] Cf. Ovid, *Ars Amatoria*, I. 633 (Hudson).

98. *fond*] loving.

101. *more cunning*] The line in Q2 is metrically deficient, and most editors adopt Q1 which is regular and makes sense; Juliet is distinguishing between real and pretended modesty. *Coy* appears in OED (v3c and v4) in the sense to entice, to affect shyness (associated with *decoy*). NCS prints Q1 on the assumption that *coying* is 'a misreading of "conyng" badly written'; Sisson supposes Shakespeare wrote *coning* which was misread as *coiing*, hence *coying*. Williams, supposing that the compositor missed the manuscript tilde here as he does elsewhere, proposes *coyning*, with the sense of 'having ability to counterfeit'. The intransitive use of the verb, extremely unusual, does not elsewhere appear in Shakespeare. Spencer compares *Tp.*, III. i. 81: Miranda, de-

I should have been more strange, I must confess,
But that thou overheard'st, ere I was ware,
My true-love passion; therefore pardon me,
And not impute this yielding to light love
Which the dark night hath so discovered.
Romeo. Lady, by yonder blessed moon I vow,
That tips with silver all these fruit-tree tops—
Juliet. O swear not by the moon, th'inconstant moon,
That monthly changes in her circled orb,
Lest that thy love prove likewise variable.
Romeo. What shall I swear by?
Juliet. Do not swear at all.
Or if thou wilt, swear by thy gracious self,
Which is the god of my idolatry,
And I'll believe thee.
Romeo. If my heart's dear love—
Juliet. Well, do not swear. Although I joy in thee,
I have no joy of this contract tonight:
It is too rash, too unadvis'd, too sudden,
Too like the lightning, which doth cease to be
Ere one can say 'It lightens'. Sweet, good night.
This bud of love, by summer's ripening breath,
May prove a beauteous flower when next we meet.
Good night, good night. As sweet repose and rest
Come to thy heart as that within my breast.
Romeo. O wilt thou leave me so unsatisfied?
Juliet. What satisfaction canst thou have tonight?
Romeo. Th'exchange of thy love's faithful vow for mine.
Juliet. I gave thee mine before thou didst request it,
And yet I would it were to give again.
Romeo. Wouldst thou withdraw it? For what purpose, love?
Juliet. But to be frank and give it thee again;
And yet I wish but for the thing I have.

104. true-love] *Q2–4;* true loves *F,Q1.* 107. blessed] *Q2–4,Q1; not in F.* vow] *Q2–4,F;* swear *Q1.* 110. circled] *Q1,Q3,4,F;* circle *Q2.*

claring herself to Ferdinand, says 'Hence, bashful cunning'. The argument of Sisson, the analogy with *Tp.* and the rarity of the intransitive form of *coyning* make *cunning* preferable.

102. *strange*] reserved, distant.

118–20. *rash . . . lightens*] Cf. Brooke, ll. 209–10, and *MND*, I. i. 145–9.

131. *frank*] (i) generous, cf. *Lr*, III. iv. 20; (ii) candidly open.

My bounty is as boundless as the sea,
My love as deep: the more I give to thee
The more I have, for both are infinite.
I hear some noise within. Dear love, adieu.
[*Nurse calls within.*]
Anon, good Nurse—Sweet Montague be true.
Stay but a little, I will come again. [*Exit Juliet.*]

Romeo. O blessed blessed night. I am afeard,
Being in night, all this is but a dream,
Too flattering sweet to be substantial.

[*Enter* JULIET *above.*]

Juliet. Three words, dear Romeo, and good night indeed.
If that thy bent of love be honourable,
Thy purpose marriage, send me word tomorrow
By one that I'll procure to come to thee,
Where and what time thou wilt perform the rite,
And all my fortunes at thy foot I'll lay,
And follow thee my lord throughout the world.

Nurse. [*Within.*] Madam.

Juliet. I come, anon—But if thou meanest not well
I do beseech thee—

Nurse. [*Within.*] Madam.

Juliet. By and by I come—
To cease thy strife and leave me to my grief.

136. S.D.] *Rowe; Cals within. F; not in Q2–4,Q1.* 138. S.D.] *Rowe; not in Q2–4,F,Q1.* 141. S.D.] *Rowe (subst.); Enter. F2; not in Q2–4,F,Q1.* 146. rite] *Q2,3,F,Q1* (right); rights *Q4.* 148. lord] *F,Q1;* L. *Q2,3;* Loue *Q4.* 149, 151. *Nurse.* [*Within.*]] *Capell; Within: F;* Madam. *Q2–4 in margin; not in Q1.* 152. strife] *Q2,3,F;* sute *Q4; not in Q1.*

133–4. *bounty . . . deep*] Cf. *AYL*, IV. i. 185–7: 'that thou didst know how many fathom deep I am in love! But it cannot be sounded; my affection hath an unknown bottom, like the Bay of Portugal.'

141. *substantial*] real not imaginary. The fear that it is all a dream suggests a link with *MND* while continuing the motif shared by these two lovers.

149, 151. *Madam.*] The repeated interruptions by the Nurse, here, are parallel to the pattern in III. iii, where she knocks repeatedly for entry, in III. v, where she warns that Lady Capulet approaches, and IV. v, where she enters to try to wake, with repeated efforts, the seemingly dead Juliet. It is a kind of miniature conceit for the tragic action as a whole.

152. *strife*] striving, effort (of loving persuasion); cf. *All's W.*, v. iii. Epilogue, l. 4: 'With strife to please you'. NCS prefers Q4's *suit* on the grounds that this is the word at this point in Brooke.

Tomorrow will I send.
Romeo. So thrive my soul—
Juliet. A thousand times good night. [*Exit Juliet.*]
Romeo. A thousand times the worse, to want thy light.
Love goes toward love as schoolboys from their books,
But love from love, toward school with heavy looks.

Enter JULIET [*above*] *again.*

Juliet. Hist! Romeo, hist! O for a falconer's voice
To lure this tassel-gentle back again.
Bondage is hoarse and may not speak aloud,
Else would I tear the cave where Echo lies
And make her airy tongue more hoarse than mine
With repetition of my Romeo's name.
Romeo. It is my soul that calls upon my name.
How silver-sweet sound lovers' tongues by night,
Like softest music to attending ears.
Juliet. Romeo.
Romeo. My nyas.
Juliet. What o'clock tomorrow

154. S.D.] *F* (*Exit*); *not in Q2–4,Q1.* 155. light] *Q2,3,F;* sight *Q4; not in Q1.* 157. toward] *Q2–4,Q1;* towards *F.* S.D.] *Malone* (*subst.*); *Enter* Juliet *againe. Q2–4,F; not in Q1.* 160. not] *Q2,3,F,Q1; not in Q4.* 162–3. than mine / With] *Q4;* then / With *Q2,3,F;* as mine, / With *Q1.* 163. Romeo's name] *Q1; Romeo Q2–4,F.* 164. *Romeo.* It] *Q2–4,F* (*subst.*); *Romeo? / Ro.* It *Q1.* soul] *Q2,3,F,Q1;* love *Q4.* 167. My nyas] *NCS* (My niess); My Neece *Q2,3,F;* My Deere *Q4;* Madame *Q1.* What] *Q2–4,F;* At what *Q1.*

159. *tassel-gentle*] a male peregrine falcon; *gentle* because nobler than the goshawk. Cf. *The Book of Hawking* (1486): 'Ther is a Fawken gentill, and a Tercell gentill, and theys be for a prynce'. The bird could be lured back to the falconer after a hunting flight by a special call. NCS thinks *hist* is Juliet's soft call, as recommended e.g. in Simon Latham, *Second Book of Faulconry* (1658), ch. xii, pp. 39–40, for its usefulness in teaching the hawk to keep close at hand and enabling one to go fowling secretly. Secrecy, they observe, is Juliet's need. The call could be a whistle, or chirrup; cf. Gervase Markham, *Country Contentments* (1675), I, ch. v, p. 30.

160. *Bondage is hoarse*] My being under my father's strict control stops me speaking loudly.

161. *cave . . . lies*] Cf. Golding's *Ovid*, III, for the story of Echo who, scorned by Narcissus, became reduced by grief to nothing but a voice and dwelt in lonely caves.

162–3.] The last word of each line is missing in Q2; Q1 seems clearly right.

167. *nyas*] Dover Wilson's emendation seems clearly right: Q2's *Neece* is a natural misinterpretation of *niesse* or

Shall I send to thee?
Romeo. By the hour of nine.
Juliet. I will not fail. 'Tis twenty year till then.
I have forgot why I did call thee back.
Romeo. Let me stand here till thou remember it.
Juliet. I shall forget, to have thee still stand there,
Remembering how I love thy company.
Romeo. And I'll still stay to have thee still forget,
Forgetting any other home but this.
Juliet. 'Tis almost morning, I would have thee gone,
And yet no farther than a wanton's bird,
That lets it hop a little from his hand
Like a poor prisoner in his twisted gyves,
And with a silken thread plucks it back again,
So loving-jealous of his liberty.
Romeo. I would I were thy bird.
Juliet. Sweet, so would I:
Yet I should kill thee with much cherishing.

169. year] *Q2* (yeare); years *Q3,4,F,Q1.* 172. forget, to] *Q3,4,F;* forget to *Q2,Q1.* 177. farther] *Q2–4;* further *F,Q1.* 178. his] *Q2–4,F;* her *Q1.* 179. Like a] *Q2,3,F,Q1;* Like *Q4.* 180. silken] *Q2–4,F;* silke *Q1, Pope.*

nyas, which Jonson spells *niaise* in *The Devil is an Ass,* I. vi. 18, and annotates marginally as 'a young Hawke tane crying out of the nest'. Dover Wilson says the term is apt 'both to young Juliet calling from her bedroom window; and as Romeo's reply to "falcon-gentle". But unlike a "tassel-gentle" which, being wild-caught, had learnt to fly, a "niess" has never flown; and the falconer has only to climb to the aerie and [it] will be his.'

172. *still*] 'yet' and 'motionless'.

177–81. *farther . . . liberty*] Capell prefers Q1, and many editors follow; but *wanton* can mean 'playful', 'capricious', and Shakespeare uses it of adults and children; *wanton* applies to boys as well as girls, and there is a famous Bronzino in the Uffizi, 'Don Garzia de Medici', a portrait of a chubby smiling boy with a small bird proudly and possessively held in his hand. Juliet seems to visualize a young boy, Cupid-like, at play (the Cupid idea only half conscious). Cf. *Tp.,* IV. i. 100–1: (Cupid swears) 'he will shoot no more, but play with sparrows, / And be a boy right out'. Here the ideas of caprice and childhood are combined with love. It is clear that *wanton* meaning 'courtesan' has the wrong tone here. The suggestion of Cupid is frequent in this part of the play (cf. II. i. 13 above and n.).

179. *gyves*] fetters.

181. *his*] Neuter form (see Abbott § 228).

Good night, good night. Parting is such sweet sorrow
That I shall say good night till it be morrow.
[*Exit Juliet.*]

Romeo. Sleep dwell upon thine eyes, peace in thy breast.
Would I were sleep and peace so sweet to rest.
The grey-ey'd morn smiles on the frowning night,
Chequering the eastern clouds with streaks of light;
And darkness fleckled like a drunkard reels

185. S.D.] *Pope; not in Q2–4,F,Q1; after l. 186 F2.*
184–7. Good . . . sorrow / That . . . morrow. / *Romeo.* Sleep . . . breast. / Would . . . rest.] *Q1* (*subst.*)*;* Good . . . night. / Parting . . . sorrow, / That . . . morrow. / *Romeo.* Sleep . . . brest. / Would . . . rest. *Q4;* Good . . . night. / Parting . . . sorrow, / That . . . morrow. / *Iu.* Sleep . . . breast. / *Ro.* Would . . . rest. *Q2;* Good . . . night. / *Ro.* Parting . . . sorrow, / That . . . morrow. / *Iu.* Sleepe . . . breast. / *Rom.* Would . . . rest. *Q3,F.* 188–91.] *As Q2,3,F; not in Q4,Q1, Pope, Camb., NCS, Riv.* 190. fleckled] *Q3,F;* fleckted *Q2.*

184–7. The printing of these lines, and of ll. 188–91, bears evident testimony to confusion in the manuscript; (i) Q2 divides the couplet ll. 186–7 between Romeo and Juliet, though it is evidently in answer to the couplet of the preceding ll. 184–5, (ii) Q2 gives two successive speech prefixes to Juliet (182b and 186), and (iii) the single l. 184 is divided into two lines in Q2. NCS is surely right in arguing 'each lover has a farewell couplet in parting, while lines 186–7 clearly belong to the same speaker' and so is Williams when he says 'the speaker who wishes to say goodnight till it be morrow is surely the speaker who has already said it many times in this scene . . . and not the speaker who has never said it and has no desire to say it or to leave the scene'. Hosley argues ('The Good Night Good Night Sequence', *SQ*, v, Jan. 1954, pp. 96–8) that the couplet at ll. 186–7 is Juliet's, and the compositor printed the speech prefix *Ro.* one line too high; and that l. 184 is divided in Q2 because Juliet speaks the first half line and Romeo the second (*Parting . . . sorrow*). As to (iii) the compositor's division need not imply two speakers of the single line.

188–91. *The grey-eyed . . . wheels*] These four lines (Version A) are repeated, with minor alterations, as the first lines of the next scene in Q2 (Version B). In Q1 they appear only once, at the beginning of the next scene, and combine elements from both versions. A is close to Golding's *Ovid* II. 172–5) which suggests the superiority of A. I further suppose that B, in Q2 and Q1 ascribed to the Friar, was marked in the manuscript for deletion and mistakenly printed; so I omit it. The analogy with III. v is a strong argument for giving the lines to Romeo; Shakespeare wishes to emphasize the separation which dawn brings to the lovers who meet at night; he wishes also to effect a transition of mood rather than the inevitably abrupt jolt which the unprepared spectator receives in the Q1 version. For a comparable instance, cf. *Ham.*, I. i. 165–7. Though they are not among Romeo's finest, the lines are characteristic of Romeo rather than the uninventive personifications of the Friar. The lines are half-recalled by *Ado*, V. iii. 25–7; and cf. Chaucer, *Knight's Tale*, ll. 1491–1496.

190. *fleckled*] a misreading in Q2.

From forth day's pathway, made by Titan's wheels.
Hence will I to my ghostly Sire's close cell,
His help to crave and my dear hap to tell. *Exit.*

[SCENE III]

Enter FRIAR [LAURENCE] *alone with a basket.*

Friar L. Now, ere the sun advance his burning eye
The day to cheer, and night's dank dew to dry,
I must upfill this osier cage of ours
With baleful weeds and precious-juiced flowers.
The earth that's nature's mother is her tomb:
What is her burying grave, that is her womb;
And from her womb children of divers kind
We sucking on her natural bosom find.
Many for many virtues excellent,
None but for some, and yet all different.
O, mickle is the powerful grace that lies

192. Sire's] *NCS, conj. Delius;* Friers *Q2–4;* Fries *F;* fathers *Q1.*

Scene III

SCENE III] *Hanmer; not in Q2–4,F,Q1.* *Location.*] *A Monastery. Rowe; Fields near a Convent. Capell; Friar Laurence's cell. Malone.* S.D.] *Q2–4,F; Enter Frier Francis. Q1.* 1. *Friar L.* Now] *F2, Rowe*[1]*; Fri.* The grey-eyed morne smiles on the frowning night, / Checkring the Easterne clowdes with streaks of light: / And fleckeld darknesse like a drunkard reeles, / From forth daies path, and *Titans* burning wheeles: / Now *Q2–4,F1,Q1* (*subst.*). 5. is] *Q2,3,F;* in *Q4; not in Q1.*

192. *ghostly Sire's*] father confessor, spiritual guide. Delius's conjecture (*Sire's*) has support from Brooke, l. 559: 'He is my gostly syre'; NCS thinks Q2 'absurd', tautological, and possibly reporter's anticipation of II. iii. 41 (*ghostly father*). Some editors adopt Q1, but this may well be reporter's anticipation of II. iii. 41 or accidental substitution.

193. *hap*] fortune.

Scene III

S.D. *Enter Friar Laurence*] The Friar is a Franciscan; his medical interests prepare us for his subsequent offer of the potion which Juliet drinks, and relate him to an important series of roles in Shakespeare, beginning with Dr Pinch and ending with Prospero.

1. *advance*] show forth.

5. *earth . . . tomb*] Proverbial; cf. Tilley E 32; but Steevens also compares Lucretius, v. 259, 'Omniparens eadem rerum commune sepulcrum'.

9. *virtues*] strengthening or healing properties in plants, waters, etc.; cf. *Ham.*, IV. vii. 141–6.

11. *mickle*] great. The passage recalls Brooke, ll. 2109–11.

powerful grace] efficacious virtue (Dr Johnson).

In plants, herbs, stones, and their true qualities.
For naught so vile that on the earth doth live
But to the earth some special good doth give;
Nor aught so good but, strain'd from that fair use,
Revolts from true birth, stumbling on abuse.
Virtue itself turns vice being misapplied,
And vice sometime's by action dignified.

Enter ROMEO.

Within the infant rind of this weak flower
Poison hath residence, and medicine power:
For this, being smelt, with that part cheers each part;
Being tasted, stays all senses with the heart.
Two such opposed kings encamp them still
In man as well as herbs: grace and rude will;
And where the worser is predominant
Full soon the canker death eats up that plant.

Romeo. Good morrow, father.

Friar L. Benedicite.
What early tongue so sweet saluteth me?
Young son, it argues a distemper'd head
So soon to bid good morrow to thy bed.
Care keeps his watch in every old man's eye,

18. sometime's] *Q1, Capell;* sometime *Q2–4,F.* 22. stays] *Q2;* slayes *Q3,4,F, Q1.* senses] *Q2,4,F,Q1;* sence *Q3.*

15. *strain'd*] perverted.

18. *And vice . . . dignified*] A faulty characteristic may under certain circumstances acquire worth through a good action.

18. S.D.] Sampson notes Shakespeare's art in 'making the victim of poison enter when poison is the subject of discourse'. Pope and some later editors place the S.D. at l. 26.

20. *Poison . . . power*] Poison has residence and healing has power.

21. *with that part*] with that quality, its odour.

22. *stays*] Mommsen defends Q2 against the *slays* of Q1 because '"To bring the heart to a stand-still, and with it all the senses", is certainly a better expression than "to slay the heart and all the senses"'; *stay* in the sense of 'to be arrested, stop, or cease' of 'an action, activity, or process' is appropriate, and instances of the word in this sense are recorded in OED for this period; also cf. the modern phrase 'cardiac arrest'. Foul case or misreading of manuscript is possible: Williams instances IV. i. 72 *slay/stay*; but Q2 makes good sense.

24. *rude will*] fleshly desire.

26. *canker*] caterpillar; cf. *Gent.* I. i. 45–6.

29. *distemper'd*] disturbed, supposedly by some imbalance of bodily humours.

And where care lodges sleep will never lie,
But where unbruised youth with unstuff'd brain
Doth couch his limbs, there golden sleep doth reign.
Therefore thy earliness doth me assure
Thou art uprous'd with some distemperature;
Or, if not so, then here I hit it right:
Our Romeo hath not been in bed tonight.

Romeo. That last is true. The sweeter rest was mine.

Friar L. God pardon sin. Wast thou with Rosaline?

Romeo. With Rosaline! My ghostly father, no.
I have forgot that name, and that name's woe.

Friar L. That's my good son. But where hast thou been then?

Romeo. I'll tell thee ere thou ask it me again.
I have been feasting with mine enemy,
Where on a sudden one hath wounded me
That's by me wounded. Both our remedies
Within thy help and holy physic lies.
I bear no hatred, blessed man, for lo,
My intercession likewise steads my foe.

Friar L. Be plain, good son, and homely in thy drift;
Riddling confession finds but riddling shrift.

Romeo. Then plainly know my heart's dear love is set
On the fair daughter of rich Capulet.
As mine on hers, so hers is set on mine,
And all combin'd save what thou must combine
By holy marriage. When, and where, and how
We met, we woo'd, and made exchange of vow
I'll tell thee as we pass; but this I pray,
That thou consent to marry us today.

32. lodges] *Q2–4,F;* lodgeth *Q1.* 51. and] *Q2–4,Q1;* rest *F.*

33. *unbruised . . . brain*] youth undamaged by the world, with a brain not yet clogged with troubles.

34. *golden sleep*] Shakespeare frequently calls sleep golden; cf. *R3*, IV. i. 84.

36. *distemperature*] mental disturbance.

48. *holy physic*] healing power as a priest—with the sacrament of marriage.

50. *steads my foe*] benefits my foe (i.e. Juliet).

51. *homely*] synonymous with *plain.*

52. *shrift*] absolution. Romeo can expect clear advice only if he clearly explains.

56. *all combin'd*] everything harmoniously united.

Friar L. Holy Saint Francis! What a change is here!
Is Rosaline, that thou didst love so dear,
So soon forsaken? Young men's love then lies
Not truly in their hearts but in their eyes.
Jesu Maria! What a deal of brine
Hath wash'd thy sallow cheeks for Rosaline.
How much salt water thrown away in waste
To season love, that of it doth not taste.
The sun not yet thy sighs from heaven clears,
Thy old groans yet ring in mine ancient ears.
Lo here upon thy cheek the stain doth sit
Of an old tear that is not wash'd off yet.
If ere thou wast thyself, and these woes thine,
Thou and these woes were all for Rosaline.
And art thou chang'd? Pronounce this sentence then:
Women may fall when there's no strength in men.
Romeo. Thou chid'st me oft for loving Rosaline.
Friar L. For doting, not for loving, pupil mine.
Romeo. And bad'st me bury love.
Friar L. Not in a grave
To lay one in, another out to have.
Romeo. I pray thee chide me not, her I love now
Doth grace for grace and love for love allow.
The other did not so.
Friar L. O, she knew well
Thy love did read by rote that could not spell.
But come young waverer, come, go with me,
In one respect I'll thy assistant be.
For this alliance may so happy prove

70. yet ring] *Q4;* yet ringing *Q2,3,F;* ring yet *Q1.* mine] *Q2;* my *Q3,4,F,Q1.*
84. not] *Q2,3,F,Q1;* no *Q4.* 85. go] *Q2,3,F,Q1;* and goe *Q4.*

63–4. *Young . . . eyes*] Cf. *MND*, I. i. 234–5, for the opposite sentiment.
68. *season*] preserve (as in pickle); with a play on the sense 'to flavour'. Cf. *All's W.*, I. i. 41–3.
69. *The sun . . . clears*] Cf. *Tit.*, III. i. 212–14.
75. *sentence*] maxim.
78. *doting . . . loving*] Cf. Lyly, *Endimion*, III. iv. 62: 'You doted then, not loued'.
84. *love . . . spell*] you knew no more about love than a child who can recite words learned by heart without being able to read them with understanding.
86. *In one respect*] In consideration of one thing.
87–8. *For . . . love*] Cf. Brooke, ll. 427–8.

To turn your households' rancour to pure love.
Romeo. O let us hence: I stand on sudden haste.
Friar L. Wisely and slow; they stumble that run fast.
Exeunt.

[SCENE IV]

Enter BENVOLIO *and* MERCUTIO.

Mer. Where the devil should this Romeo be? Came he not home tonight?

Ben. Not to his father's; I spoke with his man.

Mer. Why, that same pale hard-hearted wench, that Rosaline, torments him so that he will sure run mad.

Ben. Tybalt, the kinsman to old Capulet, hath sent a letter to his father's house.

Mer. A challenge, on my life.

Ben. Romeo will answer it.

Mer. Any man that can write may answer a letter.

Ben. Nay, he will answer the letter's master, how he dares, being dared.

Mer. Alas poor Romeo, he is already dead, stabbed with a white wench's black eye, run through the ear with a love song, the very pin of his heart cleft with the blind bow-boy's butt-shaft. And is he a man to encounter Tybalt?

88. households] *Q2–4,Q1;* houshould *F.*

Scene IV

SCENE IV] *Hanmer; not in Q2–4,F,Q1.* *Location.*] *A Street. Capell.* 1. devil] *Q2–4,F* (deule)*; not in Q1.* 4–5.] *As prose F; as verse Q2–4,Q1.* 6–7.] *As prose Q2–4,F; as verse Q1.* 14. run] *Q2–4,F;* shot *Q1.*

90. *Wisely and slow*] Proverbial: an idea the Friar repeats in different guises; cf. II. vi. 9–10, III. iii. 129–33.

Scene IV

9. *answer it*] accept the challenge. Mercutio quibblingly pretends to misunderstand Benvolio.

15. *pin*] At the centre of an archery target was a small white circle, and in the centre of that a wooden peg, the *pin*; cf. *LLL*, IV. i. 129.

16. *blind bow-boy's*] Cupid's; in *Tancred and Gismund* Cupid begins the play with an angry speech against those who 'scorne and scoffe, and shame vs euerie houre, / A brat, a bastard, and an idle boy, / A rod, a staffe, a whip to beate him out, / And to be sicke of loue, a childish toy' (I. i. 59–62). Cf. Intro., p. 59, n. 1.

butt-shaft] The heavy arrow used in butt shooting. Butt shooting was for more accuracy than clout shooting

Ben. Why, what is Tybalt?

Mer. More than Prince of Cats. O, he's the courageous captain of compliments: he fights as you sing prick-song, keeps time, distance and proportion. He rests his minim rests, one, two, and the third in your bosom: the very butcher of a silk button—a duellist, a duellist, a gentleman of the very first

18. *Ben.*] *Q1,F; Rom.* (*subst.*) *Q2–4.* 19. Cats] *Q2–4,F;* cattes, I can tel you *Q1.* 22. his minim rests] *Q2–4* (*subst.*); me his minim rest *Q1;* his minum *F.*

and consequently at a shorter distance (100–140 yards against 160–240 yards).

19. *Prince of Cats*] Cf. Nashe, *Have With You, Works,* III, p. 51: 'Tibault ... Prince of Cattes'. Warburton notes that Tybert is the name of the prince of cats in *Reynard the Fox.* In the Italian sources Tybalt's name is Tebaldo.

20. *captain of compliments*] In duelling, 'a complete master of all the laws of ceremony' (Dr Johnson). Horace S. Craig (*Univ. California Pub. in Eng.*, XI. i. 12) thinks this is an allusion to a method of the Spanish School for forming a complementary angle with one's own rapier to the angle of the opponent's, thus gaining advantage.

20–1. *pricksong*] printed music, sung carefully with attention to accuracy, in contrast to singing from memory or by ear, with more natural ease but less precision; *pricksong* also meant descant or counterpoint accompanying a simple melody (OED sv 2). Mercutio is punning on *prick* = stab, and *prick-shafts*, the arrows used in prick shooting.

21. *proportion*] rhythm; possibly with a quibble on the term referring to the ratios and angles between the lines and arcs formed by opposing fencers' motions and by their rapiers; see the illustration from Thibault's manual of 1628 reproduced in *Shakespeare's England*, II, p. 398.

22. *minim rests*] briefest possible rests; a minim was the basic short note-value in Tudor music, and it also means a note half the value of a semibreve. Mercutio continues the musical conceit, possibly not very accurately. The whole phrase means 'he will make two feints, with the briefest possible pause between each, and then he will strike' (NCS), and emphasizes the fencer's rhythmic timing.

23. *butcher ... button*] Tybalt is ridiculed by the bathos of the phrase, which hints at effeteness. There is an allusion to an episode in the career of an Italian fencing master, Rocco Bonetti, who had a fencing school in Blackfriars and who was challenged by an Englishman, Austen Baggar, as 'thou that takest upon thee to hit anie Englishman with a thrust upon anie button'. With sword and buckler Baggar struck up Bonetti's heels, cut him over the breech, and trod upon him. See *Shakespeare's England*, II, p. 396. Cf. Lyly, *Sapho and Phao*, II. iii. 9–13: 'beware of valour! hee that ... can hit a button with a thrust, and will into the field man to man ... is a shrewd fellow, and shall be well followed'.

24–5. *gentleman ... house*] of the first rank: with a subsidiary quibble on *house* as a modish name for a fencing school: Bonetti called his a *college*, as he thought it a disgrace to keep a fencing *school*. Mercutio mocks the fashionable foreign teachers, and may be implying also that Tybalt pretends to a higher social rank than he actually

house, of the first and second cause. Ah, the immortal passado, the punto reverso, the hay!

Ben. The what?

Mer. The pox of such antic lisping affecting phantasimes, these new tuners of accent. By Jesu, a very good blade, a very tall man, a very good whore! Why, is not this a lamentable thing, grandsire, that we should be thus afflicted with these strange flies, these fashion-mongers, these 'pardon-me's', who

28. antic] *Q2–4,F,Q1* (antique). phantasimes] *Williams, conj. Crow;* phantacies *Q2–4,F;* fantasticoes *Q1.* 29. accent] *Q2–4,F;* accents *Q1.* By Jesu] *Q2–4, Q1;* Jesu *F.* 33. pardon-me's] *Q1,Q3,F* (*subst.*)*;* pardons mees *Q2;* pardona-mees *Q4;* perdona-mi's *Camb.*

holds: the only first house he belongs to being a fencing school.

25. *first . . . cause*] Cf. *LLL*, I. ii. 171–2, and *The Book of Honour and Armes* (1590) by ? Sir William Segar, who reduces the *causes* for taking up quarrels among gentlemen to two: the accusation of a crime punishable by death, and a question of honour. The allusion may be more generally to duelling punctilio in the manuals of Saviolo and Carranza which is mocked in *AYL*, v. iv. 65–97. Adolph Soens, *SQ*, xx (1969), 119–27, believes there is a specific allusion to the Spanish manuals, which proceed by identifying a thing by its cause when discussing fencing evolutions; however, it is not easy to pin Mercutio down to one meaning when he is in a quibbling mood, as here.

25–6. *immortal passado*] Cf. *LLL*, I. ii. 172–3. Punning on *immortal* (i) famous, and (ii) fatal; Bobadil calls the passado 'a most desperate thrust' (*Every Man In*, I. iii. 211). The *passado* (properly *passada* in Spanish, *passata* in Italian) was a forward thrust with the sword, one foot being advanced at the same time; in the Spanish system it was the main principle of the attack, three precisely measured foot movements being recommended: 'the *pasada* of twenty four inches, the *pasada simple* of about thirty inches, and the *pasada doble*, formed of the first two, and performed by the two feet alternately' (*Shakespeare's England*, II, p. 398).

26. *punto reverso*] back-handed thrust. Cf. Saviolo's manual of 1595: 'in both these false thrusts, when he beateth them by with his rapier, you may with much sodainenesse make a passata with your left foote and your Dagger commanding his Rapier, you maie give him a punta either dritta or riversa' (K2).

hay] From Italian *hai* (= thou hast it), used when a thrust reaches the antagonist (Dr Johnson).

28. *phantasimes*] Crow's suggestion that the compositor failed to notice, or the writer failed to make clear, the tilde over *i* in manuscript *phantacies*, gains support from a similar omission in l. 6 above (*kinsman*) and II. ii. 65. *LLL*, IV. i. 92 and v. i. 18, reads *phantasime* = one full of fancies (David).

29. *tuners of accent*] fellows who speak with new-fangled inflections of voice.

30. *tall*] valiant; cf. *Tw.N.*, I. iii. 18, where a similar response is given to the affected usage.

32. *strange flies*] parasites, gaudy ephemerae; cf. Hamlet of Osric, *Ham.*, v. ii. 83.

33. *'pardon-me's'*] Q2's reading *pardons* could suggest to Q4 a misreading of *s* for *a* which yields Stratford-atte-

stand so much on the new form that they cannot sit at ease on the old bench? O their bones, their bones!

Enter ROMEO.

Ben. Here comes Romeo, here comes Romeo!

Mer. Without his roe, like a dried herring. O flesh, flesh, how art thou fishified. Now is he for the numbers that Petrarch flowed in. Laura, to his lady, was a kitchen wench—marry, she had a better love to berhyme her—Dido a dowdy, Cleopatra a gypsy, Helen and Hero hildings and harlots, Thisbe

41. was a] *Q2–4,F;* was but a *Q1*.

Bowe Italian. NCS despises translating Q2: 'Shakespeare's fops are English'. Q2's spelling may also yield phonetically *pardonnez* (*ez* = *s*).

34. *stand . . . on*] insist, with a quibble on the literal sense.

new form] Cf. *LLL*, I. i. 201–6, quibbling on the senses fashion and bench; there is play on *stand on*.

35. *sit . . . bench*] NCS cites Sir John Harington, *A Treatise of Playe* (*c.* 1597), complaining that the wainscot stools and plank forms at Court are too hard now 'great breeches' are laid aside, and pleading for upholstered seats for lords and ladies at Court.

bones] Mercutio pronounces the French *bon* so as to bring out the pun on English *bones* (cf. *LLL*, v. i. 24–5). The fashionable courtiers are in ecstasies with every trifle, crying out *good* or *well done* incessantly; they have also the *bone-ache*, venereal disease: 'Neapolitan bone-ache' in *Troil.*, II. iii. 16, 'malady of France' in *H5*, v. i. 76.

38. *Without his roe*] The name, reduced to *meo* or *O me*, becomes the cry of the lamenting lover. OED cites this passage in illustration of the sense of *roe* as the milt or sperm of male fish (sb 1 b); Mercutio still supposes Rosaline to be Romeo's beloved, so *roe-* (*saline*) is a further possible quibble. NCS suggests *without his* (*roe*) *deer*.

dried herring] In the process of curing (*drying*) the herring's roe may be removed.

39. *fishified*] Quibbling on the senses 'turned into a herring', 'become obsessed with sex', 'gone pale and bloodless'; cf. I. i. 29–30.

40. *numbers . . . flowed in*] The verses so fluently composed by Petrarch in his sonnets to his chaste love Laura de Noves.

to] in comparison with.

42. *Dido . . . dowdy*] The Queen of Carthage and love of Aeneas in Virgil. Possibly there is some joke here like that in *Tp.*, II. i. 71 ff., about 'widow Dido'.

43. *gypsy*] Cf. *Ant.*, I. i. 10, IV. xii. 28. Gypsies were supposed to be from Egypt and Cleopatra to be dark complexioned, though she was in fact of pure Macedonian blood; but Mercutio seems to be quibbling on the separate senses 'from Egypt' and 'low, sluttish woman' then in current use.

Helen and Hero] Helen's abduction by Paris was the cause of the Trojan war, sung by Homer in the *Iliad*; Hero of Sestos, celebrated in Marlowe's poem, was loved by Leander, who was drowned swimming the Hellespont.

hildings] good-for-nothings, virtually synonymous with harlots; a word

a grey eye or so, but not to the purpose. Signor Romeo, bonjour. There's a French salutation to your French slop. You gave us the counterfeit fairly last night.

Romeo. Good morrow to you both. What counterfeit did I give you?

Mer. The slip sir, the slip. Can you not conceive?

Romeo. Pardon, good Mercutio, my business was great, and in such a case as mine a man may strain courtesy.

Mer. That's as much as to say, such a case as yours constrains a man to bow in the hams.

Romeo. Meaning to curtsy.

Mer. Thou hast most kindly hit it.

Romeo. A most courteous exposition.

Mer. Nay, I am the very pink of courtesy.

Romeo. Pink for flower.

Mer. Right.

Romeo. Why, then is my pump well flowered.

51. good] *Q2–4; not in F,Q1.*

chosen partly for the comic assonance.

Thisbe] Beloved of Pyramus; their story (burlesqued by the Mechanicals in *MND*) is given in Golding's *Ovid*, IV; it is a tragic love story with affinities to *Romeo and Juliet.*

44. *grey eye*] Apparently, as a sign of approval, applied to what are now called blue eyes; cf. III. v. 19–20, where the sunlit morning is called *grey.*

44. *not to the purpose*] not worth mentioning.

46. *French slop*] wide loose breeches; cf. *Mer.V*, II. ii. 66–7, where the baron of England is mocked for having bought his round hose in France.

counterfeit] Mercutio has to explain his pun, which turns upon *slip*, a term for a counterfeit coin; cf. Greene, *A Disputation Betweene a Hee Conny-catcher and a Shee Conny-catcher* (1592): 'Counterfeyt peeces of mony . . . which the common people call slips'. Cf. *Troil.*, II. iii. 23–4.

50. *conceive*] understand.

52–3. *strain courtesy*] be unceremonious; cf. Lyly, *Mother Bombie*, III. iii. 34: 'I must straine cursie with you; I haue business, I cannot stay'.

55. *bow . . . hams*] The ham is the back of the thigh, bent in curtsying; but there is also the bawdy innuendo that Romeo's sexual exertions make him unable to stand up straight; the idea is repeated in the innuendo of l. 57, where *hit it* means 'got the joke' and 'attained the sexual target'; cf. *LLL*, IV. i. 111–33.

56. *curtsy*] pronounced like 'courtesy' and leading to the quibble on *courteous.*

57. *kindly*] Quibbling on the senses 'graciously' and 'naturally'.

59. *pink*] perfect example; quibbles develop on the senses 'flower', 'perforations decorating a leather shoe', 'rapier-thrust'.

62. *pump*] shoe; i.e. 'if pink means flower, then I may say that my pumps are ornamented with flowers'.

Mer. Sure wit, follow me this jest now, till thou hast worn out thy pump, that when the single sole of it is worn, the jest may remain after the wearing solely singular.

Romeo. O single-soled jest, solely singular for the singleness.

Mer. Come between us, good Benvolio, my wits faints.

Romeo. Switch and spurs, switch and spurs, or I'll cry a match!

Mer. Nay, if our wits run the wild-goose chase I am done. For thou hast more of the wild-goose in one of thy wits than I am sure I have in my whole five. Was I with you there for the goose?

Romeo. Thou wast never with me for anything, when thou wast not there for the goose.

Mer. I will bite thee by the ear for that jest.

Romeo. Nay, good goose, bite not.

63. Sure wit] *Q2–4,F;* Well said *Q1.* 65. solely] *Q2–4,Q1* (*subst.*); sole *F.* 69. wits faints] *Q2–4,F;* wits faile *Q1;* wits faint *Q5;* wit faints *F2.* 72. our] *Q2–4,F;* thy *Q1.* 76. Thou wast] *Q2–4,F;* Thou wert *Q1.*

65–6. *solely singular*] The quibble is on *singular* meaning 'solitary' and also 'unique'; Mercutio's phrasing also anticipates the quibbling on *single-soled* in Romeo's reply

67. *single-soled*] poor, contemptible, thin; cf. Nashe, *Have With You, Works*, I. 165, pp. 8–9: 'not in the pantofles of his prosperitie, as he was when he libeld against my Lord of Oxford, but in the single-soaled pumpes of his adversitie, with his gown cast off'.

68. *singleness*] silliness.

69. *Come between us*] Mercutio jestingly appeals for his second to intervene in the duel: a remarkable anticipation of the fatal event in the duel with Tybalt.

70. *Switch and spurs*] Urge your wits to full gallop.

70–1. *cry a match*] claim the victory.

72. *wild-goose chase*] a kind of horse race in which the leading rider chose whatever course he liked and the rest were obliged to follow him (Holt White). Nicholas Cox in *A Gentleman's Recreation* (1674) says that this chase fell into disuse, being 'found by experience so inhumane and so destructive to Horses, especially when two good horses were matched'.

74–5. *Was . . . goose*] 'Did I keep even with you?' or perhaps 'Did I score a point by calling you goose?' (Kittredge).

77. *goose*] fool, nitwit.

78. *bite . . . ear*] Usually 'to caress fondly' (OED *bite* 16) deriving from the behaviour of one horse to another (Gifford).

79. *good . . . not*] Proverbial (Tilley G 349); used as a jocular cry for mercy from an unimpressive opponent (Kittredge); cf. Nashe, *Strange Newes, Works*, I. 307, l. 9: 'Good Beare, bite not'; McKerrow thinks it ironic in tone to soothe someone's anger.

Mer. Thy wit is a very bitter sweeting, it is a most sharp sauce.

Romeo. And is it not then well served in to a sweet goose?

Mer. O here's a wit of cheveril, that stretches from an inch narrow to an ell broad.

Romeo. I stretch it out for that word 'broad', which, added to the goose, proves thee far and wide a broad goose.

Mer. Why, is not this better now than groaning for love? Now art thou sociable, now art thou Romeo; now art thou what thou art, by art as well as by nature. For this drivelling love is like a great natural that runs lolling up and down to hide his bauble in a hole.

Ben. Stop there, stop there.

Mer. Thou desirest me to stop in my tale against the hair.

Ben. Thou wouldst else have made thy tale large.

Mer. O, thou art deceived; I would have made it short; for I was come to the whole depth of my tale and meant indeed to occupy the argument no longer.

Romeo. Here's goodly gear.

Enter NURSE *and her* man [PETER].

82. then well] *Q2;* well *Q3,4,F,Q1.* in to] *Q2–4,Q1;* into *F.* 98. for] *Q2–4,Q1;* or *F.* 100. S.D. *Enter . . . man*] *Q2–4,Q1; after l. 99 F.* [PETER]] *ed.; not in Q2–4,F,Q1.*

80. *sweeting*] a sweet apple; apple sauce is a traditional accompaniment to goose; Mercutio is of course talking about the sharpness of Romeo's wit in answering proverb with proverb.

83. *cheveril*] kid leather which stretches easily; cf. *Tw.N.*, III. i. 11–12.

84. *ell*] forty-five inches. To paraphrase: 'you can make your little wit go a long way'.

85. *broad*] Quibbling on the senses 'wide', 'obvious' and 'indecent'.

91. *natural*] idiot, quibbling on *nature.*

92. *lolling*] i.e. with his tongue, or bauble, protruding pendulously (hence l. 91's *drivelling*).

92–3. *hide . . . hole*] The fool's bauble was a stick fantastically carved at one end, or with an inflated bladder attached; there is also a bawdy connotation here, as in *All's W.*, IV. v. 26–7.

95. *tale . . . hair*] Bawdy, quibbling on *tale/tail* (=penis), and the phrase 'against the hair' = against the grain.

96. *large*] Quibbling on the senses 'lengthy tale', 'large tail'.

98. *whole . . . tale*] Bawdy quibbling on *depth* and *tale.*

99. *occupy*] Quibbling on the indecent Elizabethan usage; cf. *2H4*, II. iv. 137–40.

100. *goodly gear*] Referring either to the jesting of Mercutio and Romeo ('this is good stuff') or to the appearance of the Nurse preceded by Peter

A sail! A sail!

Mer. Two. Two. A shirt and a smock.

Nurse. Peter.

Peter. Anon.

Nurse. My fan, Peter.

Mer. Good Peter, to hide her face, for her fan's the fairer face.

Nurse. God ye good morrow, gentlemen.

Mer. God ye good e'en, fair gentlewoman.

Nurse. Is it good e'en?

Mer. 'Tis no less, I tell ye; for the bawdy hand of the dial is now upon the prick of noon.

Nurse. Out upon you. What a man are you?

Romeo. One, gentlewoman, that God hath made, himself to mar.

Nurse. By my troth it is well said; 'for himself to mar' quoth a? Gentlemen, can any of you tell me where I may find the young Romeo?

Romeo. I can tell you; but young Romeo will be older when you have found him than he was when you sought him. I am the youngest of that name, for fault of a worse.

101. A sail] *Q2–4,F; Mer:* A saile *Q1.* 102. *Mer.*] *Q2–4,F; Ben: Q1.* 106. Good] *Q2–4,F;* Preethee doo good *Q1.* 107. fairer face] *Q2–4,F;* fairer of the two *Q1.* 111. ye] *Q2;* you *Q3,4,F,Q1.* 114–15. himself] *Q2–4,F;* for himselfe *Q1.* 116. well said] *Q2–4,Q1;* said *F.* 118. the] *Q2–4,F; not in Q1.*

bearing the fan ('here's a subject for mockery'); spoken in a derisory tone.

100–1.] NCS follows F in placing the S.D. before l. 100, supposing that *goodly gear* refers not to Mercutio's jests but the Nurse's 'voluminous garments and ship-like motion'. Some editors have preferred Q1 here, which ascribes l. 101 to Mercutio and l. 102 to Benvolio. The placing of the S.D. on the same line as the dialogue of l. 100 in Q2 could, but need not necessarily, support the Q1 assignment.

101. *A sail! A sail!*] A variant of the expression 'Sail ho!' used when a ship is discerned. Evidently alluding to the Nurse's appearance.

102. *shirt . . . smock*] a man and a woman.

105. *fan*] For the custom of carrying a fan cf. *LLL*, IV. i. 138.

112. *prick of noon*] i.e. the point of noon (and with a bawdy quibble). Cf. *Lucr.*, l. 781, *3H6*, I. iv. 34; the prick is the actual engraved mark on the dial.

113. *What a man*] What sort of man.

114–15. *made . . . mar*] Cf. I. ii. 13. God made man in his own image but man mars it.

122. *fault . . . worse*] Ironically altering the saying 'for want of a better';

Nurse. You say well.

Mer. Yea, is the worst well? Very well took i'faith. Wisely, wisely.

Nurse. If you be he sir, I desire some confidence with you.

Ben. She will endite him to some supper.

Mer. A bawd! A bawd! A bawd! So ho.

Romeo. What hast thou found?

Mer. No hare, sir, unless a hare, sir, in a lenten pie, that is something stale and hoar ere it be spent.

He walks by them and sings.

An old hare hoar,
And an old hare hoar,
Is very good meat in Lent.
But a hare that is hoar
Is too much for a score
When it hoars ere it be spent.

Romeo, will you come to your father's? We'll to dinner thither.

Romeo. I will follow you.

126. If you] *Q2,3,F,Q1;* If thou *Q4.* 127. endite] *Q2–4,F;* inuite *Q1.* some] *Q2–4,F; not in Q1.* 131. S.D.] *Q1; not in Q2–4,F.* 132–7.] *As Capell;* An . . . lent. / But . . . spent. *Q2–4,F;* And an . . . hore / is . . . Lent: / But . . . score, / if . . . spent. *Q1.*

the Nurse misses the jest and Mercutio mocks her for it.

126. *confidence*] Malapropism for 'conference'; cf. *Ado,* III. v. 2–3: 'I would have some confidence with you that decerns you nearly'.

127. *endite*] Jestingly Benvolio offers a malapropism for 'invite'; cf. *2H4,* II. i. 28–9: 'he is indited to dinner to the Lubber's Head'.

128–9. *So ho . . . found*] Dowden cites Madden, *Diary of Master William Silence,* p. 173: ' "As soon as he espieth her (the hare) he must cry *So how.*" Thus writes the author of *The Noble Arte* [*of Venerie*] . . . And so when Mercutio cried *So ho!* Romeo . . . asks "what hast thou found".'

130. *lenten pie*] Properly, a pie without meat to be eaten during Lent; but as NCS suggests, probably Mercutio means a hare pie eaten bit by bit surreptitiously during Lent and therefore mouldy before finished.

131. *stale*] Quibbling on the term for prostitute; cf. *Err.,* II. i. 101.

hoar] Punning on 'whore'.

spent] used up. The quibbling sense is 'a woman who has worked so long as a whore that she is physically worn out and repellent before she finally ceases to be "used" in the trade'. This dialogue looks forward to that between Pistol and Doll in *2H4,* II. iv.

132–7. *An old . . . spent*] An improvised song.

136. *too much for a score*] i.e. too mouldy to be worth paying for (NCS).

Mer. Farewell, ancient lady, farewell, lady, lady, lady.

Exeunt Mercutio and Benvolio.

Nurse. I pray you, sir, what saucy merchant was this, that was so full of his ropery?

Romeo. A gentleman, Nurse, that loves to hear himself talk, and will speak more in a minute than he will stand to in a month.

Nurse. And a speak anything against me I'll take him down, and a were lustier than he is, and twenty such jacks. And if I cannot, I'll find those that shall. Scurvy knave! I am none of his flirt-gills, I am none of his skains-mates. *She turns to Peter her man.*

141. S.D.] *Q1; Exeunt. Q2–4; Exit. Mercutio, Benuolio. F.* 142. I pray] *Q2–4,F;* Marry farewell. Pray *Q1.* 143. ropery] *Q2–4,F* (roperie)*;* roperipe *Q1;* Roguery *F4.* 147. a speak] *Q2–4,F;* hee stand to *Q1.* 150. flirt-gills] *Q2,3,F,Q1;* Gil-flirts *Q4.* 151. S.D.] *Q1; not in Q2–4,F.*

141. *lady, lady, lady*] Mercutio mocks the Nurse with this scrap of a ballad; she is no lady. T. Warton identifies the source as the Ballad of Constant Susanna, also quoted in *Tw.N.*, II. iii. 75–6: 'There dwelt a man in Babylon, of reputation great by fame; / He tooke to wife a faire woman, Susanna she was called by name; / A woman faire and vertuous: / Lady, lady, / Why should we not of her learne thus / to liue godly?' (*Roxburghe Ballads*, ed. Chappell, I, ll. 190–3).

142. *saucy merchant*] impudent fellow (*merchant* as opposed to 'gentleman' was a term of disrespect used in this way).

143. *ropery*] lewd jesting. The term is related to *rope-ripe*, which occurs in R. Wilson, *Three Ladies of London* (1584), B1: 'Thou art very pleasant and ful of thy roperipe (I would say Retorick)', where the sense is 'talk deserving of death by hanging', and to *rope-tricks*, as in *Shr.*, I. ii. 111: 'he'll rail in his rope-tricks', where, as Anne Lancashire suggests (*JEGP*, 1969, pp. 237–44), there is a quibble on *rope* = penis, also present in *1H6*, I. iii. 53, *Err.*, IV. iv. 39–40, Lyly, *Midas*, I. ii. 45, Butler, *Hudibras*, I. i. 549–52. The Nurse's word malapropizes *roguery* under the influence, perhaps, of Mercutio's insistently graphic phallic jokes.

146. *stand to*] abide by (and with a bawdy quibble, as in *All's W.*, III. ii. 40).

147. *speak*] Q1's reading makes unambiguous the bawdy connotation of *take him down*, humble him (with a bawdy quibble on the senses 'reduce his sexual appetite', 'cause detumescence'); but the joke is that the Nurse *unintentionally* expresses indecencies through unfortunate choice of words, as in Q2's version. I therefore reject Q1, which weakens the joke by making it explicit.

150. *flirt-gills*] loose women; Kittredge cites Gabriel Harvey, *Pierces Supererogation*, 1593 (ed. Grosart, II. 229): 'Yet was she not . . . such a dissolute gillian-flurtes, as this wainscot-faced Tomboy'. Nares notes *Gill* as a current and familiar term for a woman.

151. *skains-mates*] cut-throat companions; a *skain* was a long Irish knife; cf. Dekker, *Lanthorne and Candle-light* (1609), ch. 8: 'The bloudy tragedies of al these, are only acted by the

And thou must stand by too and suffer every knave to use me at his pleasure!

Peter. I saw no man use you at his pleasure; if I had, my weapon should quickly have been out. I warrant you, I dare draw as soon as another man, if I see occasion in a good quarrel, and the law on my side.

Nurse. Now afore God I am so vexed that every part about me quivers. Scurvy knave. Pray you, sir, a word—and as I told you, my young lady bid me enquire you out. What she bid me say, I will keep to myself. But first let me tell ye, if ye should lead her in a fool's paradise, as they say, it were a very gross kind of behaviour, as they say; for the gentlewoman is young. And therefore, if you should deal double with her, truly it were an ill thing to be offered to any gentlewoman, and very weak dealing.

Romeo. Nurse, commend me to thy lady and mistress. I protest unto thee—

Nurse. Good heart, and i'faith I will tell her as much. Lord, Lord, she will be a joyful woman.

Romeo. What wilt thou tell her, Nurse? Thou dost not mark me.

Nurse. I will tell her, sir, that you do protest—which, as I take it, is a gentlemanlike offer.

Romeo. Bid her devise
Some means to come to shrift this afternoon,

163. in a] *Q2–4,F;* into a *Q1.* 168. *Romeo.*] *Q2–4,Q1; Nur. F.* 176–7.] *As Delius; one line Q2–4,F; var. Q1.*

Women, who carrying long kniues or Skeanes vnder their mantles, do thus play their parts'; so Doll Tearsheet in *2H4* threatens to knife Pistol, and cf. Middleton, *The Roaring Girl*, Prologue: 'Another roars i'th'daytime, swears, stabs, gives braves'.

152–3. *use . . . pleasure*] Peter picks up the bawdy innuendo; the Nurse means 'treat me as rudely as he likes' but *use* could mean 'copulate with' as in *Tit.*, IV. ii. 40.

155. *weapon*] sword (with a bawdy quibble); cf. I. i. 32.

163. *in*] into.

fool's paradise] Cf. Marston, *The Malcontent*, V. vi. 97–9: 'Promise of matrimony by a young gallant to bring a virgin lady into a fool's paradise, make her a great woman, and then cast her off'.

167. *weak*] contemptible.

174. *protest*] NCS compares *Wiv.*, III. iv. 67, for the use of *protest* to mean 'declare love'.

177–9. *means . . . married*] Cf. Brooke, ll. 633–4.

And there she shall at Friar Laurence' cell
Be shriv'd and married. Here is for thy pains.
Nurse. No truly, sir; not a penny.
Romeo. Go to, I say you shall.
Nurse. This afternoon, sir? Well, she shall be there.
Romeo. And stay, good Nurse, behind the abbey wall.
Within this hour my man shall be with thee,
And bring thee cords made like a tackled stair,
Which to the high topgallant of my joy
Must be my convoy in the secret night.
Farewell, be trusty, and I'll quit thy pains;
Farewell. Commend me to thy mistress.
Nurse. Now God in heaven bless thee. Hark you, sir.
Romeo. What say'st thou, my dear Nurse?
Nurse. Is your man secret? Did you ne'er hear say,
Two may keep counsel, putting one away?
Romeo. I warrant thee my man's as true as steel.

Nurse. Well, sir, my mistress is the sweetest lady. Lord, Lord! When 'twas a little prating thing—O, there is a nobleman in town, one Paris, that would fain lay knife aboard; but she, good soul, had as lief see a toad, a very toad, as see him. I anger her sometimes and tell her that Paris is the properer man, but I'll warrant you, when I say so she looks as pale as any clout in the versal world. Doth not rosemary

183. stay, good] *Q2–4;* stay thou good *F;* stay thou *Q1.* 188. quit] *Q2;* quite *Q3,4,F,Q1.* 192–3.] *As Rowe; prose in Q2–4,F; not in Q1.* 194. I warrant] *F2;* Warrant *Q2–4,F; not in Q1.* man's] *Q2–4;* man *F; not in Q1.* 198. lief] *Q2–4,F* (leeue)*; not in Q1.* 198–9. see a] *Q2–4;* a see *F; not in Q1.*

185. *tackled stair*] Brooke calls it 'a corden ladder'; Dr Johnson explains: 'like stairs of rope in the tackle of a ship'; the nautical word leads to the next line's *high topgallant*, the platform on the mast from which the topgallant sail was handled, reached by a rope-ladder from the deck. Cf. *Gent.*, II. vi. 33–4.

187. *convoy*] means of conveyance.

188. *quit thy pains*] reward your effort.

193. *Two . . . away*] Proverbial, Tilley T 257; cf. *Tit.*, IV. ii. 144.

198. *lay . . . aboard*] establish his claim. Quibbles (i) on the action of the guest who, in Elizabethan times, brought his own knife, using it to mark his place at table and secure his helping, and (ii) on the term 'lay aboard' for nautical attack, as in *2H6*, IV. i. 25.

199–200. *sometimes*] Spencer notes 'the Nurse could only have heard about Romeo a few hours ago, but she talks as if the affair had been going on for some time'; cf. III. v. 239.

202. *clout . . . world*] piece of cloth

and Romeo begin both with a letter?
Romeo. Ay, Nurse, what of that? Both with an 'R'.
Nurse. Ah, mocker! That's the dog's name, 'R' is for the —No, I know it begins with some other letter; and she hath the prettiest sententious of it, of you and rosemary, that it would do you good to hear it.
Romeo. Commend me to thy lady. [*Exit Romeo.*]
Nurse. Ay, a thousand times. Peter!
Peter. Anon.
Nurse. Before, and apace. *Exeunt.*

[SCENE V]

Enter JULIET.

Juliet. The clock struck nine when I did send the Nurse,
In half an hour she promis'd to return.

205. dog's] *Q3,4,F; dog, Q2; not in Q1.* 205–6. for the—No,] *Delius, conj. Ritson;* for the no, *Q2–4,F;* for thee? No; *Theobald;* not for thee, *Hanmer;* for the nonce; *Steevens 1773, conj. Dr Johnson;* for the dog. No; *Steevens 1778, conj. Tyrwhitt; not in Q1.* 209. S.D.] *Rowe; not in Q2–4,F,Q1.* 212.] *As Q2–4,F; Peter,* take my fanne, and goe before. *Q1.*

Scene v

SCENE v] *Hanmer; not in Q2–4,F,Q1.* *Location.*] *Capulet's House. Rowe; Capulet's Garden. Capell.*

in the whole (*versal* = universal) world; cf. the modern expression 'as white as a sheet'.

205–6. *dog's name . . . No*] Though some editors print *dog-name*, Williams argues persuasively that the Q2 comma is a misreading of final *s*. I follow Ritson's punctuation. The sense is then clear: the Nurse thinks of 'R' as the dog's growl, 'ar' (see Jonson, *English Grammar*: 'R is the Dogs Letter and hirreth in the sound', Persius, *Sat.*, I. 109, and instances under 'arr' in OED). Phillip Williams in *N&Q*, Apr. 1950, suggests the Nurse just stops herself from saying the word *arse*—'with a somewhat unlooked-for show of modesty'.

207. *sententious*] The Nurse probably means *sentence*, pithy saying.

you] The possible quibble is on *U* and *R*, *yew* and *rosemary*. Kittredge suggests she is eager to repay his tip with invented compliments. In Brooke the Nurse in retailing the message to Juliet left nothing untold except 'onely one, that she forgot the taking of the golde' (l. 692).

212. *Before, and apace*] Go before me, and get a move on.

Scene v

1. *struck nine*] It was noon when the Nurse met Romeo, but we do not learn how she spent the three intervening hours.

Perchance she cannot meet him. That's not so.
O, she is lame. Love's heralds should be thoughts
Which ten times faster glides than the sun's beams
Driving back shadows over lowering hills.
Therefore do nimble-pinion'd doves draw Love,
And therefore hath the wind-swift Cupid wings.
Now is the sun upon the highmost hill
Of this day's journey, and from nine till twelve
Is three long hours, yet she is not come.
Had she affections and warm youthful blood
She would be as swift in motion as a ball:
My words would bandy her to my sweet love,
And his to me.
But old folks, many feign as they were dead—
Unwieldy, slow, heavy, and pale as lead.

Enter NURSE [*and* PETER].

O God she comes. O honey Nurse, what news?
Hast thou met with him? Send thy man away.
Nurse. Peter, stay at the gate. [*Exit Peter.*]
Juliet. Now good sweet Nurse—O Lord why look'st thou sad?
Though news be sad, yet tell them merrily,
If good, thou sham'st the music of sweet news
By playing it to me with so sour a face.
Nurse. I am aweary, give me leave awhile.
Fie, how my bones ache. What a jaunce have I!

4. heralds] *Q2–4,Q1;* Herauld *F.* 11. Is three] *Q3,4;* Is there *Q2;* I three *F; not in Q1.* 15–16.] *As Rowe; M.* And his . . . dead *Q2,3;* And his . . . dead *Q4;* And his . . . folkes, / Many . . . dead *F; not in Q1.* 17. S.D.] *Theobald; Enter Nurse. Q2–4,F,Q1.* 20. S.D.] *Theobald; not in Q2–4,F,Q1.* 23. sham'st] *Q4,F;* shamest *Q2,3; not in Q1.* 25. aweary] *Q2–4,F;* weary *Q1.* 26. jaunce] *Q2,3;* iaunt *Q4,F,Q1.* I] *Q2;* I had *Q3,4,F,Q1.*

7. *doves draw Love*] Doves were sacred to Venus and were depicted drawing her chariot; cf. *Ven.*, ll. 153, 1190.

9. *Now . . . hill*] Cf. Golding's *Ovid*, II. 84–7: 'the morning way Lyes steepe vpright, so that the steedes . . . haue much adoe to climb against the Hyll'.

14. *bandy*] strike (as in tennis, following the previous line's *ball*).

16. *feign*] make themselves appear (OED sv v. II. 9).

25. *give me leave*] let me alone.

26. *jaunce*] A noun from the verb *jaunse* or *jaunce* (cf. *R2*, v. v. 94). OED offers no other instance of *jaunce* from the period, and suggests that Q2's spelling here may be a misreading of manuscript *jaunte*. Hosley suggests it is a colloquial development from the plural form *jaunts* (=trudge about).

Juliet. I would thou hadst my bones and I thy news.
Nay come, I pray thee, speak: good, good Nurse, speak.
Nurse. Jesu, what haste. Can you not stay awhile?
Do you not see that I am out of breath?
Juliet. How art thou out of breath when thou hast breath
To say to me that thou art out of breath?
The excuse that thou dost make in this delay
Is longer than the tale thou dost excuse.
Is thy news good or bad? Answer to that,
Say either, and I'll stay the circumstance.
Let me be satisfied: is't good or bad?

Nurse. Well, you have made a simple choice. You know not how to choose a man. Romeo? No, not he. Though his face be better than any man's, yet his leg excels all men's, and for a hand and a foot and a body, though they be not to be talked on, yet they are past compare. He is not the flower of courtesy, but I'll warrant him as gentle as a lamb. Go thy ways, wench, serve God. What, have you dined at home?

Juliet. No, no. But all this did I know before.
What says he of our marriage? What of that?
Nurse. Lord, how my head aches! What a head have I:
It beats as it would fall in twenty pieces.
My back o' t'other side—ah, my back, my back!
Beshrew your heart for sending me about
To catch my death with jauncing up and down.
Juliet. I'faith I am sorry that thou art not well.
Sweet, sweet, sweet Nurse, tell me, what says my
love?
Nurse. Your love says like an honest gentleman,

41. leg excels] *Q2–4;* legs excels *F; not in Q1.* 41–2. a body] *Q2,3,F;* body *Q4;* a baudie *Q1.* 44. as a] *Q2–4;* a *F; not in Q1.* 47. this] *Q2–4;* this this *F; not in Q1.* 51. ah] *Q2–4* (a); O *F; not in Q1.* 53. jauncing] *Q2,3;* iaunting *Q4,F; not in Q1.* 54. not well] *Q2–4;* so well *F; not in Q1.*

29. *stay*] wait.

36. *stay the circumstance*] wait for the details.

38. *simple*] foolish.

40–2. *face . . . body*] Ironically reminiscent of Juliet's speech at II. ii. 40–7.

42. *not . . . talked on*] not worth talking about.

44–5. *Go thy ways*] Well, off you go.

And a courteous, and a kind, and a handsome,
And I warrant a virtuous—Where is your mother?
Juliet. Where is my mother? Why, she is within.
Where should she be? How oddly thou repliest.
'Your love says, like an honest gentleman,
"Where is your mother?" '
Nurse. O God's lady dear,
Are you so hot? Marry, come up, I trow.
Is this the poultice for my aching bones?
Henceforward do your messages yourself.
Juliet. Here's such a coil. Come, what says Romeo?
Nurse. Have you got leave to go to shrift today?
Juliet. I have.
Nurse. Then hie you hence to Friar Laurence' cell.
There stays a husband to make you a wife.
Now comes the wanton blood up in your cheeks.
They'll be in scarlet straight at any news.
Hie you to church. I must another way
To fetch a ladder by the which your love
Must climb a bird's nest soon when it is dark.
I am the drudge, and toil in your delight,
But you shall bear the burden soon at night.
Go. I'll to dinner. Hie you to the cell.
Juliet. Hie to high fortune! Honest Nurse, farewell. *Exeunt.*

59–60.] *As Rowe;* Where . . . be? / How . . . repliest: *Q2–4;* Where . . . Mother? / Why . . . be? / How . . . repli'st: *F; var. Q1.* 75. climb] *Q2,4, Q1;* climde *Q3,F.*

63. *Marry, come up, I trow*] Expressions of impatience; cf. I. ii. 74.

66. *coil*] fuss.

72. *They'll . . . news*] Any sudden news always makes your cheeks scarlet.

75. *bird's nest*] Juliet's bedroom; the imagery of birds is associated with her in II. ii. *passim*, in III. ii. 14, and III. v. 1–35.

77. *bear the burden*] Quibbling on 'do the work' and 'bear the weight of your lover'; cf. *Ant.*, I. v. 21.

[SCENE VI]

Enter FRIAR [LAURENCE] *and* ROMEO.

Friar L. So smile the heavens upon this holy act
That after-hours with sorrow chide us not.
Romeo. Amen, amen, but come what sorrow can,
It cannot countervail the exchange of joy
That one short minute gives me in her sight.
Do thou but close our hands with holy words,
Then love-devouring death do what he dare:
It is enough I may but call her mine.
Friar L. These violent delights have violent ends
And in their triumph die, like fire and powder,
Which as they kiss consume. The sweetest honey
Is loathsome in his own deliciousness,
And in the taste confounds the appetite.
Therefore love moderately; long love doth so.
Too swift arrives as tardy as too slow.

Enter JULIET *somewhat fast and embraces Romeo.*

Here comes the lady. O, so light a foot
Will ne'er wear out the everlasting flint.
A lover may bestride the gossamers
That idles in the wanton summer air
And yet not fall; so light is vanity.

Scene VI

SCENE VI] *Hanmer; not in Q2–4,F,Q1.* *Location.*] *The Monastery. Rowe; Friar Laurence's cell. Capell.* 12. loathsome] *Q2,3,F;* lothsomnesse *Q4; not in Q1.* 15. S.D.] *As Q1; Enter* Iuliet *Q2–4,F.*

3. *come . . . can*] let whatever sorrow come that conceivably may.

4. *It . . . joy*] It cannot counterbalance the joy I receive. (The emphasis on dark omens is marked.)

9. *These . . . ends*] Proverbial; cf. Tilley B 262, N 321, and II. ii. 118–20.

10. *triumph*] high-point of spectacular elation, flash point of an explosive.

powder] gunpowder.

11–13. *honey . . . appetite*] Cf. Tilley H 560.

14. *long love doth so*] Cf. Tilley L 559.

17. *ne'er . . . flint*] Cf. *2H6*, II. iv. 8–9, 34–6.

18. *gossamers*] threads of spider's web. The idea is reminiscent of I. iv. 99–103, II. ii. 28–32.

19. *wanton*] playful.

20. *light*] (i) trivial, worthless, (ii) the opposite of heavy.

vanity] the pleasures of this world; cf. Ecclesiastes i. 2, ii. 1.

Juliet. Good even to my ghostly confessor.
Friar L. Romeo shall thank thee, daughter, for us both.
Juliet. As much to him, else is his thanks too much.
Romeo. Ah, Juliet, if the measure of thy joy
Be heap'd like mine, and that thy skill be more
To blazon it, then sweeten with thy breath
This neighbour air, and let rich music's tongue
Unfold the imagin'd happiness that both
Receive in either by this dear encounter.
Juliet. Conceit more rich in matter than in words
Brags of his substance, not of ornament.
They are but beggars that can count their worth,
But my true love is grown to such excess
I cannot sum up sum of half my wealth.
Friar L. Come, come with me and we will make short work,
For, by your leaves, you shall not stay alone
Till holy church incorporate two in one. [*Exeunt.*]

23. else is] *Q2,3;* else in *Q4,F; not in Q1.* 24. *Romeo.*] *Q2–4; Fri. F; not in Q1.* 27. music's] *Q4,F;* musicke *Q2,3; not in Q1.* 33. such] *Q2–4;* such such *F; not in Q1.* 34. sum of] *Q2,3;* some of *Q4,F; not in Q1.* 37. S.D.] *Q1 (subst.); not in Q2–4,F.*

21. *ghostly*] spiritual; cf. II. ii. 192, II. iii. 41.

22. *Romeo . . . both*] Romeo shall return Juliet's greeting with a kiss on behalf of the Friar.

23. *As . . . much*] Juliet considers that Romeo exceeded his brief and included a kiss from himself; she restores the balance by giving him one back.

26. *blazon*] Literally, to describe a coat of arms in proper heraldic terms; hence, describe the rich hues of joy.

breath] i.e. in speech.

30–1. *Conceit . . . ornament*] Imagination, when richer in substance than words, is proud of meaning, not verbal ornamentation.

32. *They . . . worth*] Cf. *Ant.*, I. i. 15.

34. *I . . . wealth*] I cannot compute the total of even half my wealth: cf. Sidney, *Astrophil and Stella*, Sonnet 85, l. 10: 'See Beauties totall summe summ'd in her face'.

[ACT III]

[SCENE I]

Enter MERCUTIO, BENVOLIO *and* Men.

Ben. I pray thee, good Mercutio, let's retire;
The day is hot, the Capels are abroad,
And if we meet we shall not 'scape a brawl,
For now these hot days is the mad blood stirring.

Mer. Thou art like one of these fellows that, when he enters the confines of a tavern, claps me his sword upon the table and says 'God send me no need of thee!' and by the operation of the second cup draws him on the drawer, when indeed there is no need.

Ben. Am I like such a fellow?

Mer. Come, come, thou art as hot a Jack in thy mood as any in Italy; and as soon moved to be moody, and as soon moody to be moved.

Ben. And what to?

Mer. Nay, and there were two such, we should have none shortly, for one would kill the other. Thou? Why,

ACT III

Scene I

ACT III SCENE I] *Rowe; not in Q2–4,F,Q1.* *Location.*] *The street. Rowe.* 2. Capels are] *Q1;* Capels *Q2,3;* Capulets *Q4,F.* 3–4.] *As Rowe; prose in Q2–4,F; not in Q1.* 5. these] *Q2–4,F;* those *Q1.* 9. him] *Q2–4,F;* it *Q1.*

2. *The day is hot*] 'It is observed, that in Italy almost all assassinations are committed during the heat of summer' (Dr Johnson). Reed cites Sir Thomas Smith, *The Common-welth of England* (1583): 'in the warme time people for the most part be more unruly'.

Capels] *Capels* for *Capulets* appears in Brooke and at v. i. 18 below.

8. *operation*] intoxicating effect.

9. *drawer*] waiter who draws and serves wine or ale.

12. *moved*] provoked.

moody] irascible.

15. *two*] Punning on Benvolio's *to* in l. 14.

thou wilt quarrel with a man that hath a hair more or a hair less in his beard than thou hast. Thou wilt quarrel with a man for cracking nuts, having no other reason but because thou hast hazel eyes. What eye but such an eye would spy out such a quarrel? Thy head is as full of quarrels as an egg is full of meat, and yet thy head hath been beaten as addle as an egg for quarrelling. Thou hast quarrelled with a man for coughing in the street, because he hath wakened thy dog that hath lain asleep in the sun. Didst thou not fall out with a tailor for wearing his new doublet before Easter; with another for tying his new shoes with old riband? And yet thou wilt tutor me from quarrelling!

Ben. And I were so apt to quarrel as thou art, any man should buy the fee simple of my life for an hour and a quarter.

Mer. The fee simple! O simple!

Enter TYBALT, PETRUCHIO *and* Others.

Ben. By my head, here comes the Capulets.

Mer. By my heel, I care not.

Tyb. Follow me close, for I will speak to them.
Gentlemen, good e'en: a word with one of you.

Mer. And but one word with one of us? Couple it with

30. from] *Q2–4,F;* of *Q1.*

21. *eye*] Punning on Benvolio's *I* of l. 10; but what he accuses Benvolio of is more applicable to himself; it will be confirmed by his reaction to Tybalt's *consortest* at l. 44.

22–3. *as full . . . meat*] Proverbial; cf. Tilley K 149; *meat* = food.

23. *addle*] rotten.

26. *dog*] Cf. I. i. 7 and n.

27–8. *wearing . . . Easter*] The penitential period of Lent, before Easter, yields the adjective *lenten* = dismal (of clothing); new fashions came out at Easter.

31–3. *any . . . quarter*] my life would not be worth an hour and a quarter's purchase.

34. *fee simple*] Literally, an estate belonging absolutely to its owner; hence, absolute possession.

simple] feeble.

S.D. *Petruchio*] Also named as Capulet's guest in I. v. 130; but Shakespeare gives him no speaking part. See Intro., p. 14.

36. *By my heel*] A scornful oath (cf. *Ado,* III. iv. 44); i.e. he will not take to his heels; cf. the exchange between Sampson and Gregory at I. i. 30–5.

something, make it a word and a blow.

Tyb. You shall find me apt enough to that, sir, and you will give me occasion.

Mer. Could you not take some occasion without giving?

Tyb. Mercutio, thou consortest with Romeo.

Mer. Consort? What, dost thou make us minstrels? And thou make minstrels of us, look to hear nothing but discords. Here's my fiddlestick, here's that shall make you dance. Zounds, consort!

Ben. We talk here in the public haunt of men.
Either withdraw unto some private place,
Or reason coldly of your grievances,
Or else depart. Here all eyes gaze on us.

Mer. Men's eyes were made to look, and let them gaze.
I will not budge for no man's pleasure, I.

Enter ROMEO.

Tyb. Well, peace be with you, sir, here comes my man.

Mer. But I'll be hang'd, sir, if he wear your livery.
Marry, go before to field, he'll be your follower.
Your worship in that sense may call him 'man'.

Tyb. Romeo, the love I bear thee can afford
No better term than this: thou art a villain.

Romeo. Tybalt, the reason that I have to love thee
Doth much excuse the appertaining rage
To such a greeting: villain am I none,
Therefore farewell. I see thou knowest me not.

48. Zounds] *Q2–4;* Come *F; var. Q1.*

59. love] *Q2–4,F;* hate *Q1.*

40. *word . . . blow*] Proverbial; cf. Tilley W 763.

44. *consortest with*] art a close companion of.

45. *minstrels*] Mercutio finds an insulting quibble: *consort* was the collective noun for a group of hired musicians, classed as menials.

47. *fiddlestick*] For similar puns on fencing and music cf. II. iv. 20–3, where Mercutio is talking about Tybalt.

55. *my man*] i.e. the man I am after.

56. *wear your livery*] (i) as if by *man* Tybalt means 'manservant', (ii) be of your sort: *a coward*—a quibble on *livery/liver* leads towards 'lily-livered'.

57. *he'll . . . follower*] (i) quibbling on *man* as personal attendant, (ii) he'll eagerly follow to fight the duel. Cf. Lyly, *Sapho and Phao*, II. iii. 9–13, as cited in n. to II. iv. 23.

60. *villain*] imputing menial birth and base conduct.

62. *Doth . . . rage*] Goes far to excuse me from reacting with the degree of anger appropriate.

Tyb. Boy, this shall not excuse the injuries
That thou hast done me, therefore turn and draw.

Romeo. I do protest I never injuried thee,
But love thee better than thou canst devise
Till thou shalt know the reason of my love.
And so, good Capulet, which name I tender
As dearly as mine own, be satisfied.

Mer. O calm, dishonourable, vile submission:
Alla stoccata carries it away! [*He draws.*]
Tybalt, you rat-catcher, will you walk?

Tyb. What wouldst thou have with me?

Mer. Good King of Cats, nothing but one of your nine lives. That I mean to make bold withal, and, as you shall use me hereafter, dry-beat the rest of the eight. Will you pluck your sword out of his pilcher by the ears? Make haste, lest mine be about your ears ere it be out.

Tyb. I am for you. [*He draws.*]

Romeo. Gentle Mercutio, put thy rapier up.

Mer. Come sir, your passado. [*They fight.*]

Romeo. Draw, Benvolio, beat down their weapons.
Gentlemen, for shame, forbear this outrage.
Tybalt, Mercutio! The Prince expressly hath

67. injuried] *Q2; injured Q3,4,F,Q1 (subst.), Pope.* 68. love] *Q2–4,Q1;* lou'd *F.* 71. mine] *Q2;* my *Q3,4,F; not in Q1.* 73. stoccata] *Knight; stucatho Q2–4,F; stockado Q1.* S.D.] *Capell; not in Q2–4,F,Q1.* 82. S.D.] *Rowe (Drawing); not in Q2–4,F,Q1.* 84. S.D.] *Capell; not in Q2–4,F,Q1.*

67. *injuried*] Mommsen defends this Q2 reading, and Crow notes it to be a 'good Elizabethan verb', as OED examples show.

68. *devise*] imagine.

70. *tender*] value.

73. *Alla stoccata*] A technical term for a thrust, in the Italian fencing manuals.

carries it away] wins the day.

74. *rat-catcher*] Cf. II. iv. 19 n.

walk] withdraw (to fight a duel).

75. *What . . . me?*] Tybalt's reluctance to react to Mercutio's insults persists.

76–7. *nine lives*] A proverbial superstition; cf. Tilley C 154.

77–8. *That . . . eight*] 'One of them I mean to take; and then, according as you treat me well or ill, I'll spare your eight other lives or thrash you until you have lost them all' (Kittredge).

79. *pilcher*] an outer garment of leather (OED sb 1), hence, a scabbard.

79–80. *by the ears*] 'suggests a reluctant sword' (NCS); presumably ears = hilt.

84. *Come . . . passado*] Come sir, show the thrust you make such a fuss about. Cf. II. iv. 25–6 and n.

Forbid this bandying in Verona streets.
Hold, Tybalt! Good Mercutio!
Tybalt under Romeo's arm thrusts Mercutio in.
A Follower. Away Tybalt. *Exit Tybalt* [*with his followers*].
Mer. I am hurt.
A plague o' both your houses. I am sped.
Is he gone, and hath nothing?
Ben. What, art thou hurt?
Mer. Ay, ay, a scratch, a scratch. Marry, 'tis enough.
Where is my page? Go villain, fetch a surgeon.
[*Exit Page.*]
Romeo. Courage, man, the hurt cannot be much.

Mer. No, 'tis not so deep as a well, nor so wide as a church door, but 'tis enough, 'twill serve. Ask for me tomorrow and you shall find me a grave man. I am peppered, I warrant, for this world. A plague o' both your houses. Zounds, a dog, a rat, a mouse, a cat, to scratch a man to death. A braggart, a

88. Forbid this] *Q2;* Forbid *Q3,4;* Forbidden *F; not in Q1.* 89. S.D.] *ed.; Tybalt . . . in and flies. Q1; not in Q2–4,F.* 90. *A Follower.* Away Tybalt.] *Spencer; Petruchio.* Away *Tybalt. Williams, conj. Greg; Away* Tybalt. *Q2–4; Exit Tybalt. F (as S.D.); not in Q1.* 92. o' both your] *Dyce;* a both *Q2–4;* a both the *F;* of both the *F2;* on your *Q1.* 95. S.D.] *Capell; not in Q2–4,F,Q1.* 101. Zounds] *Q5;* sounds *Q2–4;* What *F; not in Q1.*

88. *bandying*] Cf. II. v. 14 and n.

89. S.D. *thrusts Mercutio in.*] Cf. *Tw.N.*, III. iv. 261–2: 'he gives me the stuck in'.

90. S.D.] Q2 prints *Away Tybalt* in the centre of the page with a line space before and after it, as if a S.D. (on the next page, F4r, '*Enter* Benuolio' is set out in identical manner). Editors either substitute the detailed, interesting S.D. from Q1 or normalize *Away* to *Exit* or assume with Greg that a speech prefix is missing. Possibly this is a Shakespearean imperative S.D. like that in v. iii. 17: *Whistle boy.*

92. *both your houses*] *your* is supplied by analogy with ll. 100–1, 108 and 110; corruption in Q2 at l. 90 shows that the compositor found the manuscript difficult to decipher. The repetition of *your houses* stresses the thematic importance of the event, and Mercutio's perception of the irony of his death for someone else's cause.

sped] done for.

94. *scratch*] Quibbling again on Tybalt as a cat, cf. l. 102 below.

97–8. *wide . . . door*] Cf. Tilley B 93, 'as broad as a barn door'. Mercutio's variant may be because he is thinking of his own funeral.

98–9. *Ask . . . man*] Cf. *Bishop's Bible*, Job vii. 21: 'Behold, nowe must I sleepe in the dust, and if thou sekest me to morowe in the morning, I shal not be' (J. G. McManaway, *N&Q*, ns 3, 1956, p. 57). The quibble on *grave* is especially apt from Mercutio, who cannot be grave even about his own death.

rogue, a villain, that fights by the book of arithmetic—why the devil came you between us? I was hurt under your arm.

Romeo. I thought all for the best.

Mer. Help me into some house, Benvolio,
Or I shall faint. A plague o' both your houses,
They have made worms' meat of me.
I have it, and soundly too. Your houses!

Exit [Mercutio with Benvolio].

Romeo. This gentleman, the Prince's near ally,
My very friend, hath got this mortal hurt
In my behalf—my reputation stain'd
With Tybalt's slander—Tybalt that an hour
Hath been my cousin. O sweet Juliet,
Thy beauty hath made me effeminate
And in my temper soften'd valour's steel.

Enter BENVOLIO.

Ben. O Romeo, Romeo, brave Mercutio is dead,
That gallant spirit hath aspir'd the clouds
Which too untimely here did scorn the earth.

Romeo. This day's black fate on mo days doth depend:
This but begins the woe others must end.

Enter TYBALT.

Ben. Here comes the furious Tybalt back again.

109–10.] *As Q2–4,F;* They . . . it, / And . . . houses! *Dyce; var. Q1.* 110. S.D.] *Rowe; Exit. Q2–4,F; Exeunt. Q1.* 112. got this] *Q2;* gott his *Q3;* got his *Q4,F;* tane this *Q1.* 115. cousin] *Q2–4,F;* kinsman *Q1.* 118. Mercutio is] *Q2–4,Q1;* Mercutio's is *F.* 121. mo] *Q2–4,F;* more *Q1.* 122. S.D.] *Q1,F; not in Q2–4.*

103–4. *book of arithmetic*] fencing manual; cf. II. iv. 21 and n.

109. *worms' meat*] Cf. Tilley M 253, 'A man is nothing but worm's meat', and *1H4*, v. iv. 85–6.

110. *I have it*] Cf. II. iv. 26 and n. on *hai.*

111. *ally*] relative.

114–15. *Tybalt that . . . cousin*] i.e. as a result of the marriage which has just taken place; *cousin* = kinsman.

117. *temper*] (i) disposition, (ii) process by which steel is hardened; cf. I. i. 85 n.

119. *aspir'd*] risen up to. The Marlovian style of this speech is evident; Malone compares *Tamburlaine*, pt. I, 432: 'And both our soules aspire celestiall thrones'.

121. *depend*] impend; cf. *Troil.*, II. iii. 17.

Romeo. Again, in triumph, and Mercutio slain.
Away to heaven respective lenity,
And fire-ey'd fury be my conduct now!
Now, Tybalt, take the 'villain' back again
That late thou gav'st me, for Mercutio's soul
Is but a little way above our heads,
Staying for thine to keep him company.
Either thou, or I, or both must go with him.
Tyb. Thou wretched boy, that didst consort him here,
Shalt with him hence.
Romeo. This shall determine that.
They fight. Tybalt falls.
Ben. Romeo, away, be gone,
The citizens are up, and Tybalt slain!
Stand not amaz'd. The Prince will doom thee death
If thou art taken. Hence, be gone, away!
Romeo. O, I am fortune's fool.
Ben. Why dost thou stay?
Exit Romeo.

Enter Citizens.

Citizen. Which way ran he that kill'd Mercutio?
Tybalt, that murderer, which way ran he?
Ben. There lies that Tybalt.
Citizen. Up, sir, go with me.
I charge thee in the Prince's name obey.

Enter PRINCE, MONTAGUE, CAPULET, *their* Wives *and* All.

Prince. Where are the vile beginners of this fray?

124. Again] *Capell;* He gan *Q2;* He gon *Q3,4,F;* A liue *Q1;* He gay *Hoppe;* He yare *Williams.* 126. fire-ey'd] *Q1* (fier eyed)*;* fier end *Q2;* fier and *Q3;* fire and *Q4,F.* 128. gav'st] *F,Q1;* gavest *Q2–4.* 131. Either] *Q2–4,F;* Or *Q1.* 142. name] *Q2–4;* names *F; not in Q1.*

124. *Again*] Capell's emendation is attractive because the misreading of manuscript *A* as *He* is plausible, and *Again* (taking up Benvolio's last word) makes good sense. I note that in F, III. v. 219, occurs the misprint *Hlack* for *Alack*.

125. *respective lenity*] considerations of mildness.

126. *conduct*] guide.

138. *fortune's fool*] the helpless victim of fortune's mockery and abuse; cf. *Lr*, IV. vi. 191–2: 'what, a prisoner? I am even / The natural fool of fortune'.

Ben. O noble Prince, I can discover all
The unlucky manage of this fatal brawl.
There lies the man, slain by young Romeo,
That slew thy kinsman brave Mercutio.
Lady Cap. Tybalt, my cousin, O my brother's child!
O Prince, O husband, O, the blood is spill'd
Of my dear kinsman. Prince, as thou art true,
For blood of ours shed blood of Montague.
O cousin, cousin.
Prince. Benvolio, who began this bloody fray?
Ben. Tybalt, here slain, whom Romeo's hand did slay.
Romeo, that spoke him fair, bid him bethink
How nice the quarrel was, and urg'd withal
Your high displeasure. All this uttered
With gentle breath, calm look, knees humbly bow'd,
Could not take truce with the unruly spleen
Of Tybalt, deaf to peace, but that he tilts
With piercing steel at bold Mercutio's breast,
Who, all as hot, turns deadly point to point
And, with a martial scorn, with one hand beats
Cold death aside, and with the other sends
It back to Tybalt, whose dexterity
Retorts it. Romeo, he cries aloud
'Hold, friends! Friends part!' and swifter than his tongue
His agile arm beats down their fatal points

148. *Lady Cap.*] *ed.; Capu. Wi. Q2–4,F; M: Q1.* 149. O Prince, O husband] *Capell;* O Prince, O Cozen, husband *Q2–4,F* (*subst.*)*;* Vnhappie sight? Ah *Q1.* 153. bloody] *Q2–4; not in F,Q1.* 160. Tybalt] *Q2–4;* Tybalts *F; not in Q1.* 168. agile] *Q1,Q4* (agill)*;* aged *Q2,3,F.*

144. *discover*] reveal.

149. *O husband*] Dyce suggests the redundant unmetrical *cousin* was caught from the line before; on the other hand Shakespeare's first and second thoughts may have both been printed here.

153. *who . . . fray*] The parallel with I. i is insistent; once again Benvolio is required to give an account of an affray between Capulets and Montagues.

156. *nice*] trivial.

160–1. *Tybalt . . . breast*] Benvolio suppresses the fact that Mercutio provoked Tybalt; in Brooke two bands from the opposed families meet (ll. 961–1036), Tybalt urges his men on to fight; Romeo, walking with his friends, hears the riot, runs to it, and cries 'part frendes, helpe frendes to part the fray' whereupon Tybalt attacks him ferociously. Mercutio is not present in Brooke's version, and Benvolio is not named.

And 'twixt them rushes; underneath whose arm
An envious thrust from Tybalt hit the life
Of stout Mercutio; and then Tybalt fled,
But by and by comes back to Romeo,
Who had but newly entertain'd revenge,
And to't they go like lightning: for, ere I
Could draw to part them, was stout Tybalt slain,
And as he fell did Romeo turn and fly.
This is the truth, or let Benvolio die.

Lady Cap. He is a kinsman to the Montague.
Affection makes him false. He speaks not true.
Some twenty of them fought in this black strife
And all those twenty could but kill one life.
I beg for justice, which thou, Prince, must give.
Romeo slew Tybalt. Romeo must not live.

Prince. Romeo slew him, he slew Mercutio.
Who now the price of his dear blood doth owe?

Mont. Not Romeo, Prince, he was Mercutio's friend;
His fault concludes but what the law should end,
The life of Tybalt.

Prince. And for that offence
Immediately we do exile him hence.
I have an interest in your hearts' proceeding;
My blood for your rude brawls doth lie a-bleeding.
But I'll amerce you with so strong a fine
That you shall all repent the loss of mine.
I will be deaf to pleading and excuses;
Nor tears nor prayers shall purchase out abuses.
Therefore use none. Let Romeo hence in haste,

178. *Lady Cap.*] *ed.; Ca. Wi. Q2–4; Cap. Wi. F; Mo: Q1.* 186. *Mont.*] *Q4; Capu. Q2,3,F; La. Cap. Rowe; La. Mont. Theobald; not in Q1.* 190. hearts'] *Q2–4,F;* hates *Q1;* heats' *Hanmer.* 194. I] *Q1,Q4;* It *Q2,3,F.* 195. out] *Q2–4;* our *F;* for *Q1.*

170. *envious*] full of enmity.

174. *like lightning*] Cf. Brooke, l. 1031: 'Even as two thunderboltes'.

186. *Mont.*] Q2's *Capu.* is an obvious error.

190. *hearts'*] NCS compares III. ii. 73, where Q2 reads *heart* and Q1 wrongly *hate*.

191. *My blood*] Mercutio is his blood-relative.

192. *amerce*] penalize.

193. *loss of mine*] my loss.

195. *purchase out*] buy off the penalty for.

Else, when he is found, that hour is his last.
Bear hence this body, and attend our will.
Mercy but murders, pardoning those that kill. *Exeunt.*

[SCENE II]

Enter JULIET *alone.*

Juliet. Gallop apace, you fiery-footed steeds,
Towards Phoebus' lodging. Such a waggoner
As Phaeton would whip you to the west
And bring in cloudy night immediately.
Spread thy close curtain, love-performing night,
That runaway's eyes may wink, and Romeo
Leap to these arms untalk'd-of and unseen.

199. but] *Q2–4;* not *F; var. Q1.*

Scene II

SCENE II] *Rowe; not in Q2–4,F,Q1.* *Location.*] *An Apartment in Capulet's House. Rowe; Capulet's Garden. Capell.* 2. Towards] *Q2–4,F;* To *Q1.*

198. *Bear . . . body*] Although Mercutio is carried off stage to die, Tybalt's corpse remains as a strong focus of attention until the scene ends; the action of bearing him off gives visual emphasis to the turning point of the action: the dark second half of the play begins. At the same time, the action does not pause: Juliet's soliloquy of longing for Romeo, in III. ii, uttered while his sentence of banishment still rings in our ears, is an astonishingly powerful dramatic juxtaposition.

Scene II

1. *Gallop apace*] Cf. Marlowe, *Edward II*, l. 1738: 'Gallop a pace bright *Phoebus* through the skie'. See the discussion of the speech, Intro., pp. 58–60 above.

fiery-footed] Cf. Golding's *Ovid*, II. 491, where the chariot-horses of Phoebus are called 'firiefooted'.

2. *lodging*] night's resting place (OED sb 3).

waggoner] Golding's word for Phaeton.

3–4. *Phaeton . . . immediately*] Cf. *3H6*, I. iv. 34, II. vi. 11–13. The irony implicit in Juliet's invocation of the Phaeton story is notable.

5. *love-performing*] i.e. for the enacting of love. Cf. Daniel, *Rosamond*, ll. 432–4: 'night . . . / Who with her sable mantle friendly couers / The sweet-stolne sports, of ioyfull meeting Louers'.

6. *runaway's*] Editors, in Johnson's phrase, have frolicked in conjecturing emendations, but this famous crux still resists solution. Warburton explains that *runaway's* refers to the sun which has at last turned and run before the irresistible onset of night, and compares *Mer.V.*, II. vi. 47: 'For the close night doth play the runaway'. Among suggestions which may claim graphical plausibility is *cunningest* (Dover Wilson) = most scandal-mongering and curious. Some interpret *runaway's* as referring to Night

Lovers can see to do their amorous rites
By their own beauties; or, if love be blind,
It best agrees with night. Come, civil night,
Thou sober-suited matron, all in black,
And learn me how to lose a winning match
Play'd for a pair of stainless maidenhoods.
Hood my unmann'd blood, bating in my cheeks,
With thy black mantle, till strange love grow bold,
Think true love acted simple modesty.
Come night, come Romeo, come thou day in night,
For thou wilt lie upon the wings of night
Whiter than new snow upon a raven's back.

9. By] *Q4; And by Q2,3,F; not in Q1.* if love be] *Q2,3,F;* of love to *Q4; not in Q1.* 13. maidenhoods] *Q2,3,F;* maiden-heads *Q4; not in Q1.* 15. grow] *Q2–4,F;* grown *Rowe; not in Q1.* 19. new snow upon] *Q2,3,F;* snow upon *Q4;* new snow on *F2; not in Q1.*

whose eyes are stars, or to Romeo; Delius thinks it plural, meaning 'vagabonds at night'. Phaeton in the chariot of the sun is a runaway, and Cupid is called a runaway often (cf. Lyly, *Sapho and Phao*, v. ii. 72–4, *Gallathea*, II. ii. 9–11, Spenser, *Faerie Queene*, III. vi. 11–26) and this is an acceptable interpretation here: cf. *Cym.*, II. iv. 87–91: 'The roof o'th'chamber / With golden cherubins is fretted; her andirons— / I had forgot them—were two winking Cupids / Of silver, each on one foot standing, nicely / Depending on their brands.' Dowden's suggested punctuation makes *That* a demonstrative pronoun (= yonder) and the whole phrase an interjection '—That runaway's eyes may wink—'.

7. *Leap*] Cf. Marlowe, *Tragedy of Dido*, v. i. 1587–8: 'if thou wilt stay, / Leap in mine armes, mine armes are open wide'.

8–9. *Lovers . . . beauties*] Cf. Marlowe, *Hero and Leander*, I. 191: 'darke night is *Cupid's* day'.

8. *amorous rites*] Cf. ibid., II. 64.

9. *if . . . blind*] Cf. I. i. 169 and n.

10. *civil*] grave, decently solemn (Johnson).

12. *lose a winning match*] i.e. win her beloved by surrendering to him; cf. Marlowe, *Hero and Leander*, II. 293–4: 'Treason was in her thought, / And cunningly to yeeld herself she sought'.

14. *Hood . . . bating*] Terms from falconry. An untrained (*unmanned*) hawk would flutter its wings (*bate*) when taken out of doors unless a hood was drawn over its head: so night will cover Juliet's blushing cheeks; cf. *Shr.*, IV. i. 177–80: 'Another way I have to man my haggard, / To make her come, and know her keeper's call, / That is, to watch her, as we watch these kites / That bate and beat, and will not be obedient'.

unmann'd] (i) untrained, as above, (ii) as yet without her husband.

15. *strange*] unfamiliar, shy.

16. *acted*] A past participle, not a preterite.

17. *day in night*] Cf. v. iii. 85–6, and Sonnet 27; or Marlowe, *Hero and Leander*, II. 240: 'Rich iewels in the darke are soonest spide'.

19. *Whiter . . . back*] Cf. I. v. 47.

new snow] NCS prefers Q4, believing *new* to be a first shot which Shakespeare marked (or should have marked) for deletion: 'One cannot

Come gentle night, come loving black-brow'd night,
Give me my Romeo; and when I shall die
Take him and cut him out in little stars,
And he will make the face of heaven so fine
That all the world will be in love with night,
And pay no worship to the garish sun.
O, I have bought the mansion of a love
But not possess'd it, and though I am sold,
Not yet enjoy'd. So tedious is this day
As is the night before some festival
To an impatient child that hath new robes
And may not wear them. O, here comes my Nurse.

Enter NURSE *with cords, wringing her hands.*

And she brings news, and every tongue that speaks
But Romeo's name speaks heavenly eloquence.
Now, Nurse, what news? What hast thou there?
The cords that Romeo bid thee fetch?

Nurse. Ay, ay, the cords.

Juliet. Ay me, what news? Why dost thou wring thy hands?

Nurse. Ah weraday, he's dead, he's dead, he's dead!
We are undone, lady, we are undone.
Alack the day, he's gone, he's kill'd, he's dead.

Juliet. Can heaven be so envious?

21. I] *Q2,3,F;* hee *Q4; not in Q1.* 31. S.D.] *As Williams; Enter Nurse with cords. Q2–4,F; Enter Nurse wringing her hands with the ladder of cordes in her lap. Q1.* 37. weraday] *Q2;* welady *Q3,4,F; not in Q1.* he's dead, he's dead, he's dead] *Q2–4;* he's dead, he's dead *F; var. Q1.*

have *old* snow on a raven's back'; but the function of *new* here is to emphasize the brilliant whiteness of the snow; F2 corrects the metre.

21. *I*] Juliet quibbles on *death* as also meaning sexual ecstasy: she prays that Romeo may share the experience with her, in death like a rocket soaring up into the night sky and exploding into innumerable stars, outgoing the final climax in Ovid's *Metamorphoses*, the apotheosis of Caesar into a 'goodly shyning starre' (xv. 955). Romeo will experience a metamorphosis into shining immortality, yet she seems to think of herself as mortally ephemeral—if she thinks of herself at all—in this moment of intense adoration of her lover. Q4's *he* lacks the element of tragic premonition of their shared fate expressed in Q2.

22–5. *Take . . . sun*] Cf. II. ii. 20–2.

30–1. *an impatient . . . wear them*] Cf. Lyly, *Euphues and his England* (ed. Bond), p. 158: 'To love women & neuer enioy them, is as much as to . . . be delighted with faire apparel, & neuer wear it'.

31. S.D. with cords . . . hands] See Intro., p. 8.

Nurse. Romeo can,
Though heaven cannot. O Romeo, Romeo,
Who ever would have thought it? Romeo!
Juliet. What devil art thou that dost torment me thus?
This torture should be roar'd in dismal hell.
Hath Romeo slain himself? Say thou but 'Ay'
And that bare vowel 'I' shall poison more
Than the death-darting eye of cockatrice.
I am not I if there be such an 'I',
Or those eyes shut that makes thee answer 'Ay'.
If he be slain say 'Ay', or if not, 'No'.
Brief sounds determine of my weal or woe.
Nurse. I saw the wound, I saw it with mine eyes
—God save the mark—here on his manly breast.
A piteous corse, a bloody piteous corse,
Pale, pale as ashes, all bedaub'd in blood,
All in gore-blood. I swounded at the sight.
Juliet. O break, my heart. Poor bankrupt, break at once.
To prison, eyes, ne'er look on liberty.
Vile earth to earth resign, end motion here,
And thou and Romeo press one heavy bier.
Nurse. O Tybalt, Tybalt, the best friend I had.
O courteous Tybalt, honest gentleman.
That ever I should live to see thee dead.
Juliet. What storm is this that blows so contrary?
Is Romeo slaughter'd and is Tybalt dead?
My dearest cousin and my dearer lord?

49. shut] *Capell;* shot *Q2–4,F; not in Q1.* 51. of my] *F,Q5;* my *Q2–4; not in Q1.* 60. one] *Q4;* on *Q2,3,F; not in Q1.* bier] *Q4,F* (beere)*;* beare *Q2,3; not in Q1.*

40. *envious*] full of enmity.

Romeo can] i.e. by killing Tybalt.

47. *the . . . cockatrice*] a fabulous serpent (also called a basilisk) proverbial for slaying by sight (Tilley C 495); cf. *Tw.N.*, III. iv. 185–6: 'they will kill one another by the look, like cockatrices'.

48–50. *I am . . . 'No'*] Cf. *R2*, IV. i. 201: 'Ay, no, no, ay; for I must nothing be'.

53. *God . . . mark*] A proverbial apologetic phrase used when something unlucky, improper or disagreeable has been mentioned. The Nurse dwells in detail on the scene, all the same.

56. *gore*] clotted.

59. *Vile earth . . . resign*] Cf. Ecclesiastes xii. 7: 'Then shall the dust return to the earth as it was'.

62. *honest*] honourable.

Then dreadful trumpet sound the general doom,
For who is living if those two are gone?

Nurse. Tybalt is gone and Romeo banished.
Romeo that kill'd him, he is banished.

Juliet. O God! Did Romeo's hand shed Tybalt's blood?

Nurse. It did, it did, alas the day, it did.

Juliet. O serpent heart, hid with a flowering face.
Did ever dragon keep so fair a cave?
Beautiful tyrant, fiend angelical,
Dove-feather'd raven, wolvish-ravening lamb!
Despised substance of divinest show!
Just opposite to what thou justly seem'st!
A damned saint, an honourable villain!
O nature what hadst thou to do in hell
When thou didst bower the spirit of a fiend
In mortal paradise of such sweet flesh?
Was ever book containing such vile matter
So fairly bound? O, that deceit should dwell
In such a gorgeous palace.

Nurse. There's no trust,

72. *Nurse.*] *Q1; not in Q2–4,F.* 73. *Juliet.* O] *Q1; Nur.* O *Q2–4,F.* heart] *Q2–4,F;* hate *Q1.* 74. Did] *F2; Iu.* Did *Q2–4,F; not in Q1.* 76. Dove-feather'd raven] *Theobald (subst.);* Rauenous douefeatherd rauē *Q2,3,F (subst.);* Ravenous doue, feathred Rauen *Q4; not in Q1.* 79. damned] *Q4;* dimme *Q2,3;* dimne *F; not in Q1.* 81. bower] *Q2,3,F;* power *Q4; not in Q1.* 85–7.] *As Capell;* Theres . . . men, / All . . . dissemblers, *Q2–4,F;* There's no trust, / No faith, no honesty in men; all naught, / All perjured, all dissemblers, all forsworn *Daniel, conj. Fleay; var. Q1.*

67. *dreadful trumpet*] 'the last trump' (1 Corinthians xv. 52).

72. *Nurse*] In Q2 the prefixes for Nurse and Juliet appear one line low so that *it did* is continued to Juliet, and the questioner answers herself. Q1 is correct.

73. *serpent . . . face*] Proverbial; Whitney, *A Choice of Emblemes* (1586), illustrates and quotes Virgil, *Ecl.*, iii. 93 ('latet anguis in herba'); cf. *2H6*, III. i. 228–30, *Mac.*, I. v. 62–3.

75. *tyrant*] ruffian (OED sb 4 b).

76. *Dove-feather'd*] The emendation removes Shakespeare's first draft version.

wolvish-ravening] Cf. Matthew vii. 15: 'Beware of false prophets, which come to you in sheep's clothing, but inwardly they are ravening wolves'.

77. *Despised . . . show*] Despicable reality masked as divine.

78. *justly*] exactly.

79. *damned*] The shortened form *damnd* in the manuscript would have made the misreading easier.

83. *book*] Cf. I. iii. 87–8.

85. *palace*] Cf. V. iii. 107.

85–7. *There's . . . dissemblers*] Capell's arrangement is closest to Q2; Hosley supposes that the phrase *all naught* is Shakespeare's first thought

No faith, no honesty in men. All perjur'd,
All forsworn, all naught, all dissemblers.
Ah, where's my man? Give me some aqua vitae.
These griefs, these woes, these sorrows make me old.
Shame come to Romeo.

Juliet. Blister'd be thy tongue
For such a wish. He was not born to shame.
Upon his brow shame is asham'd to sit,
For 'tis a throne where honour may be crown'd
Sole monarch of the universal earth.
O, what a beast was I to chide at him.

Nurse. Will you speak well of him that kill'd your cousin?

Juliet. Shall I speak ill of him that is my husband?
Ah, poor my lord, what tongue shall smooth thy name
When I thy three-hours wife have mangled it?
But wherefore, villain, didst thou kill my cousin?
That villain cousin would have kill'd my husband.
Back, foolish tears, back to your native spring,
Your tributary drops belong to woe
Which you mistaking offer up to joy.
My husband lives, that Tybalt would have slain,
And Tybalt's dead, that would have slain my husband.
All this is comfort. Wherefore weep I then?
Some word there was, worser than Tybalt's death,
That murder'd me. I would forget it fain,
But O, it presses to my memory
Like damned guilty deeds to sinners' minds.
Tybalt is dead and Romeo—banished.
That 'banished', that one word 'banished',
Hath slain ten thousand Tybalts: Tybalt's death

95. at him] *Q2–4;* him *F; not in Q1.* 106. Tybalt's] *Q2–4; Tybalt F; not in Q1.* 108. word there was] *Q2;* words there was *Q3,4,F; not in Q1.*

which he had neglected to delete from his foul papers.

87. *naught*] wicked.

88. *aqua vitae*] brandy. The Nurse calls again for aqua vitae at IV. v. 16; there is a hint of comedy in her prompt seizure of legitimate, 'medicinal' excuses for strong drink. In *Tw.N.*, II. v. 176, Sir Toby regards a liking for aqua vitae as proverbial among midwives.

89. *griefs . . . old*] Cf. Falstaff's protestations in *1H4*, II. iv. 223–5.

90–1. *Blister'd . . . wish*] Cf. Brooke, ll. 1145–6.

98. *smooth*] speak well of (and 'stroke soothingly', contrasting with l. 99's *mangled*).

103. *tributary*] in tribute.

Was woe enough, if it had ended there.
Or if sour woe delights in fellowship
And needly will be rank'd with other griefs,
Why follow'd not, when she said 'Tybalt's dead',
Thy father or thy mother, nay or both,
Which modern lamentation might have mov'd?
But with a rearward following Tybalt's death,
'Romeo is banished': to speak that word
Is father, mother, Tybalt, Romeo, Juliet,
All slain, all dead. Romeo is banished,
There is no end, no limit, measure, bound,
In that word's death. No words can that woe sound.
Where is my father and my mother, Nurse?

Nurse. Weeping and wailing over Tybalt's corse.
Will you go to them? I will bring you thither.

Juliet. Wash they his wounds with tears? Mine shall be spent
When theirs are dry, for Romeo's banishment.
Take up those cords. Poor ropes, you are beguil'd,
Both you and I, for Romeo is exil'd.
He made you for a highway to my bed,
But I, a maid, die maiden-widowed.
Come, cords, come, Nurse, I'll to my wedding bed,
And death, not Romeo take my maidenhead.

Nurse. Hie to your chamber. I'll find Romeo
To comfort you. I wot well where he is.
Hark ye, your Romeo will be here at night.
I'll to him. He is hid at Laurence' cell.

121. with] *Q2–4;* which *F; not in Q1.* 128. corse] *Q2,3* (course), *Q4;* coarse *F,Q1.* 130. tears?] *Q2;* teares: *Q3,4,F; not in Q1.* 136. cords] *Q2;* cord *Q3,4,F; not in Q1.*

117. *needly . . . griefs*] Proverbial; cf. Tilley C 571. Kittredge compares Chaucer, *Troilus*, I. 708–9.

120. *modern*] commonplace.

121. *rearward*] Literally, the rear-guard of a formation of soldiers, hence, a further source of pain after the bad news of Tybalt.

126. *word's death*] i.e. the death involved in the word *banished*.

sound] (i) plumb the depths of, (ii) utter, express.

130. *Wash . . . tears?*] As interrogative, these words are consistent with Juliet's feelings earlier in the scene, as at l. 90 or 126. As non-interrogative on the other hand, Juliet must be understood as saying 'let them weep over Tybalt'.

Juliet. O find him, give this ring to my true knight
And bid him come to take his last farewell. *Exeunt.*

[SCENE III]

Enter FRIAR [LAURENCE].

Friar L. Romeo, come forth, come forth, thou fearful man.
Affliction is enamour'd of thy parts
And thou art wedded to calamity.

Enter ROMEO.

Romeo. Father, what news? What is the Prince's doom?
What sorrow craves acquaintance at my hand
That I yet know not?
Friar L. Too familiar
Is my dear son with such sour company.
I bring thee tidings of the Prince's doom.
Romeo. What less than doomsday is the Prince's doom?
Friar L. A gentler judgement vanish'd from his lips:
Not body's death but body's banishment.
Romeo. Ha! Banishment! Be merciful, say 'death'.
For exile hath more terror in his look,
Much more than death. Do not say 'banishment'.
Friar L. Hence from Verona art thou banished.
Be patient, for the world is broad and wide.

Scene III

SCENE III] *Rowe; not in Q2–4,F,Q1.* *Location.*] *The Monastery. Rowe; Friar Laurence's cell. Capell.* S.D.] *Q1; Enter Frier and Romeo. Q2–4,F.* 3. S.D.] *Q1; not in Q2–4,F.* 15. Hence] *Q1;* Here *Q2–4,F.*

2–3. *Affliction . . . calamity*] The Friar's affectionate quibbles on *enamoured* and *wedded* unintentionally reinforce the idea of fate having marked Romeo; there is also anticipation of v. iii. 102–5 where Romeo thinks of death as amorous of Juliet, seeking her as his paramour. These ironically unconscious echoes and anticipations intensify in the second half of the play.

2. *parts*] attractive qualities.

4. *doom*] judgement.

16. *Be . . . wide*] From Brooke, ll. 1443–4; cf. *R2*, I. iii. 275–6, where Gaunt similarly comforts banished Bolingbroke.

Romeo. There is no world without Verona walls
But purgatory, torture, hell itself;
Hence 'banished' is banish'd from the world,
And world's exile is death. Then 'banished'
Is death, misterm'd. Calling death 'banished'
Thou cut'st my head off with a golden axe
And smilest upon the stroke that murders me.
Friar L. O deadly sin, O rude unthankfulness.
Thy fault our law calls death, but the kind Prince,
Taking thy part, hath rush'd aside the law
And turn'd that black word 'death' to banishment.
This is dear mercy and thou seest it not.
Romeo. 'Tis torture and not mercy. Heaven is here
Where Juliet lives, and every cat and dog
And little mouse, every unworthy thing,
Live here in heaven and may look on her,
But Romeo may not. More validity,
More honourable state, more courtship lives
In carrion flies than Romeo. They may seize
On the white wonder of dear Juliet's hand
And steal immortal blessing from her lips,
Who, even in pure and vestal modesty
Still blush, as thinking their own kisses sin.
But Romeo may not, he is banished.

26. rush'd] *Q2–4,F,Q1;* brush'd *Collier*[2]. 37. blessing] *Q2–4,F;* kisses *Q1.* 40–3.] *See note below.*

17. *There . . . walls*] Cf. *Troil.*, I. i. 2–3: 'Why should I war without the walls of Troy / That find such cruel battle here within?'

19. *banished*] Romeo's agonized repetitions of this word are parallel to Juliet's in III. ii. 112–31.

20. *world's exile*] i.e. exile from the world.

26. *rush'd*] thrust violently. A possible compositorial error for *thrust*. Other possibilities include *pushed* and *brushed*.

30–2. *cat . . . look on her*] Proverbial; cf. Tilley C 141: 'A cat may look at a king'.

33. *validity*] value.

34. *state*] rank.

courtship] the state befitting a courtier (OED sv b 2).

35. *flies*] A similar intensity of focus on a fly occurs in *Tit.*, III. ii. 53–80.

39. *Still*] Ever.

their own] i.e. the kisses one lip gives the other when they are closed.

40–3. *But Romeo . . . death?*] Q2 reads *This may flies do, when I from this must flie, / And sayest thou yet, that exile is not death? / But Romeo may not, he is banished. / Flies may do this, but I from this must flie: / They are freemen, but I am banished.* Capell was the first to propose that Shakespeare's first version, meant for deletion, had been acci-

Flies may do this, but I from this must fly.
They are free men but I am banished.
And say'st thou yet that exile is not death?
Hadst thou no poison mix'd, no sharp-ground knife,
No sudden mean of death, though ne'er so mean,
But 'banished' to kill me? 'Banished'?
O Friar, the damned use that word in hell.
Howling attends it. How hast thou the heart,
Being a divine, a ghostly confessor,
A sin-absolver, and my friend profess'd,
To mangle me with that word 'banished'?
Friar L. Thou fond mad man, hear me a little speak.
Romeo. O, thou wilt speak again of banishment.
Friar L. I'll give thee armour to keep off that word,
Adversity's sweet milk, philosophy,
To comfort thee though thou art banished.
Romeo. Yet 'banished'? Hang up philosophy.
Unless philosophy can make a Juliet,
Displant a town, reverse a Prince's doom,
It helps not, it prevails not. Talk no more.
Friar L. O, then I see that mad men have no ears.
Romeo. How should they when that wise men have no eyes?
Friar L. Let me dispute with thee of thy estate.
Romeo. Thou canst not speak of that thou dost not feel.

43. say'st] *Q3–4,F;* sayest *Q2; not in Q1.* 48. Howling attends] *Q2–4,Q1;* Howlings attends *F.* 52. Thou] *Q1,Q4;* Then *Q2,3,F.* a little] *Q2–4; not in F,Q1.* 61. mad men] *Q1,Q3,4,F;* mad man *Q2.* 62. that] *Q2,Q1; not in Q3,4,F.* 63. dispute] *Q2–4,Q1;* dispaire *F.*

dentally printed; he omitted the first three lines of Q2. I suppose that, having already written *And sayest . . . death?*, Shakespeare revised *This may . . . flie* by expanding it into the last three lines of the passage; he did not clearly delete *This may . . . flie* and he did not clearly indicate where his three-line revision was to be placed; it was mistakenly placed after, not before, *And sayest . . . death?* NCS supposes that the last three lines were Shakespeare's first shot. Other editors suppose the line *Flies . . . flie* to be a second version of *This may flies . . . flie* and so must be preferred, and the line *They . . . banished* a version of *But Romeo . . . banished.*

45. *mean*] Quibbling on (i) method, (ii) sordid, base.

59. *Displant*] Transplant.

62. *wise . . . eyes*] The proverb was 'Discreet women have neither eyes nor ears'; cf. Tilley W 683.

63. *dispute . . . estate*] discuss your situation with you.

Wert thou as young as I, Juliet thy love,
An hour but married, Tybalt murdered,
Doting like me, and like me banished,
Then mightst thou speak, then mightst thou tear thy hair
And fall upon the ground as I do now,
Taking the measure of an unmade grave. *Knock.*

Friar L. Arise, one knocks. Good Romeo, hide thyself.

Romeo. Not I, unless the breath of heartsick groans
Mist-like infold me from the search of eyes. *Knock.*

Friar L. Hark how they knock.—Who's there?—Romeo, arise,
Thou wilt be taken.—Stay awhile.—Stand up. *Knock.*
Run to my study.—By and by.—God's will,
What simpleness is this?—I come, I come. *Knock.*
Who knocks so hard? Whence come you, what's your will?

Nurse. [*Within.*] Let me come in and you shall know my errand.
I come from Lady Juliet.

Friar L. Welcome then.

Enter NURSE.

Nurse. O holy Friar, O, tell me, holy Friar,
Where is my lady's lord, where's Romeo?

Friar L. There on the ground, with his own tears made drunk.

Nurse. O, he is even in my mistress' case,

65. I] *Q2–4,Q1; not in F.* thy] *Q2–4,Q1;* my *F.* 70. S.D.] *Rowe (subst.); Enter Nurse, and knocke. Q2,3,F; Nurse knocks. Q4,Q1.* 73. S.D.] *Q4,F; They knocke. Q2,3; var. Q1.* 75. S.D.] *F; Slud knock. Q2,3 (subst.); Knocke againe. Q4; not in Q1.* 77. S.D.] *Q2–4,F; not in Q1.* 82. Where is] *Q1;* Wheres *Q2–4,F.*

70. *Taking . . . grave*] i.e. as Romeo lies stretched on the ground in despair.

74–7. *Hark . . . come*] The Friar addresses Romeo, and the unseen person knocking, alternately.

75. S.D.] Gericke conjectures that Q2's *Slud* may be a misreading of *Slye*, the actor who evidently played under his own name in *Shr.* Harold Jenkins suggests *Still*, which is attractive.

76. *By and by*] in a moment.

77. *simpleness*] foolishness.

Just in her case. O woeful sympathy,
Piteous predicament. Even so lies she,
Blubbering and weeping, weeping and blubbering.
Stand up, stand up. Stand, and you be a man.
For Juliet's sake, for her sake, rise and stand.
Why should you fall into so deep an O? *He rises.*

Romeo. Nurse.

Nurse. Ah sir, ah sir, death's the end of all.

Romeo. Spak'st thou of Juliet? How is it with her?
Doth not she think me an old murderer
Now I have stain'd the childhood of our joy
With blood remov'd but little from her own?
Where is she? And how doth she? And what says
My conceal'd lady to our cancell'd love?

Nurse. O, she says nothing, sir, but weeps and weeps,
And now falls on her bed, and then starts up,
And Tybalt calls, and then on Romeo cries,
And then down falls again.

Romeo. As if that name,
Shot from the deadly level of a gun,
Did murder her, as that name's cursed hand
Murder'd her kinsman. O, tell me, Friar, tell me,
In what vile part of this anatomy
Doth my name lodge? Tell me that I may sack

85–6. O woeful . . . predicament.] *Q2–4,F,Q1; Friar.* Oh woeful . . . predicament! *Steevens 1778, conj. Farmer.* 90. S.D.] *Q1; not in Q2–4,F.* 92. Spak'st] *Q2–4,Q1;* Speak'st *F.* 93. not she] *Q2–4,F;* she not *Q1.* 97. cancell'd] *Q2–4,Q1;* conceal'd *F.* 101–2. As if . . . gun] *Rowe; one line in Q2–4,F,Q1.* 102. deadly] *Q2–4,Q1;* dead *F.*

85–6. *O . . . predicament*] Any emendation would be against all available textual evidence. Steevens accepts Farmer's conjecture that 'such language must necessarily belong to the Friar'. Ulrici disagrees, finding it characteristic that the Nurse should use a 'few grand, high-sounding phrases', even if for once they are correctly employed.

88–90. *Stand . . . O*] The Nurse unwittingly makes a series of bawdy quibbles on *Stand* and *O* (cf. *Wiv.*, IV. i. 46–9).

93. *old*] (i) hardened (OED sb 5), (ii) great (OED sb 6).

97. *cancell'd*] a legal term: 'made null and void'; cf. *Lucr.*, l. 26.

102. *level*] line of aim.

105–6. *In . . . lodge*] Cf. II. ii. 38–51: the parallel with Juliet's meditation is acutely ironic; cf. also *Lr*, III. vi. 75–8.

The hateful mansion.
Friar L. Hold thy desperate hand.
Art thou a man? Thy form cries out thou art.
Thy tears are womanish, thy wild acts denote
The unreasonable fury of a beast.
Unseemly woman in a seeming man,
And ill-beseeming beast in seeming both!
Thou hast amaz'd me. By my holy order,
I thought thy disposition better temper'd.
Hast thou slain Tybalt? Wilt thou slay thyself?
And slay thy lady that in thy life lives,
By doing damned hate upon thyself?
Why rail'st thou on thy birth, the heaven and earth?
Since birth, and heaven, and earth all three do meet
In thee at once; which thou at once wouldst lose.
Fie, fie, thou sham'st thy shape, thy love, thy wit,
Which, like a usurer, abound'st in all,
And usest none in that true use indeed
Which should bedeck thy shape, thy love, thy wit.
Thy noble shape is but a form of wax
Digressing from the valour of a man;

109. denote] *Q1,Q4,F;* deuote *Q2,3.* 116. that . . . lives,] *F4;* that . . . lies, *Q2–4,F;* too, that liues in thee? *Q1.* 118. rail'st] raylest *Q2–4; not in Q1.* 121. sham'st] *F;* shamest *Q2–4; not in Q1.*

107. *mansion*] Cf. III. ii. 26, an ironic echo.

Here Q1 has the S.D. *He offers to stab himselfe, and Nurse snatches the dagger away.* There is nothing in the dialogue (or the characterization of the Nurse generally) to prepare for or to support this intervention by the Nurse; indeed this piece of business looks like a gratuitous and distracting bid on the part of the actor in the unauthorized version to claim extra attention to himself when the audience should be concentrating on Romeo and the Friar. To retain this S.D. in the text seems neither necessary or defensible, so I omit it.

108–12. *Art . . . both*] Cf. Brooke, ll. 1353–8.

112. *ill-beseeming*] unnatural and inappropriate.

118. *Why . . . birth*] Cf. Brooke, l. 1327: 'The time and place of byrth, he fiersly did reprove'. Shakespeare, recalling Brooke, did not notice that his own Romeo has not railed against his *birth*, though he has (in ll. 101–7) railed against his *name*. Cf. Intro., p. 38.

122. *like a usurer*] because he does not put talents to their proper use. Quibbling on *use* = interest on money (OED sb 4).

125–6. *form . . . man*] waxwork figure, if it deviates from what makes a man a man—valour.

Thy dear love sworn but hollow perjury,
Killing that love which thou hast vow'd to cherish;
Thy wit, that ornament to shape and love,
Misshapen in the conduct of them both,
Like powder in a skilless soldier's flask
Is set afire by thine own ignorance,
And thou dismember'd with thine own defence.
What, rouse thee, man. Thy Juliet is alive,
For whose dear sake thou wast but lately dead.
There art thou happy. Tybalt would kill thee,
But thou slew'st Tybalt. There art thou happy.
The law that threaten'd death becomes thy friend
And turns it to exile. There art thou happy.
A pack of blessings light upon thy back;
Happiness courts thee in her best array;
But like a mishav'd and a sullen wench
Thou pouts upon thy fortune and thy love.
Take heed, take heed, for such die miserable.

137. slew'st] *Q1,F;* slewest *Q2–4.* happy] *Q2–4,F;* happy too *Q1.* 138. becomes] *Q2–4;* became *F; not in Q1.* 139. turns] *Q2,4;* turne *Q3;* turn'd *F; not in Q1.* 140. of] *Q2–4,Q1;* or *F.* blessings] *Q2,4,Q1;* blessing *Q3,F.* light] *Q2,3,F;* lights *Q4,Q1.* 142. mishav'd] *Q2,3;* misbehau'd *Q4,Q1;* mishaped *F.* a sullen] *F2;* sullen *Q2–4,F,Q1.* 143. pouts upon] *Q4;* puts up *Q2,3;* poutst upon *Q5;* puttest up *F;* frownst upon *Q1.*

130. *Misshapen . . . conduct*] Going awry in the guidance.

131–2. *powder . . . ignorance*] Alluding to the danger in loading a matchlock gun. The soldier carried a flask of ordinary 'corned' gunpowder at the waist and, looped on the third finger of the left hand, a yard of match (lighted at both ends). Powder was poured into the barrel, primed with touchpowder, and the bullet rammed down. A spark from the burning residue of the previous shot might run back through the live powder and set off the flask in the soldier's hand; or the weapon would overheat after seven or eight shots so that the barrel itself might ignite the powder on contact; or the lighted match on the left hand (with which he steadied the gun barrel during loading) might ignite carelessly poured powder. (See C. G. Cruikshank, *Elizabeth's Army*, 1946, p. 106, T. R. Henn, *The Living Image*, 1972, pp. 91–2.) Cf. gunpowder images at II. vi. 9–11 and V. i. 63–5.

142. *mishav'd*] Crow (pp. 15–16) argues from Shakespeare's use of *Haviour* that *mishav'd* has the right to stand here; it is recorded in OED as in use in the sixteenth century in the sense of 'misbehaved'. F2 has *a sullen* which corrects the metre.

143. *pouts*] A common second person singular in Shakespeare (Abbott § 340). Sisson notes 'The copy clearly read *pouts up̄* which the compositor misread as the familiar phrase *puts up* (bears patiently). Had the copy read

Go, get thee to thy love as was decreed,
Ascend her chamber—hence, and comfort her.
But look thou stay not till the Watch be set,
For then thou canst not pass to Mantua,
Where thou shalt live till we can find a time
To blaze your marriage, reconcile your friends,
Beg pardon of the Prince and call thee back,
With twenty hundred thousand times more joy
Than thou wentst forth in lamentation.
Go before, Nurse. Commend me to thy lady
And bid her hasten all the house to bed,
Which heavy sorrow makes them apt unto.
Romeo is coming.

Nurse. O lord, I could have stay'd here all the night
To hear good counsel. O, what learning is.
My lord, I'll tell my lady you will come.

Romeo. Do so, and bid my sweet prepare to chide.

Nurse offers to go in and turns again.

Nurse. Here sir, a ring she bid me give you, sir.
Hie you, make haste, for it grows very late. *Exit.*

Romeo. How well my comfort is reviv'd by this.

Friar L. Go hence, good night, and here stands all your state:
Either be gone before the Watch be set,
Or by the break of day disguis'd from hence.
Sojourn in Mantua. I'll find out your man,
And he shall signify from time to time
Every good hap to you that chances here.
Give me thy hand. 'Tis late. Farewell. Good night.

Romeo. But that a joy past joy calls out on me,
It were a grief so brief to part with thee.
Farewell. *Exeunt.*

151. the] *Q2,4;* thy *Q3,F; not in Q1.* 158. the] *Q2–4;* this *Q1; not in F.* 161. S.D.] *Q1; not in Q2–4,F.* 162. bid] *Q2,3,F;* bids *Q4;* bad *Q1.* 163. S.D.] *Q1; not in Q2–4,F.* 167. disguis'd] *Q3,4,F;* disguise *Q2; not in Q1.*

poutst the error would hardly have been possible.'

150. *blaze*] proclaim in public.

[SCENE IV]

Enter CAPULET, LADY CAPULET *and* PARIS.

Cap. Things have fallen out, sir, so unluckily
That we have had no time to move our daughter.
Look you, she lov'd her kinsman Tybalt dearly,
And so did I. Well, we were born to die.
'Tis very late. She'll not come down tonight.
I promise you, but for your company,
I would have been abed an hour ago.
Paris. These times of woe afford no times to woo.
Madam, good night. Commend me to your daughter.
Lady Cap. I will, and know her mind early tomorrow.
Tonight she's mew'd up to her heaviness.
Paris offers to go in and Capulet calls him again.
Cap. Sir Paris, I will make a desperate tender
Of my child's love. I think she will be rul'd
In all respects by me; nay, more, I doubt it not.
Wife, go you to her ere you go to bed,
Acquaint her here of my son Paris' love,
And bid her—mark you me?—on Wednesday next—
But soft—what day is this?
Paris. Monday, my lord.
Cap. Monday! Ha ha! Well, Wednesday is too soon.
A Thursday let it be, a Thursday, tell her,
She shall be married to this noble earl.
Will you be ready? Do you like this haste?

Scene IV

SCENE IV] *Rowe; not in Q2–4,F,Q1.* *Location.*] *A room in Capulet's house. Capell.* S.D.] *As Rowe; Enter old* Capulet, *his wife and* Paris. *Q2–4,F,Q1 (subst.).* 8. woo] *Q2,3,F,Q1* (wooe); woe *Q4.* 10. *Lady Cap.*] *ed.; La. Q2–4; Lady. F; not in Q1.* 11. she's] *Q2;* she is *Q3,4,F; not in Q1.* S.D.] *Q1; not in Q2–4,F.* 13. be] *Q1,Q3,4,F;* me *Q2.* 16. here of] *Q2,4,F;* hereof *Q3;* with *Q1;* ear of *NCS.*

2. *move*] persuade.

11. *mew'd up*] The mews were the hawk-houses in which hawks were kept at night; cf. *Shr.*, I. i. 87.

12. *desperate tender*] The tender is literally hopeless in the circumstances we know but Capulet does not; Shakespeare stresses the arbitrary and sudden change of Capulet's mind, emphasized in the Q1 S.D.

We'll keep no great ado—a friend or two.
For, hark you, Tybalt being slain so late,
It may be thought we held him carelessly,
Being our kinsman, if we revel much.
Therefore we'll have some half a dozen friends
And there an end. But what say you to Thursday?
Paris. My lord, I would that Thursday were tomorrow.
Cap. Well, get you gone. A Thursday be it then.
Go you to Juliet ere you go to bed,
Prepare her, wife, against this wedding day.
Farewell, my lord.—Light to my chamber, ho!
Afore me, it is so very late that we
May call it early by and by. Good night. *Exeunt.*

[SCENE V]

Enter Romeo *and* Juliet *aloft at the window.*

Juliet. Wilt thou be gone? It is not yet near day.
It was the nightingale and not the lark
That pierc'd the fearful hollow of thine ear.
Nightly she sings on yond pomegranate tree.
Believe me, love, it was the nightingale.

23. We'll] *Q1,Q3,4,F;* Well *Q2, Mommsen.* 34. very] *Q2–4;* very very *Q1; not in F.*

Scene v

Scene v] *Rowe; not in Q2–4,F,Q1.* *Location.*] *The Garden. Rowe; Juliet's Chamber looking to the Garden. Theobald.* S.D.] *Camb.; Enter* Romeo *and* Iuliet *aloft. Q2–4,F; Enter Romeo and Iuliet at the window Q1.*

27. *half a dozen friends*] Shakespeare is not following Brooke here; cf. IV. ii. 2 n., where he seems to be remembering Brooke again.

34. *Afore me*] Indeed (a light oath).

34–5. *very . . . by*] Proverbial; cf. *Tw.N.*, II. iii. 1–10, especially 'Not to be abed after midnight is to be up betimes' (1–2).

Scene v

1–7. *Wilt . . . nightingale*] J. W. Lever (*Sh.S.*, 6, pp. 82–3) compares Eliot, *Ortho-Epia*, p. 149, where, after quoting lines on the lark (cf. l. 22 n. below), Eliot has: 'Harke, harke, tis some other bird that sings now. / Tis a blacke-bird or a Nightingale. / The Nightingale sings not but evening and morning. / Where is she I pray thee? / Tis a Nightingale I heard her record. / Seest thou not her sitting on a sprig?'

3. *fearful*] timorous.

Romeo. It was the lark, the herald of the morn,
No nightingale. Look, love, what envious streaks
Do lace the severing clouds in yonder east.
Night's candles are burnt out, and jocund day
Stands tiptoe on the misty mountain tops.
I must be gone and live, or stay and die.
Juliet. Yond light is not daylight, I know it, I.
It is some meteor that the sun exhales
To be to thee this night a torchbearer
And light thee on thy way to Mantua.
Therefore stay yet: thou need'st not to be gone.
Romeo. Let me be ta'en, let me be put to death,
I am content, so thou wilt have it so.
I'll say yon grey is not the morning's eye,
'Tis but the pale reflex of Cynthia's brow.
Nor that is not the lark whose notes do beat
The vaulty heaven so high above our heads.
I have more care to stay than will to go.
Come death, and welcome. Juliet wills it so.
How is't, my soul? Let's talk. It is not day.
Juliet. It is, it is. Hie hence, begone, away.

10. mountain] *Q2,Q1;* Mountaines *Q3,4,F.* 13. exhales] *Q1,Q3,4,F;* exhale *Q2;* exhaled *Hosley.* 19. yon] *Q2,3,F,Q1;* you *Q4.* the] *Q1,Q3,4,F;* the the *Q2.* 20. brow] *Q2–4,F,Q1;* bow *Collier*[2]. 21. the] *Q2–4; not in F; var. Q1.*

7. *envious*] malicious.

9. *Night's candles*] The stars; cf. *Mac.*, II. i. 4–5: 'There's husbandry in heaven; / Their candles are all out'.

13. *meteor . . . exhales*] Meteors were thought to be the product of corruption in the sublunary world (cf. Middleton, *The Changeling*, v. iii. 154–5: 'Beneath the stars, upon yon meteor / Ever hung my fate, 'mongst things corruptible'); they were contrasted to the pure and fixed stars and were of ill omen, as in *Caes.*, II. i. 44: 'The exhalations, whizzing in the air'.

19. *grey*] Cf. II. ii. 188: 'the grey-ey'd morn'.

20. *reflex*] reflection.

brow] forehead; cf. *2H6*, III. i. 155, 'cloudy brow', *Cor.*, II. i. 50, 'the forehead of the morning', and *Lr*, II. ii. 103, 'Phoebus' front'. Collier's conjecture *bow* supposes a misprint in Q2 because 'a *brow* would not occasion a *pale reflex*'; the crescent moon/bow image appeals to nineteenth-century taste.

22. *vaulty heaven*] J. W. Lever, *Sh.S.*, 6, p. 82, compares Eliot's quotation from Du Bartas in *Ortho-Epia*, p. 147: 'La gentile Alouëtte auec son tyre-lire / Tire l'yre a l'iré, & tiri-lyrant vire / Vers la voûte du Ciel, puis son vol vers ce lieu / Vire, & desire dire, adieu Dieu, adieu Dieu.' Cf. also Sonnet 29.

23. *care*] desire.

It is the lark that sings so out of tune,
Straining harsh discords and unpleasing sharps.
Some say the lark makes sweet division.
This doth not so, for she divideth us.
Some say the lark and loathed toad change eyes.
O, now I would they had chang'd voices too,
Since arm from arm that voice doth us affray,
Hunting thee hence with hunt's-up to the day.
O now be gone, more light and light it grows.
Romeo. More light and light: more dark and dark our woes.

Enter NURSE *hastily.*

Nurse. Madam.
Juliet. Nurse?
Nurse. Your lady mother is coming to your chamber.
The day is broke, be wary, look about. [*Exit.*]
Juliet. Then, window, let day in and let life out.
Romeo. Farewell, farewell, one kiss and I'll descend.
He goes down.
Juliet. Art thou gone so? Love, lord, ay husband, friend,
I must hear from thee every day in the hour,
For in a minute there are many days.

35. light it] *Q2–4,Q1;* it light *F.* 36. S.D.] *Q1 (after l. 59); Enter Madame and Nurse. Q2–4,F.* 40. S.D.] *Theobald; not in Q2–4,F,Q1.* 42. S.D.] *Q1 (subst.); not in Q2–4,F.* 43. Love, . . . friend,] *Q2–4,F;* my Lord, my Loue, my Frend? *Q1;* Love, Lord ah Husband, Friend *F2, Rowe.*

29. *division*] execution of a rapid melodic passage in music (OED sb 7); with a quibble on the sense 'to separate'.

31. *Some . . . eyes*] Warburton notes that the toad has very fine eyes and the lark very ugly ones, and supposes this to be the source of the 'common saying among the people'.

33. *affray*] frighten.

34. *hunt's-up*] The morning song to awaken a newly married wife (Cotgrave) derived from the song originally used to wake huntsmen, and the name of a ballad for that occasion.

36. S.D.] The Q2 reading probably stands for 'Enter Nurse, calling *Madame*' in the MS. (Greg, *First Folio*, p. 230).

42. S.D. *He goes down*] Romeo uses the rope ladder; Juliet must then quickly pull it up again and conceal it.

43. *ay*] As it stands Q2 makes sense; *friend* means 'lover, paramour' as in *Meas.*, I. iv. 29: 'He hath got his friend with child'. Juliet uses *ay* as an intensifier. Elsewhere the affirmative is spelt *I* in Q2; some editors choose F2's *ah*, some Q1's *my*, some suppose Q2's *ay* to mean 'ever', some print 'love-lord, aye husband-friend'.

O, by this count I shall be much in years
Ere I again behold my Romeo.

Romeo. Farewell.
I will omit no opportunity
That may convey my greetings, love, to thee.

Juliet. O think'st thou we shall ever meet again?

Romeo. I doubt it not, and all these wōes shall serve
For sweet discourses in our times to come.

Juliet. O God, I have an ill-divining soul!
Methinks I see thee, now thou art so low,
As one dead in the bottom of a tomb.
Either my eyesight fails, or thou look'st pale.

Romeo. And trust me, love, in my eye so do you.
Dry sorrow drinks our blood. Adieu, adieu.
Exit.

Juliet. O Fortune, Fortune! All men call thee fickle;
If thou art fickle, what dost thou with him
That is renown'd for faith? Be fickle, Fortune,
For then I hope thou wilt not keep him long,
But send him back.

Enter LADY CAPULET.

Lady Cap. Ho, daughter, are you up?

Juliet. Who is't that calls? It is my lady mother.
Is she not down so late, or up so early?
What unaccustom'd cause procures her hither?
She goeth down from the window.

51. think'st] *Q2,Q1;* thinkest *Q3,4,F.* 53. times] *Q2;* time *Q3,4,F,Q1.* 54. *Juliet.*] *Q1,Q4,F; Ro. Q2,3.* 57. look'st] *Q1,F;* lookest *Q2–4.* 64. *Lady Cap.*] *ed.; La. Q2–4; Lad. F; Moth: Q1.* 65. It is] *Q2–4,Q1;* Is it *F.* 67. hither] *Q2,4,F;* either *Q3; not in Q1.* S.D.] *Q1; not in Q2–4,F.*

46. *count*] method of calculation.

52–3. *all . . . come*] Proverbial; cf. Tilley R 73.

54. *Juliet*] The catchword in Q2 sig H3 is '*Iu.* O' which supports Q1.

59. *Dry . . . blood*] Cf. *MND*, III. ii. 97: 'sighs of love that costs the fresh blood dear'; and Marlowe, *Tragedy of Dido*, II. i. 298–300: 'Theban Niobe, / Who for her sonnes death wept out life and breath, / And drie with griefe was turnd into a stone'. Every sigh was supposed to draw away a drop of blood from the heart.

67. S.D. *She . . . window*] Juliet withdraws at the upper level and descends unseen, reappearing on the stage to answer her mother's repeated call. The ensuing action is obviously too important and powerful to be per-

Lady Cap. Why, how now Juliet?

[*Enter* JULIET.]

Juliet. Madam, I am not well.
Lady Cap. Evermore weeping for your cousin's death?
What, wilt thou wash him from his grave with tears?
And if thou couldst, thou couldst not make him live.
Therefore have done: some grief shows much of love,
But much of grief shows still some want of wit.
Juliet. Yet let me weep for such a feeling loss.
Lady Cap. So shall you feel the loss but not the friend
Which you weep for.
Juliet. Feeling so the loss,
I cannot choose but ever weep the friend.
Lady Cap. Well, girl, thou weepst not so much for his death
As that the villain lives which slaughter'd him.
Juliet. What villain, madam?
Lady Cap. That same villain Romeo.
Juliet. Villain and he be many miles asunder.
God pardon him. I do with all my heart.
And yet no man like he doth grieve my heart.
Lady Cap. That is because the traitor murderer lives.
Juliet. Ay madam, from the reach of these my hands.
Would none but I might venge my cousin's death.
Lady Cap. We will have vengeance for it, fear thou not.
Then weep no more. I'll send to one in Mantua,
Where that same banish'd runagate doth live,
Shall give him such an unaccustom'd dram

68. *Lady Cap.*] *ed.; La. Q2–4; Lad. F; Moth: Q1.* S.D.] *Williams; not in Q2–4,F,Q1.* 69. *Lady Cap.*] *ed.; La. Q2–4; Lad. F; Moth: Q1.* 75. *Lady Cap.*] *ed.; La. Q2–4; Lad. F; not in Q1.* 78. *Lady Cap.*] *ed.; La. Q2–4,F; Moth: Q1.* 80. *Lady Cap.*] *ed.; La. Q2–4; Lad. F; Moth: Q1.* 82. him] *Q4; not in Q2,3,F,Q1.* 84. *Lady Cap.*] *ed.; La. Q2–4; Lad. F; not in Q1.* murderer] *Q2; not in Q3,4,F,Q1.* 87. *Lady Cap.*] *ed.; La. Q2–4; Lad. F; Moth: Q1.* 90. unaccustom'd] *Q2,3,F;* accustom'd *Q4; not in Q1.*

formed at the upper level; the transition simply makes the main stage now Juliet's bedroom seen from the inside.

70–1. *What . . . live*] Cf. Brooke, l. 1797.

74. *feeling*] heartfelt.

75. *feel . . . friend*] you will feel your loss but not feel him, warm and alive.

77. *friend*] A quibble (i) cousin, (ii) lover.

88. *Mantua*] Lady Capulet cannot, naturalistically speaking, yet know Romeo's destination, for which he has set off only moments earlier.

That he shall soon keep Tybalt company;
And then I hope thou wilt be satisfied.
Juliet. Indeed I never shall be satisfied
With Romeo, till I behold him—dead—
Is my poor heart so for a kinsman vex'd.
Madam, if you could find out but a man
To bear a poison, I would temper it—
That Romeo should upon receipt thereof
Soon sleep in quiet. O, how my heart abhors
To hear him nam'd, and cannot come to him
To wreak the love I bore my cousin
Upon his body that hath slaughter'd him.
Lady Cap. Find thou the means and I'll find such a man.
But now I'll tell thee joyful tidings, girl.
Juliet. And joy comes well in such a needy time.
What are they, I beseech your ladyship?
Lady Cap. Well, well, thou hast a careful father, child;
One who to put thee from thy heaviness
Hath sorted out a sudden day of joy,
That thou expects not, nor I look'd not for.
Juliet. Madam, in happy time. What day is that?
Lady Cap. Marry, my child, early next Thursday morn
The gallant, young, and noble gentleman,

94. him—dead—] *Pope;* him. Dead *Q2–4,F;* him, dead *Q1.* 103. *Lady Cap.*] *ed.; Mo. Q2–4,F; var. Q1.* 104. tidings] *Q2,3,F;* tiding *Q4;* newes *Q1.* 106. I beseech] *Q4;* beseech *Q2,3,F; not in Q1.* 107. *Lady Cap.*] *ed.; M. Q2,3; Mo. Q4,F; Moth: Q1.* 111. that] *Q2–4,Q1;* this *F.* 112. *Lady Cap.*] *ed.; M. Q2,3; Mo. Q4,F; Moth: Q1.*

94. *With . . . dead*] Juliet intends to deceive her mother, as in other exchanges in this episode, but there is a further irony of which she is unaware: the next time she sees Romeo he is dead. Lady Capulet understands Juliet to mean 'I never shall be satisfied with Romeo till I behold him dead; dead is my poor heart so for a kinsman vexed,' but Juliet quibbles on *be satisfied*: (i) have enough of, (ii) be at peace over, and on *kinsman*: (i) husband, (ii) cousin. Her private meaning is: (1) 'I never shall have enough of Romeo', (2) 'I never shall be satisfied with Romeo till I behold him', (3) 'till I behold him, dead is my poor heart so for a kinsman vexed'.

97. *temper*] (i) mix, (ii) modify, reduce effect of.

106. *I beseech*] Q4 perfects the metre.

107. *careful*] solicitous.

108. *heaviness*] grief.

110. *expects*] The second person singular can commonly be in this form; cf. I. v. 8, or *Ham.*, I. iv. 53 ('Revisits').

111. *in . . . time*] how fortunate!

The County Paris, at Saint Peter's Church,
Shall happily make thee there a joyful bride.

Juliet. Now by Saint Peter's Church, and Peter too,
He shall not make me there a joyful bride.
I wonder at this haste, that I must wed
Ere he that should be husband comes to woo.
I pray you tell my lord and father, madam,
I will not marry yet. And when I do, I swear
It shall be Romeo, whom you know I hate,
Rather than Paris. These are news indeed.

Lady Cap. Here comes your father, tell him so yourself,
And see how he will take it at your hands.

Enter CAPULET *and* NURSE.

Cap. When the sun sets the earth doth drizzle dew,
But for the sunset of my brother's son
It rains downright.
How now, a conduit, girl? What, still in tears?
Evermore showering? In one little body
Thou counterfeits a bark, a sea, a wind.
For still thy eyes, which I may call the sea,
Do ebb and flow with tears. The bark thy body is,
Sailing in this salt flood, the winds thy sighs,
Who raging with thy tears and they with them,

115. happily] *Q2,F;* happly *Q3,4; not in Q1.* there] *Q2–4,Q1; not in F.* 119. woo] *Q2–4;* woe *F; not in Q1.* 124. *Lady Cap.*] *ed.; M. Q2,3; Mer. Q4; Mo. F; Moth: Q1.* 126. earth] *Q2,3,F;* Ayre *Q4; not in Q1.* 128–9. It . . . downright. / How . . . tears] *Q4,F; one line Q2,3; not in Q1.* 131. counterfeits] *Q2* (countefaits); counterfaits *Q3,4,F; not in Q1.* 135. thy] *Q2–4;* the *F; var. Q1.*

126. *earth*] Cf. *Lucr.*, l. 1226: 'But as the earth doth weep, the sun being set'; Spenser in *The Shepheardes Calender*, January, l. 41, has 'And from mine eyes the drizling teares descend', and Golding's *Ovid*, x, 5: 'His torch with drizling smoke / Was dim'. It is not plausible that MS. *ayre* could have been misread as *earth*.

129. *conduit*] Cf. Brooke, ll. 1805–6: 'So that my payned hart by conduites of the eyne / No more henceforth, as wont it was, shall gush forth dropping bryne'. City fountains were often made in the form of a human figure, and there were several in Shakespeare's London; cf. I. i. 83 and n.; also *Tit.*, II. iv. 29–30: 'And notwithstanding all this loss of blood— / As from a conduit with three issuing spouts', and *Caes.*, II. ii. 76–9.

130–7. *In . . . body*] Cf. *Tit.*, III. i. 222–30.

131. *counterfeits*] presentst a likeness of; cf. l. 110 n.

bark] A generic term for any small sailing vessel; cf. V. iii. 118; Romeo's final image is ominously prepared for.

Without a sudden calm will overset
Thy tempest-tossed body. How now, wife?
Have you deliver'd to her our decree?

Lady Cap. Ay sir, but she will none, she gives you thanks.
I would the fool were married to her grave.

Cap. Soft. Take me with you, take me with you, wife.
How? Will she none? Doth she not give us thanks?
Is she not proud? Doth she not count her blest,
Unworthy as she is, that we have wrought
So worthy a gentleman to be her bride?

Juliet. Not proud you have, but thankful that you have.
Proud can I never be of what I hate,
But thankful even for hate that is meant love.

Cap. How, how, how, how? Chopp'd logic? What is this?
'Proud' and 'I thank you' and 'I thank you not'
And yet 'not proud'? Mistress minion you,
Thank me no thankings nor proud me no prouds,
But fettle your fine joints 'gainst Thursday next
To go with Paris to Saint Peter's Church,
Or I will drag thee on a hurdle thither.
Out, you green-sickness carrion! Out, you baggage!

137. wife] *Q2,3,F,Q1;* wise *Q4.* 139. *Lady Cap.*] *ed.; La. Q2–4; Lady. F; Moth: Q1.* gives] *Q3,4,F;* giue *Q2; not in Q1.* 145. bride] *Q2;* Bridegroome *Q3,4,F; not in Q1.* 147. hate] *Q2–4,Q1;* have *F.* 149. How, how, how, how?] *Q2 (subst.); How now, how now Q3,4,F; not in Q1.* Chopp'd] *Q2–4,F* (chopt)*;* chop *Q1.* 151. And . . . you] *Q2–4; not in F; var. Q1.*

140. *married . . . grave*] Kittredge thinks the phrase conventional, and compares Sidney, *Arcadia* (1590), sig. 20v: 'Shee . . . assured her mother, she would first be bedded in her graue, then wedded to Demagoras'.

141. *Take . . . you*] Let me understand you.

145. *bride*] In Shakespeare's time *bride* could be used of a man.

149. *Chopp'd logic*] OED records the verbal form of *chop* in such instances as 'Ye logyke chopped' and 'chopping logick'. Dowden cites Awdelay, *Fraternitye of Vacabondes* (1561), p. 15, New Sh. Soc. Reprint: 'Choplogyke is he that when his mayster rebuketh him of hys fault he wyll geve him xx words for one'. A chop-logic is a contentious, sophistical arguer.

151. *minion*] spoiled minx, hussy.

153. *fettle . . . joints*] *fettle* = groom (of horses) (OED v 1); hence 'get yourself ready'.

156. *green-sickness*] Adjectival, from the noun denoting chlorosis, anaemia in young women, hence, immature and foolish. Polonius makes the same criticism of *his* daughter in *Ham.*, I. iii. 101.

You tallow-face!
Lady Cap. Fie, fie. What, are you mad?
Juliet. Good father, I beseech you on my knees.
She kneels down.
Hear me with patience but to speak a word.
Cap. Hang thee young baggage, disobedient wretch!
I tell thee what—get thee to church a Thursday
Or never after look me in the face.
Speak not, reply not, do not answer me.
My fingers itch. Wife, we scarce thought us blest
That God had lent us but this only child;
But now I see this one is one too much,
And that we have a curse in having her.
Out on her, hilding.
Nurse. God in heaven bless her.
You are to blame, my lord, to rate her so.
Cap. And why, my Lady Wisdom? Hold your tongue,
Good Prudence! Smatter with your gossips, go.
Nurse. I speak no treason.
Cap. O God 'i' good e'en!
Nurse. May not one speak?
Cap. Peace, you mumbling fool!
Utter your gravity o'er a gossip's bowl,
For here we need it not.
Lady Cap. You are too hot.

157. You] *Q2–4,F;* out you *Q1.* *Lady Cap.*] *ed.; La. Q2–4; Lady. F; not in Q1.* 158. S.D.] *Q1; not in Q2–4,F.* 160. *Cap.*] *ed.; Fa. Q2–4,F; var. Q1.* 170. *Cap.*] *Q1; Fa. Q2–4,F.* 171. gossips] *Q2–4,Q1;* gossip *F.* 172. *Cap.* O] *Q1;* Father, ô *Q2,3,F (subst.); Fa.* O *Q4.* 173. *Nurse.*] *Q4; not in Q2,3,F,Q1. Cap.*] *ed.; Fa. Q2–4,F; not in Q1.* 174 bowl] *Q2–4,Q1;* bowles *F.* 175. *Lady Cap.*] *ed.; Wi. Q2–4; La. F; Mo: Q1.*

157. *tallow-face*] Juliet's pallor results from shock and weeping.

165. *only child*] Cf. I. ii. 14–15, I. iii. 72 n.

168. *hilding*] jade.

169. *rate*] berate, upbraid.

171. *Smatter*] Prattle, chatter.

172. *Cap.*] Q2 failed to recognize that in the MS. *Father* was a speech prefix, hence on the next line *Nurse* seemed redundant as a speech prefix and was omitted. Evidently Q1 was not consulted. Cf. III. ii. 72 n., III. i. 90 n.

174. *gravity*] wise advice.

gossip's bowl] i.e. when visiting your cronies.

Cap. God's bread, it makes me mad! Day, night, work, play,
Alone, in company, still my care hath been
To have her match'd. And having now provided
A gentleman of noble parentage,
Of fair demesnes, youthful and nobly lign'd,
Stuff'd, as they say, with honourable parts,
Proportion'd as one's thought would wish a man—
And then to have a wretched puling fool,
A whining mammet, in her fortune's tender,
To answer 'I'll not wed, I cannot love,
I am too young, I pray you pardon me!'
But, and you will not wed, I'll pardon you!
Graze where you will, you shall not house with me.
Look to't, think on't, I do not use to jest.
Thursday is near. Lay hand on heart. Advise.
And you be mine I'll give you to my friend;

176. *Cap.*] *Q1; Fa. Q2–4,F.* 176–7. work, play, / Alone,] *Hoppe;* houre, tide, time, worke, play, / Alone *Q2–4,F;* early, late, at home, abroad, / Alone, *Q1;* late, early, / At home, abroad, alone, *Pope.* 180. lign'd] *This ed., conj. Jenkins;* liand *Q2;* allied *Q3,4,F;* trainde *Q1;* limb'd *Hosley;* lianc'd *conj. Capell.*

176. *God's bread*] i.e. bread consecrated in the Communion service.

176–7. *Day . . . company*] Hoppe's emendation produces metrical regularity and is defended by Dover Wilson: 'the hand of Shakespeare, it seems, having written "Day, night", doodled with "houre, tide, time"; rejected each in turn; but omitted to score the rejects out, because the mind then flowed on without further difficulty' ('The New Way', p. 82). Cf. *2H6*, I. i. 26–7: 'By day, by night, waking and in my dreams, / In courtly company or at my beads', which supports a decision to amend here in *Rom.*

177–8. *still . . . match'd*] Cf. Lyly, *Euphues, The Anatomy of Wit* (ed. Bond), p. 227, ll. 17–18: 'Mine onely care hath bene hetherto to match thee'.

180. *lign'd*] Sisson comments: 'The *liand* of Q2 was easily misread by an unintelligent compositor for *traind* in his copy', but Crow argues 'Shakespeare meant that the County was well connected, had noble "*liens de famille*", was nobly *lien'd*'. Jenkins doubts whether this is possible in English at this date, and supposes Shakespeare wrote *lind* or *lignd* (OED sb^{2} IV b) past participle (adjective) from the noun *line*, often spelt *ligne*, in this sense. It goes with *nobly*. Hosley supposes a misreading of *limd*, finding the spelling *lims* in Q2 at v. iii. 36. I find Jenkins's suggestion a refinement of Crow's and so I adopt it. The fact that Paris is a highly suitable match in terms of family and social position is consistently stressed in the play.

181. *Stuff'd*] Cf. *Ado*, I. i. 48.

184. *mammet*] puppet.

fortune's tender] when good fortune is offered her.

190. *Advise*] Consider.

And you be not, hang! Beg! Starve! Die in the streets!
For by my soul I'll ne'er acknowledge thee,
Nor what is mine shall never do thee good.
Trust to't, bethink you. I'll not be forsworn. *Exit.*

Juliet. Is there no pity sitting in the clouds
That sees into the bottom of my grief?
O sweet my mother, cast me not away,
Delay this marriage for a month, a week,
Or if you do not, make the bridal bed
In that dim monument where Tybalt lies.

Lady Cap. Talk not to me, for I'll not speak a word.
Do as thou wilt, for I have done with thee. *Exit.*

Juliet. O God, O Nurse, how shall this be prevented?
My husband is on earth, my faith in heaven.
How shall that faith return again to earth
Unless that husband send it me from heaven
By leaving earth? Comfort me, counsel me.
Alack, alack, that heaven should practise stratagems
Upon so soft a subject as myself.
What sayst thou? Hast thou not a word of joy?
Some comfort, Nurse.

Nurse. Faith, here it is.
Romeo is banish'd, and all the world to nothing
That he dares ne'er come back to challenge you.
Or if he do, it needs must be by stealth.
Then, since the case so stands as now it doth,
I think it best you married with the County.
O, he's a lovely gentleman.
Romeo's a dishclout to him. An eagle, madam,
Hath not so green, so quick, so fair an eye
As Paris hath. Beshrew my very heart,
I think you are happy in this second match,

194. never] *Q2,3,F;* ever *Q4,Q1.* 202. *Lady Cap.*] *ed.; Mo. Q2–4,F; Moth: Q1.* 212–13. Faith . . . is. / Romeo . . . nothing] *F; one line in Q2–4; var. Q1.* 215. by] *Q2,3,F;* my *Q4; not in Q1.*

205. *faith in heaven*] i.e. my marriage vows are registered in heaven (*faith* = plighted faithfulness to Romeo).

206–8. *How . . . earth*] How can my vows be revoked unless by Romeo's death?

209. *stratagems*] tricks, plots.

213. *all . . . nothing*] the odds are a million to one.

For it excels your first; or, if it did not,
Your first is dead, or 'twere as good he were
As living here and you no use of him.

Juliet. Speakest thou from thy heart?

Nurse. And from my soul too, else beshrew them both.

Juliet. Amen.

Nurse. What?

Juliet. Well, thou hast comforted me marvellous much.
Go in, and tell my lady I am gone,
Having displeas'd my father, to Laurence' cell,
To make confession and to be absolv'd.

Nurse. Marry, I will; and this is wisely done. *Exit.*

Juliet. Ancient damnation! O most wicked fiend,
Is it more sin to wish me thus forsworn,
Or to dispraise my lord with that same tongue
Which she hath prais'd him with above compare
So many thousand times? Go, counsellor.
Thou and my bosom henceforth shall be twain.
I'll to the Friar to know his remedy.
If all else fail, myself have power to die. *Exit.*

225. here] *Q2–4,F;* hence *Hanmer; not in Q1.* 226. Speakest] *Q3,4,F;* Speakst *Q2,Q1.* 227. else] *Q2;* or else *Q3,4,F,Q1.* 234. S.D.] *Q4; not in Q2,3,F; She lookes after Nurse. Q1.* 235. wicked] *Q2–4,F;* cursed *Q1.* 236. Is it] *Q2–4,Q1;* It is *F.*

227. *them both*] i.e. my heart and soul.

235. *Ancient damnation*] Wicked old woman.

240. *twain*] separated.

[ACT IV]

[SCENE I]

Enter FRIAR [LAURENCE] *and* PARIS.

Friar L. On Thursday, sir? The time is very short.
Paris. My father Capulet will have it so,
And I am nothing slow to slack his haste.
Friar L. You say you do not know the lady's mind.
Uneven is the course. I like it not.
Paris. Immoderately she weeps for Tybalt's death,
And therefore have I little talk'd of love,
For Venus smiles not in a house of tears.
Now sir, her father counts it dangerous
That she do give her sorrow so much sway,
And in his wisdom hastes our marriage
To stop the inundation of her tears
Which, too much minded by herself alone,
May be put from her by society.
Now do you know the reason of this haste.
Friar L. I would I knew not why it should be slow'd—
Look sir, here comes the lady toward my cell.

Enter JULIET.

ACT IV

Scene I

SCENE I] *Rowe; not in Q2–4,F,Q1.* *Location.*] *The Monastery. Rowe; Friar Laurence's cell. Capell.* S.D.] *Q2–4,F,Q1* (*subst.*) (*Enter Frier and Countie* Paris.). 7. talk'd] *Q1;* talke *Q2–4,F.* 10. do] *Q2;* doth *Q3,4,F,Q1.* 17. toward] *Q2;* towards *Q3,4,F;* to *Q1.*

2. *father*] i.e. prospective father-in-law.

3. *nothing . . . haste*] I am by no means reluctant, lest I check his haste.

8. *Venus . . . tears*] Quibbling on astrological terms: the planet Venus sheds no beneficent influence; *house* is the term for the twelve parts into which the heavens were divided, each with a sign of the zodiac identifying it.

13–14. *too . . . society*] Cf. the concern at Romeo's melancholy in I. i. 135–40.

Paris. Happily met, my lady and my wife.
Juliet. That may be, sir, when I may be a wife.
Paris. That may be, must be, love, on Thursday next.
Juliet. What must be, shall be.
Friar L. That's a certain text.
Paris. Come you to make confession to this father?
Juliet. To answer that, I should confess to you.
Paris. Do not deny to him that you love me.
Juliet. I will confess to you that I love him.
Paris. So will ye, I am sure, that you love me.
Juliet. If I do so, it will be of more price
Being spoke behind your back than to your face.
Paris. Poor soul, thy face is much abus'd with tears.
Juliet. The tears have got small victory by that,
For it was bad enough before their spite.
Paris. Thou wrong'st it more than tears with that report.
Juliet. That is no slander, sir, which is a truth,
And what I spake, I spake it to my face.
Paris. Thy face is mine, and thou hast slander'd it.
Juliet. It may be so, for it is not mine own.—
Are you at leisure, holy father, now,
Or shall I come to you at evening mass?
Friar L. My leisure serves me, pensive daughter, now.—
My lord, we must entreat the time alone.
Paris. God shield I should disturb devotion.
Juliet, on Thursday early will I rouse ye;
Till then, adieu, and keep this holy kiss. *Exit.*
Juliet. O shut the door, and when thou hast done so,
Come weep with me, past hope, past cure, past help!

33. no] *Q2,3,F,Q1; not in Q4.* 34. my] *Q2–4,Q1;* thy *F.* 40. we] *Q2–4,Q1;* you *F.* 45. cure] *Q1;* care *Q2–4,F.*

21. *What . . . be*] Proverbial; cf. Tilley M 1331.

36. *not . . . own*] Juliet privately means that it belongs to Romeo.

38. *evening mass*] Possibly a literal rendering of *missa vespertina* (NCS), or meant generally for divine service (rather than the mass, which is not normally celebrated in the evening).

40. *entreat . . . alone*] ask to be allowed privacy.

45. *cure*] Q2's *care* in the less common sense 'oversight with a view to protection' (OED sb 4) might be acceptable, and a range of senses of *care* is played upon in *R2*, IV. i. 194–9; still, *cure*, 'treatment directed towards recovery' (OED sb II 5 b) seems pre-

Friar L. O Juliet, I already know thy grief;
It strains me past the compass of my wits.
I hear thou must—and nothing may prorogue it—
On Thursday next be married to this County.
Juliet. Tell me not, Friar, that thou hearest of this,
Unless thou tell me how I may prevent it.
If in thy wisdom thou canst give no help,
Do thou but call my resolution wise,
And with this knife I'll help it presently.
God join'd my heart and Romeo's, thou our hands;
And ere this hand, by thee to Romeo's seal'd,
Shall be the label to another deed,
Or my true heart with treacherous revolt
Turn to another, this shall slay them both.
Therefore, out of thy long-experienc'd time
Give me some present counsel, or behold:
'Twixt my extremes and me this bloody knife
Shall play the umpire, arbitrating that
Which the commission of thy years and art
Could to no issue of true honour bring.
Be not so long to speak. I long to die
If what thou speak'st speak not of remedy.
Friar L. Hold, daughter. I do spy a kind of hope
Which craves as desperate an execution
As that is desperate which we would prevent.
If, rather than to marry County Paris,
Thou hast the strength of will to slay thyself,
Then is it likely thou wilt undertake
A thing like death to chide away this shame,

47. strains] *Q2–4;* streames *F; not in Q1.* 54. with this] *Q2–4;* with'his *F; not in Q1.* 56. Romeo's] *Q2–4;* Romeo *F; not in Q1.* 72. slay] *Q1,Q4;* stay *Q2,3,F.*

ferable, especially when taken with l. 51's *tell me how I may prevent it* and IV. v. 65 below. There is a proverb, 'past cure past care', which is reversed in *LLL*, v. ii. 28 (Q,F) indicating the close association of the two words.

48. *prorogue*] postpone.

54. *presently*] instantly.

57. *label*] Literally, a supplementary codicil to a legal document (OED sb 2), hence a deed cancelling the first marriage.

59. *both*] i.e. hand and heart.

62. *extremes*] intense difficulties.

64. *commission*] authority deriving from.

That cop'st with death himself to scape from it.
And if thou dar'st, I'll give thee remedy.

Juliet. O, bid me leap, rather than marry Paris,
From off the battlements of any tower,
Or walk in thievish ways, or bid me lurk
Where serpents are. Chain me with roaring bears,
Or hide me nightly in a charnel-house
O'ercover'd quite with dead men's rattling bones,
With reeky shanks and yellow chapless skulls.
Or bid me go into a new-made grave,
And hide me with a dead man in his shroud—
Things that, to hear them told, have made me tremble—
And I will do it without fear or doubt,
To live an unstain'd wife to my sweet love.

Friar L. Hold then. Go home, be merry, give consent
To marry Paris. Wednesday is tomorrow;
Tomorrow night look that thou lie alone.
Let not the Nurse lie with thee in thy chamber.
Take thou this vial, being then in bed,
And this distilling liquor drink thou off;
When presently through all thy veins shall run

76. dar'st] *F;* darest *Q2–4;* doost *Q1.* 78. off] *Q1;* of *Q2–4,F.* any] *Q2–4,F;* yonder *Q1.* 81. hide] *Q2–4,F;* shut *Q1.* 83. chapless] *Q1* (chaples), *Q4;* chapels *Q2,3,F.* 85. shroud] *Q4;* graue *F; not in Q2,3; var. Q1;* tomb *Williams, conj. Malone.* 92. the] *Q2;* thy *Q3,4,F,Q1.* 94. distilling] *Q2–4,F;* distilled *Q1.*

75. *cop'st*] associatest, facest.

79. *thievish ways*] paths infested with robbers.

81. *charnel-house*] a small building attached to a church in which were deposited skulls and bones found when digging new graves in the churchyard.

83. *chapless*] without the lower jaw.

85. *shroud*] Q2 omits the final word of this line. Malone's conjecture *tomb* is repetitious, though distinguishing *grave*, the individual burial spot, from *tomb*, a structure above ground or a vault (v. ii. 29 has 'Poor living corse, clos'd in a dead man's tomb.'). Q4's *shroud* is supported by IV. iii. 42–3: 'bloody Tybalt . . . festering in his shroud' and v. iii. 97: 'Tybalt, liest thou there in thy bloody sheet?' The idea of sharing a *shroud* with a festering corpse is extremely gruesome and Italianate, certainly, but this is not therefore an objection, since the previous ll. 81–3 are also gruesome. In addition, *shroud* develops a new idea in the sequence beginning at l. 77, whereas *tomb* or *grave* does not. The subterranean link of *shroud* with *sheet* suggests that Juliet will dare such a bed with such a partner rather than commit adultery and inwardly be 'stained'. The conceit is typical of character and author.

94. *distilling*] permeating the body (OED v 3).

A cold and drowsy humour, for no pulse
Shall keep his native progress, but surcease:
No warmth, no breath shall testify thou livest,
The roses in thy lips and cheeks shall fade
To wanny ashes, thy eyes' windows fall
Like death when he shuts up the day of life.
Each part depriv'd of supple government
Shall stiff and stark and cold appear, like death,
And in this borrow'd likeness of shrunk death
Thou shalt continue two and forty hours
And then awake as from a pleasant sleep.
Now when the bridegroom in the morning comes
To rouse thee from thy bed, there art thou, dead.
Then as the manner of our country is,
In thy best robes, uncover'd on the bier
Thou shall be borne to that same ancient vault
Where all the kindred of the Capulets lie.
In the meantime, against thou shalt awake,
Shall Romeo by my letters know our drift

98. breath] *Q1,Q3,4,F;* breast *Q2.* thy] *Q2;* the *Q3,4,F; not in Q1.* 100. wanny] *Hoppe, conj. Kellner;* many *Q2,3,F;* paly *Q4; not in Q1.* 101. shuts] *Q2–4;* shut *F; not in Q1.* 110. In] *Q3,4,F;* Is *Q2; not in Q1.* 110–11. bier / Thou] *Hanmer;* Beere, Be borne to buriall in thy kindreds graue: / Thou *Q2–4,F; var. Q1.* 111. shall] *Q2;* shalt *Q3,4,F; not in Q1.*

96. *humour*] fluid.

97. *native*] natural.

99. *roses . . . fade*] When Romeo in v. iii. 95 sees crimson in Juliet's lips and cheeks, it is returning, not, as he thinks, about to fade.

100. *wanny*] I assume that the compositor was deceived by the spelling *Too* (= to) into misreading the first letter of the manuscript adjective. If the error *is* graphic, then the graphic outline of Q2's *many* makes *wany* in Shakespeare's MS. plausible: *wany* is a variant of the Elizabethan adjective *wanny* = 'pale, pallid' (OED). Yet Q4's reading is a very shrewd guess (as at l. 85 above), and may well be right. Cf. Brooke, l. 957, 'rak'd up, in ashes pale and ded'.

102. *supple government*] power of movement.

105. *two and forty*] McGinn (Furness, p. 428) and Marsh (cited by Dowden) argue from calculations of the time scheme of the action that the figure should be two and fifty or two and thirty, respectively. It is possible that Shakespeare or the compositor made a slip for *four and twenty*. See Intro., p. 54.

109–10. *manner . . . bier*] Cf. Brooke, ll. 2523–5.

110–11. *bier . . . vault*] Q2's additional words are a first version accidentally printed.

113. *against*] in anticipation of the time when.

And hither shall he come, and he and I
Will watch thy waking, and that very night
Shall Romeo bear thee hence to Mantua,
And this shall free thee from this present shame,
If no inconstant toy nor womanish fear
Abate thy valour in the acting it.

Juliet. Give me, give me! O tell not me of fear.

Friar L. Hold. Get you gone. Be strong and prosperous
In this resolve. I'll send a friar with speed
To Mantua with my letters to thy lord.

Juliet. Love give me strength, and strength shall help afford.
Farewell, dear father. *Exeunt.*

[SCENE II]

Enter CAPULET, LADY CAPULET, NURSE *and two or three* Servingmen.

Cap. So many guests invite as here are writ.
[*Exit Servingman.*]
Sirrah, go hire me twenty cunning cooks.

Ser. You shall have none ill, sir, for I'll try if they can lick their fingers.

Cap. How! Canst thou try them so?

Ser. Marry sir, 'tis an ill cook that cannot lick his own

115–16. and he . . . waking,] *Q2–4; not in F,Q1.* 115. and he] *Q3,4;* an he *Q2.* 116. waking] *Q3,4;* walking *Q2.* 119. toy] *Q2,3,F;* joy *Q4; not in Q1.* 121. not me] *Q2,3,F;* me not *Q4; not in Q1.* fear] *Q2–4;* care *F; not in Q1.*

Scene II

SCENE II] *Rowe; not in Q2–4,F,Q1.* *Location.*] *Hall in Capulet's house. Capell.*
1. S.D.] *Capell (subst.); not in Q2–4,F,Q1.*

119. *inconstant toy*] whim that interferes with your firmness; cf. Brooke, l. 2190.

Scene II

2. *twenty cunning cooks*] But in III. iv. Capulet planned a very small event. Shakespeare may be remembering Brooke, ll. 2281–7, or be emphasizing Capulet's impulsiveness; *cunning* = skilled.

6–7. *'tis . . . fingers*] Proverbial (cf. Tilley C 636), for one who has no faith in his work. Kittredge notes a

fingers; therefore he that cannot lick his fingers goes not with me.

Cap. Go, be gone. *Exit Servingman.*
We shall be much unfurnish'd for this time.
What, is my daughter gone to Friar Laurence?

Nurse. Ay, forsooth.

Cap. Well, he may chance to do some good on her.
A peevish self-will'd harlotry it is.

Enter JULIET.

Nurse. See where she comes from shrift with merry look.

Cap. How now, my headstrong: where have you been gadding?

Juliet. Where I have learnt me to repent the sin
Of disobedient opposition
To you and your behests, and am enjoin'd
By holy Laurence to fall prostrate here,
To beg your pardon. Pardon, I beseech you.
Henceforward I am ever rul'd by you.
She kneels down.

Cap. Send for the County, go tell him of this.
I'll have this knot knit up tomorrow morning.

Juliet. I met the youthful lord at Laurence' cell,
And gave him what becomed love I might,
Not stepping o'er the bounds of modesty.

Cap. Why, I am glad on't. This is well. Stand up.
This is as't should be. Let me see the County.
Ay, marry. Go, I say, and fetch him hither.

9. S.D.] *Q1; not in Q2–4,F.*
17. me] *Q2,3,F; not in Q4,Q1.*
14. self-will'd] *Q2–4,Q1;* selfe-wild *F.*
22. S.D.] *Q1; not in Q2–4,F.*

subsidiary meaning 'to lick one's fingers' = sly and crooked profit-making.

10. *unfurnish'd*] unprepared in arrangements and provisions.

14. *self-will'd*] Q2's spelling *self-wield* is eccentric but unambiguous; cf. *1H4*, III. i. 198–9: 'a peevish / self will'd harlotry, one that no persuasion can do good upon'.

harlotry] good-for-nothing.

24. *tomorrow morning*] Juliet's act of humility, on the Friar's instructions, has the unforeseen and disastrous effect of prompting Capulet to this impetuous advance of the day of marriage.

26. *becomed*] An adjective meaning 'befitting, becoming': the only example cited by OED is the present one. Perhaps a coinage.

Now afore God, this reverend holy Friar,
All our whole city is much bound to him.
Juliet. Nurse, will you go with me into my closet,
To help me sort such needful ornaments
As you think fit to furnish me tomorrow?
Lady Cap. No, not till Thursday. There is time enough.
Cap. Go, Nurse, go with her. We'll to church tomorrow.
Exeunt Juliet and Nurse.
Lady Cap. We shall be short in our provision,
'Tis now near night.
Cap. Tush I will stir about,
And all things shall be well, I warrant thee, wife.
Go thou to Juliet, help to deck up her.
I'll not to bed tonight, let me alone.
I'll play the housewife for this once.—What ho!—
They are all forth. Well, I will walk myself
To County Paris, to prepare up him
Against tomorrow. My heart is wondrous light
Since this same wayward girl is so reclaim'd. *Exeunt.*

31. reverend holy] *Q2–4,F;* holy reuerent *Q1.* 36. *Lady Cap.*] *ed.; Mo. Q2–4,F; Moth: Q1.* 37. *Cap.*] *ed.; Fa. Q2–4,F; Capo: Q1.* S.D.] *Q1 (subst.), F; Exeunt. Q2–4.* 38. *Lady Cap.*] *ed.; Mo. Q2–4,F; Moth: Q1.* 39. *Cap.*] *ed.; Fa. Q2–4,F; Capo: Q1.* 45. up him] *Q2–4;* him up *F; not in Q1.*

31–2. *Now . . . him*] Cf. Brooke, ll. 2249–50.

33. *closet*] private room.

33–4. *will . . . ornaments*] Cf. Brooke, ll. 2234–5.

39. *'Tis . . . night*] Malone notes that in III. v Romeo parted at daybreak; Juliet went immediately afterwards to the Friar, where he supposes she could have stayed no longer than two hours; she is now just returned, yet it is *near night.* Clarke suggests that the mention of evening mass, the Friar's directions for action *tomorrow night,* and Capulet's talk of preparations for the wedding which has been advanced to *tomorrow,* all prepare the mind for the accelerated passing of time which underscores the accelerating action; cf. IV. i. 105 n.

45. *up him*] Some editors find the F reading preferable since the pronoun is not emphatic. NCS compares *Tp.,* III. iii. 56: 'to belch up you', and l. 41 above, and cites Franz 444.

[SCENE III]

Enter JULIET *and* NURSE.

Juliet. Ay, those attires are best. But, gentle Nurse,
I pray thee leave me to myself tonight,
For I have need of many orisons
To move the heavens to smile upon my state,
Which, well thou know'st, is cross and full of sin.

Enter LADY CAPULET.

Lady Cap. What, are you busy, ho? Need you my help?
Juliet. No madam, we have cull'd such necessaries
As are behoveful for our state tomorrow.
So please you, let me now be left alone
And let the Nurse this night sit up with you,
For I am sure you have your hands full all
In this so sudden business.
Lady Cap. Good night.
Get thee to bed and rest, for thou hast need.
Exeunt [Lady Capulet and Nurse].
Juliet. Farewell. God knows when we shall meet again.
I have a faint cold fear thrills through my veins
That almost freezes up the heat of life.
I'll call them back again to comfort me.
—Nurse!—What should she do here?
My dismal scene I needs must act alone.
Come, vial.
What if this mixture do not work at all?

Scene III

SCENE III] *Rowe; not in Q2–4,F,Q1.* *Location.] Juliet's chamber. Rowe.* 5. know'st] *F;* knowest *Q2–4; not in Q1.* S.D.] *Rowe; Enter Mother. Q2–4,F,Q1.* 6. *Lady Cap.*] *ed.; Mo. Q2–4,F; Moth: Q1.* 12. *Lady Cap.*] *ed.; Mo. Q2–4,F; Moth: Q1.* 13. S.D.] *Capell; Exeunt. Q2–4,F; Exit. Q1.* 16. life] *Q2–4;* fire *F; not in Q1.* 20–1.] *As Hanmer; one line in Q2–4,F; var. Q1.*

1–5. *But . . . sin*] A close imitation of Brooke, ll. 2325–33.

3. *orisons*] prayers.

15. *faint cold*] causing faintness and coldness.

21. *What . . . all*] Cf. Brooke, ll. 2361–2.

Shall I be married then tomorrow morning?
No! No! This shall forbid it. Lie thou there.
[*She lays down a knife.*]
What if it be a poison which the Friar
Subtly hath minister'd to have me dead,
Lest in this marriage he should be dishonour'd,
Because he married me before to Romeo?
I fear it is. And yet methinks it should not,
For he hath still been tried a holy man.
How if, when I am laid into the tomb,
I wake before the time that Romeo
Come to redeem me? There's a fearful point!
Shall I not then be stifled in the vault,
To whose foul mouth no healthsome air breathes in,
And there die strangled ere my Romeo comes?
Or, if I live, is it not very like,
The horrible conceit of death and night
Together with the terror of the place,
As in a vault, an ancient receptacle
Where for this many hundred years the bones
Of all my buried ancestors are pack'd,
Where bloody Tybalt yet but green in earth
Lies festering in his shroud; where, as they say,
At some hours in the night spirits resort—
Alack, alack! Is it not like that I
So early waking, what with loathsome smells,
And shrieks like mandrakes torn out of the earth,

22. Shall . . . morning?] *Q2–4,F;* Must I of force be married to the Countie? *Q1.* 23. S.D.] *Johnson (subst.); not in Q2–4,F,Q1.* 40. this] *Q2;* these *Q3,4,F; not in Q1.*

33–5. *Shall . . . comes*] A close imitation of Brooke, ll. 2370–6.

37. *conceit of*] fantastic thought aroused by.

39–41. *vault . . . pack'd*] Cf. Brooke, ll. 2371–4.

42. *green in earth*] freshly buried. Possibly quibbling on the colour.

44. *spirits*] Cf. Brooke, ll. 2392–3.

47. *mandrakes*] The mysterious properties attributed to the mandrake plant are many and ancient, among the most prominent being the belief that when dug up it shrieked. By some accounts this was fatal to whoever heard it (cf. *2H6*, III. ii. 310: 'Would curses kill as doth the mandrake's groan'), by others it induced madness (cf. Webster, *The Duchess of Malfi*, II, v. 1–2). Sir Thomas Browne, *Vulgar Errors*, II. 6, remarks that the notion that mandrakes shriek is ridiculous, 'arising perhaps from a small and stridulous

That living mortals, hearing them, run mad—
O, if I wake, shall I not be distraught,
Environed with all these hideous fears,
And madly play with my forefathers' joints,
And pluck the mangled Tybalt from his shroud,
And, in this rage, with some great kinsman's bone
As with a club dash out my desperate brains?
O look, methinks I see my cousin's ghost
Seeking out Romeo that did spit his body
Upon a rapier's point! Stay, Tybalt, stay!
Romeo, Romeo, Romeo, here's drink! I drink to thee!

She falls upon her bed within the curtains.

49. O . . . wake] *Hanmer;* O . . . walke *Q2,3,F;* Or . . . wake *Q4; var. Q1.* 51. joints] *Q2,3,F;* joynes *Q4;* bones *Q1.* 57. a] *Q2–4;* my *F; not in Q1.* 58. Romeo, Romeo, Romeo, here's drink!] *Q2–4,F* (*subst.*); *Romeo* I come, this doe *Q1;* Romeo, Romeo, Romeo, *Knight*[2], *conj. Dyce; Romeo, Romeo,* heeres drinke, *Williams, conj. Nicholson.* S.D.] *Q1; not in Q2–4,F.*

noise, which being firmly rooted, it maketh upon divulsion of parts'. He notes, and dismisses, the belief that they grow under gallows and places of execution. J. J. Munro, op. cit., p. xvii, cites Sir B. W. Richardson's opinion (after experimentation) that a certain kind of Greek mandrake, called *death-wine* by the ancient Greeks, could have served as the source of the potion used by Juliet. The Greeks used it for surgical operations as we use chloroform, 'a dose having the effect of causing apparent death'.

49. *wake*] Q2's error *walke* is paralleled by IV. i. 116.

58. *Romeo . . . thee*] Q1 is attractive as an anticipation of Antony's 'Eros! I come, my queen.—Eros! Stay for me' (*Ant.*, IV. ii. 50). Dyce suggests that a marginal S.D. *here drinke* was fitted into the dialogue. A minimal emendation to secure metrical regularity is often adopted, but I would argue that the extra-long line is deliberate, expressive of frenzied emotion.

58. S.D. *bed . . . curtains*] The Q1 directions do not indicate whether the bed is brought on for the scene (the simplest solution) or whether the curtains are those of an opening in the tiring-house façade, or whether a projecting, curtained structure was used. The tomb will occupy the same area of the stage in Act V: but it must be large enough to accommodate several bodies which must be visible to the audience. It will probably need to be larger than the bed, and could be erected after V. i: it does not need to be dismantled before the play ends.

[SCENE IV]

Enter LADY CAPULET *and* NURSE.

Lady Cap. Hold, take these keys and fetch more spices, Nurse.
Nurse. They call for dates and quinces in the pastry.

Enter CAPULET.

Cap. Come, stir, stir, stir, the second cock hath crow'd!
The curfew bell hath rung, 'tis three o'clock.
Look to the bak'd meats, good Angelica:
Spare not for cost.
Nurse. Go, you cot-quean, go,
Get you to bed. Faith, you'll be sick tomorrow
For this night's watching.
Cap. No, not a whit. What, I have watch'd ere now
All night for lesser cause, and ne'er been sick.
Lady Cap. Ay, you have been a mouse-hunt in your time;

Scene IV

SCENE IV] *Rowe; not in Q2–4,F,Q1.* *Location.*] *A Hall. Rowe.* S.D.] *Q2–4,F (Enter Lady of the house, and Nurse.); Enter Nurse with hearbs, Mother. Q1.* 1. *Lady Cap.*] *ed.; La. Q2–4; Lady. F; Moth: Q1.* 6. *Nurse.*] *Q2–4,F,Q1; La. Cap. / Singer, conj. Jackson.* 10. lesser] *Q2;* lesse *Q3,4,F; not in Q1.* 11. *Lady Cap.*] *ed.; La. Q2–4,F; Moth: Q1.*

2. *pastry*] place where pastry is made.

3. *second cock*] 3 a.m. Tusser, *Husbandry* (1573), says cocks crow 'At midnight, at three, and an hower ere day'.

4. *curfew bell*] The same bell that rings the curfew rings at morning light.

6. *Nurse.*] Ascription of this speech to the Nurse has been disputed by Z. Jackson on the grounds that she would not dare to call her master a *cot-quean*, a man who meddles with domestic affairs. Yet the touch of vulgarity suggests the Nurse, and it is wholly consistent with the presentation of the domestic affairs and manners of the Capulet household that he should involve himself and that she should banter with her master. There is doubt about which of the women is called Angelica. Spencer suggests that if Capulet is addressing the Nurse, the effect might be comic, 'for Angelica was the pagan princess of exquisite beauty and heartless coquetry who came to sow dissension among the Christian princes in Ariosto's *Orlando Furioso*'.

8. *watching*] lack of sleep.

11. *a . . . time*] a prowler in your rakish youth (like a cat at night). *Mouse* was an amorous term for woman, as in *Ham.*, III. iv. 183: 'Pinch wanton on your cheek; call you his mouse'.

But I will watch you from such watching now.
Exeunt Lady Capulet and Nurse.
Cap. A jealous-hood, a jealous-hood!

Enter three or four Servingmen *with spits and logs and baskets.*

Now fellow, what is there?
1 Ser. Things for the cook, sir, but I know not what.
Cap. Make haste, make haste! [*Exit 1 Servingman.*]
—Sirrah, fetch drier logs!
Call Peter, he will show thee where they are.
2 Ser. I have a head, sir, that will find out logs
And never trouble Peter for the matter.
Cap. Mass and well said! A merry whoreson, ha.
Thou shalt be loggerhead! [*Exit 2 Servingman.*]
—Good faith! 'Tis day!
Play music.
The County will be here with music straight,
For so he said he would. I hear him near.
Nurse! Wife! What ho! What, Nurse I say!

Enter NURSE.

Go waken Juliet, go, and trim her up.
I'll go and chat with Paris. Hie, make haste,

13. hood! . . . there?] *As Capell; one line prose Q2–4;* hood, / Now . . . there? *F; var. Q1.* what is] *Q2–4;* what *F; var. Q1.* 14. *1 Ser.*] *ed.; Fel. Q2–4,F; Ser: Q1.* 15. S.D.] *Capell; not in Q2–4,F,Q1.* 17. *2 Ser.*] *ed.; Fel. Q2–4,F; Ser: Q1.* 20. S.D. [*Exit 2 Servingman.*]] *Camb.; not in Q2–4,F,Q1.* faith] *Q4;* father *Q2,3,F; not in Q1.*

13. *jealous-hood*] OED suggests either *hood* as the type of the female head, or alluding to the use of a hood as a disguise for a jealous spy; cf. mad-cap, sly-boots. Capulet is chortling at his wife's quick response to his boasts of youthful amorous escapades; perhaps the *-hood* suffix means simply 'your *quality* (as a jealous wife)', as in *ladyhood, knighthood,* as Harold Brooks suggests, privately.

17. *I . . . logs*] He means 'I am good at finding logs'; the other sense is 'I am a blockhead'.

20. *loggerhead*] blockhead. Capulet makes the obvious punning jest.

faith] NCS suppose *faith* in the MS. was misread as *fath.* The oath *good father* does not occur elsewhere in Shakespeare. Cf. III. v. 172 n.

21. *straight*] immediately.

Make haste! The bridegroom he is come already.
Make haste I say. [*Exeunt Capulet and Servingmen.*]

[Scene V]

[*Nurse goes to curtains.*]

Nurse. Mistress! What, mistress! Juliet! Fast, I warrant her, she.
Why, lamb, why, lady, fie! You slug-abed!
Why, love I say! Madam! Sweetheart! Why, bride!
What, not a word? You take your pennyworths now.
Sleep for a week; for the next night, I warrant,
The County Paris hath set up his rest
That you shall rest but little! God forgive me!
Marry and amen. How sound is she asleep!
I needs must wake her. Madam, madam, madam!
Ay, let the County take you in your bed,
He'll fright you up, i'faith. Will it not be?
What, dress'd, and in your clothes, and down again?
I must needs wake you. Lady! Lady! Lady!
Alas, alas! Help, help! My lady's dead!

26–7.] *As F; one line in Q2–4; not in Q1.* 27. S.D.] *Rowe; not in Q2–4,F,Q1.*

Scene V

SCENE V] *Pope; not in Q2–4,F,Q1.* *Location.*] *Scene draws and discovers Juliet on a bed. Rowe; Juliet's chamber; the curtains closed about the bed. NCS.* S.D.] *Spencer; Undraws the curtains. Camb. (l. 11); Enter Nurse. Hanmer; not in Q2–4,F,Q1.*
9. needs must] *Q2;* must needs *Q3,4,F;* must *Q1.*

S.D.] It is convenient to mark a new scene for ease of reference, but the Nurse has not in fact left the stage; cf. I. v. 1 and n., II. ii. 1 and n.

1. *Fast*] fast asleep.

2–3. *lamb . . . sweetheart*] Cf. I. iii. 3–4 and n.

4. *pennyworths*] small allowances.

6. *set . . . rest*] determined; with quibbles on (i) the phrase from card-play meaning 'to stake everything'; (ii) take a rest, relax; (iii) take up one's abode, as in Lodge, *Rosalynde* (1590, ed. Greg, 1907, p. 51): 'Aliena resolved there to set up her rest . . . and so became mistress of the farm'; (iv) the term for preparing to fire the musket, where a support was fixed in the ground, on which the heavy barrel was *rested* before taking aim—this yields bawdy applications like those on 'shooting' in *LLL*, IV. i. 101–32; (v) Partridge, sv *set up*, supposes an allusion to couching a lance for the charge in tilting, but he concurs in finding a bawdy innuendo. The jest on setting up rest to prevent rest also occurs in Nashe, *Terrors of the Night*, *Works*, I. 384, l. 34; and cf. *Mer.V.*, II. ii. 95: 'I have set up my rest to run away'.

7. *God forgive me*] The Nurse apologizes for her lewd jest; cf. I. iii. 2–4; there are further bawdy quibbles on *take you* (l. 10) and *fright you up* (l. 11).

O weraday that ever I was born.
Some aqua vitae, ho! My lord! My lady!

Enter LADY CAPULET.

Lady Cap. What noise is here?
Nurse. O lamentable day!
Lady Cap. What is the matter?
Nurse. Look, look! O heavy day!
Lady Cap. O me, O me! My child, my only life.
Revive, look up, or I will die with thee.
Help, help! Call help!

Enter CAPULET.

Cap. For shame, bring Juliet forth, her lord is come.
Nurse. She's dead, deceas'd! She's dead! Alack the day!
Lady Cap. Alack the day! She's dead, she's dead, she's dead!
Cap. Ha! Let me see her. Out alas. She's cold,
Her blood is settled and her joints are stiff.
Life and these lips have long been separated.
Death lies on her like an untimely frost
Upon the sweetest flower of all the field.
Nurse. O lamentable day!
Lady Cap. O woeful time!
Cap. Death, that hath ta'en her hence to make me wail
Ties up my tongue and will not let me speak.

Enter FRIAR [LAURENCE] *and* PARIS *and* Musicians.

Friar L. Come, is the bride ready to go to church?
Cap. Ready to go, but never to return.

15. weraday] *Q2; weleaday Q3; weladay Q4,F;* alack the day *Q1.* 16. S.D] *Camb.; Enter Mother. F,Q1; not in Q2–4.* 17. *Lady Cap.*] *ed.; Mo. Q2–4,F; not in Q1.* 18. *Lady Cap.*] *ed.; Mo. Q2–4,F; Moth: Q1.* 19. *Lady Cap.*] *ed.; Mo. Q2–4,F; not in Q1.* 22. *Cap.*] *Q1; Fa. Q2–4,F.* 24. *Lady Cap.*] *ed.; M. Q2,3,F; Mo. Q4; Nur: Q1.* 25. *Cap.*] *Q1; Fa. Q2–4,F.* 30. *Lady Cap.*] *ed.; Mo. Q2–4,F; not in Q1.* 31. *Cap.*] *ed.; Fa. Q2–4,F; not in Q1.* 32. S.D.] *Q4* (*subst.*)*; Enter Frier and the Countie. Q2,3,F,Q1* (*subst.*). 34. *Cap.*] *Q1; Fa. Q2–4,F.*

15. *weraday*] alas.

16. *aqua vitae*] brandy; cf. III. ii. 88.

28–9. *Death . . . field*] Cf. Marlowe, *Jew of Malta*, I. 621–3: 'A faire young maid scarce 14 yeares of age, / The sweetest flower in *Citherea's* field, / Cropt from the pleasures of the fruitful earth'.

O son, the night before thy wedding day
Hath Death lain with thy wife. There she lies,
Flower as she was, deflowered by him.
Death is my son-in-law, Death is my heir.
My daughter he hath wedded. I will die,
And leave him all: life, living, all is Death's.

Paris. Have I thought long to see this morning's face,
And doth it give me such a sight as this?

Lady Cap. Accurs'd, unhappy, wretched, hateful day.
Most miserable hour that e'er time saw
In lasting labour of his pilgrimage.
But one, poor one, one poor and loving child,
But one thing to rejoice and solace in,
And cruel Death hath catch'd it from my sight.

Nurse. O woe! O woeful, woeful, woeful day.
Most lamentable day. Most woeful day
That ever, ever I did yet behold.
O day, O day, O day, O hateful day.
Never was seen so black a day as this.
O woeful day, O woeful day.

Paris. Beguil'd, divorced, wronged, spited, slain.
Most detestable Death, by thee beguil'd,
By cruel, cruel thee quite overthrown.
O love! O life! Not life, but love in death!

Cap. Despis'd, distressed, hated, martyr'd, kill'd.
Uncomfortable time, why cam'st thou now
To murder, murder our solemnity?

36. There] *Q2–4,F;* see, where *Q1.* 41. long] *Q1,Q3,4,F;* loue *Q2.* 43. *Lady Cap.*] *ed.; Mo. Q2–4,F; var. Q1.* 46. loving] *Q2–4,F;* living *Johnson 1771; not in Q1.* 49–50.] *All at once cry out and wring their hands/All cry:* And all our joy, and all our hope is dead,/Dead, lost, undone, absented, wholy fled, *Q1.* 59. *Cap.*] *ed.; Fat. Q2–4,F; var. Q1.*

36. *Death . . . wife*] Cf. v. iii. 102–5.

41. *long*] This is in Brooke (l. 2274) and in Q1, and develops the impression of emotional impatience felt by Paris, though of course in the play the period of waiting for the wedding day has been short; cf. IV. ii. 39 n.

45. *lasting labour*] unceasing toil.

49–64. *O woe . . . buried*] Probably, as White suggests, a parody of Jasper Heywood's translation of Seneca's tragedies (1581); cf. *MND*, v. i. 168–79. Q1 dialogue differs, divided between *Paris* (8), *Cap.* (2), *All cry* (2), *Cap.* (5), *Cap.* (5), *Moth.* (5). Thus only two lines are spoken in chorus.

55. *Beguil'd*] Disappointed, cheated, of a hoped-for future.

60. *Uncomfortable*] Devoid of consolation.

61. *solemnity*] ceremony (of marriage), festal occasion.

O child, O child! My soul and not my child,
Dead art thou. Alack, my child is dead,
And with my child my joys are buried.

Friar L. Peace, ho, for shame. Confusion's cure lives not
In these confusions. Heaven and yourself
Had part in this fair maid, now heaven hath all,
And all the better is it for the maid.
Your part in her you could not keep from death,
But heaven keeps his part in eternal life.
The most you sought was her promotion,
For 'twas your heaven she should be advanc'd,
And weep ye now, seeing she is advanc'd
Above the clouds, as high as heaven itself?
O, in this love you love your child so ill
That you run mad, seeing that she is well.
She's not well married that lives married long,
But she's best married that dies married young.
Dry up your tears, and stick your rosemary
On this fair corse, and, as the custom is,
All in her best array bear her to church.
For though fond nature bids us all lament,
Yet nature's tears are reason's merriment.

Cap. All things that we ordained festival

65. cure] *Theobald; care Q2–4,F; not in Q1.* 72. should] *Q2–4;* shouldst *F; not in Q1.* 81. All in] *Rowe;* And in *Q2–4,F;* In all *Q1.* 82. fond] *F2;* some *Q2–4,F; not in Q1.* us all] *Q2–4;* all us *F; not in Q1.* 84. *Cap.*] *ed.; Fa. Q2–4,F; var. Q1.*

65. *Confusion's*] Calamity's.

66. *confusions*] uncontrolled outbursts.

67. *maid*] The Friar coolly preserves the secret of the marriage.

69. *Your part*] i.e. her mortal body.

71. *promotion*] advancement to the happiest state possible.

72. *For . . . advanc'd*] For it was your idea of bliss she should be advanced in rank (i.e. by marrying Paris).

76. *well*] A proverbial saying (Tilley H 347); cf. *Ant.*, II. v. 31–2: 'we use / To say the dead are well', *Mac.*, IV. iii. 177, 179.

79. *rosemary*] The herb was a symbol of remembrance (cf. *Ham.*, IV. v. 172–3) and was used at funerals, as well as weddings (the Nurse associates rosemary with Romeo in II. iv. 202–3).

80–1. *custom . . . church*] Cf. IV. i. 109 and n.

82. *fond*] weak and foolish, indulgent. The Q2–4, F reading *some* makes nonsense but might be a misreading of a manuscript *fond.*

nature] natural affection.

83. *Yet . . . merriment*] Natural affection prompts us all to lament, yet reason bids us rejoice; cf. *Tw.N.*, I. v. 61–6.

84. *festival*] i.e. for festal purposes (adjectival form).

Turn from their office to black funeral:
Our instruments to melancholy bells,
Our wedding cheer to a sad burial feast;
Our solemn hymns to sullen dirges change,
Our bridal flowers serve for a buried corse,
And all things change them to the contrary.

Friar L. Sir, go you in, and madam, go with him,
And go, Sir Paris. Every one prepare
To follow this fair corse unto her grave.
The heavens do lour upon you for some ill;
Move them no more by crossing their high will.

Exeunt all but the Nurse and Musicians, casting rosemary on Juliet and shutting the curtains.

1 Mus. Faith, we may put up our pipes and be gone.

Nurse. Honest good fellows, ah put up, put up,
For well you know this is a pitiful case.

1 Mus. Ay, by my troth, the case may be amended.

Exit Nurse.

Enter PETER.

95. S.D.] *ed.; Exeunt manet. Q2,3; Exeunt manent Musici. Q4; Exeunt. F; They all but the Nurse goe foorth, casting Rosemary on her and shutting the Curtens. Q1.* 96. *1 Mus.*] *ed.; Musi. Q2–4; Mu. F; not in Q1.* 99. *1 Mus.*] *ed.; Fid. Q2–4; Mu. F; 1. Q1.* by my] *Q1,Q3,4,F;* my my *Q2.* S.D. *Exit Nurse.*] *Q1; Exit omnes Q2; Exeunt omnes. Q3,4; not in F.* S.D. PETER] *Q4,F; Will Kemp. Q2,3; Seruingman Q1.*

86–9. *Our . . . corse*] Cf. Brooke, ll. 2507–14.

87. *cheer*] banquet.

88. *solemn*] fitting to the ceremony (here, a wedding). Cf. Malory, *Arthur*, VII. xxxvi. 270: 'The Bisshop of Caunterbury made the weddyng . . . with grete sollempnytee' (OED).

94. *ill*] sin (which you have committed).

95. S.D.] The Q1 version of this scene is very garbled, preserving only fragments of the Q2 dialogue and an outline of the action; this S.D. may record a detail of an original and authentic production, however.

96. *put . . . pipes*] The use of the phrase does not imply that the musicians are pipers: it was proverbial (Tilley P 345) for 'desist', 'pack up'; the jest occurs in Nashe, *Summer's Last Will*, *Works*, III. 263, where Harvest leads out his chorus of reapers and says 'We were as good euen put vp our pipes, and sing Merry, merry, for we shall get no money'. The Musicians are identified (ll. 127 ff.) by generic names, as strings: possibly one of them doubles as a singer (see l. 134).

98. *case*] state of affairs.

99. *case . . . amended*] Quibbling on (i) *case* in l. 98, (ii) the fiddler's instrument case which needs repair, (iii) the proverb (Tilley C 111) 'The case is altered'.

S.D.] Dover Wilson speculates that Q2's *Exit omnes* indicates that what follows is a later addition, possibly by

Peter. Musicians, O musicians, 'Heart's ease', 'Heart's ease'! O, and you will have me live, play 'Heart's ease'.

1 Mus. Why 'Heart's ease'?

Peter. O musicians, because my heart itself plays 'My heart is full'. O play me some merry dump to comfort me.

1 Mus. Not a dump we! 'Tis no time to play now.

Peter. You will not then?

1 Mus. No.

Peter. I will then give it you soundly.

1 Mus. What will you give us?

Peter. No money, on my faith, but the gleek! I will give you the minstrel.

1 Mus. Then will I give you the serving-creature.

Peter. Then will I lay the serving-creature's dagger on

100. *Peter.*] *Q2–4,F; Ser: Q1 (to end of scene).* 103. *1 Mus.*] *ed.; Fidler. Q2–4; Mu. F; not in Q1.* 105. full] *Q2,3,F;* full of woe *Q4; not in Q1.* 105–6. O play . . . me] *Q2–4; not in F; var. Q1.* 107. *1 Mus.*] *ed.; Minstrels. Q2–4; Mu. F; 1. Q1.* 109. *1 Mus.*] *ed.; Minst. Q2; Min. Q3,4; Mu. F; 1. Q1.* 111. *1 Mus.*] *ed.; Minst. Q2; Min. Q3,4; Mu. F; 1. Q1.* 114. *1 Mus.*] *ed.; Minstrel. Q2; Min. Q3,4; Mu. F; not in Q1.* 115. lay] *Q2,3,F;* say *Q4; not in Q1.*

Nashe. Spencer notes that l. 99 sounds like an exit line. The parallels with Nashe are strong, but not peculiar to this passage. The Q2 reading *Enter Will Kemp* might indicate that if this was an addition it was designed for Kemp's benefit. Will Kemp played Peter and was famous in comic parts; he was a sharer in the company; see Intro., p. 14.

100. *Heart's ease*] A popular song of the time; the words are lost, the tune is preserved in Playford, *The English Dancing Master* (1651), and is reprinted in E. W. Naylor, *Shakespeare and Music* (1896), p. 193.

104–5. '*My . . . full*'] Q4 offers to complete a song-title; Steevens identifies it with 'A Pleasant New Ballad of Two Lovers' which has a line 'Hey hoe! my heart is full of woe!' The date of the song is not demonstrably early enough to make the conjecture certain; NCS notes (in defence of preferring Q4) 'probably the foul papers gave enough to remind the prompter, or Kemp, what should be quoted'.

105. *dump*] A dismal tune; Peter makes a contradiction in terms.

110. *soundly*] thoroughly (with a quibble on *sound*, as they are musicians).

112. *gleek*] gesture of contempt.

113. *minstrel*] A contemptuous term, many minstrels being vagabonds; cf. III. i. 45.

your pate. I will carry no crotchets. I'll re you, I'll fa you. Do you note me?

1 Mus. And you re us and fa us, you note us.

2 Mus. Pray you put up your dagger and put out your wit.

Peter. Then have at you with my wit. I will dry-beat you with an iron wit, and put up my iron dagger. Answer me like men.

'When griping griefs the heart doth wound,
And doleful dumps the mind oppress,
Then music with her silver sound'—

Why 'silver sound'? Why 'music with her silver sound'? What say you, Simon Catling?

1 Mus. Marry, sir, because silver hath a sweet sound.

Peter. Prates. What say you, Hugh Rebeck?

2 Mus. I say 'silver sound' because musicians sound for silver.

118. *1 Mus.*] *ed.; Minst. Q2; Min. Q3,4; Mu. F; 1. Q1.* 119. *2 Mus.*] *ed.; 2. M. Q2–4,F; not in Q1.* 120. *Peter.* Then . . . I] *Q4;* Then . . . wit. *Peter.* I *Q2,3,F; var. Q1.* 123–5. When . . . sound] *As verse Q1; as prose Q2–4,F.* 124. And . . . oppress] *Q1; not in Q2–4,F.* 128. *1 Mus.*] *ed.; Minst. Q2; Min. Q3,4; Mu. F; 1. Q1.* 129. Prates] *Q2;* Pratest *Q3,F;* Pratee *Q4;* Pretie *Q1.* 130. *2 Mus.*] *ed.; 2. M. Q2–4,F; 2. Q1.*

116. *carry . . . crotchets*] endure none of your quirks (with a quibble on the term in music for a quarter-note).

116–17. *re . . . fa*] Names of notes in the musical scale used comically as verbs.

117. *note*] pay attention and understand (with an obvious quibble).

118. *you note us*] NCS explains '*You* and *us* are emphatic'.

119. *put out*] display, put forth.

120. *dry-beat*] thrash; cf. III. i. 78; possibly quibbling on *dry* = stupid as in *AYL*, II. vii. 38–40.

121. *iron wit*] Cf. Nashe, *Unfortunate Traveller*, *Works*, II. 261, l. 24; Peter presumably means 'strong'.

123–5. '*When . . . sound*'] The opening of a poem 'In commendation of Musick' by Richard Edwardes (1523–66) which appears in *The Paradyse of Daynty Deuises* (1576). Keyboard music for '*When griping griefs*' is included in Denis Stevens, *The Mulliner Book* (1951). Greg supports Q1: Shakespeare 'did not trouble to write more than the first and last lines of this popular stanza' (*The Editorial Problem*, p. 62).

125. *silver sound*] Cf. Nashe, *The Unfortunate Traveller*, *Works*, II. 222, l. 6: 'This siluer-sounding tale made such sugred harmonie in his eares that . . . he could haue found in his hart to haue packt vp hys pipes and to haue gone to heauen without a bait'.

127. *Catling*] 'A small lute-string' (Steevens).

129, 132. *Prates*] Q2 makes good sense. [*He*] *prates* serves the purpose better than the supposedly ironic *Pretty*, which is from Q1, and an easier reading.

129. *Rebeck*] An early kind of fiddle.

Peter. Prates too. What say you, James Soundpost?

3 Mus. Faith, I know not what to say.

Peter. O, I cry you mercy, you are the singer. I will say for you. It is 'music with her silver sound' because musicians have no gold for sounding.

'Then music with her silver sound
With speedy help doth lend redress.' *Exit.*

1 Mus. What a pestilent knave is this same.

2 Mus. Hang him, Jack. Come, we'll in here, tarry for the mourners, and stay dinner. *Exeunt.*

132. Prates] *Q2;* Pratest *Q3,F;* Pratee *Q4;* Prettie *Q1.* 133. *3 Mus.*] *ed.; 3. M. Q2–4; 3. Mu. F; 3. Q1.* 139. *1 Mus.*] *ed.; Min. Q2–4; Mu. F; var. Q1.* 140. *2 Mus.*] *ed.; M. 2. Q2–4,F; 1. Q1.*

132. *Soundpost*] 'A small peg of wood fixed beneath the bridge of a violin or similar instrument' (OED).

134. *singer*] Hence, unable to *say* anything: Peter displays his iron wit.

136. *sounding*] making music (with a quibble on jingling in their purses).

[ACT V]

[SCENE I]

Enter Romeo.

Romeo. If I may trust the flattering truth of sleep
My dreams presage some joyful news at hand.
My bosom's lord sits lightly in his throne
And all this day an unaccustom'd spirit
Lifts me above the ground with cheerful thoughts.
I dreamt my lady came and found me dead—
Strange dream that gives a dead man leave to think!—
And breath'd such life with kisses in my lips
That I reviv'd and was an emperor.
Ah me, how sweet is love itself possess'd
When but love's shadows are so rich in joy.

Enter Balthasar, *Romeo's* man, *booted.*

News from Verona! How, now Balthasar,
Dost thou not bring me letters from the Friar?

ACT V

Scene 1

Act V Scene 1] *Rowe; not in Q2–4,F,Q1.* *Location.*] *Mantua. Rowe; A street. Capell.* 1. truth] *Q2–4,F;* Eye *Q1.* 4. this day] *Q2–4;* thisan day *F; not in Q1.* unaccustom'd] *Q2–4;* uccustom'd *F; not in Q1.* 7. dream that gives] *Q2,3,F;* dreames that giues *Q4;* dreames that giue *Q1.* 11. S.D.] *Q1 (subst.); Enter Romeos man. Q2,3,F (subst.); Enter* Romeos *man* Balthazer. *Q4.*

1–9. *If . . . emperor*] J. W. Hales compares Chaucer, *Troilus*, v. 1164–9, where Troilus has an intuition of good fortune which is tragically disappointed.

1. *flattering . . . sleep*] encouraging reports that truth manifests itself to us in sleep. OED (sv v 7) records *flatter*, 'to inspire with hope, usually on insufficient grounds'; cf. Sonnet 87.

3. *bosom's lord*] love.

sits . . . throne] Cf. *Tw.N.*, i. i. 37–8: 'liver, brain, and heart, / These sovereign thrones', alluding to the belief that the seat of passion was the liver, of thought the brain, of love the heart.

8. *breath'd . . . lips*] Cf. Marlowe, *Hero and Leander*, ii. 3: 'He kist her, and breath'd life into her lips'.

How doth my lady? Is my father well?
How doth my Juliet? That I ask again,
For nothing can be ill if she be well.

Bal. Then she is well and nothing can be ill.
Her body sleeps in Capels' monument,
And her immortal part with angels lives.
I saw her laid low in her kindred's vault
And presently took post to tell it you.
O pardon me for bringing these ill news,
Since you did leave it for my office, sir.

Romeo. Is it e'en so? Then I defy you, stars!
Thou know'st my lodging. Get me ink and paper,
And hire posthorses. I will hence tonight.

Bal. I do beseech you sir, have patience.
Your looks are pale and wild and do import
Some misadventure.

Romeo. Tush, thou art deceiv'd.
Leave me, and do the thing I bid thee do.
Hast thou no letters to me from the Friar?

15. doth my Juliet] *Pope;* doth my Lady *Juliet Q2–4, F;* fares my *Juliet Q1.* 19. lives] *Q2–4;* liue *F; var. Q1.* 24. defy] *Q1;* denie *Q2–4,F.* you] *Q2–4,F;* my *Q1.* 25. know'st] *F;* knowest *Q2–4; not in Q1.*

15. *my Juliet*] The compositor accidentally duplicated *lady* from l. 14; there is no justification for adopting Q1's whole phrase, however, with Steevens.

17. *well*] Cf. IV. v. 76 and n.

21. *presently*] immediately.

23. *for my office*] as my duty.

24. *defy*] Every argument *except* an appeal to graphic similarity between the manuscript forms of *deny* and *defy* shows *defy* to be preferable. Evidently, Romeo admits the influence of the stars (*Is it e'en so?*). His hysterical reactions to news of his banishment in III. iii (tearing his hair and falling on the ground, despite the Friar's counsel of 'patience') might be a precedent for supposing him here equally hysterical, rather than the resolved, furious and defiant hero of III. i. 125–6: 'Away to heaven respective lenity, / And fire-ey'd fury be my conduct now'. Yet by this late stage of the play Romeo has clear awareness of the powerful influence of the stars; the parallel with III. i. 125–6 is striking: on receiving the news Romeo is death-defying. In Brooke Romeo's reaction to news of the banishment is 'He cryed out (with open mouth) against the starres above' and 'He blamed all the world, and all he did defye'. Cf. *Ham.*, v. ii. 211: 'we defy augury'.

25–6. *Get . . . posthorses*] Cf. Brooke, ll. 2604, 2612.

27. *have patience*] show fortitude.

Bal. No, my good lord.
Romeo. No matter. Get thee gone.
And hire those horses. I'll be with thee straight.
Exit Balthasar.
Well, Juliet, I will lie with thee tonight.
Let's see for means. O mischief thou art swift
To enter in the thoughts of desperate men.
I do remember an apothecary—
And hereabouts a dwells—which late I noted
In tatter'd weeds, with overwhelming brows,
Culling of simples. Meagre were his looks,
Sharp misery had worn him to the bones,
And in his needy shop a tortoise hung,
An alligator stuff'd, and other skins
Of ill-shap'd fishes; and about his shelves
A beggarly account of empty boxes,
Green earthen pots, bladders, and musty seeds,
Remnants of packthread, and old cakes of roses
Were thinly scatter'd to make up a show.
Noting this penury, to myself I said,
'And if a man did need a poison now,
Whose sale is present death in Mantua,
Here lives a caitiff wretch would sell it him'.
O, this same thought did but forerun my need,
And this same needy man must sell it me.
As I remember, this should be the house.

33. S.D.] *As Q1; after* lord *in Q2–4,F.* 38. a] *Q2–4; not in F,Q1.*

39. *weeds*] clothes.

overwhelming] overhanging, beetling.

40. *Culling of simples*] Gathering medicinal herbs.

42–4. *tortoise . . . fishes*] Cf. Nashe, *Have With You, Works*, III. 67: 'The next rat he seazd on hee made an Anatomie of, . . . and after hanged her ouer his head in his studie, in stead of an Apothecaries Crocodile, or dride Alligatur'. Steevens refers to plate iii in Hogarth's *Marriage à la Mode*, and says 'I have met with the alligator, tortoise, &c., hanging up in the shop of an ancient apothecary at Limehouse'. These curiosities were regularly displayed in apothecaries' shops.

45. *beggarly account*] wretchedly small number.

47. *packthread*] twine used for securing parcels or bundles.

cakes of roses] rose-petals compressed into cake-form and used as perfume.

51. *Whose . . . death*] Of which the sale is punishable by instant death.

52. *caitiff*] miserable, pitiable.

Being holiday, the beggar's shop is shut.
What ho! Apothecary!

Enter Apothecary.

Apoth. Who calls so loud?
Romeo. Come hither, man. I see that thou art poor.
Hold, there is forty ducats. Let me have
A dram of poison, such soon-speeding gear
As will disperse itself through all the veins,
That the life-weary taker may fall dead,
And that the trunk may be discharg'd of breath
As violently as hasty powder fir'd
Doth hurry from the fatal cannon's womb.
Apoth. Such mortal drugs I have, but Mantua's law
Is death to any he that utters them.
Romeo. Art thou so bare and full of wretchedness,
And fear'st to die? Famine is in thy cheeks,
Need and oppression starveth in thy eyes,
Contempt and beggary hangs upon thy back.
The world is not thy friend, nor the world's law;
The world affords no law to make thee rich;
Then be not poor, but break it, and take this.
Apoth. My poverty, but not my will consents.
Romeo. I pay thy poverty and not thy will.
Apoth. Put this in any liquid thing you will
And drink it off and if you had the strength

57. S.D.] *Q1,F; not in Q2–4.* 69. fear'st] *F;* fearest *Q2–4; var. Q1.* 70. starveth in] *Q2–4,F;* stareth in *Rowe; var. Q1.* 76. pay] *Q1,Q4;* pray *Q2,3,F.*

59. *forty ducats*] a considerable sum (which the Courtesan in *Err.*, IV. iii. 78, 91, says is the value of her diamond ring, and 'forty ducats is too much to lose'). In Brooke the sum is fifty crowns, in Boaistuau fifty ducats. Evidently Shakespeare preferred to remember *Err.*, where the line can have memorable effect. The ducat was a gold coin, so called in several European countries though originally Venetian.

60. *soon-speeding gear*] quick-working stuff; cf. Brooke, l. 2585.

61. *disperse . . . veins*] Cf. Daniel, *Rosamond*, l. 603 (cited in n. to V. iii. 92).

64–5. *violently . . . womb*] Cf. II. vi. 9–10, III. iii. 131–2.

67. *he*] man; cf. Abbott (§ 224) and *Shr.*, III. ii. 230–1.

utters] sells, dispenses.

70. *starveth*] are hungry (Dowden).

71. *Contempt and beggary*] Contemptible beggary.

74. *it*] i.e. the law.

77–9. *Put . . . straight*] Cf. Brooke, ll. 2587–8. Steevens compares Chaucer,

Of twenty men it would dispatch you straight.
Romeo. There is thy gold—worse poison to men's souls,
Doing more murder in this loathsome world
Than these poor compounds that thou mayst not sell.
I sell thee poison, thou hast sold me none.
Farewell, buy food, and get thyself in flesh.
Come, cordial, and not poison, go with me
To Juliet's grave, for there must I use thee. *Exeunt.*

[SCENE II]

Enter FRIAR JOHN.

Friar J. Holy Franciscan Friar, Brother, ho!

Enter FRIAR LAURENCE.

Friar L. This same should be the voice of Friar John.
Welcome from Mantua. What says Romeo?
Or, if his mind be writ, give me his letter.
Friar J. Going to find a barefoot brother out,
One of our order, to associate me,
Here in this city visiting the sick,
And finding him, the searchers of the town,
Suspecting that we both were in a house
Where the infectious pestilence did reign,

81. murder] *Q2,3,F* (murther); murthers *Q4; not in Q1.*

Scene II

SCENE II] *Pope; not in Q2–4,F,Q1.* *Location.*] *The monastery near Verona. Rowe; Friar Laurence's cell. Capell.* S.D. *Enter* FRIAR JOHN.] *Q1; Enter Frier* John *to Frier* Lawrence *Q2–4,F.* 1. S.D. *Enter* FRIAR LAURENCE.] *Q2–4,F; not in Q1.*

Pardoner's Tale, 859–67, where the pothecary similarly dispenses a strong and violent poison, of which an amount the size of 'a corn of whete' is fatal.

84. *get . . . flesh*] grow plump (OED).

Scene II

4. *mind*] message.

5–12. *Going . . . stay'd*] Cf. Brooke, ll. 2488–99.

5. *barefoot brother*] Franciscan.

6. *associate*] accompany; the rule of the order forbade him to travel without the company of another friar; cf. Brooke, l. 2490.

8. *searchers*] persons appointed to view dead bodies and report on the cause of death (OED sb 1 e).

Seal'd up the doors and would not let us forth,
So that my speed to Mantua there was stay'd.

Friar L. Who bare my letter then to Romeo?

Friar J. I could not send it—here it is again—
Nor get a messenger to bring it thee,
So fearful were they of infection.

Friar L. Unhappy fortune! By my brotherhood,
The letter was not nice but full of charge,
Of dear import, and the neglecting it
May do much danger. Friar John, go hence,
Get me an iron crow and bring it straight
Unto my cell.

Friar J. Brother, I'll go and bring it thee. *Exit.*

Friar L. Now must I to the monument alone.
Within this three hours will fair Juliet wake.
She will beshrew me much that Romeo
Hath had no notice of these accidents,
But I will write again to Mantua,
And keep her at my cell till Romeo come.
Poor living corse, clos'd in a dead man's tomb. *Exit.*

[SCENE III]

Enter PARIS *and his* Page, *with flowers and sweet water.*

Paris. Give me thy torch, boy. Hence and stand aloof.
Yet put it out, for I would not be seen.

12. my] *Q2,3,F;* may *Q4; not in Q1.* 14. could] *Q2,3,F;* cold *Q4; not in Q1.*

Scene III

SCENE III] *Rowe; not in Q2–4,F,Q1.* *Location.*] *A Churchyard, in it, a noble Monument belonging to the Capulets. Rowe.* S.D.] *Q1; Enter* Paris *and his Page. Q2–4,F.* 1. aloof] *Q2–4;* aloft *F; not in Q1.*

12. *speed . . . was stay'd*] successful progress was prevented.

18. *nice*] trivial.

charge] importance.

19. *dear import*] momentous consequence.

21. *crow*] short crowbar; cf. *Err.*, III. i. 80, where Antipholus of Ephesus tells his servant to get him a crow to break down the locked door of his house.

Scene III

S.D. *sweet*] perfumed.

1. *stand aloof*] keep at a distance.

Under yond yew trees lay thee all along,
Holding thy ear close to the hollow ground;
So shall no foot upon the churchyard tread,
Being loose, unfirm, with digging up of graves,
But thou shalt hear it. Whistle then to me
As signal that thou hear'st something approach.
Give me those flowers. Do as I bid thee. Go.

Page. I am almost afraid to stand alone
Here in the churchyard. Yet I will adventure. [*Retires.*]

Paris strews the tomb with flowers.

Paris. Sweet flower, with flowers thy bridal bed I strew.
O woe, thy canopy is dust and stones
Which with sweet water nightly I will dew,
Or wanting that, with tears distill'd by moans.
The obsequies that I for thee will keep
Nightly shall be to strew thy grave and weep.

Page whistles.

The boy gives warning something doth approach.
What cursed foot wanders this way tonight,
To cross my obsequies and true love's rite?
What, with a torch? Muffle me, night, awhile.

[*Paris retires.*]

Enter ROMEO *and* BALTHASAR *with a torch, a mattock and a crow of iron.*

3. yond yew trees] *Pope;* yond young Trees *Q2–4,F;* this Ew-tree *Q1;* yond yeug Trees *Williams.* 4. Holding] *Q2–4,F;* keeping *Q1.* 8. hear'st] *Rowe*[2]*;* hearest *Q2–4,F; not in Q1.* 11. S.D. [*Retires.*]] *Capell; not in Q2–4,F,Q1.* *Paris . . . flowers.*] *Q1; not in Q2–4,F.* 17. S.D.] *Q2–4,F* (*Whistle Boy.*)*; Boy whistles and calls.* My Lord. *Q1.* 19. way] *Q2–4;* wayes *F;* was *Q1.* 20. rite] *Q2–4,F* (right)*;* rites *Q1.* 21. S.D. [*Paris retires.*]] *Capell; not in Q2–4,F,Q1.* BALTHASAR . . . *iron.*] *Q1;* Peter *Q2,3,F;* Balthazer *his man. Q4.*

3. *yew*] The sixteenth-century spelling *yeugh* or *yeug* could have been misread as *young*; Q1 and the context make the emendation certain.

all along] at full length.

12. *Sweet . . . strew*] Cf. *Ham.*, v. i. 237, where Gertrude scatters flowers in Ophelia's grave.

14. *sweet*] perfumed.

20. *cross*] thwart, interrupt.

21. S.D. *Paris retires*] The ironic parallel with II. ii is strong: there Romeo, concealed by darkness, observes and overhears Juliet; here Paris, from much the same position, observes and overhears Romeo at her tomb.

S.D. *Balthasar*] Q2's *Peter* may indicate that Kemp doubled the parts: the actor who took *Peter* was still

Romeo. Give me that mattock and the wrenching iron.
Hold, take this letter. Early in the morning
See thou deliver it to my lord and father.
Give me the light. Upon thy life I charge thee,
Whate'er thou hear'st or seest, stand all aloof
And do not interrupt me in my course.
Why I descend into this bed of death
Is partly to behold my lady's face
But chiefly to take thence from her dead finger
A precious ring, a ring that I must use
In dear employment. Therefore hence, be gone.
But if thou jealous dost return to pry
In what I farther shall intend to do,
By heaven I will tear thee joint by joint,
And strew this hungry churchyard with thy limbs.
The time and my intents are savage-wild,
More fierce and more inexorable far
Than empty tigers or the roaring sea.
Bal. I will be gone, sir, and not trouble ye.
Romeo. So shalt thou show me friendship. Take thou that.
Live, and be prosperous, and farewell, good fellow.
Bal. For all this same, I'll hide me hereabout.
His looks I fear, and his intents I doubt.
[*Balthasar retires.*]
Romeo. Thou detestable maw, thou womb of death
Gorg'd with the dearest morsel of the earth,
Thus I enforce thy rotten jaws to open,
And in despite I'll cram thee with more food.
Romeo opens the tomb.

22. that] *Q2; the Q3,4,F; this Q1.* 26. hear'st] *F;* hearest *Q2–4; not in Q1.* 34. farther] *Q2–4;* further *F; var. Q1.* 40, 43. *Bal.*] *Q1,Q4; Pet. Q2,3,F.* 40. ye] *Q2;* you *Q3,4,F,Q1.* 44. S.D.] *Hanmer; not in Q2–4,F,Q1.* 48. S.D.] *Q1 (l. 44); not in Q2–4,F.*

thought of as *Peter* even though now taking the different role of *Balthasar.*

26. *all aloof*] The parallel with Paris and his Page (l. 1) is emphasized.

32. *dear*] personally important.

33. *jealous*] suspicious.

38–9. *More . . . sea*] Cf. *John,* III. i. 260: (hold) 'a fasting tiger safer by the tooth' and II. i. 451: 'The sea enraged is not half so deaf' (as we).

45. *maw*] gullet.

womb] belly.

48. *in despite*] to spite thee (because already gorged with food).

more food] i.e. his own body.

S.D. *Romeo . . . tomb*] Romeo has

Paris. This is that banish'd haughty Montague
That murder'd my love's cousin—with which grief
It is supposed the fair creature died—
And here is come to do some villainous shame
To the dead bodies. I will apprehend him.
Stop thy unhallow'd toil, vile Montague.
Can vengeance be pursu'd further than death?
Condemned villain, I do apprehend thee.
Obey, and go with me, for thou must die.

Romeo. I must indeed, and therefore came I hither.
Good gentle youth, tempt not a desperate man.
Fly hence and leave me. Think upon these gone.
Let them affright thee. I beseech thee, youth,
Put not another sin upon my head
By urging me to fury. O be gone.
By heaven I love thee better than myself,
For I come hither arm'd against myself.
Stay not, be gone, live, and hereafter say
A mad man's mercy bid thee run away.

Paris. I do defy thy conjuration
And apprehend thee for a felon here.

Romeo. Wilt thou provoke me? Then have at thee, boy!
They fight.

Page. O Lord, they fight! I will go call the Watch.
[*Exit Page.*]

Paris. O, I am slain! If thou be merciful,
Open the tomb, lay me with Juliet. [*Paris dies.*]

60. these] *Q2–4;* those *F; not in Q1.* 68. conjuration] *Capell;* coniurations *Q1;* commiration *Q2;* commisseration *Q3,4,F;* commination *Williams, conj. Mommsen.* 70. S.D.] *Q1; not in Q2–4,F.* 71. *Page.*] *Q4; Pet. F; Boy: Q1; not in Q2,3.* O . . . Watch] *Q1,Q4,F; O . . . Watch Q2,3 (as S.D.).* S.D.] *Capell; not in Q2–4,F,Q1.* 73. S.D.] *Theobald; not in Q2–4,F,Q1.*

tools and speaks of *enforcing* the tomb's *rotten jaws*, which suggests that the tomb has solid doors or gates. The scene requires that the bodies are visible once the tomb is open; Romeo will then place the body of Paris beside Tybalt and Juliet, and when he dies the tableau is complete.

52–3. *come to do . . . bodies*] Cf. Brooke, ll. 2793–98.

56. *apprehend*] arrest.

65. *arm'd . . . myself*] i.e. with the poison for suicide.

68. *conjuration*] Q2's reading is nonsense, and emendations attempt to reconstruct the MS. word which

Romeo. In faith I will. Let me peruse this face.
Mercutio's kinsman, noble County Paris!
What said my man, when my betossed soul
Did not attend him, as we rode? I think
He told me Paris should have married Juliet.
Said he not so? Or did I dream it so?
Or am I mad, hearing him talk of Juliet,
To think it was so? O, give me thy hand,
One writ with me in sour misfortune's book.
I'll bury thee in a triumphant grave.
A grave? O no, a lantern, slaughter'd youth.
For here lies Juliet, and her beauty makes
This vault a feasting presence, full of light.
Death, lie thou there, by a dead man interr'd.
How oft when men are at the point of death
Have they been merry! Which their keepers call
A lightning before death. O how may I
Call this a lightning? O my love, my wife,
Death that hath suck'd the honey of thy breath
Hath had no power yet upon thy beauty.
Thou art not conquer'd. Beauty's ensign yet
Is crimson in thy lips and in thy cheeks,

94. art] *Q2–4;* are *F; not in Q1.*

might yield it. Sisson calls it a 'mere matter of minims', which leaves little to choose between *coniuration* and *commination*; but meanings are also important, and *commination*, 'a threatening', seems less appropriate, as a response to Romeo's speech, than *coniuration*, 'solemn entreaty'. Cf. *H5*, I. ii. 23–9: 'We charge you in the name of God, take heed . . . Under this conjuration speak, my lord'.

84. *lantern*] 'a spacious . . . turret full of windows' (Steevens); to Romeo the dark tomb is turned by Juliet's presence into a great hall in a palace, brilliantly lit for a feast; the source of light is Juliet herself.

86. *presence*] presence chamber.

89. *keepers*] jailors, or sick-nurses at death-beds.

90. *lightning*] 'That exhilaration or revival of the spirits . . . supposed to occur . . . before death' (OED vbl sb 2 b); proverbial (Tilley L 277).

92–6. *Death . . . there*] Cf. Daniel, *Rosamond*, ll. 603–7: 'The poyson soone disperc'd through all my vaines, / Had dispossess'd my liuing senses quite: / When naught respecting death, the last of paines, / Plac'd his pale collours, th'ensigne of his might, / Vpon hys new-got spoyle before his right'; and ll. 673–9: 'Ah how me thinks I see death dallying seekes, / To entertaine itselfe in loues sweet place: / Decayed Roses of discoloured cheekes, / Doe yet retaine deere notes of former grace: / And ougly death sits faire within her face; / Sweet remnants resting of vermilion red, / That

And Death's pale flag is not advanced there.
Tybalt, liest thou there in thy bloody sheet?
O, what more favour can I do to thee
Than with that hand that cut thy youth in twain
To sunder his that was thine enemy?
Forgive me, cousin. Ah, dear Juliet,
Why art thou yet so fair? Shall I believe
That unsubstantial Death is amorous,
And that the lean abhorred monster keeps
Thee here in dark to be his paramour?
For fear of that I still will stay with thee,
And never from this palace of dim night
Depart again. Here, here, will I remain
With worms that are thy chambermaids. O here
Will I set up my everlasting rest
And shake the yoke of inauspicious stars
From this world-wearied flesh. Eyes, look your last.
Arms, take your last embrace! And lips, O you
The doors of breath, seal with a righteous kiss

100. thine] *Q2–4;* thy *F; not in Q1.* 102. Shall I believe] *Theobald;* I will beleeue, / Shall I beleeue *Q2–4,F;* O I beleeue *Q1;* I will believe *Pope.* 107. palace] *Q3,4,F;* pallat *Q2; not in Q1.* 107–8. night / Depart] *Q4, Camb.;* night. / Depart againe, come lye thou in my arme, / Heer's to thy health, where ere thou tumblest in. / O true Appothecarie! / Thy drugs are quicke. Thus with a kisse I die. / Depart *Q2,3,F; not in Q1.*

death it selfe, doubts whether she be dead.' Cf. also *Lucr.*, ll. 402–6.

97. *Tybalt . . . sheet*] Cf. IV. iii. 42–3; Juliet lies beside Tybalt in the tomb.

102. *Why . . . believe*] In Q2 *I will believe* is Shakespeare's first shot, accidentally included by copyist or compositor.

106. *still*] always.

107. *palace*] Presumably *pallac* was misread from the MS. as *pallat*, a simple error; also cf. III. ii. 85, and v. iii. 84 n. Hosley defends *pallat* as 'an image which supports the theme that Juliet's wedding is indeed her grave'. R. Smallwood, *SQ*, XXVI (1975), 298, would agree and compares *John*, III. iv. 26: 'the couch of lasting night'.

108. *Depart again*] The lines printed in Q2 after l. 107 and omitted here are a first version incorporated in the fuller version of ll. 108–20; possibly *tumblest in* is the germ of the shipwreck metaphor developed in ll. 117–18.

109. *worms . . . chambermaids*] Cf. *Ham.*, IV. iii. 20–2.

110. *set up . . . rest*] resolve to remain here for ever (with a quibble as at IV. v. 6).

112–15. *Eyes . . . Death*] Cf. Daniel, *Rosamond*, ll. 659–72; Sidney, *Astrophil and Stella*, Sonnet 85, ll. 9–14.

114–15. *seal . . . Death*] make an everlasting bargain with all-devouring death; *engrossing* = (i) purchasing in gross, in large quantities, (ii) writing a legal document, (iii) illegally monopolizing or amassing.

A dateless bargain to engrossing Death.
Come, bitter conduct, come unsavoury guide,
Thou desperate pilot now at once run on
The dashing rocks thy seasick weary bark.
Here's to my love! [*He drinks.*] O true apothecary,
Thy drugs are quick. Thus with a kiss I die.
[*He*] *falls.*

Enter FRIAR [LAURENCE] *with lantern, crow and spade.*

Friar L. Saint Francis be my speed. How oft tonight
Have my old feet stumbled at graves. Who's there?
Bal. Here's one, a friend, and one that knows you well.
Friar L. Bliss be upon you. Tell me, good my friend,
What torch is yond that vainly lends his light
To grubs and eyeless skulls? As I discern,
It burneth in the Capels' monument.
Bal. It doth so, holy sir, and there's my master,
One that you love.
Friar L. Who is it?
Bal. Romeo.
Friar L. How long hath he been there?
Bal. Full half an hour.
Friar L. Go with me to the vault.
Bal. I dare not, sir.
My master knows not but I am gone hence,
And fearfully did menace me with death
If I did stay to look on his intents.
Friar L. Stay then, I'll go alone. Fear comes upon me.
O, much I fear some ill unthrifty thing.

119. S.D.] *Theobald; not in Q2–4,F,Q1.* 120. S.D.] *Q1* (*Falls.*)*; not in Q2–4,F.* S.D. *Enter . . . spade.*] *Q2–4,F; Enter Fryer with a Lanthorne. Q1.* 135. Fear comes] *Q2–4;* feares comes *F; var. Q1.* 136. unthrifty] *Q2;* unluckie *Q3,4,F; not in Q1.*

116. *bitter conduct*] The vial of poison will be his *guide* to death, the pilot of l. 117 guiding his *bark* (body).

117–18. *Thou . . . bark*] Cf. Sidney, *Astrophil and Stella*, Sonnet 85, ll. 1–4; Brooke, ll. 799–808, especially l. 808's 'sea beaten barke'; and *Oth.*, v. ii. 270–1: 'Here is my journey's end, here is my butt, / And very sea-mark of my utmost sail'.

120. *quick*] Quibbling on (i) swift, (ii) live.

122. *stumbled*] An evil omen; cf. *R3*, III. iv. 86.

125. *What torch*] In Brooke, ll. 2695–6.

126. *grubs*] worms.

136. *unthrifty*] unfortunate; cf. Spenser, *Faerie Queene*, I. iv. 35.

Bal. As I did sleep under this yew tree here
I dreamt my master and another fought,
And that my master slew him.
Friar L. Romeo!

Friar stoops and looks on the blood and weapons.

Alack, alack, what blood is this which stains
The stony entrance of this sepulchre?
What mean these masterless and gory swords
To lie discolour'd by this place of peace?
Romeo! O, pale! Who else? What, Paris too?
And steep'd in blood? Ah what an unkind hour
Is guilty of this lamentable chance?
The lady stirs.

JULIET *rises.*

Juliet. O comfortable Friar, where is my lord?
I do remember well where I should be,
And there I am. Where is my Romeo?
Friar L. I hear some noise. Lady, come from that nest
Of death, contagion, and unnatural sleep.
A greater power than we can contradict
Hath thwarted our intents. Come, come away.
Thy husband in thy bosom there lies dead,
And Paris too. Come, I'll dispose of thee
Among a sisterhood of holy nuns.
Stay not to question, for the Watch is coming.
Come, go, good Juliet. I dare no longer stay.
Juliet. Go, get thee hence, for I will not away.

Exit Friar Laurence.

What's here? A cup clos'd in my true love's hand?
Poison, I see, hath been his timeless end.
O churl. Drunk all, and left no friendly drop
To help me after? I will kiss thy lips.
Haply some poison yet doth hang on them

137. yew] *Pope;* yong *Q2–4,F; not in Q1;* yeug *Williams.* 139. S.D.] *Q1; not in Q2–4,F.* 147. S.D.] *Q1; not in Q2–4,F.* 160. S.D.] *Dyce (after l. 160); after l. 159 Q2–4,F; not in Q1.* 163. Drunk] *Q2;* drinke *Q3,4,F,Q1.* left] *Q2–4,F;* leaue *Q1.*

145. *unkind*] unnatural.

To make me die with a restorative. [*She kisses him.*]
Thy lips are warm!

Watchman. [*Within.*] Lead, boy. Which way?

Juliet. Yea, noise? Then I'll be brief. O happy dagger.
This is thy sheath. There rust, and let me die.
She stabs herself and falls.

Enter Page *and* Watchmen.

Page. This is the place. There, where the torch doth burn.

1 Watchman. The ground is bloody. Search about the churchyard.
Go, some of you: whoe'er you find, attach.
[*Exeunt some Watchmen.*]
Pitiful sight! Here lies the County slain
And Juliet bleeding, warm, and newly dead,
Who here hath lain this two days buried.
Go tell the Prince. Run to the Capulets.
Raise up the Montagues. Some others search.
[*Exeunt some Watchmen.*]
We see the ground whereon these woes do lie,
But the true ground of all these piteous woes
We cannot without circumstance descry.

Enter [*several* Watchmen *with*] BALTHASAR.

2 Watchman. Here's Romeo's man. We found him in the churchyard.

166. S.D.] *Capell; not in Q2–4,F,Q1.* 169. This is] *Q2,4;* Tis is *Q3;* 'Tis in *F; var. Q1.* rust] *Q2–4,F;* Rest *Q1.* S.D. *She . . . falls.*] *Q1; Kils herselfe. F; not in Q2–4.* 171. *1 Watchman.*] *ed.; Watch. Q2–4,F,Q1.* 172. S.D.] *Hanmer; not in Q2–4,F,Q1.* 175. this] *Q2;* these *Q3,4,F; not in Q1.* 177. S.D. *Capell; not in Q2–4,F,Q1.* 180. S.D.] *Q1* (*Enter one with Romeos Man.*), *Rowe; Enter Romeos man. Q2–4,F.* 181. *2 Watchman.*] *ed.; Watch. Q2–4,F; 1. Q1.*

169. *rust*] Dover Wilson thinks *rust* 'hideously unpoetical'; but I find it vivid, fierce, bearing traces of Juliet's earlier attentiveness to the factual details of physical decay in death: it also completes the motif of Death as rival to Romeo; Death *lies with* Juliet, as her passionate *This is thy sheath* acknowledges. The Q1 reading has of course inferior authority.

179. *ground*] Quibbling on (i) cause, (ii) earth, as in l. 178.

180. *circumstance*] detailed information.

1 Watchman. Hold him in safety till the Prince come hither.

Enter another Watchman *with* FRIAR LAURENCE.

3 Watchman. Here is a friar that trembles, sighs and weeps.
We took this mattock and this spade from him
As he was coming from this churchyard's side.
1 Watchman. A great suspicion. Stay the friar too.

Enter the PRINCE [*and* Attendants].

Prince. What misadventure is so early up,
That calls our person from our morning rest?

Enter CAPULET *and* LADY CAPULET [*and* Servants].

Cap. What should it be that is so shriek'd abroad?
Lady Cap. O, the people in the street cry 'Romeo',
Some 'Juliet', and some 'Paris', and all run
With open outcry toward our monument.
Prince. What fear is this which startles in our ears?
1 Watchman. Sovereign, here lies the County Paris slain,
And Romeo dead, and Juliet, dead before,
Warm, and new kill'd.
Prince. Search, seek, and know how this foul murder comes.
1 Watchman. Here is a friar, and slaughter'd Romeo's man,
With instruments upon them fit to open
These dead men's tombs.

182. *1 Watchman.*] *ed.; Chief watch. Q2–4,F; Capt: Q1.* 183. *3 Watchman.*] *Q2–4,F; 1. Q1.* 185. churchyard's] *Q2;* Church-yard *Q3,4,F; not in Q1.* 186. *1 Watchman.*] *ed.; Chief watch. Q2–4; Con. F; Cap: Q1.* too] *F;* too too *Q2–4; not in Q1.* 188. morning] *Q2,3;* mornings *Q4,F; var. Q1.* S.D.] *Capell; Enter Capels Q2,3; Enter Capulet and his Wife Q4,F,Q1* (*subst.*). 189. is so shriek'd] *Daniel, conj. Camb.;* is so shrike *Q2;* they so shrike *Q3,4,F; var. Q1.* 190. *Lady Cap.*] *ed.; Wife. Q2–4,F; Moth: Q1.* 192. our] *Q2–4;* out *F; not in Q1.* 193. our] *Capell;* your *Q2–4,F; not in Q1.* 194, 198. *1 Watchman.*] *ed.; Watch. Q2–4,F* (*subst.*)*; Capt: Q1* (*subst.*). 198. slaughter'd] *Q4,F;* Slaughter *Q2,3; not in Q1.* 200.] *As Q4,F; Q2,3 add S.D. Enter Capulet and his wife.*

185. *this churchyard's side*] this side of the churchyard.

189. *shriek'd*] Q2 probably represents a misreading of *shrikd* as *shrike.* Adoption of Q3 is indefensible; *shrieks* is spelt *shrikes* at IV. iii. 47.

193. *startles*] sounds startlingly.

198. *slaughter'd*] The Q2 compositor took *Slaughter* to be the name of Romeo's servant.

Cap. O heavens! O wife, look how our daughter bleeds!
This dagger hath mista'en, for lo, his house
Is empty on the back of Montague,
And it mis-sheathed in my daughter's bosom.
Lady Cap. O me! This sight of death is as a bell
That warns my old age to a sepulchre.

Enter MONTAGUE [*and* Servants].

Prince. Come, Montague, for thou art early up
To see thy son and heir now early down.
Mont. Alas, my liege, my wife is dead tonight.
Grief of my son's exile hath stopp'd her breath.
What further woe conspires against mine age?
Prince. Look, and thou shalt see.
Mont. O thou untaught! What manners is in this,
To press before thy father to a grave?
Prince. Seal up the mouth of outrage for a while
Till we can clear these ambiguities
And know their spring, their head, their true descent,
And then will I be general of your woes
And lead you, even to death. Meantime forbear,
And let mischance be slave to patience.
Bring forth the parties of suspicion.
Friar L. I am the greatest, able to do least,
Yet most suspected, as the time and place
Doth make against me, of this direful murder.
And here I stand, both to impeach and purge
Myself condemned and myself excus'd.
Prince. Then say at once what thou dost know in this.
Friar L. I will be brief, for my short date of breath
Is not so long as is a tedious tale.
Romeo, there dead, was husband to that Juliet,

201. heavens] *Q2;* heaven *Q3,4,F; not in Q1.* 204. it] *Q2;* is *Q3,4,F;* it is *Q1.* 205. *Lady Cap.*] *ed.; Wife. Q2,F; Wi. Q3,4; not in Q1.* 206. S.D.] *Capell; Enter Mountague. Q2–4,F,Q1 (subst.).* 208. now early] *Q3,4,F;* now earling *Q2;* more early *Q1.* 211. mine] *Q2;* my *Q3,4,F; var. Q1.* 213. is in] *Q2–4,Q1;* in is *F.* 215. mouth] *Q2,3,F;* moneth *Q4; var. Q1.*

215. *outrage*] passionate outcry; cf. *1H6,* IV. i. 126: 'this immodest clamorous outrage'.

220. *let . . . patience*] submit to misfortune with patience.

And she, there dead, that Romeo's faithful wife.
I married them, and their stol'n marriage day
Was Tybalt's doomsday, whose untimely death
Banish'd the new-made bridegroom from this city;
For whom, and not for Tybalt, Juliet pin'd.
You, to remove that siege of grief from her,
Betroth'd and would have married her perforce
To County Paris. Then comes she to me
And with wild looks bid me devise some mean
To rid her from this second marriage,
Or in my cell there would she kill herself.
Then gave I her—so tutor'd by my art—
A sleeping potion, which so took effect
As I intended, for it wrought on her
The form of death. Meantime I writ to Romeo
That he should hither come as this dire night
To help to take her from her borrow'd grave,
Being the time the potion's force should cease.
But he which bore my letter, Friar John,
Was stay'd by accident, and yesternight
Return'd my letter back. Then all alone
At the prefixed hour of her waking
Came I to take her from her kindred's vault,
Meaning to keep her closely at my cell
Till I conveniently could send to Romeo.
But when I came, some minute ere the time
Of her awakening, here untimely lay
The noble Paris and true Romeo dead.
She wakes; and I entreated her come forth
And bear this work of heaven with patience,
But then a noise did scare me from the tomb
And she, too desperate, would not go with me
But, as it seems, did violence on herself.

231. that] *Q4;* thats *Q2,3,F; var. Q1.* 239. mean] *Q2;* meanes *Q3,4,F,Q1.* 257. awakening] *Q2;* awaking *Q3,4,F; not in Q1.* 261. scare] *Q2–4;* scarre *F; not in Q1.*

246. *as*] Cf. *Caes.*, v. i. 71–2: 'This is my birthday; as this very day / Was Cassius born'; Abbott (§ 114) notes *as* to be used redundantly with definitions of time.

All this I know; and to the marriage
Her Nurse is privy; and if aught in this
Miscarried by my fault, let my old life
Be sacrific'd some hour before his time
Unto the rigour of severest law.

Prince. We still have known thee for a holy man.
Where's Romeo's man? What can he say to this?

Bal. I brought my master news of Juliet's death,
And then in post he came from Mantua
To this same place, to this same monument.
This letter he early bid me give his father
And threaten'd me with death, going in the vault,
If I departed not and left him there.

Prince. Give me the letter, I will look on it.
Where is the County's Page that rais'd the Watch?
Sirrah, what made your master in this place?

Page. He came with flowers to strew his lady's grave
And bid me stand aloof, and so I did.
Anon comes one with light to ope the tomb
And by and by my master drew on him,
And then I ran away to call the Watch.

Prince. This letter doth make good the Friar's words:
Their course of love, the tidings of her death,
And here he writes that he did buy a poison
Of a poor pothecary, and therewithal
Came to this vault to die and lie with Juliet.
Where be these enemies? Capulet, Montague,
See what a scourge is laid upon your hate,
That heaven finds means to kill your joys with love;
And I, for winking at your discords too,
Have lost a brace of kinsmen. All are punish'd.

Cap. O brother Montague, give me thy hand.
This is my daughter's jointure, for no more
Can I demand.

264–7.] *As Pope;* All . . . priuie: / And . . . fault, / Let . . . time, *Q2–4,F; not in Q1.* 267. his] *Q2,Q1;* the *Q3,4,F.*

269. *still*] always.
293. *winking at*] shutting my eyes to.
296. *jointure*] the portion the bridegroom brings the bride; the handclasp of friendship and reconciliation is all Capulet asks.

Mont. But I can give thee more,
For I will raise her statue in pure gold,
That whiles Verona by that name is known,
There shall no figure at such rate be set
As that of true and faithful Juliet.
Cap. As rich shall Romeo's by his lady's lie,
Poor sacrifices of our enmity.
Prince. A glooming peace this morning with it brings:
The sun for sorrow will not show his head.
Go hence to have more talk of these sad things.
Some shall be pardon'd, and some punished,
For never was a story of more woe
Than this of Juliet and her Romeo. *Exeunt.*

298. raise] *Q4,F;* raie *Q2,3;* erect *Q1.* 300. such] *Q2,Q1;* that *Q3,4,F.* 302. *Cap.*] *Q3,4,F,Q1; Capel. Q2.* Romeo's . . . lady's] *Q2–4; Romeo* . . . Lady *F,Q1.* 304. glooming] *Q2–4,F;* gloomie *Q1.* 309. S.D.] *F; not in Q2–4,Q1.*

298. *raise*] cause to be made. Brooke has *raise* but Hosley prefers *raie* (= array) and thinks the effigies are to be high-relief figures on sarcophagi.

300. *at . . . set*] be so highly valued and esteemed.

302. *As rich*] Capulet will provide a golden figure of Romeo; cf. Brooke, ll. 3013–14.

304. *glooming*] Cf. Spenser, *Faerie Queene*, I. i. 14, where the Redcross Knight approaches the dark cave and his armour 'made / A litle glooming light, much like a shade, / By which he saw the vgly monster plaine'. The associations of this cave and the tomb in the play, of the lovers' victory over the monster death and the knight's victory over Error ('For light she hated as the deadly bale') may have subconsciously prompted Shakespeare to use 'glooming'.

305. *sun . . . head*] Cf. *R3*, v. iii. 277–8; Golding's *Ovid*, II. 419: to mark the fall of Phaeton 'A day did pass without the Sunne'.

307. *Some . . . punished*] In Brooke the Nurse is banished (for concealing the marriage), Peter allowed to go free, the apothecary hanged, the Friar released; he becomes a hermit and dies five years later.

APPENDIX I

The Queen Mab speech in Q1

Mer: Ah then I see Queene Mab hath bin with you.
Ben: Queene Mab whats she?
She is the Fairies Midwife and doth come
In shape no bigger than an Aggat stone
On the forefinger of a Burgomaster,
Drawne with a teeme of little Atomi,
A thwart mens noses when they lie a sleepe.
Her waggon spokes are made of spinners webs,
The couer, of the winges of Grashoppers,
The traces are the Moone-shine watrie beames,
The collers crickets bones, the lash of filmes,
Her waggoner is a small gray coated flie,
Not halfe so big as is a little worme,
Pickt from the lasie finger of a maide,
And in this sort she gallops vp and downe
Through Louers braines, and then they dream of loue:
O're Courtiers knees: who strait on cursies dreame
O're Ladies lips, who dreame on kisses strait:
Which oft the angrie Mab with blisters plagues,
Because their breathes with sweetmeats tainted are:
Sometimes she gallops ore a Lawers lap,
And then dreames he of smelling out a sute,
And sometime comes she with a tithe pigs taile,
Tickling a Parsons nose that lies a sleepe,
And then dreames he of another benefice:
Sometime she gallops ore a souldiers nose,
And then dreames he of cutting forraine throats,
Of breaches ambuscados, countermines,
Of healthes fiue fadome deepe, and then anon
Drums in his eare: at which he startes and wakes,
And sweares a Praier or two and sleepes againe.
This is that Mab that makes maids lie on their backes,
And proues them women of good cariage. (the night,

This is the verie Mab that plats the manes of Horses in
And plats the Elfelocks in foule sluttish haire,
Which once vntangled much misfortune breedes.
Rom: Peace, peace, thou talkst of nothing.

APPENDIX II

Extracts from Brooke's *Romeus and Juliet*, 1562

THE TRAGICALL HISTORYE OF ROMEUS AND JULIET

written first in Italian by Bandell, and nowe in Englishe by Ar. Br.

In aedibus Richardi Tottelli. Cum Privilegio

[1562]

TO THE READER

The God of all glorye created universallye all creatures, to settle forth his prayse, both those whiche we esteme profitable in use and pleasure, and also those, whiche we accompte noysome, and lothsome. But principally he hath appointed man, the chiefest instrument of his honour, not onely, for ministryng matter thereof in man himselfe: but aswell in gatheryng out of other, the occasions of publishing Gods goodnes, wisdome, & power. And in like sort, everye dooyng of man hath by Goddes dyspensacion some thynge, whereby God may, and ought to be honored. So the good doynges of the good, & the evil actes of the wicked, the happy successe of the blessed, and the wofull procedinges of the miserable, doe in divers sorte sound one prayse of God. And as eche flower yeldeth hony to the bee: so every exaumple ministreth good lessons, to the well disposed mynde. The glorious triumphe of the continent man upon the lustes of wanton fleshe, incourageth men to honest restraynt of wyld affections, the shamefull and wretched endes of such, as have yelded their libertie thrall to fowle desires, teache men to witholde them selves from the hedlong fall of loose dishonestie. So, to lyke effect, by sundry meanes, the good mans exaumple byddeth men to be good, and the evill mans mischefe, warneth men not to be evyll. To this good ende, serve all ill endes, of yll begynnynges. And to this ende (good Reader) is this tragicall matter written, to describe unto thee a coople of unfortunate lovers, thralling themselves to unhonest desire, neglecting the authoritie and advise of parents and frendes, conferring their principall counsels with dronken gossyppes, and superstitious friers (the naturally fitte instruments of unchastitie) attemptyng all adventures of peryll, for thattaynyng of their wished lust, usyng auriculer confession (the kay of whoredome, and treason) for furtheraunce of theyr purpose, abusyng the honorable name of lawefull mariage, the cloke the shame of stolne contractes, finallye, by all meanes of unhonest lyfe, hastyng to most unhappye deathe. This president (good Reader) shalbe to thee, as the slaves of Lacedemon, oppressed with excesse of drinke, deformed and altered from likenes of men, both in mynde, and use of body, were to the free borne children, so shewed to them by their parentes, to thintent to rayse in them an hatefull lothyng of so filthy beastlynes. Hereunto if you applye it, ye shall deliver my dooing from offence, and profit your selves. Though I saw the same argument lately set foorth on stage with more commendation, then I can looke for: (being there much better set forth then I have or can dooe) yet the same matter penned as it is, may serve to lyke good effect, if the readers do brynge with them lyke myndes, to consider it. which hath the more incouraged me to publishe it, suche as it is.

Ar. Br.

THE ARGUMENT

Love hath inflamed twayne by sodayn sight.
And both do graunt the thing that both desyre.
They wed in shrift by counsell of a frier.
Yong Romeus clymes fayre Juliets bower by night.
Three monthes he doth enjoy his cheefe delight.
By Tybalts rage, provoked unto yre,
He payeth death to Tybalt for his hyre.
A banisht man he scapes by secret flight.
New mariage is offred to his wyfe:
She drinkes a drinke that seemes to reve her breath.
They bury her, that sleping yet hath lyfe.
Her husband heares the tydinges of her death.
He drinkes his bane. And she with Romeus knyfe,
When she awakes, her selfe (alas) she sleath.

ROMEUS AND JULIET

There is beyonde the Alps, a towne of auncient fame
Whose bright renoune yet shineth cleare, Verona men it name,
Bylt in an happy time, bylt on a fertile soyle,
Maynteined by the heavenly fates, and by the townish toyle.
The fruitfull hilles above, the pleasant vales belowe,
The silver streame with chanell depe, that through the towne doth flow,

The store of springes that serve for use, and eke for ease
And other moe commodities which profite may and please,
Eke many certaine signes of thinges betyde of olde,
To fyll the houngry eyes of those that curiously beholde
Doe make this towne to be preferde above the rest
Of Lumbard townes, or at least compared with the best.
In which while Escalus, as prince alone dyd raigne,
To reache rewarde unto the good, to pay the lewde with payne,
Alas (I rewe to thinke) an heavy happe befell
Which Boccace skant (not my rude tong) were able forth to tell.
Within my trembling hande, my penne doth shake for feare
And on my colde amased head, upright doth stand my heare.
But sith she doth commaunde, whose hest I must obaye,
In moorning verse, a wofull chaunce to tell I will assaye.
Helpe learned Pallas, helpe, ye muses with your arte,
Helpe all ye damned feendes to tell, of joyes retournd to smart,
Helpe eke ye sisters three, my skillesse penne t'indyte
For you it causd which I (alas) unable am to wryte.
There were two auncient stockes, which Fortune high dyd place
Above the rest, indewd with welth, and nobler of their race,
Loved of the common sort, loved of the Prince alike,
And like unhappy were they both, when Fortune list to strike.
Whose prayse with equall blast, fame in her trumpet blew:
The one was cliped Capelet, and thother Montagew.
A wonted use it is, that men of likely sorte
(I wot not by what furye forsd) envye eche others porte.
So these, whose egall state bred envye pale of hew,
And then of grudging envyes roote, blacke hate and rancor grewe.
As of a little sparke, oft ryseth mighty fyre,
So of a kyndled sparke of grudge, in flames flashe out theyr yre,
And then theyr deadly foode, first hatchd of trifling stryfe
Did bathe in bloud of smarting woundes, it re[a]ved breth and lyfe.
No legend lye I tell, scarce yet theyr eyes be drye
That did behold the grisly sight, with wet and weping eye.
But when the prudent prince, who there the scepter helde,
So great a new disorder in his common weale behelde
By jentyl meane he sought, their choler to asswage,
And by perswasion to appease, their blameful furious rage.
But both his woords and tyme, the prince hath spent in vayne
So rooted was the inward hate, he lost his buysy payne.
When frendly sage advise, ne jentyll woords avayle,

By thondring threats, and princely powre their courage gan he quayle,
In hope that when he had the wasting flame supprest,
In time he should quyte quench the sparks that boornd within their brest.
Now whilst these kyndreds do remayne in this estate,
And eche with outward frendly shew dooth hyde his inward hate,
One Romeus, who was of race a Montague,
Upon whose tender chyn, as yet, no manlyke beard there grewe,
Whose beauty and whose shape so farre the rest did stayne,
That from the cheefe of Veron youth he greatest fame dyd gayne,
Hath founde a mayd so fayre (he found so foule his happe)
Whose beauty, shape, and comely grace, did so his heart entrappe,
That from his owne affayres, his thought she did remove,
Onely he sought to honor her, to serve her, and to love.
To her he writeth oft, oft messengers are sent:
At length (in hope of better spede) himselfe the lover went
Present to pleade for grace, which absent was not founde,
And to discover to her eye his new receaved wounde.
But she that from her youth was fostred evermore
With vertues foode, and taught in schole of wisdomes skilfull lore,
By aunswere did cutte of[f] thaffections of his love,
That he no more occasion had so vayne a sute to move.
So sterne she was of chere, (for all the payne he tooke)
That in reward of toyle, she would not geve a frendly looke. . . .

In sighs, in teares, in plainte, in care, in sorow and unrest,
He mones the daye, he wakes the long and wery night,
So deepe hath love with pearcing hand, ygravd her bewty bright
Within his brest, and hath so mastred quite his hart
That he of force must yeld as thrall, no way is left to start.
He can not staye his steppe, but forth still must he ronne,
He languisheth and melts awaye, as snow against the sonne,
His kyndred and al[l]yes do wonder what he ayles,
And eche of them in frendly wise, his heavy hap bewayles.
But one emong the rest, the trustiest of his feeres,
Farre more then he with counsel fild, and ryper of his yeeres,
Gan sharply him rebuke, suche love to him he bare
That he was felow of his smart, and partner of his care.
What meanst thou Romeus (quoth he) what doting rage
Dooth make thee thus consume away, the best parte of thine age,
In seking her that scornes, and hydes her from thy sight,

Not forsing all thy great expence, ne yet thy honor bright,
Thy teares, thy wretched lyfe, ne thine unspotted truth
Which are of force (I weene) to move the hardest hart to ruthe.
Now for our frendships sake, and for thy health I pray
That thou hencefoorth become thyne owne, O geve no more away
Unto a thankeles wight, thy precious free estate.
In that thou lovest such a one, thou seemst thy selfe to hate,
For she doth love els where, (and then thy time is lorne)
Or els (what booteth thee to sue) loves court she hath forsworne. . . .

But sow no more thy paynes in such a barrayne soyle
As yeldes in harvest time no crop in recompence of toyle.
Ere long the townishe dames together will resort,
Some one of bewty, favour, shape, and of so lovely porte
With so fast fixed eye, perhaps thou mayst beholde,
That thou shalt quite forget thy love, and passions past of olde.
The yong mans lystning eare receivde the [w]holesome sounde,
And reasons truth yplanted so, within his head had grounde
That now with healthy coole ytempred is the heate
And piecemeale weares away the greefe that erst his heart dyd freate.
To his approved frend, a solemne othe he plight:
At every feast ykept by day, and banquet made by night,
At pardons in the churche, at games in open streate,
And every where he would resort where Ladies wont to meete.
Eke should his savage heart lyke all indifferently,
For he would view and judge them all with unallured eye.
How happy had he been had he not been forsworne
But twyse as happy had he been had he been never borne,
For ere the Moone could thryse her wasted hornes renew,
False Fortune cast for him poore wretch, a myschiefe newe to brewe.
The wery winter nightes restore the Christmas games,
And now the season doth invite to banquet townish dames.
And fyrst in Capels house, the chiefe of all the kyn
Sparth for no cost, the wonted use of banquets to begyn.
No Lady fayre or fowle, was in Verona towne,
No knight or gentleman of high or lowe renowne
But Capilet himselfe hath byd unto his feast,

Or by his name in paper sent, appoynted as a geast.
Yong damsels thether flocke, of bachelers a rowte,
Not so much for the banquets sake, as bewties to searche out.
But not a Montagew would enter at his gate,
For as you heard, the Capilets, and they were at debate,
Save Romeus, and he in maske with hidden face,
The supper done, with other five dyd prease into the place.
When they had maskd a whyle, with dames in courtly wise
All dyd unmaske, the rest dyd shew them to theyr ladies eyes.
But bashfull Romeus, with shamefast face forsooke
The open prease, and him withdrew into the chambers nooke.
But brighter then the sunne, the waxen torches shone
That mauger what he could, he was espyd of every one. . . .

The Capilets disdayne the presence of theyr foe [183]
Yet they suppresse theyr styrred yre, the cause I do not knowe.
Perhaps toffend theyr gestes the courteous knights are loth,
Perhaps they stay from sharpe revenge, dreadyng the Princes wroth,
Perhaps for that they shamd to exercise theyr rage
Within their house, gainst one alone and him of tender age. . . .

At length he saw a mayd, right fayre of perfect shape [197]
Which Theseus, or Paris would have chosen to their rape,
Whom erst he never sawe, of all she pleasde him most.
Within himselfe he said to her, thou justly mayst thee boste
Of perfit shapes renoune, and Beauties sounding prayse,
Whose like ne hath, ne shalbe seene, ne liveth in our dayes.
And whilest he fixd on her his partiall perced eye,
His former love, for which of late he ready was to dye,
Is nowe as quite forgotte, as it had never been.
The proverbe saith, unminded oft are they that are unseene
And as out of a planke a nayle a nayle doth drive,
So novell love out of the minde the auncient love doth rive.
This sodain kindled fyre in time is wox so great,
That onely death and both theyr blouds might quench the fiery heate.
When Romeus saw himselfe in this new tempest tost
Where both was hope of pleasant port, and daunger to be lost,
He doubtefull, ska[r]sely knew what countenance to keepe;
In Lethies floud his wonted flames were quenchd and drenched deepe.

Yea he forgets himselfe, ne is the wretch so bolde
To aske her name, that without force hath him in bondage folde.
Ne how tunloose his bondes doth the poore foole devise,
But onely seeketh by her sight to feede his houngry eyes.
Through them he swalloweth downe loves sweete empoysonde baite,
How surely are the wareles wrapt by those that lye in wayte?
So is the poyson spred throughout his bones and vaines,
That in a while (alas the while) it hasteth deadly paines.
Whilst Juliet (for so this gentle damsell hight)
From syde to syde on every one dyd cast about her sight.
At last her floting eyes were ancored fast on him,
Who for her sake dyd banishe health and fredome from eche limme.
He in her sight did seeme to passe the rest as farre
As Phoebus shining beames do passe the brightnes of a starre.
In wayte laye warlike love with golden bowe and shaft,
And to his eare with steady hand the bowstring up he raft.
Till now she had escapde his sharpe inflaming darte,
Till now he listed not assaulte her yong and tender hart.
His whetted arrow loosde, so touchd her to the quick,
That through the eye it strake the hart, and there the hedde did sticke.
It booted not to strive, for why, she wanted strength:
The weaker aye unto the strong of force must yeld at length.
The pomps now of the feast her heart gyns to despyse
And onely joyeth when her eyen meete with her lovers eyes.
When theyr new smitten heartes had fed on loving gleames,
Whilst passing too and fro theyr eyes ymingled were theyr beames,
Eche of these lovers gan by others lookes to knowe
That frendship in their brest had roote, and both would have it grow.
When thus in both theyr harts had Cupide made his breache
And eche of them had sought the meane to end the warre by speache,
Dame Fortune did assent theyr purpose to advaunce,
With torche in hand a comly knight did fetch her foorth to daunce.
She quit her selfe so well, and with so trim a grace,
That she the cheefe prayse wan that night from all Verona race.
The whilst our Romeus, a place had warely wonne

Nye to the seate where she must sit, the daunce once beyng donne
Fayre Juliet tourned to her chayre with pleasant cheere
And glad she was her Romeus approched was so neere.
At thone side of her chayre, her lover Romeo
And on the other side there sat one cald Mercutio,
A courtier that eche where was highly had in pryce,
For he was coorteous of his speche, and pleasant of devise
Even as a Lyon would emong the lambes be bolde,
Such was emong the bashfull maydes, Mercutio to beholde.
With frendly gripe he ceasd fayre Juliets snowish hand.
A gyft he had that nature gave him in his swathing band,
That frosen mountayne yse was never halfe so cold
As were his handes, though nere so neer the fire he dyd them holde.
As soone as had the knight the vyrgins right hand raught
Within his trembling hand her left hath loving Romeus caught,
For he wist well himselfe for her abode most payne
And well he wist she loved him best, unles she list to fayne.
Then she with tender hand his tender palme hath prest,
What joy trow you was graffed so in Romeus cloven brest?
The soodain sweete delight hath stopped quite his tong
Ne can he claime of her his right, ne crave redresse of wrong.
But she espyd straight waye, by chaunging of his hewe
From pale to red, from red to pale, and so from pale anewe,
That vehment love was cause, why so his tong dyd stay
And so much more she longde to heare what love could teache him saye.
When she had longed long, and he long held his peace,
And her desire of hearing him, by sylence dyd encrease,
At last with trembling voyce and shamefast chere, the mayde
Unto her Romeus tournde her selfe, and thus to him she sayde.
O blessed be the time of thy arrivall here:
But ere she could speake forth the rest, to her love drewe so nere
And so within her mouth, her tong he glewed fast,
That no one woord could scape her more, then what already past.
In great contented ease the yong man straight is rapt,
What chaunce (quoth he) unware to me O lady myne is hapt?
That geves you worthy cause, my cumming here to blisse?
Fayre Juliet was come agayne unto her selfe by this.
Fyrst ruthfully she lookd, then sayd with smylyng cheere

Mervayle no whit my heartes delight, my onely knight and fere,
Mercutio's ysy hande had all to frosen myne
And of thy goodnes thou agayne hast warmed it with thine.
Whereto with stayed brow, gan Romeus to replye
If so the gods have graunted me suche favour from the skye,
That by my being here, some service I have donne
That pleaseth you I am as glad, as I a realme had wonne.
O wel bestowed tyme, that hath the happy hyre,
Which I woulde wysh if I might have, my wished harts desire,
For I of God woulde crave, as pryse of paynes forpast,
To serve, obey, and honour you, so long as lyfe shall last.
As proofe shall teache you playne, if that you like to trye
His faltles truth, that nill for ought, unto his lady lye,
But if my tooched hand, have warmed yours some dele,
Assure your self the heat is colde, which in your hand you fele
Compard to suche quick sparks and glowing furious gleade
As from your bewties pleasaunt eyne, love caused to proceade
Which have so set on fyre, eche feling parte of myne,
That lo, my mynde doeth melt awaye, my utwerd parts doe pyne
And but you helpe all whole, to ashes shall I toorne,
Wherfore (alas) have ruth on him, whom you do force to boorne.
Even with his ended tale, the torches daunce had ende,
And Juliet of force must part from her new chosen frend.
His hand she clasped hard, and all her partes did shake,
When laysureles with whispring voyce thus did she aunswer make:
You are no more your owne (deare frend) then I am yours,
(My honor saved) prest tobay your will, while life endures.
Lo, here the lucky lot that seld true lovers finde,
Eche takes away the others hart, and leaves the owne behinde.
A happy life is love if God graunt from above,
That hart with hart by even waight doo make exchaunge of love.
But Romeus gone from her, his heart for care is colde,
He hath forgot to aske her name that hath his hart in holde.
With forged careles cheere, of one he seekes to knowe,
Both how she hight, and whence she came, that him enchaunted so
So hath he learned her name, and knowth she is no geast,
Her father was a Capilet, and master of the feast.
Thus hath his foe in choyse to geve him lyfe or death
That scarsely can his wofull brest keepe in the lively breath.
Wherfore with piteous plaint feerce Fortune doth he blame
That in his ruth and wretched plight doth seeke her laughing game. . . .

As carefull was the mayde what way were best devise [341]
To learne his name, that intertaind her in so gentle wise,
Of whome her hart received so deepe, so wyde a wounde.
An auncient dame she calde to her, and in her eare gan rounde.
This olde dame in her youth, had nurst her with her mylke,
With slender nedle taught her sow, and how to spin with silke.
What twayne are those (quoth she) which prease unto the doore,
Whose pages in theyr hand doe beare, two toorches light before?
And then as eche of them had of his houshold name,
So she him namde yet once agayne, the yong and wyly dame,
And tell me who is he with vysor in his hand,
That yonder doth in masking weede besyde the window stand?
His name is Romeus, (said she) a Montegewe
Whose fathers pryde first styrd the strife which both your housholdes rewe.
The woord of Montegew, her joyes did overthrow,
And straight in steade of happy hope, dyspayre began to growe.
What hap have I quoth she, to love my fathers foe?
What, am I wery of my wele? what, doe I wishe my woe?
But though her grievous paynes distraind her tender hart
Yet with an outward shewe of joye she cloked inward smart,
And of the courtlyke dames her leave so courtly tooke,
That none dyd gesse the sodain change by changing of her looke.
Then at her mothers hest to chamber she her hyde,
So well she faynde, mother ne nurce, the hidden harme descride.
But when she should have slept as wont she was, in bed,
Not halfe a winke of quiet slepe could harber in her hed. . . .

The mayde had scarsely yet ended the wery warre, [433]
Kept in her heart by striving thoughtes, when every shining starre
Had payd his borowed light, and Phebus spred in skies
His golden rayes, which seemd to say, now time it is to rise.
And Romeus had by this forsaken his wery bed,
Where restles he a thousand thoughts had forged in his hed.
And while with lingring step by Juliets house he past,
And upward to her windowes high his gredy eyes did cast,
His love that looked for him there gan he straight espie.
With pleasant cheere eche greeted is, she followeth with her eye
His parting steppes, and he oft looketh backe againe,
But not so oft as he desyres; warely he doth refraine.
What life were lyke to love, if dred of jeopardy

Ysowred not the sweete, if love were free from jelosy.
But she more sure within, unseene of any wight,
When so he comes, lookes after him, till he be out of sight.
In often passing so, his busy eyes he threw,
That every pane and tooting hole the wily lover knew.
In happy houre he doth a garden plot espye,
From which, except he warely walke, men may his love descrye,
For lo, it fronted full upon her leaning place,
Where she is woont to shew her heart by cheerefull frendly face.
And lest the arbors might theyr secret love bewraye,
He doth keepe backe his forward foote from passing there by daye.
But when on earth the night her mantel blacke hath spred,
Well armd he walketh foorth alone, ne dreadfull foes doth dred.
Whom maketh love not bold, naye whom makes he not blynde?
He reveth daungers dread oft times out of the lovers minde.
By night he passeth here, a weeke or two in vayne
And for the missing of his marke, his griefe hath him nye slaine.
And Juliet that now doth lacke her hearts releefe,
Her Romeus pleasant eyen (I meene) is almost dead for greefe.
Eche day she chaungeth howres, (for lovers keepe an howre)
When they are sure to see theyr love, in passing by their bowre.
Impacient of her woe, she hapt to leane one night
Within her window, and anon the Moone did shine so bright
That she espyde her love, her hart revived, sprang
And now for joy she clappes her handes, which erst for woe she wrang.
Eke Romeus, when he sawe his long desired sight,
His moorning cloke of mone cast off, hath clad him with delight.
Yet dare I say, of both, that she rejoyced more:
His care was great, hers twise as great, was all the tyme before,
For whilst she knew not why he dyd himselfe absent,
Ay douting both his health and lyfe, his death she dyd lament.
For love is fearefull oft, where is no cause of feare
And what love feares, that love laments, as though it chaunced weare. . . .

Now whilst with bitter teares her eyes as fountaynes ronne,
With whispering voyce, ybroke with sobs, thus is her tale begonne.
Oh Romeus (of your lyfe) too lavas sure you are,
That in this place, and at thys tyme to hasard it you dare,
What if your dedly foes, my kynsmen, saw you here?

Lyke Lyons wylde, your tender partes asonder would they teare.
In ruth and in disdayne, I weary of my life,
With cruell hand my moorning hart would perce with bloudy knyfe.
For you myne owne once dead, what joy should I have here?
And eke my honor staynde which I then lyfe doe holde more deare.
Fayre lady myne dame Juliet my lyfe (quod he)
Even from my byrth committed was to fatall sisters three.
They may in spyte of foes, draw foorth my lively threed
And they also, who so sayth nay, asonder may it shreed.
But who to reave my lyfe, his rage and force would bende,
Perhaps should trye unto his payne how I it could defende.
Ne yet I love it so, but alwayes, for your sake,
A sacrifice to death I would my wounded corps betake.
If my mishappe were such, that here, before your sight,
I should restore agayne to death, of lyfe my borowde light,
This one thing and no more my parting sprite would rewe:
That part he should, before that you by certaine triall knew
The love I owe to you, the thrall I languish in
And how I dread to loose the gayne which I doe hope to win
And how I wishe for lyfe, not for my propre ease,
But that in it, you might I love, you honor, serve and please
Tyll dedly pangs the sprite out of the corps shall send.
And therupon he sware an othe, and so his tale had ende.
Now love and pitty boyle, in Juliets ruthfull brest,
In windowe on her leaning arme, her weary hed doth rest,
Her bosome bathd in teares, to witnes inward payne,
With dreary chere to Romeus, thus aunswerd she agayne.
Ah my deere Romeus, keepe in these woordes (quod she)
For lo, the thought of such mischaunce, already maketh me
For pitty and for dred welnigh to yelde up breath.
In even ballance peysed are my life and eke my death,
For so my hart is knitte, yea, made one selfe with yours
That sure there is no greefe so small, by which your mynde endures,
But as you suffer payne, so I doe beare in part,
(Although it lessens not your greefe), the halfe of all your smart.
But these thinges overpast, if of your health and myne
You have respect, or pitty ought my teary weping eyen,
In few unfained woords, your hidden mynd unfolde,
That as I see your pleasant face, your heart I may beholde.
For if you doe intende my honor to defile

In error shall you wander still, as you have done this whyle,
But if your thought be chaste, and have on vertue ground,
If wedlocke be the ende and marke which your desire hath found,
Obedience set aside, unto my parentes dewe,
The quarell eke that long agoe betwene our housholdes grewe,
Both me and myne I will all whole to you betake
And following you where so you goe, my fathers house forsake.
But if by wanton love, and by unlawfull sute,
You thinke in ripest yeres to plucke my maydenho[o]ds dainty frute,
You are begylde, and now your Juliet you beseekes
To cease your sute, and suffer her to live emong her likes.
Then Romeus, whose thought was free from fowle desyre
And to the top of vertues haight, did worthely aspyre
Was fild with greater joy, then can my pen expresse
Or, till they have enjoyed the like, the hearers hart can gesse.
And then with joyned hands heavd up into the skies
He thankes the Gods, and from the heavens for vengeance downe he cries,
If he have other thought, but as his lady spake,
And then his looke he toornd to her, and thus did aunswer make.
Since Lady that you like to honor me so much,
As to accept me for your spouse, I yeld my selfe for such.
In true witnes wherof, because I must depart,
Till that my deede do prove my woord, I leave in pawne my hart.
To morrow eke betimes, before the sunne arise,
To fryer Lawrence will I wende, to learne his sage advise.
He is my gostly syre, and oft he hath me taught
What I should doe in things of wayght, when I his ayde have sought.
And at this selfe same houre, I plyte you here my fayth:
I wil be here (if you thinke good) to tell you what he sayth.
She was contented well, els favour found he none
That night, at lady Juliets hand, save pleasant woordes alone.
This barefoote fryer gyrt with cord his grayish weede,
For he of Frauncis order was, a fryer as I reede,
Not as the most was he, a grosse unlearned foole,
But doctor of divinitie proceded he in schoole.
The secretes eke he knew, in natures woorkes that loorke,
By magiks arte most men supposd that he could wonders woorke.

Ne doth it ill beseeme devines those skils to know
If on no harmefull deede they do such skilfulnes bestow.
For justly of no arte can men condemne the use
But right and reasons lore crye out agaynst the lewd abuse.
The bounty of the fryer and wisdom hath so wonne
The townes folks herts, that welnigh all to fryer Lawrence ronne
To shrive them selfe the olde, the yong, the great and small.
Of all he is beloved well, and honord much of all.
And for he did the rest in wisdome farre exceede,
The prince by him (his counsell cravde) was holpe at time of neede.
Betwixt the Capilets and him great frendship grew:
A secret and assured frend unto the Montegue.
Loved of this yong man more then any other gest,
The frier eke of Verone youth aye liked Romeus best,
For whom he ever hath, in time of his distres,
(As erst you heard) by skilfull lore, found out his harmes redresse.
To him is Romeus gonne, ne stayth he till the morowe,
To him he paynteth all his case, his passed joy and sorow, . . .

And then with weping eyes he prayes his gostly syre
To further and accomplish all theyr honest hartes desire.
A thousand doutes and moe in thold mans hed arose,
A thousand daungers like to come, the olde man doth disclose,
And from the spousall rites he redeth him refrayne:
Perhaps he shalbe bet advisde within a weeke or twayne.
Advise is banishd quite from those that followe love,
Except advise to what they like theyr bending mynde do move.
As well the father might have counseld him to stay
That from a mountaines top thrown downe, is falling halfe the way,
As warne his frend to stop, amyd his race begonne,
Whom Cupid with his smarting whip enforceth foorth to ronne.
Part wonne by earnest sute, the fryer doth graunt at last.
And part, because he thinkes the stormes so lately overpast,
Of both the housholdes wrath, this mariage might apease,
So that they should not rage agayne, but quite for ever cease.
The respite of a day, he asketh to devyse
What way were best, unknowne to ende so great an enterprise. . . .

Yong Romeus powreth foorth his hap and his mishap,

Into the friers brest, but where shall Juliet unwrap
The secretes of her hart? to whom shall she unfolde,
Her hidden burning love, and eke her thought and cares so colde?
The nurce of whom I spake within her chaumber laye,
Upon the mayde she wayteth still; to her she doth bewray
Her new received wound, and then her ayde doth crave.
In her she saith it lyes to spill, in her her life to save.
Not easely she made the froward nurce to bowe
But wonne at length, with promest hyre she made a solemne vowe
To do what she commaundes, as handmayd of her hest,
Her mistres secrets hide she will, within her covert brest.
To Romeus she goes; of him she doth desyre,
To knowe the meane of mariage, by councell of the fryre.
On Saterday, quod he, if Juliet come to shrift,
She shalbe shrived and maried, how lyke you noorse this drift?
Now by my truth (quod she) gods blessing have your hart
For yet in all my life I have not heard of such a part. . . .

[*They plan that Juliet shall pretend to go to shrift.*]

I know her mother will in no case say her nay,
I warrant you she shall not fayle to come on Saterday.
And then she sweares to him, the mother loves her well,
And how she gave her sucke in youth she leaveth not to tell.
A prety babe (quod she), it was when it was yong,
Lord how it could full pretely have prated with it tong,
A thousand times and more I laid her on my lappe,
And clapt her on the buttocke soft and kist where I did clappe
And gladder then was I of such a kisse forsooth,
Then I had been to have a kisse of some olde lechers mouth.
And thus of Juliets youth began this prating noorse,
And of her present state to make a tedious long discoorse.
For though he pleasure tooke in hearing of his love,
The message aunswer seemed him to be of more behove.
But when these Beldams sit at ease upon theyr tayle,
The day and eke the candle light before theyr talke shall fayle
And part they say is true, and part they do devise,
Yet boldly do they chat of both when no man checkes theyr lyes.
Then he .vi. crownes of gold out of his pocket drew
And gave them her, a slight reward (quod he) and so adiew.
In seven yeres twise tolde she had not bowd so lowe,

Her crooked knees, as now they bowe, she sweares she will bestowe
Her crafty wit, her time, and all her busy payne,
To helpe him to his hoped blisse, and, cowring downe agayne,
She takes her leave, and home she hyes with spedy pace.
The chaumber doore she shuts, and then she saith with smyling face,
Good newes for thee, my gyrle, good tidinges I thee bring,
Leave of thy woonted song of care and now of pleasure sing.
For thou mayst hold thy selfe the happiest under sonne
That in so little while, so well so worthy a knight hast wonne.
The best yshapde is he, and hath the fayrest face,
Of all this towne, and there is none hath halfe so good a grace,
So gentle of his speche, and of his counsell wise,
And still with many prayses more she heaved him to the skies.
Tell me els what (quod she) this evermore I thought,
But of our mariage say at once, what aunswer have you brought?
Nay, soft, quoth she, I feare your hurt by sodain joye.
I list not play quoth Juliet, although thou list to toye.
How glad trow you was she, when she had heard her say
No farther of then Saterday, differred was the day.
Againe the auncient nurce doth speake of Romeus,
And then (said she) he spake to me, and then I spake him thus.
Nothing was done or said, that she hath left untolde,
Save onely one, that she forgot the taking of the golde.
There is no losse quod she, (sweete wench) to losse of time,
Ne in thine age shalt thou repent so much of any crime.
For when I call to mynde, my former passed youth
One thing there is which most of all doth cause my endles ruth.
At sixtene yeres I first did choose my loving feere,
And I was fully ripe before, (I dare well say) a yere.
The pleasure that I lost, that yere so overpast,
A thousand times I have bewept, and shall while lyfe doth last.
In fayth it were a shame, yea sinne it were ywisse,
When thou mayst live in happy joy to set light by thy blisse.
She that this mornyng could her mistres mynde disswade,
Is now becomme an Oratresse, her lady to perswade. . . .

Thus to the fryers cell, they both foorth walked bin: [743]
He shuts the doore as soone as he and Juliet were in.

But Romeus her frend was entred in before
And there had wayted for his love, two howers large and more.
Eche minute seemde an howre, and every howre a day:
Twixt hope he lived and despayre, of cumming or of stay. . . .

So lovers live in care, in dread, and in unrest [793]
And dedly warre by striving thoughts they kepe within their brest.
But wedlocke is the peace wherby is freedome wonne,
To do a thousand pleasant thinges that should not els be donne.
The newes of ended warre these two have h[e]ard with joy
But now they long the fruite of peace with pleasure to enjoy.
In stormy wind and wave, in daunger to be lost,
Thy stearles ship (O Romeus) hath been long while betost.
The seas are now appeasd, and thou by happy starre
Art comme in sight of quiet haven and, now the wrackfull barre
Is hid with swelling tyde, boldly thou mayst resort
Unto thy wedded ladies bed, thy long desyred port.
God graunt no follies mist, so dymme thy inward sight,
That thou do misse the chanell, that doth leade to thy delight.
God graunt no daungers rocke, ylurking in the darke,
Before thou win the happy port, wracke thy sea beaten barke.
A servant Romeus had, of woord and deede so just,
That with his life (if nede requierd) his master would him trust.
His faithfulnes had oft our Romeus proved of olde
And therfore all that yet was done unto his man he tolde,
Who straight as he was charged, a corden ladder lookes
To which he hath made fast two strong and crooked yron hookes.
The bryde to send the nurce at twylight fayleth not,
To whom the bridegroome geven hath, the ladder that he got,
And then to watch for him appointeth her an howre
For whether Fortune smyle on him, or if she list to lowre,
He will not misse to comme to his appoynted place,
Where wont he was to take by stelth the view of Juliets face.
How long these lovers thought the lasting of the day,
Let other judge that woonted are lyke passions to assay.
For my part, I do gesse eche howre seemes twenty yere
So that I deeme, if they might have (as of Alcume we heare)
The sunne bond to theyr will, if they the heavens might gyde,
Black shade of night and doubled darke should straight all over hyde.
Thappointed howre is comme, he clad in riche araye,

Walkes toward his desyred home, good Fortune gyde his way.
Approching nere the place from whence his hart had life,
So light he wox, he lept the wall, and there he spyde his wife,
Who in the windowe watcht the cumming of her lorde,
Where she so surely had made fast the ladder made of corde
That daungerles her spouse the chaumber window climes,
Where he ere then had wisht himselfe above ten thousand times.
The windowes close are shut, els looke they for no gest,
To light the waxen quariers, the auncient nurce is prest,
Which Juliet had before prepared to be light,
That she at pleasure might beholde her husbandes bewty bright. . . .

The blyndfyld goddesse that with frowning face doth fraye, [911]
And from theyr seate the mighty kinges throwes downe with hedlong sway,
Begynneth now to turne, to these her smyling face,
Nedes must they tast of great delight, so much in Fortunes grace.
If Cupid, God of love, be God of pleasant sport,
I thinck O Romeus Mars himselfe envies thy happy sort.
Ne Venus justly might, (as I suppose) repent,
If in thy stead (O Juliet) this pleasant time she spent.
  Thus passe they foorth the night in sport, in joly game:
The hastines of Phoebus steeds in great despyte they blame.
And now the virgins fort hath warlike Romeus got,
In which as yet no breache was made by force of canon shot,
And now in ease he doth possesse the hoped place.
How glad was he, speake you that may your lovers parts embrace. . . .

  The summer of their blisse, doth last a month or twayne
But winters blast with spedy foote doth bring the fall agayne.
Whom glorious fortune erst had heaved to the skies
By envious fortune overthrowne on earth now groveling lyes.
She payd theyr former greefe with pleasures doubled gayne,
But now for pleasures usery ten folde redoubleth payne.
  The prince could never cause those housholds so agree,
But that some sparcles of their wrath, as yet remaining bee
Which lye this while rak'd up, in ashes pale and ded,

Till tyme do serve that they agayne in wasting flame may spred.
At holiest times, men say most heynous crimes are donne;
The morowe after Easter day the mischiefe new begonne.
A band of Capilets did meete (my hart it rewes)
Within the walles, by Pursers gate, a band of Montagewes.
The Capilets as cheefe, a yong man have chose out,
Best exercisd in feates of armes, and noblest of the rowte,
Our Juliets unkles sonne that cliped was Tibalt.
He was of body tall and strong, and of his courage halt.
They neede no trumpet sounde to byd them geve the charge,
So lowde he cryde with strayned voyce and mouth outstretched large.
Now, now, (quod he) my frends, our selfe so let us wreake,
That of this dayes revenge, and us, our childrens heyres may speake.
Now once for all let us their swelling pride asswage,
Let none of them escape alive; then he with furious rage
And they with him gave charge, upon theyr present foes,
And then forthwith a skyrmishe great upon this fray arose.
For loe, the Montagewes thought shame away to flye,
And rather then to live with shame, with prayse did choose to dye.
The woordes that Tybalt usd to styre his folke to yre,
Have in the brestes of Montagewes kindled a furious fyre.
With Lyons hartes they fight, warely themselfe defende,
To wound his foe, his present wit and force eche one doth bend.
This furious fray is long, on each side stoutly fought,
That whether part had got the woorst full doutfull were the thought.
The noyse hereof anon, throughout the towne doth flye
And partes are taken on every side, both kinreds thether hye.
Here one doth gaspe for breth, his frend bestrideth him,
And he hath lost a hand, and he another maymed lim,
His leg is cutte whilst he strikes at an other full
And whom he would have thrust quite through hath cleft his cracked skull.
Theyr valiant harts forbode theyr foote to geve the grounde,
With unappauled cheere they tooke full deepe and doutfull wounde.
Thus foote by foote long while, and shield to shield set fast,
One foe doth make another faynt but makes him not agast.
And whilst this noyse is ryfe in every townes mans eare,

Eke walking with his frendes, the noyse doth wofull Romeus heare.
With spedy foote he ronnes unto the fray apace,
With him those fewe that were with him he leadeth to the place.
They pittie much to see the slaughter made so greate,
That wetshod they might stand in blood on eyther side the streate.
Part frendes (sayd he) part frendes, helpe frendes to part the fray
And to the rest, enough (he cryes) now time it is to staye.
Gods farther wrath you styrre, beside the hurt you feele
And with this new uprore confounde all this our common wele.
But they so busy are in fight so egar and feerce.
That through theyr eares his sage advise no leysure had to pearce.
Then lept he in the throng, to part, and barre the blowes,
As well of those that were his frendes as of his dedly foes.
As soone as Tybalt had our Romeus espyde,
He threw a thrust at him that would have past from side to side,
But Romeus ever went (douting his foes) well armde
So that the swerd (kept out by mayle) hath nothing Romeus harmde.
Thou doest me wrong (quoth he) for I but part the fraye,
Not dread, but other waighty cause my hasty hand doth stay.
Thou art the cheefe of thine, the noblest eke thou art:
Wherfore leave of thy malice now, and helpe these folke to parte.
Many are hurt, some slayne, and some are like to dye.
No, coward, traytor boy (quoth he) straight way I mynd to trye
Whether thy sugred talke, and tong so smothely fylde,
Against the force of this my swerd shall serve thee for a shylde.
And then at Romeus hed, a blow he strake so hard,
That might have clove him to the brayne but for his cunning ward.
It was but lent to him that could repay agayne
And geve him death for interest, a well forborne gayne. . . .

Even as two thunderboltes, throwne downe out of the skye,
That through the ayre the massy earth and seas have power to flye,
So met these two, and while they chaunge a blowe or twayne,
Our Romeus thrust him through the throte and so is Tybalt slayne.
Loe here the ende of those that styrre a dedly stryfe:

Who thyrsteth after others death, himselfe hath lost his life.
The Capilets are quaylde, by Tibalts overthrowe,
The courage of the Mountagewes, by Romeus sight doth growe,
The townes men waxen strong, the prince doth send his force,
The fray hath end, the Capilets do bring the brethles corse,
Before the prince and crave that cruell dedly payne
May be the guerdon of his falt, that hath their kinsman slaine.
The Montagewes do pleade, theyr Romeus voyde of falt,
The lookers on do say, the fight begonne was by Tybalt,
The prince doth pawse, and then geves sentence in a while,
That Romeus, for sleying him should goe into exyle.
His foes would have him hangde, or sterve in prison strong,
His frendes do think (but dare not say) that Romeus hath wrong.
Both housholds straight are charged on payne of losing lyfe,
Theyr bloudy weapons layd aside, to cease the styrred stryfe.
This common plag[u]e is spred, through all the towne anon,
From side to syde the towne is fild with murmour and with mone. . . .

But how doth moorne emong the moorners Juliet?
How doth she bathe her brest in teares? what depe sighes doth she fet?
How doth she tear her heare? her weede how doth she rent?
How fares the lover hearing of her lovers banishment?
How wayles she Tibalts death, whom she had loved so well?
Her hearty greefe and piteous plaint, cunning I want to tell
For delving depely now in depth of depe dispayre,
With wretched sorowes cruell sound she fils the empty ayre
And to the lowest hell, downe falles her heavy crye,
And up unto the heavens haight her piteous plaint doth flye. . . .

And then agayne, wroth with her selfe, with feble voyce gan say.
Ah cruell murthering tong, murthrer of others fame,
How durst thou once attempt to tooch the honor of his name?
Whose dedly foes doe yelde him dewe and earned prayse,
For though his fredome be bereft, his honor not decayes.
Why blamst thou Romeus for sleying of Tybalt,
Since he is gyltles quite of all, and Tybalt beares the falt?
Whether shall he (alas), poore banishd man, now flye?
What place of succor shall he seeke beneth the starry skye,
Synce she pursueth him, and him defames by wrong

That in distres should be his fort, and onely rampier strong?
Receive the recompence, O Romeus, of thy wife,
Who, for she was unkind her selfe, doth offer up her lyfe.
In flames of yre, in sighes, in sorow and in ruth,
So to revenge the crime she did commit against thy truth.
These said, she could no more, her senses all gan fayle
And dedly panges began straight way her tender hart assayle
Her limmes she stretched forth, she drew no more her breath,
Who had been there, might well have seene the signes of present death.
The nurce that knew no cause, why she absented her,
Did doute lest that some sodain greefe too much tormented her.
Eche where but where she was the carefull Beldam sought,
Last, of the chamber where she lay, she haply her bethought,
Where she with piteous eye, her nurce childe did beholde:
Her limmes stretched out, her utward parts as any marble colde.
The nurce supposde that she had payde to death her det
And then as she had lost her wittes, she cryed to Juliet.
Ah my dere hart (quoth she) how greeveth me thy death?
Alas what cause hast thou thus soone to yelde up living breath?
But while she handled her, and chafed every part,
She knew there was some sparke of life by beating of her hart,
So that a thousand times she cald upon her name.
There is no way to helpe a traunce, but she hath tryde the same. . . .

Alas my tender nurce, and trusty frend (quoth she)
Art thou so blinde, that with thine eye, thou canst not easely see
The lawfull cause I have, to sorow and to moorne,
Since those the which I hyld most deere I have at once forlorne?
Her nurce then aunswerd thus. Me thinkes it sits you yll,
To fall in these extremities that may you gyltles spill,
For when the stormes of care, and troubles do aryse,
Then is the time for men to know, the foolish from the wise.
You are accounted wise, a foole am I your nurce
But I see not how in like case I could behave me wurse.
Tibalt your frend is ded, what, weene you by your teares,
To call him backe againe? thinke you that he your crying heares?
You shall perceve the falt, (if it be justly tryde)
Of his so sodayn death, was in his rashnes and his pryde.
Would you that Romeus, him selfe had wronged so,
To suffer himselfe causeles to be outraged of his foe

To whom in no respect, he ought a place to geve?
Let it suffise to thee fayre dame, that Romeus doth live,
And that there is good hope that he, within a while,
With greater glory shalbe calde home from his hard exile.
How wel yborne he is, thy selfe I know canst tell,
By kindred strong, and well alyed, of all beloved well.
With patience arme thy selfe, for though that Fortunes cryme,
Without your falt, to both your greefes depart you for a time,
I dare say for amendes of all your present payne
She will restore your owne to you, within a month or twayne,
With such contented ease, as never erst you had.
Wherfore rejoyce a while in hope, and be ne more so sad.
And that I may discharge your hart of heavy care
A certaine way I have found out, my paynes ne will I spare
To learne his present state, and what in time to comme
He mindes to doe, which knowne by me, you shall know all and somme. . . .

By this, unto his cell, the nurce, with spedy pace, [1277]
Was comme the nerest way: she sought no ydel resting place.
The fryer sent home the newes of Romeus certain helth
And promesse made (what so befell) he should that night by stelth
Comme to his wonted place that they in nedefull wise
Of theyr affayres in time to comme, might thorowly devyse.
Those joyfull newes, the nurce brought home with mery joy
And now our Juliet joyes to thinke, she shall her love enjoye.
The fryer shuts fast his doore, and then to him beneth,
That waytes to heare the doutefull newes of lyfe or els of death,
Thy hap quoth he, is good, daunger of death is none
But thou shalt live, and doe full well, in spite of spitefull fone.
This onely payne for thee was erst proclaymde aloude,
A banishd man, thou mayst thee not within Verona shroude.
These heavy tydinges heard, his golden lockes he tare
And, like a frantike man, hath torne the garmentes that he ware.
And as the smitten deere, in brakes is waltring found,
So waltreth he, and with his brest doth beate the troden grounde.
He rises eft, and strikes his head against the wals,
He falleth downe againe, and lowde for hasty death he cals.
Come spedy death (quoth he) the readiest leache in love,
Since nought can els beneth the sunne the ground of griefe remove,

Of lothsome life breake downe the hated staggering stayes,
Destroy, destroy at once the lyfe that faintly yet decayes.
But you (fayre dame) in whome dame nature dyd devise,
With cunning hand to woorke, that might seeme wondrous in our eyes,
For you I pray the Gods, your pleasures to increase,
And all mishap, with this my death, for evermore to cease. . . .

Therewith, a cloude of sighes, he breathd into the skies
And two great streames of bitter teares, ran from his swollen eyes.
These thinges, the auncient fryre, with sorow saw, and heard,
Of such begynning eke, the ende, the wise man greatly feard.
But loe, he was so weake, by reason of his age,
That he ne could by force, represse the rigour of his rage.
His wise and frendly woordes, he speaketh to the ayre
For Romeus so vexed is, with care and with dispayre,
That no advise can perce, his close forstopped eares,
So now the fryer doth take his part, in shedding ruthfull teares.
With colour pale, and wan, with armes full hard yfold,
With wofull cheere, his wayling frend, he standeth to beholde.
And then, our Romeus, with tender handes ywrong,
With voyce, with plaint made horce, with sobs, and with a foltring tong,
Renewd with novel mone the dolours of his hart,
His outward dreery cheere bewrayde, his store of inward smart.
Fyrst, nature did he blame, the author of his lyfe,
In which his joyes had been so scant, and sorowes aye so ryfe;
The time and place of byrth, he fiersly did reprove,
He cryed out (with open mouth) against the starres above;
The fatall sisters three, he said, had done him wrong,
The threed that should not have been sponne they had drawne foorth too long.
He wished that he [ne] had before this time been borne,
Or that as soone as he wan light, his life he had forlorne. . . .

He blamed all the world, and all he did defye
But Juliet, for whom he lived, for whom eke would he dye.
When after raging fits, appeased was his rage,
And when his passions (powred forth) gan partly to asswage
So wisely did the fryre unto his tale replye,
That he straight cared for his life, that erst had care to dye.

Art thou, quoth he, a man? thy shape saith so thou art:
Thy crying and thy weping eyes, denote a womans hart,
For manly reason is quite from of thy mynd outchased,
And in her stead affections lewd, and fansies highly placed,
So that I stoode in doute this howre (at the least)
If thou a man, or women wert, or els a brutish beast.
A wise man in the midst of troubles and distres,
Still standes not wayling present harme, but seeks his harmes redres. . . .

[*The lovers spend the night in Juliet's bedchamber.*]

But now (somewhat too soone) in farthest East arose [1703]
Fayre Lucifer, the golden starre that Lady Venus chose,
Whose course appoynted is, with spedy race to ronne,
A messenger of dawning daye, and of the rysing sonne.
Then freshe Aurora, with her pale and silver glade,
Did clear the skyes, and from the earth, had chased ougly shade.
When thou ne lookest wide, ne closely dost thou winke,
When Phoebus from our hemysphere, in westerne wave doth sinke.
What cooller then the heavens do shew unto thine eyes,
The same, (or like) saw Romeus in farthest Esterne skyes.
As yet, he saw no day, he could he call it night,
With equall force, decreasing darke, fought with increasing light.
Then Romeus in armes his lady gan to folde,
With frendly kisse, and ruthfully she gan her knight beholde.
With solemne othe they both theyr sorowfull leave do take;
They sweare no stormy troubles shall theyr steady frendship shake.
Then carefull Romeus, agayne to cell retoornes,
And in her chamber secretly our joyles Juliet moornes.
Now hugy cloudes of care, of sorow, and of dread,
The clearnes of their gladsome harts hath wholy overspread.
When golden crested Phoebus bosteth him in skye,
And under earth, to scape revenge, his dedly foe doth flye,
Then hath these lovers day an ende, their night begonne,
For eche of them to other is, as to the world the sunne.
The dawning they shall see, ne sommer any more,
But blackfaced night with winter rough, (ah) beaten over sore.
The wery watch discharged, did hye them home to slepe,
The warders, and the skowtes were chargde theyr place and coorse to keepe,
And Verone gates awyde, the porters had set open.

When Romeus had of hys affayres with frier Lawrence spoken,
Warely he walked forth, unknowne of frend or foe,
Clad like a merchant venterer, from top even to the toe.
He spurd apace, and came withouten stop or stay,
To Mantua gates, where lighted downe, he sent his man away
With woords of comfort, to his olde afflicted syre:
And straight in mynd to sojorne there, a lodgeing doth he hyre,
And with the nobler sort he doth himselfe acquaint,
And of his open wrong receaved, the Duke doth heare his plaint. . . .

In absence of her knight, the lady no way could [1781]
Kepe trewce betwene her greefes and her, though nere so fayne she would;
And though with greater payne she cloked sorowes smart,
Yet did her paled face disclose the passions of her hart. . . .

[*Juliet's parents decide she is melancholy because she is not yet married.*]

And Capilet the maydens sire, within a day or twayne, [1876]
Conferreth with his frendes, for mariage of his daughter,
And many gentlemen there were, with busy care that sought her;
Both, for the mayden was well shaped, yong, and fayre,
As also well brought up, and wise, her fathers onely heyre.
Emong the rest was one inflamde with her desire,
Who County Paris cliped was, an Earle he had to syre.
Of all the suters, him the father liketh best,
And easely unto the Earle he maketh his behest,
Both of his owne good will, and of his frendly ayde,
To win his wife unto his will, and to perswade the mayde.
The wife dyd joy to heare the joyfull husband say,
How happy hap, how meete a match, he had found out that day,
Ne did she seeke to hyde her joyes within her hart,
But straight she hyeth to Juliet; to her she telles apart,
What happy talke (by meane of her) was past no rather
Betwene the woing Paris, and her carefull loving father.
The person of the man, the fewters of his face,
His youthfull yeres, his fayrenes, and his port and semely grace,
With curious wordes she payntes before her daughters eyes,
And then with store of vertues prayse she heaves him to the skyes.
She vauntes his race, and gyftes, that Fortune did him geve,
Wherby (she saith) both she and hers, in great delight shall live.
When Juliet conceived her parentes whole entent,
Wherto, both love, and reasons right, forbod her to assent,

Within her selfe she thought, rather then be forsworne,
With horses wilde, her tender partes asonder should be torne.
Not now with bashfull brow (in wonted wise) she spake,
But with unwonted boldnes, straight into these woordes she brake.
Madame, I marvell much, that you so lavasse are
Of me your childe, (your jewel once, your onely joy and care,)
As thus to yelde me up, at pleasure of another,
Before you know if I doe like, or els mislike my lover.
Doo what you list, but yet of this assure you still,
If you do as you say you will, I yelde not there untill.
For had I choyse of twayne, farre rather would I choose,
My part of all your goodes, and eke my breath and lyfe to lose,
Then graunt that he possesse of me the smallest part; . . .

So deepe this aunswere made the sorowes downe to sinke
Into the mothers brest, that she ne knoweth what to thinke
Of these her daughters woords, but all appalde she standes,
And up unto the heavens she throwes her wondring head and handes,
And nigh besyde her selfe her husband hath she sought.
She telles him all; she doth forget ne yet she hydeth ought.
The testy old man, wroth, disdainfull without measure,
Sendes forth his folke in haste for her, and byds them take no leysure:
Ne on her teares or plaint, at all to have remorse,
But (if they can not with her will,) to bring the mayde perforce.
The message heard, they part, to fetch that they must fet,
And willingly with them walkes forth obedient Juliet.
Arrived in the place, when she her father saw,
Of whom (as much as duety would) the daughter stoode in awe,
The servauntes sent away, (the mother thought it meete),
The wofull daughter all bewept, fell groveling at his feete,
Which she doth washe with teares as she thus groveling lyes:
So fast, and eke so plenteously distill they from her eyes.
When she to call for grace her mouth doth think to open,
Muet she is; for sighes and sobs her fearefull talke have broken.
The syre, whose swelling wroth her teares could not asswage,
With fiery eyen, and skarlet cheekes, thus spake her in his rage,
Whilst ruthfully stood by the maydens mother mylde,
Listen (quoth he) unthankfull and thou disobedient childe; . . .

Such care thy mother had, so deere thou wert to me,
That I with long and earnest sute provided have for thee
One of the greatest lordes, that wonnes about this towne,
And for his many vertues sake, a man of great renowne.
Of whom, both thou and I, unworthy are too much,
So riche ere long he shalbe left, his fathers welth is such.
Such is the noblenes, and honor of the race,
From whence his father came, and yet thou playest in this case,
The dainty foole, and stubberne gyrle; for want of skill,
Thou dost refuse thy offred weale, and disobay my will.
Even by his strength I sweare, that fyrst did geve me lyfe
And gave me in my youth the strength, to get thee on my wyfe,
Onlesse by Wensday next, thou bende as I am bent,
And at our castle cald Free towne, thou freely doe assent
To Counte Paris sute, and promise to agree
To whatsoever then shall passe, twixt him, my wife, and me,
Not onely will I geve all that I have away
From thee, to those that shall me love, me honor, and obay,
But also too so close, and to so hard a gaole,
I shall thee wed, for all thy life, that sure thou shalt not fayle
A thousand times a day to wishe for sodayn death,
And curse the day, and howre when first thy lunges did geve thee breath.
Advise thee well, and say that thou art warned now,
And thinke not that I speake in sport, or mynd to breake my vowe. . . .

[*Juliet consults the Friar.*]

When too and fro in mynde he dyvers thoughts had cast,
With tender pity and with ruth his hart was wonne at last.
He thought he rather would in hasard set his fame,
Then suffer such adultery. Resolving on the same,
Out of his closet straight, he tooke a litele glasse,
And then with double hast retornde where wofull Juliet was;
Whom he hath found welnigh in traunce, scarce drawing breath,
Attending still to heare the newes of lyfe or els of death.
Of whom he did enquire of the appointed day.
On Wensday next (quod Juliet) so doth my father say:
I must geve my consent, but (as I do remember)
The solemne day of mariage is, the tenth day of September.
Deere daughter, quoth the fryer, of good chere see thou be,
For loe, sainct Frauncis of his grace hath shewde a way to me,

By which I may both thee, and Romeus together,
Out of the bondage which you feare assuredly deliver. . . .

Receive this vyoll small, and keepe it as thine eye,
And on thy mariage day before the sunne doe cleare the skye,
Fill it with water full, up to the very brim,
Then drinke it of, and thou shalt feele, throughout eche vayne and lim
A pleasant slumber slide, and quite dispred at length,
On all thy partes, from every part reve all thy kindly strength.
Withouten moving thus thy ydle parts shall rest,
No pulse shall goe, ne hart once beate within thy hollow brest,
But thou shalt lye as she that dyeth in a traunce:
Thy kinsmen, and thy trusty frendes shall wayle the sodain chaunce:
Thy corps then will they bring to grave in this church yarde,
Where thy forefathers long agoe a costly tombe preparde,
Both for him selfe, and eke for those that should come after,
Both deepe it is, and long and large, where thou shall rest my daughter,
Till I to Mantua sende for Romeus, thy knight.
Out of the tombe both he and I will take thee forth that night.
And when out of thy slepe thou shalt awake agayne,
Then mayst thou goe with him from hence, and healed of thy payne,
In Mantua lead with him unknowne a pleasant life,
And yet perhaps in time to comme, when cease shall all the strife,
And that the peace is made twixt Romeus and his foes,
My selfe may finde so fit a time these secretes to dysclose,
Both to my prayse, and to thy tender parentes joy,
That daungerles, without reproche, thou shalt thy love enjoy. . . .

[*Juliet tells her parents she will marry Paris.*]

At length the wished time of long hoped delight,
(As Paris thought) drew nere, but nere approched heavy plight.
Against the bridall day the parentes did prepare
Such rich attyre, such furniture, such store of dainty fare,
That they which did behold the same the night before
Did thinke and say, a man could scarcely wishe for any more.
Nothing did seeme to deere, the deerest thinges were bought,

And (as the written story saith) in dede there wanted nought,
That longd to his degree and honor of his stocke.
But Juliet, the whilst, her thoughts within her brest did locke;
Even from the trusty nurce, whose secretnes was tryde,
The secret counsell of her hart the nurce childe seekes to hide.
For sith, to mocke her dame, she dyd not sticke to lye,
She thought no sinne with shew of truth, to bleare her nurces eye.
In chamber secretly the tale she gan renew,
That at the doore she tolde her dame, as though it had been trew.
The flattring nurce did prayse the fryer for his skill,
And said that she had done right well by wit to order will.
She setteth foorth at large the fathers furious rage,
And eke she prayseth much to her, the second mariage;
And County Paris now she praiseth ten times more,
By wrong, then she her selfe, by right, had Romeus praysde before. . . .

These wordes and like, the nurce did speake, in hope to please,
But greatly did these wicked wordes the ladies mynde disease,
But ay she hid her wrath, and seemed well content,
When dayly dyd the naughty nurce new argumentes invent.
But when the bryde perceved her howre approched nere,
She sought (the best she could) to fayne, and temperd so her cheere,
That by her outward looke, no living wight could gesse
Her inward woe, and yet anew renewde is her distresse.
Unto her chaumber doth the pensive wight repayre,
And in her hand a percher light the nurce beares up the stayre.
In Juliets chamber was her wonted use to lye,
Wherfore her mistres, dreading that she should her work descrye,
As sone as she began her pallet to unfold,
Thinking to lye that night, where she was wont to lye of olde,
Doth gently pray her seeke her lodgeing some where els;
And lest she crafty should suspect, a ready reason telles.
Dere frend (quoth she) you knowe, to morow is the day
Of new contract, wherfore this night, my purpose is to pray
Unto the heavenly myndes, that dwell above the skyes,
And order all the course of thinges, as they can best devyse,
That they so smyle upon the doynges of to morow,

That all the remnant of my lyfe, may be exempt from sorow.
Wherfore I pray you leave me here alone this night,
But see that you to morow comme before the dawning light,
For you must curle my heare, and set on my attyre.
And easely the loving nurse, dyd yelde to her desire,
For she within her hed dyd cast before no doute;
She little knew the close attempt, her nurce childe went about.
  The nurce departed once, the chamber doore shut close,
Assured that no living wight, her doing myght disclose,
She powred forth into the vyole of the fryer,
Water, out of a silver ewer, that on the boord stoode by her.
The slepy mixture made, fayre Juliet doth it hyde,
Under her bolster soft, and so unto her bed she hyed:
Where divers novel thoughts arise within her hed,
And she is so invironed about with deadly dred,
That what before she had resolved undoutedly,
That same she calleth into doute, and lying doutfully
Whilst honest love did strive with dred of dedly payne,
With handes ywrong, and weping eyes, thus gan she to complaine.
What, is there any one beneth the heavens hye,
So much unfortunate as I? so much past hope as I? . . .

What doe I knowe (quoth she) if that this powder shall
Sooner or later then it should or els not woorke at all?
And then my craft descride as open as the day,
The peoples tale and laughing stocke shall I remayne for aye.
And what know I (quoth she) if serpentes odious,
And other beastes and wormes that are of nature venemous,
That wonted are to lurke, in darke caves under grounde,
And commonly, as I have heard, in dead mens tombes are found,
Shall harme me, yea or nay, where I shall lye as ded.
Or how shall I, that alway have in so freshe ayre been bred,
Endure the lothsome stinke of such an heaped store
Of carkases, not yet consumde, and bones that long before
Intombed were, where I my sleping place shall have,
Where all my auncesters doe rest, my kindreds common grave?
Shall not the fryer and my Romeus, when they come,
Fynd me (if I awake before) ystifled in the tombe?
  And whilst she in these thoughtes doth dwell somewhat to long,

The force of her ymagining, anon dyd waxe so strong,
That she surmysde she saw out of the hollow vaulte,
(A griesly thing to looke upon), the carkas of Tybalt,
Right in the selfe same sort, that she few dayes before
Had seene him in his blood embrewde, to death eke wounded sore.
And then, when she agayne within her selfe had wayde
That quicke she should be buried there, and by his side be layde,
All comfortles, for she shall living feere have none,
But many a rotten carkas, and full many a naked bone,
Her dainty tender partes gan shever all for dred,
Her golden heares did stand upright, upon her chillish hed.
Then pressed with the feare that she there lived in,
A sweat as colde as mountaine yse, pearst through her tender skin,
That with the moysture hath wet every part of hers,
And more besides, she vainely thinkes, whilst vainely thus she feares,
A thousand bodies dead have compast her about,
And lest they will dismember her, she greatly standes in dout.
But when she felt her strength began to weare away,
By little and little, and in her hart her feare increased ay,
Dreading that weakenes might, or foolish cowardise,
Hinder the execution of the purposde enterprise,
As she had frantike been, in hast the glasse she caught,
And up she dranke the mixture quite, withouten farther thought.
Then on her brest she crost her armes long and small,
And so, her senses fayling her, into a traunce did fall.
And when that Phoebus bright heaved up his seemely hed,
And from the East in open skies his glistring rayes dispred,
The nurce unshut the doore, for she the key did keepe,
And douting she had slept to long, she thought to breake her slepe.
Fyrst, softly dyd she call, then lowder thus did crye,
Lady, you slepe to long, (the Earle) will rayse you by and by,
But wele away, in vayne unto the deafe she calles,
She thinkes to speake to Juliet, but speaketh to the walles.
If all the dredfull noyse, that might on earth be found,
Or on the roaring seas, or if the dredfull thunders sound
Had blowne into her eares, I thinke they could not make,
The sleping wight before the time by any meanes awake:
So were the sprites of lyfe shut up, and senses thrald,

Wherwith the seely carefull nurce was wondrously apalde.
She thought to daw her now as she had donne of olde,
But loe, she found her parts were stiffe, and more then marble colde,
Neither at mouth nor nose, found she recourse of breth;
Two certaine argumentes were these, of her untimely death.
Wherfore as one distraught, she to her mother ranne,
With scratched face, and heare betorne, but no woord speake she can.
At last (with much a doe) dead (quoth she) is my childe.
Now, out alas (the mother cryde) and as a Tyger wilde,
Whose whelpes whilst she is gonne out of her denne to prey,
The hunter gredy of his game, doth kill or cary away:
So, rageing forth she ranne, unto her Juliets bed,
And there she found her derling, and her onely comfort ded.
Then shriked she out as lowde, as serve her would her breth,
And then (that pity was to heare) thus cryde she out on death.
Ah cruell death (quoth she) that thus against all right
Hast ended my felicitie, and robde my hartes delight,
Do now thy worst to me, once wreake thy wrath for all,
Even in despite I crye to thee thy vengeance let thou fall.
Wherto stay I (alas) since Juliet is gone?
Wherto live I since she is dead, except to wayle and mone?
Alacke, dere chyld, my teares for thee shall never cease;
Even as my dayes of life increase, so shall my plaint increase.
Such store of sorow shall afflict my tender hart,
That dedly panges when they assayle, shall not augment my smart.
Then gan she so to sobbe, it seemde her hart would brast,
And while she crieth thus, behold the father at the last,
The County Paris, and of gentilmen a route,
And ladies of Verona towne, and country round about,
Both kindreds and alies, thether apace have preast,
For by theyr presence there they sought to honor so the feast.
But when the heavy newes the bydden geastes did heare,
So much they mournd, that who had seene theyr countnance and theyr cheere,
Might easely have judgde, by that that they had seene,
That day the day of wrath, and eke of pity to have beene.
But more then all the rest the fathers hart was so
Smit with the heavy newes, and so shut up with sodain woe,

That he ne had the powre his daughter to bewepe,
Ne yet to speake, but long is forsd, his teares and plaint to kepe. . . .

The towne of Juliets byrth was wholy busied,
About her obsequies, to see theyr darlyng buried.
Now is the parentes myrth quite chaunged into mone,
And now to sorow is retornde the joy of every one.
And now the wedding weedes for mourning weedes they chaunge,
And Hymene into a Dyrge, alas it seemeth straunge.
In steade of mariage gloves, now funerall gloves they have,
And whom they should see maried, they follow to the grave.
The feast that should have been of pleasure and of joy,
Hath every dish, and cup, fild full of sorow and annoye.
  Now throughout Italy this common use they have,
That all the best of every stocke are earthed in one grave;
For every houshold, if it be of any fame,
Doth bylde a tombe, or digge a vault that beares the housholdes name;
Wherein (if any of that kindred hap to dye)
They are bestowde, els in the same no other corps may lye.
The Capilets her corps in such a one dyd lay,
Where Tybalt slayne of Romeus was layde the other day.
An other use there is, that whosoever dyes,
Borne to their church with open face, upon the beere he lyes
In wonted weede attyrde, not wrapt in winding sheete. . . .

[*Romeo's man sees Juliet and goes to Mantua to tell Romeo the news. Friar John is caught by quarantine and fails to deliver the message. Romeo gets the poison and returns to Verona.*]

When he approched nere, he warely lighted downe,
And even with the shade of night he entred Verone towne,
Where he hath found his man, wayting when he should comme,
With lanterne, and with instruments, to open Juliets toomme.
Helpe Peter, helpe, quod he, helpe to remove the stone,
And straight when I am gone fro thee, my Juliet to bemone,
See that thou get thee hence, and on the payne of death,
I charge thee that thou comme not nere, whyle I abyde beneath,
Ne seeke thou not to let thy masters enterprise,
Which he hath fully purposed to doe, in any wise.
Take there a letter, which, as soone as he shall ryse,

Present it in the morning to my loving fathers eyes;
Which unto him perhaps farre pleasanter shall seeme,
Than eyther I do mynd to say, or thy gros[s]e head can deeme.
  Now Peter, that knew not the purpose of his hart,
Obediently a little way withdrew himselfe apart,
And then our Romeus, (the vault stone set upright)
Descended downe, and in his hand he bare the candle light.
And then with piteous eye, the body of his wyfe
He gan beholde, who surely was the organ of his lyfe;
For whom unhappy now he is, but erst was blyst.
He watred her with teares, and then an hundred times her kyst,
And in his folded armes, full straightly he her plight,
But no way could his greedy eyes be filled with her sight.
His fearfull handes he layd upon her stomacke colde,
And them on divers parts besyde, the wofull wight did hold.
But when he could not fynd the signes of lyfe he sought,
Out of his cursed box he drewe the poyson that he bought;
Wherof he gredely devowrde the greater part,
And then he cryde with dedly sigh, fetcht from his mourning hart:
Oh Juliet, of whom the world unwoorthy was,
From which, for worldes unworthines thy worthy gost dyd passe,
What death more pleasant could my hart wish to abyde,
Then that which here it suffreth now, so nere thy frendly syde?
Or els so glorious tombe, how could my youth have craved,
As in one selfe same vaulte with thee haply to be ingraved?
What Epitaph more worth, or halfe so excellent,
To consecrate my memorye, could any man invente,
As this, our mutuell, and our piteous sacrifice
Of lyfe, set light for love.—But while he talketh in this wise,
And thought as yet a while his dolors to enforce,
His tender hart began to faynt, prest with the venoms force,
Which little and little gan to overcomme hys hart,
And whilst his busy eyne he threwe about to every part,
He saw hard by the corce of sleping Juliet,
Bold Tybalts carkas dead, which was not all consumed yet.
To whom (as having life) in this sort speaketh he:
Ah cosin dere Tybalt whereso thy restles sprite now be,
With stretched handes to thee for mercy now I crye,
For that before thy kindly howre I forced thee to dye.
But if with quenched lyfe, not quenched be thine yre,
But with revengeing lust as yet thy hart be set on fyre,

What more amendes, or cruell wreke desyrest thou
To see on me, then this which here is shewd forth to thee now?
Who reft by force of armes from thee thy living breath,
The same with his owne hand (thou seest) doth poyson himselfe to death.
And for he caused thee in tombe too soone to lye,
Too soone also, yonger then thou, himselfe he layeth by.
These said, when he gan feele the poysons force prevayle,
And little and little mastred lyfe, for aye beganne to fayle,
Kneeling upon his knees, he said with voyce full lowe.
Lord Christ, that so to raunsome me descendedst long agoe
Out of thy fathers bosome, and in the virgins wombe
Didst put on fleshe, Oh let my plaint out of this hollow toombe,
Perce through the ayre, and graunt my sute may favour finde;
Take pity on my sinnefull and my poore afflicted mynde.
For well enough I know, this body is but clay,
Nought but a masse of sinne, to frayle, and subject to decay.
Then pressed with extreme greefe, he threw with so great force,
His overpressed parts upon his ladies wayled corps,
That now his wekened hart, weakened with tormentes past,
Unable to abyde this pang, the sharpest and the last,
Remayned quite deprived, of sense and kindly strength,
And so the long imprisond soule hath freedome wonne at length.
Ah cruell death, too soone, too soone was this devorce,
Twixt youthfull Romeus heavenly sprite, and his fayre earthy corse.
The fryer that knew what time the powder had been taken,
Knew eke the very instant when the sleper should awaken,
But wondring that he could no kind of aunswer heare,
Of letters, which to Romeus his fellow fryer did beare,
Out of sainct Frauncis church hymselfe alone dyd fare,
And for the opening of the tombe, meete instrumentes he bare.
Approching nigh the place, and seeing there the lyght,
Great horror felt he in his hart, by straunge and sodaine sight
Tyll Peter (Romeus man) his coward hart made bolde,
When of his masters being there, the certain newes he tolde.
There hath he been (quoth he) this halfe howre at the least,
And in this time I dare well say his plaint hath still increast.
Then both they entred in, where they (alas) dyd fynde,
The bretheles corps of Romeus, forsaken of the mynde;
Where they have made such mone, as they may best conceve,

That have with perfect frendship loved, whose frend, feerce death dyd reve.
But whilst with piteous playnt, they Romeus fate bewepe,
An howre too late fayre Juliet awaked out of slepe,
And much amasde to see in tombe so great a light,
She wist not if she saw a dreame, or sprite that walkd by night.
But cumming to her selfe, she knew them, and said thus:
What, fryer Lawrence, is it you? where is my Romeus?
And then the auncient frier, that greatly stoode in feare,
Lest if they lingred over long, they should be taken there,
In few plaine woordes, the whole that was betyde he tolde,
And with his fingar shewd his corps out stretched, stiffe, and colde,
And then perswaded her with pacience to abyde
This sodain great mischaunce, and sayth that he will soone provyde
In somme religious house for her a quiet place,
Where she may spend the rest of lyfe, and where in time percase
She may with wisdomes meane, measure her mourning brest,
And unto her tormented soule call backe exiled rest.
But loe, as soone as she had cast her ruthfull eye
On Romeus face, that pale and wan, fast by her side dyd lye,
Straight way she dyd unstop the conduites of her teares,
And out they gushe; with cruell hand she tare her golden heares.
But when she neither could her swelling sorow swage,
Ne yet her tender hart abyde her sickenes furious rage,
Falne on his corps, she lay long panting on his face,
And then with all her force and strength, the ded corps dyd embrace,
As though with sighes, with sobs, with force and busy payne,
She would him rayse, and him restore from death to lyfe agayne.
A thousand times she kist his mouth as cold as stone,
And it unkist agayne as oft, then gan she thus to mone.
Ah pleasant prop of all my thoughtes, ah onely ground
Of all the sweete delightes, that yet in all my lyfe I found,
Did such assured trust within thy hart repose,
That in this place, and at this time, thy churchyarde thou hast chose,
Betwixt the armes of me, thy perfect loving make?
And thus by meanes of me to ende thy lyfe, and for my sake? . . .

And when our Juliet would continue still her mone, [2761]

The fryer and the servant fled, and left her there alone,
For they a sodayne noyse, fast by the place did heare,
And lest they might be taken there, greatly they stoode in feare.
When Juliet saw her selfe left in the vaulte alone,
That freely she might worke her will, for let or stay was none,
Then once for all, she tooke the cause of all her harmes,
The body dead of Romeus, and claspd it in her armes.
Then she with earnest kisse, sufficiently did prove,
That more then by the feare of death she was attaint by love.
And then past deadly feare, for lyfe ne had she care,
With hasty hand she did draw out the dagger that he ware.
O welcome death (quoth she) end of unhappines,
That also art beginning of assured happines;
Feare not to darte me nowe, thy stripe no longer stay,
Prolong no longer now my lyfe, I hate this long delaye,
For straight my parting sprite, out of this carkas fled,
At ease shall finde my Romeus sprite, among so many ded.
And thou my loving lord, Romeus my trusty feer,
If knowledge yet doe rest in thee, if thou these woordes dost heer,
Receve thou her, whom thou didst love so lawfully,
That causd (alas) thy violent death although unwillingly;
And therfore willingly offers to thee her gost,
To thend that no wight els but thou, might have just cause to boste
Thinjoying of my love, which ay I have reserved,
Free from the rest, bound unto thee, that hast it well deserved:
That so our parted sprites, from light that we see here,
In place of endlesse light and blisse, may ever live yfere.
These said, her ruthlesse hand through gyrt her valiant hart.
Ah, Ladies, helpe with teares to wayle the ladies dedly smart.
She grones, she stretcheth out her limmes, she shuttes her eyes,
And from her corps the sprite doth flye. what should I say? she dyes.
The watchemen of the towne, the whilst are passed by,
And through the gates the candel light within the tombe they spye:
Wherby they did suppose, inchaunters to be comme,
That with prepared instrumentes had opened wide the tombe,
In purpose to abuse the bodies of the ded,
Which by theyr science ayde abusde, do stand them oft in sted.

Theyr curious harts desire the trueth herof to know,
Then they by certaine steppes descend, where they do fynd below,
In clasped armes ywrapt the husband and the wyfe,
In whom as yet they seemd to see somme certaine markes of lyfe.
But when more curiously with leysure they did vew,
The certainty of both theyr deathes, assuredly they knew.
Then here and there so long with carefull eye they sought,
That at the length hidden they found the murthrers so they thought.
In dongeon depe that night they lodgde them under grounde,
The next day do they tell the prince the mischefe that they found.
The newes was by and by throughout the towne dyspred,
Both of the takyng of the fryer, and of the two found ded.
Thether might you have seene whole housholdes forth to ronne,
For to the tombe where they did heare this wonder straunge was donne,
The great, the small, the riche, the poore, the yong, the olde,
With hasty pace do ronne to see, but rew when they beholde,
And that the murtherers to all men might be knowne,
Like as the murders brute abrode through all the towne was blowne,
The prince did straight ordaine, the corses that wer founde
Should be set forth upon a stage, hye raysed from the grounde,
Right in the selfe same fourme, (shewde forth to all mens sight)
That in the hollow valt they had been found that other night,
And eke that Romeus man, and fryer Lawrence should
Be openly examined, for els the people would
Have murmured, or faynd there were some wayghty cause,
Why openly they were not calde, and so convict by lawes.
The holy fryer now, and reverent by his age,
In great reproche set to the shew upon the open stage,
(A thing that ill beseemde a man of silver heares)
His beard as whyte as mylke he bathes, with great fast-falling teares:
Whom straight the dredfull Judge commaundeth to declare
Both how this murther hath been donne, and who the murthrers are,
For that he nere the tombe was found at howres unfitte,
And had with hym those yron tooles, for such a purpose fitte.
The frier was of lively sprite, and free of speche,

The Judges woordes appald him not, ne were his wittes to seeche.
But with advised heed, a while fyrst did he stay,
And then with bold assured voyce, aloude thus gan he say.
My lordes, there is not one emong you, set togyther,
So that (affection set aside) by wisdome he consider
My former passed lyfe, and this my extreme age,
And eke this heavy sight, the wreke of frantike Fortunes rage,
But that, amased much, doth wonder at this chaunge,
So great, so sodainly befalne, unlooked for, and straunge.
For I, that in the space of lx. yeres and tenne,
Since first I did begin, to soone, to leade my lyfe with men,
And with the worldes vaine thinges, my selfe I did acquaint,
Was never yet, in open place, at any time attaynt
With any cryme, in waight, as heavy as a rushe,
Ne is there any stander by, can make me gylty blushe,
(Although before the face of God, I doe confesse,
My selfe to be the sinfulst wretch of all this mighty presse.)
When readiest I am, and likeliest to make
My great accompt, which no man els for me shall undertake;
When wormes, the earth, and death doe cite me every howre,
Tappeare before the judgement seate of everlasting powre,
And falling ripe I steppe upon my graves brinke,
Even then, am I, most wretched wight, (as eche of you doth thinke)
Through my most haynous deede, with hedlong sway throwne downe,
In greatest daunger of my lyfe, and domage of renowne. . . .

Thus much I thought to say, to cause you so to know, [2881]
That neither these my piteous teares, though nere so fast they flowe,
Ne yet these yron tooles, nor the suspected time,
Can justly prove the murther donne, or damne me of the cryme. . . .

And then the auncient frier began to make dyscourse, [2915]
Even from the first of Romeus, and Juliets amours. . . .

And for the proofe of thys his tale, he doth desyer [2965]
The Judge, to send forthwith to Mantua for the fryer,
To learne his cause of stay, and eke to reade his letter,

And more beside, to thend that they might judge his cause the better,
He prayeth them depose the nurce of Juliet,
And Romeus man, whom at unwares besyde the tombe he met.
Then Peter not so much as erst he was, dysmayd:
My lordes (quoth he) too true is all, that fryer Laurence sayd.
And when my maister went into my mystres grave,
This letter that I offer you, unto me then he gave,
Which he himselfe dyd write as I do understand,
And charged me to offer them unto his fathers hand.
The opened packet doth conteyne in it the same,
That erst the skilfull frier said, and eke the wretches name
That had at his request, the dedly poyson sold,
The price of it, and why he bought, his letters playne have tolde.
The case unfolded so, and open now it lyes,
That they could wish no better proofe, save seeing it with theyr eyes.
So orderly all thinges were tolde and tryed out,
That in the prease there was not one, that stoode at all in doute.
The wyser sort to councell called by Escalus,
Have geven advyse, and Escalus sagely decreeth thus.
The nurse of Juliet, is banisht in her age,
Because that from the parentes she dyd hyde the mariage,
Which might have wrought much good, had it in time been knowne,
Where now by her concealing it, a mischeefe great is growne;
And Peter, for he dyd obey his masters hest,
In woonted freedome had good leave to lead his lyfe in rest:
Thapothecary, high is hanged by the throte,
And for the paynes he tooke with him, the hangman had his cote.
But now what shall betyde of this gray-bearded syre?
Of fryer Lawrence thus araynde, that good barefooted fryre?
Because that many times he woorthely did serve
The commen welth, and in his lyfe was never found to swerve,
He was discharged quyte, and no marke of defame
Did seeme to blot, or touch at all, the honor of his name.
But of him selfe he went into an Hermitage,
Two myles from Veron towne, where he in prayers past forth his age,
Tyll that from earth to heaven, his heavenly sprite dyd flye.

Fyve yeres he lived an Hermite, and an Hermite dyd he dye.
The straungenes of the chaunce, when tryed was the truth
The Montagewes and Capelets hath moved so to ruth,
That with their emptyed teares, theyr choler and theyr rage,
Was emptied quite, and they whose wrath no wisdom could asswage,
Nor threatning of the prince, ne mynd of murthers donne,
At length, (so mighty Jove it would) by pitye they are wonne.
And lest that length of time might from our myndes remove
The memory of so perfect, sound, and so approved love,
The bodies dead removed from vaulte where they did dye,
In stately tombe, on pillers great, of marble rayse they hye.
On every syde above, were set and eke beneath,
Great store of cunning Epitaphes, in honor of theyr death.
And even at this day the tombe is to be seene,
So that among the monumentes that in Verona been,
There is no monument more worthy of the sight,
Then is the tombe of Juliet, and Romeus her knight.